Contents

KU-203-701

OPPOSITE BO-KAAP **PREVIOUS PAGE** TABLE MOUNTAIN

Introduction to
Cape Town
the Winelands & the Garden Route

Cape Town is southern Africa's most beautiful, most romantic and most visited city. Its precolonial Khoikhoi inhabitants recognized its extraordinary physical setting when they referred to Table Mountain, the city's emblematic landmark, as Hoerikwaggo – the mountain in the sea. If the landscape doesn't take your breath away, its high-octane activities, from paragliding to kitesurfing should do the trick, and that's before you've sampled the nightlife. Which isn't to say Cape Town is just about adrenaline. Away from the thrills and pumping party scene, you'll find a city boasting breathtaking beaches, rolling vineyards and fine museums – enough to keep you busy over an extended visit. Despite this, most visitors find the time to escape the city – to the Winelands, to sample South Africa's celebrated wines and further east along the Garden Route, whose draw includes unparalleled whale-watching, crashing seascapes, dappled forests and – at its culmination – lions, leopards and elephants in the best game reserve in the southern half of the country.

Cape Town has a rich urban texture too, etched in its diverse **architecture**. In the suburbs, shimmering white Cape Dutch homesteads, rooted in seventeenth-century northern European traditions, characterize the grand estates of the Constantia Winelands; in the city, Muslim slaves, freed in the nineteenth century, added their minarets to the centre's skyline; and the English, who invaded and freed these slaves, introduced Georgian and Victorian buildings. In the tight terraces of the Bo-Kaap quarter and the tenements of District Six, the coloured descendants of slaves evolved a unique, evocatively Capetonian brand of jazz, which is well worth catching live. Indeed great sounds, along with high standards of accommodation, smart restaurants, laidback cafés and a vibrant gay scene, make visiting Cape Town a truly cosmopolitan experience.

ABOVE BEACH HUTS, MUIZENBERG

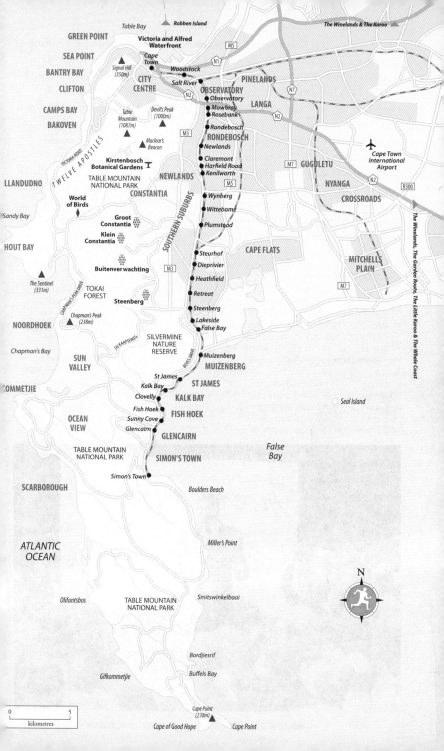

But despite a reputation for greater **liberalism** and racial tolerance during the apartheid era than the rest of the country, Cape Town has paradoxically been the slowest city in South Africa to embrace post-apartheid multiracialism. Ever since the mid-seventeenth century when Jan van Riebeeck, leader of the first whites to settle in South Africa, thought of digging a canal across the Cape Peninsula to cut it off from the rest of Africa, Cape Town has stood aloof from the rest of the country. For 350 years Cape Town's white establishment endeavoured to maintain an illusion that the city was somehow really European, despite its location.

Under apartheid, black (as opposed to coloured) South Africans were actively excluded from the Western Cape, which is why today **Africans** are still a minority in the Mother City, though they constitute the overwhelming majority in South Africa. For most Capetonians, living in crowded **townships** and **shantytowns**, poverty and sky-high crime rates are part of everyday life.

CINE CITY

Following the success of *U-Carmen eKhayelitsha* at the Berlin Film Festival in 2005, Cape Town was not only lauded for showing its grittier face on film, but Hollywood directors began to realize the city's **chameleon-like** ability to re-create anything from French boulevards to hectic New York traffic. Cape Town was subsequently able to stand in for 35 diverse locations for the 2005 Nicolas Cage movie *Lord of War*, including Bolivia, Beirut, Berlin, the Caribbean, Sierra Leone, Indonesia, Odessa and New York City.

Nowadays, Capetonians are increasingly spotting major **Hollywood names** in bars along the Atlantic seaboard beaches, as *24*, starring Kiefer Sutherland, *Blood Diamond* with Leonardo DiCaprio and Jennifer Connolly, and Clint Eastwood-directed *Invictus*, starring Matt Damon and Morgan Freeman, have been shot in the city. Following the arrival of the world-class R350m Cape Town Film Studios in 2011, the city has hosted the filming of major Hollywood productions, including *Dredd* and *Long Walk to Freedom*, while the fourth season of TV drama *Homeland* began shooting in the Mother City in 2014.

ABOVE IDRIS ELBA IN *MANDELA: LONG WALK TO FREEDOM* **OPPOSITE** OSTRICHES NEAR OUDTSHOORN

What to see

Table Mountain, frequently mantled by its "tablecloth" clouds, is the solid core of Cape Town, dividing the city into distinct zones, with public gardens, wilderness, forests, hiking routes, vineyards and desirable residential areas. To its north lies the **city centre**, home to the city's most important museums and galleries, and with a buzzing street life – buskers, hawkers and market traders. In the adjacent **Bo-Kaap** Muslim quarter, colourful terraces and restaurants serving local curries add piquancy to the city's heart. A stone's throw from the centre, the **V&A Waterfront** is Cape Town's most popular spot for shopping, eating and drinking in a highly picturesque setting among the piers and quays of a working harbour. It's also the embarkation point for catamarans to **Robben Island**, the site of Nelson Mandela's notorious incarceration. The rocky shore west of the Waterfront is occupied by the inner-city suburbs of **Green Point**, **De Waterkant** and **Sea Point**, home to some of the peninsula's oldest and best restaurants, their back-streets crammed with backpacker lodges, B&Bs and hotels. Equally good for accommodation, but more leafy and upmarket in comparison, the **City Bowl suburbs** gaze down from the Table Mountain foothills across the central business district to the ships in Duncan Dock.

South from Sea Point, a coastal road traces the chilly **Atlantic seaboard** under the heights of the Twelve Apostles and past some of Cape Town's most expensive suburbs and spectacular beaches to Hout Bay. From here, the road merges with the precipitous **Chapman's Peak Drive**, ten dramatically snaking kilometres of Victorian engineering carved into the western cliffsides of the Table Mountain massif, high above the crashing waves. To the east, across Table Mountain, the exceptionally beautiful **Kirstenbosch National Botanical Gardens** creep up the lower slopes, as do the **Constantia Winelands** a little further south, while the middle-class **southern suburbs** stretch down the peninsula as far as Muizenberg. The scenic Metrorail train line cuts through these suburbs and continues along the **False Bay seaboard**, passing through village-like **Kalk Bay**, with its intact harbour and working fishing community, and **Fish Hoek**, which has the best bathing beach along the eastern peninsula, before the final stop at the historic settlement of **Simon's Town**.

Most visitors see only the areas that were classified under apartheid as "white" and which still remain relatively safe and salubrious. But the townships of the **Cape Flats** to the east of the city can be visited on guided tours, and if you really want to get under the skin of the African areas, you can enjoy the hospitality of any of several B&Bs in **Xhosa homes**.

Beyond the city, the beautiful **Winelands** lie just an hour east of the Cape Flats, rich in elegant examples of Cape Dutch architecture, wonderful wines and excellent restaurants. Southeast of Cape Town you can take the picturesque coastal route, winding around massive sea-cliffs, to reach Hermanus, the largest settlement on the **Whale Coast**, and a fabulous spot for shore-based whale-watching.

After Cape Town, the best-known tourist feature of the Western Cape is the **Garden Route**, a drive along the N2 from Cape Town all the way to Port Elizabeth in the Eastern Cape. The Garden Route can be driven in a day, but to cover it so quickly would mean missing its essence, which lies off the road in its coastal towns, lagoons, mountains and ancient forests on the stretch between **Mossel Bay** and **Storms River Mouth**. The highlight along here, at the easternmost section of the Garden Route National Park, is **Tsitsikamma**, where the dark Storms River opens spectacularly into the Indian Ocean. Public transport along the Garden Route is better than anywhere in the country, partly because the route is a single stretch of freeway, and tour operators along the way have begun turning it into the country's most concentrated strip for packaged **adventure sports** and **outdoor activities**. Parallel to the Garden Route, **Route 62** provides a thoroughly rewarding inland alternative, traversing some of the most dramatic mountain passes in the region and taking in a number of picturesque Little Karoo *dorps*.

But the ultimate destination at the eastern end of the region, to which both the Garden Route and Route 62 lead, is **Addo Elephant National Park**, where sightings of elephants are virtually guaranteed, and there's a chance of seeing lions, buffalo and rhinos, among other wildlife.

When to go

Cape Town has a **Mediterranean climate**, the warm, dryish summers balanced by cool wet winters. Come prepared for hot days in winter and cold snaps in summer, and pack a jumper and jacket whatever time of year you come. The **southeaster**, the cool summer wind that blows in across False Bay, forms a major obsession for Capetonians. Its fickle moods can singlehandedly determine what kind of day you're going to have, and when it gusts at over 60kph you won't want to be outdoors, let alone on the beach. Conversely,

ANIMAL ATTRACTIONS

In Cape Town you're never far from the Table Mountain National Park and although this is no longer lion country (the last one was shot in the 1720s), you can still see countless varieties of animals, birds and reptiles here and along the city's coastline.

Commonest of the peninsula's large mammals are **baboons**, which number between three and four hundred and are mostly seen in the Cape of Good Hope section of the park. Another common species are **dassies**, or rock hyraxes, the fluffy beasts that resemble large guinea pigs and routinely sun themselves around the Upper Cable Station on Table Mountain. Of the scores of other mammals present, including **caracals**, **genets**, **polecats**, **Cape foxes** and some twenty species of **mice**, among the ones you'll most likely see are **Cape Mountain zebras**, **bontebok** (a large antelope) and **mongooses**.

Moving offshore, **African penguins** can be seen in high numbers at the colony in Boulders Bay and along the coastline to Hermanus. The city's most famous and glorious marine mammals, however, are the hefty **southern right whales** that arrive in False Bay during their calving season (peak period mid-Aug and mid-Oct), while **dolphins** are commonly spotted off the coast. And if you're willing to go under, you'll discover that False Bay is one of the best places in the country to meet a **great white shark** face to face on a shark-diving excursion.

its gentler incarnation as the so-called **Cape Doctor** brings welcome relief on humid summer days, and lays the famous cloudy tablecloth on top of Table Mountain. The **Garden Route** falls within overlapping weather systems and as a result has rain throughout the year, falling predominantly at night, to water the lush vegetation that gives the region its name.

For sun and swimming, the best time to visit is from **October to mid-December** and **mid-January to Easter**, when it's light long into the evening and there's an average of ten hours of sunshine a day. Between mid-December and mid-January, the whole region becomes congested as the nation takes its annual seaside holiday. In Cape Town, this is serious party time, with plenty of **major festivals** and events; if this is when you plan to visit, arrange accommodation and transport well in advance, and expect to pay considerably more for your bed than during the rest of the year.

Despite its shorter daylight hours, the **autumn** period, from April to mid-May, has a lot going for it: the southeaster drops and air temperatures remain pleasantly warm and the light is sharp and bright. For similar reasons the **spring** month of September can be very agreeable, with the added attraction that following the winter rains the peninsula tends to be at its greenest. Although spells of heavy rain occur in **winter** (June and July), it tends to be relatively mild, with temperatures rarely falling below 6°C. Glorious sunny days with crisp blue skies are common, and you won't see bare wintry trees either: indigenous vegetation is evergreen and gardens flower year-round. It's also in July that the first migrating **whales** begin to appear along the southern Cape coast, usually staying till the end of November.

Author picks

Although he's lived there for over a decade, our author is constantly amazed by Cape Town, where he's watched a whale breach during his morning coffee, trodden grapes with a high court judge and run into a baboon during a morning jog. Chance encounters aside, here are some of the other things that make his adopted home so special…

Best Table in town No café in Cape Town offers better views of Table Mountain, or better coffee, than *Common Ground*. **See p.120**

Top wildlife experience The five-day Whale Trail in De Hoop Nature Reserve is stunningly beautiful throughout the year – and sublime in season when there are whales around every corner. **See p.179**

Nightmare at the opera Catch any theatrical production by Brett Bailey, one of the country's most exciting directors, whose dark adaptation of Verdi's *Macbeth* has electrified audiences at home and across Europe. **See p.129**

Foulest-mouthed musicians Zef-rap crew Die Antwoord have stormed the world with Cape Flats slang, but still perform at home. **See p.264**

Tree-hugging overnight stay Hide out in the boughs of virgin forest at *Teniqua Treetops*, a romantic experiment in sustainable living. **See p.198**

Wettest seafood The small deck at *Harbour House Restaurant* in Kalk Bay jetties out over the crashing surf, with the risk of a drenching at high tide. **See p.122**

Go out on a limb The beautiful timber and steel Tree Canopy Walkway sways gently in the wind as it meanders through the forest canopy at Kirstenbosch Botanical Gardens. **See p.79**

Safari style The glass bedroom walls at boutique-hotel-in-the-bush *Kwandwe Private Game Reserve* are all that separates you from the Big Five. **See p.249**

> Our author recommendations don't end here. We've flagged up our favourite places – a perfectly sited hotel, an atmospheric café, a special restaurant – throughout the guide, highlighted with the ★ symbol.

ABOVE FROM TOP *KWANDWE ECCA LODGE*; DIE ANTWOORD; DE HOOP NATURE RESERVE

18
things not to miss

It's not possible to see everything that Cape Town and the Garden Route have to offer in one trip – and we don't suggest you try. What follows is a selective and subjective taste of the highlights, including outstanding national parks, spectacular wildlife, thrilling adventure sports and beautiful architecture. All entries have a page reference to take you straight into the Guide, where you can find out more. Coloured numbers refer to chapters in the Guide section.

9

10

11

SANDBOARDING
Page 140

One of the newest and most exciting rides for adrenaline junkies – boarding at speed down the peninsula's dunes.

6 THE BO-KAAP
Page 46

Meander through the city's oldest and brightest quarter.

7 PENGUINS
Pages 102

Teeming with African penguins, Boulders Beach offers a surreal landscape of enormous sea-worn rocks and fine, safe swimming.

8 CAPE POINT
Page 103

Roam the treacherous rocky promontory south of Cape Town and experience one of the most dramatic viewpoints in the country.

9 WINELANDS
Page 149

The Western Cape's wine estates combine stunning scenery, Cape Dutch architecture and some fine and affordable vintages.

10 ELEPHANTS
Page 244

Addo Elephant National Park, the world-famous reserve at the end of the Garden Route, has some three hundred pachyderms to marvel at.

11 MOTHER CITY QUEER PROJECTS
Page 145

The biggest and most outrageous ball of the year – Cape Town's straight-friendly gay party.

ROUTE 62 THROUGH THE LITTLE KAROO

Basics

Getting there

Most overseas visitors to Cape Town travel there by air, either on a direct flight or via Johannesburg, which is connected to Cape Town by frequent domestic flights (see p.24). There are no direct services from North America, but a nonstop flight from the UK makes the twelve-hour-plus journey a little more bearable. It can be cheaper, however, to fly via mainland Europe or Africa.

Airfares always depend on the **season**, with the highest prices and greatest demand in June, July, August, December and the first week of January. Prices drop during the "shoulder" season in May and September. You get the best prices during the low season in October, November and the last three weeks of January till March.

Flights from the UK and Ireland

From London there are nonstop flights with British Airways (🌐 ba.com), South African Airways (🌐 flysaa.com) and Virgin Atlantic (🌐 virgin -atlantic.com) to Cape Town. **Flying time** from the UK to Cape Town is around twelve hours and average high-low-season scheduled direct fares from London start at £800/500. You can save up to £400 by flying via mainland Europe, Africa or Asia, and enduring at least one change of plane, often in Johannesburg.

There are no direct flights from **Ireland**, but a number of European and Middle Eastern carriers fly to Cape Town via their hub airports.

Flights from the US and Canada

There are no direct flights **from the US**, but there are nonstop **flights** from New York (JFK) and Washington (IAD) to Johannesburg operated by South African Airways (SAA). These take between fifteen and seventeen hours. Most other flights stop off in Europe, the Middle East or Asia and involve a change of plane. On flights from the US to Cape Town via Jo'burg, expect the high-low-season return fares to start from $2500/1400 for Washington, DC, and $2000/1700 for New York, depending on season; you might save from $200 to as much as $900 if you fly **via Europe**.

From Canada, you'll have to change planes in the US, Europe or Asia on hauls that can last up to thirty hours. Return fares from Vancouver to Cape Town start at $1900.

Flights from Australia and New Zealand

There are nonstop flights **from Sydney** (which take 14hr) and **Perth** (just under 11hr) to **Johannesburg**, with onward connections to **Cape Town**; New Zealanders also tend to fly via Sydney. South African Airways (SAA) and Qantas (🌐 quantas.com.au) both serve South Africa from Australia. Several Asian, African and Middle Eastern airlines fly to Cape Town via their hub cities, and tend to be less expensive, but their routings often entail long stopovers.

Cape Town is not a cheap destination for travellers from Australia and New Zealand; high-low-season fares start at around Aus$3000/2000 for a return direct flight **from Sydney** to Cape Town via Johannesburg, and a flight to Europe with a stopover in South Africa, or even an RTW ticket, may represent better value than a straight-forward return. More affordable routes include Perth to Johannesburg via Singapore (Tiger Airways and Qatar) and Sydney or Melbourne to Johannesburg via Kuala Lumpur (Air Asia and Cathay Pacific).

AGENTS AND OPERATORS

Abercrombie & Kent Australia ☎ 1300 851 924, 🌐 abercrombiekent.com.au; UK ☎ 0845 485 1551, 🌐 abercrombiekent.co.uk; US ☎ 1 800 554 7016, 🌐 abercrombiekent.com. Classy operator whose packages feature Cape Town, Johannesburg, Kruger and luxury rail travel.

Adventure Center US ☎ 1 800 228 8747, 🌐 adventurecenter .com. Wide variety of affordable packages, including luxury rail journeys from Victoria Falls or Johannesburg to Cape Town.

A BETTER KIND OF TRAVEL

At Rough Guides we are passionately committed to travel. We believe it helps us understand the world we live in and the people we share it with – and of course tourism is vital to many developing economies. But the scale of modern tourism has also damaged some places irreparably, and climate change is accelerated by most forms of transport, especially flying. All Rough Guides' flights are carbon-offset, and every year we donate money to a variety of environmental charities.

Africa Travel Centre UK ☎ 020 7843 3500, ⊛ africatravel.co.uk.
Experienced Africa specialists, who are agents for many South
Africa-based overland operators.

Bales Worldwide UK ☎ 0844 488 1137, ⊛ balesworldwide.com.
High-quality escorted tours.

Cox & Kings UK ☎ 020 7873 5000, ⊛ coxandkings.co.uk;
US ☎ 1 800 999 1758, ⊛ coxandkingsusa.com. Stylish operator with
classic luxury journeys, including a twelve-day Cape Town to
Johannesburg excursion and deluxe safaris.

Destinations Ireland ☎ 01 435 0092, ⊛ destinations.ie. Specialists
in long-haul destinations, including South Africa.

Exodus UK ☎ 0845 287 3647, ⊛ exodus.co.uk. Small-group
adventure tour operator with trips in and around Cape Town, excursions to
the country's wildlife reserves and activity packages such as horseriding,
kloofing (canyoning), mountain biking and surfing.

Expert Africa UK ☎ 020 8232 9777; US ☎ 1 800 242 2434,
⊛ expertafrica.com. Small-group tours for independent travellers,
as well as tailor-made trips. Strong on Cape Town and the
Western Cape.

Explore Worldwide UK ☎ 0843 775 1343, ⊛ explore.co.uk;
US ☎ 1 800 715 1746, ⊛ exploreworldwide.com. Good range of
small-group tours, expeditions and safaris, staying mostly in small hotels
and taking in Cape Town and around.

Goway Travel Experiences US ☎ 1 800 557 2841, ⊛ goway.com.
Wide range of packages from three to fourteen days taking in the Western
Cape and Eastern Cape game reserves.

Joe Walsh Tours Ireland ☎ 01 241 0800, ⊛ joewalshtours.ie.
Budget fares as well as beach and safari packages in the Western and
Eastern Cape provinces.

Kuoni Travel UK ☎ 0844 488 0581, ⊛ kuoni.co.uk. Flexible
package holidays, including safaris, escorted tours and a three-night Cape
Town package. Good deals for families.

North South Travel UK ☎ 01245 608 291, ⊛ northsouthtravel
.co.uk. Discounted fares worldwide. Profits are used to support
projects in the developing world, especially the promotion of
sustainable tourism.

Okavango Tours and Safaris UK ☎ 020 8347 4030, ⊛ okavango
.com. Top-notch outfit with on-the-ground knowledge of sub-Saharan
Africa, offering fully flexible and individual tours across the country,
including the Western Cape.

On the Go Tours UK ☎ 020 7371 1113, ⊛ onthegotours.com.
Group and tailor-made tours to South Africa including a 22-day overland
safari from Cape Town to Victoria Falls.

Rainbow Tours UK ☎ 020 7666 1250, ⊛ rainbowtours.co.uk.
Knowledgeable and sensitive South Africa specialists whose trips
emphasize ecofriendly and community-based tourism, including
the "Footsteps of a Legend" tour, which pays tribute to Nelson
Mandela.

STA Travel UK ☎ 0333 321 0099, US ☎ 1800 781 4040, Australia
☎ 134 782, New Zealand ☎ 0800 474 400, South Africa ☎ 0861
781 781; ⊛ statravel.co.uk. Worldwide specialists in independent
travel; also student IDs, travel insurance, car rental, rail passes and more.
Good discounts for students and under-26s.

Trailfinders UK ☎ 0207 368 1200, Ireland ☎ 021 464 8800;
⊛ trailfinders.com. One of the best-informed and most efficient agents
for independent travellers.

Tribes UK ☎ 01473 890 499, ⊛ tribes.co.uk; US ☎ 1800 474 2056.
Unusual and off-the-beaten-track fair-trade safaris and cultural tours,
including Alternative Cape Town.

USIT Ireland ☎ 01 602 1906, Australia ☎ 1800 092 499; ⊛ usit.ie.
Ireland's main student and youth travel specialists.

Wildlife Worldwide UK ☎ 0845 130 6982, ⊛ wildlifeworldwide
.com. Tailor-made trips for wildlife and wilderness enthusiasts, including
a Garden Route self-drive package and excursions taking in national parks
and the Winelands.

Arrival

Cape Town International Airport, Cape Town's international and domestic airport (CPT; ⊛ acsa.co.za) lies 22km east of the city centre. A bureau de change is open to coincide with international arrivals; there are also ATMs here and a tourist information desk. The major car rental firms have desks inside the international terminal. Pre-booking a vehicle is essential, especially during the week when there is a big demand from domestic business travellers, and over the mid-December to mid-January and Easter peak seasons.

Metered 24-hour taxis operated by Touch Down Taxis (☎ 021 919 4659), an association of independent **cab companies** officially authorized by the airport, rank in reasonable numbers outside both terminals and charge around R250 for the trip into the city.

The cheapest transport from the airport is the **MyCiTi bus** (every 20min; 4.20am–9pm; R60–70; ☎ 0800 65 64 63, ⊛ myciti.org.za) operated by the city, which goes to the Civic Centre on Hertzog Boulevard, opposite the central train and bus station, and has connections further afield (see opposite). More expensive but considerably more convenient are the door-to-door **shuttle services** which offer transport around Cape Town, including airport transfers (see p.22).

Mobile phone rental is available at the international and domestic terminals from Vodashop Rentafone (⊛ rentafone.net) or Cellucity (⊛ b4i .travel) and can be organized beforehand for collection on arrival. Several car rental companies include free mobile rental (you only pay for calls) in their deals, and you can also rent GPS units.

Getting around

Cape Town's public transport system consists of a bus network that serves the city centre, the City Bowl, the northern suburbs and the Atlantic Seaboard, as well as a train line that runs through the southern suburbs and down the False Bay seaboard as far as Simon's Town.

For some attractions, you'll still need a **car** or else to rely on tours, or **minibus** and **metered taxis**. For getting further afield, there are several decent **intercity bus** lines as well as the **Baz Bus** backpacker service that gets to some places the intercity buses don't reach.

City transport

Although Cape Town's city centre is compact enough to get around on foot, many of the major attractions are spread along the considerable length of the peninsula and require transport to get there. Between them, the **MyCiTi rapid bus service**, introduced in 2011, and **Metrorail**, a single train line down the peninsula, offer a relatively comprehensive trunk service that covers much of Cape Town.

The **Golden Acre** shopping complex, at the junction of Strand and Adderley streets in the heart of Cape Town, can be a confusing muddle, but this, and the nearby **Civic Centre**, are where all rail and most bus transport (both intercity and from elsewhere in the city) and most minibus taxis converge. Everything you need for your next move is within two or three blocks of here, including tourist information (see p.38).

Buses

The **MyCiTi Bus** (☎080 065 6463, ⊛myciti.org.za) is a safe and comprehensive commuter system that operates daily from 5am to 10pm. Emulating a rail system, with stations along dedicated trunk roads, MyCiTi is part of the government's initiative to improve public transport in South Africa's major centres. Frequent buses service the **city centre**, **City Bowl suburbs**, **Atlantic Seaboard** and **Northern Suburbs** and provide a reliable transport alternative to cars, which most middle-class Capetonians rely on even for short distances. **Frequencies** vary from route to route but buses operate every 10 to 20 minutes during peak periods (6.30–8.30am & 4–6pm) and every 20 to 30 minutes during the off-peak period that falls between these times and over weekends. Importantly MyCiTi is the only safe public transport option in the evening and more routes are being added as the system evolves.

Cash is not accepted on buses and you'll need a **myconnect card**, which you load with credit to cover fares based on distance travelled. Fares range from R5 for routes within the city centre to R10 from the centre to Hout Bay or Table View and R60 to the airport. Cards can be bought for R25 from MyCiTi stations as well as the airport and visitor information centres in town, and can be refunded after your stay – you'll need your receipt.

To use the card you tap your card against validators marked "in" when you board, and again on one marked "out" when you get off.

The MyCiTi **website** has user-friendly and up-to-date **information** on fares, routes and timetables.

GO TOPLESS

The open-top, hop-on, hop-off red **City Sightseeing Bus** (☎021 511 6000, ⊛citysightseeing. co.za; 1-day ticket R150, children R70) is an extremely convenient and, on a fine day, fun way of getting to the major sights. It's also a great way to get around with kids – the headphone commentary runs one channel for adults and another for children, which features the voices of Blatjan Baboon and Madisa Mongoose among others. They operate two tours; buses leave from the Two Oceans Aquarium at the Waterfront.

The Blue Mini Peninsula Tour (daily May to mid-Sept every 35min, mid-Sept to early May every 20–25min; 9am–3.25pm) stops at Cape Town Tourism in Burg Street, *The Mount Nelson Hotel*, Kirstenbosch, World of Birds, Imizamo Yethu Township, Mariner's Wharf in Hout Bay, Camps Bay and Sea Point.

The Red City Centre Tour (daily May to mid-Sept every 20min, mid-Sept to April every 15min; 9am–5.15pm) stops at Cape Town Tourism, St George's Cathedral, SA Museum, Jewish Museum, District Six Museum, Castle of Good Hope, Gold Museum, Cableway, Camps Bay, Sea Point.

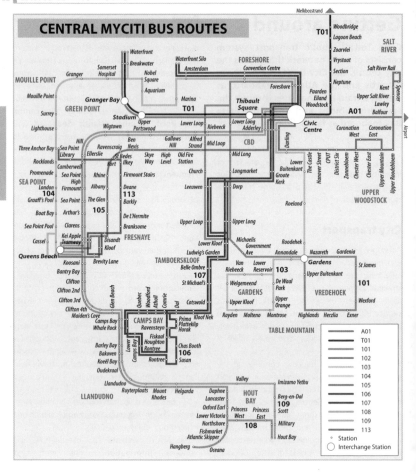

CENTRAL MYCITI BUS ROUTES

Taxis

The term "**taxi**" refers, somewhat confusingly, to conventional metered cars, jam-packed minibuses and *rikkis*.

Metered taxis

You will find regulated company-owned and independent **metered taxis** at the **taxi ranks** around town, including the Waterfront, the train station and Greenmarket Square. You can also hail one off the street, but to ensure you are using a regulated taxi, phone to be picked up (see box opposite). Taxis must have the driver's name and identification clearly on display and the meter clearly visible. **Fares** work out at around R12–15 per kilometre.

Minibus taxis

Minibus taxis are cheap, frequent and bomb up and down the main routes at tearaway speeds. They can be hailed from the street – you'll recognize them from the whistling, hooting and booming music – or boarded at the central taxi rank, above the Cape Town train station. Once you've boarded, pay the assistant who sits near the driver and tell where you want to get off. **Fares** are R7–10 for most trips. As well as risky driving, be prepared for **pickpockets** working the taxi ranks.

Rikkis and shuttle buses

Rikkis are ex-London taxi cabs, operating all hours and aimed principally at tourists; you need to

ENGLISH/AFRIKAANS STREET NAMES

Many towns along the Garden Route have **bilingual street names** with English and Afrikaans alternatives sometimes appearing along the same road. Often the Afrikaans name will bear little resemblance to the English one, something it's worth being aware of when trying to map read. In Cape Town you'll also find Afrikaans direction signs; for example signs for the airport will sometimes use the Afrikaans word "Lughawe".

We have included a list of Afrikaans terms you may encounter on signage in "Language" (see p.270).

book them by telephone (☎086 174 5547, ⓦ rikkis .co.za). They offer private rides and operate within three distinct areas: central (City Bowl and the Atlantic seaboard as far as Hout Bay); the southern suburbs (Claremont and Constantia); plus in and around Hout Bay. They also offer airport shuttles (R210 one way).

In the same vein but a little cheaper, the **Backpacker Bus** (booking two days ahead recommended; ☎082 809 9185, ⓦ backpackerbus.co.za) offers particularly good value transport for groups, from backpacker lodges to Kirstenbosch (one person return R280, two people R350, five or more R90pp return) and Stellenbosch (one person return R420, two people R480, five or more R140 per person return). They have a well-priced airport shuttle service, which runs 24 hours a day as required to accommodate flight arrivals and departures (R180 one way for the first person, two people R280, three people R300, five or more R70pp one way).

Trains

Cape Town's suburban **train** service is run by **Metrorail** (timetable information ☎0800 656 463, ⓦ capemetrorail.co.za). The only route likely to be useful to visitors is the relatively reliable if slightly run-down line that sets off from Cape Town station down through the southern suburbs and all the way down the False Bay seaboard as far as Simon's Town. Three other lines run east from Cape Town to Strand (through Bellville), to the Cape Flats, and to the outlying towns of Stellenbosch and Paarl; however, the journeys aren't recommended, as they run through some of the less safe areas of the Flats. Even on a False Bay train, never board an empty carriage.

The service to the False Bay seaboard must be one of the world's greatest urban train journeys. It reaches the coast at Muizenberg and continues south to Simon's Town, sometimes so spectacularly close to the ocean that you can feel the spray and peer into rock pools. The stretch of the line to Fish Hoek is well served, with several trains an hour. Services to Simon's Town run every forty to sixty minutes.

There are no signposts to the stations on the streets, so if you're staying in the southern suburbs, ask for directions at your accommodation. Tickets must be bought at the station before boarding – you're best off in the first-class carriages, which are reasonably priced (for example, Cape Town–Muizenberg is about R12 one way). Third class (curiously, there's no second class) tends to be more crowded, and in the mornings is often filled with the harmonies of domestic workers singing on their way to work.

Intercity buses

Baz Bus (☎0861 229 287, ⓦ bazbus.com) operates an extremely useful hop-on, hop-off service daily between Cape Town and Port Elizabeth in both

RELIABLE TAXI SERVICES

The three companies listed below run a prompt, 24-hour service, seven days a week, unless otherwise stated.

City Cabs ☎ 021 202 2222, ⓦ citycabsa.co.za. One of the best radio-controlled taxi services, operating 24 hours. Fares are R12 a kilometre with a minimum fee if booked in advance. When taken off the street you can usually bargain and get extremely competitive fares.

Excite Taxis ☎ 021 448 4444, ⓦ excitetaxis.co.za. Fares are R9 a kilometre within their normal operating area (city centre to southern suburbs), but there may be an additional charge if your

pick-up or drop-off point is further flung than this.

Rikkis ☎ 0861 745 547, ⓦ rikkis.co.za. Rikkis has one of the lowest fare-structures in town and operates in Hout Bay and the southern suburbs (24 hours, seven days). Fares are calculated at R10 a zone: so a ride from the Waterfront to the City Bowl, for example, would set you back about R60.

After 10pm there is an extra charge of R80.

directions, via Mossel Bay, George, Knysna, Plettenberg Bay, Storms River and Jeffrey's Bay, with other stops possible along the N2. The service is aimed squarely at backpackers, with buses stopping off at hostels en route. The Cape Town–Port Elizabeth fare is R1550 one way, though there are also better-value seven-, fourteen- and 21-day passes costing R1700, R2700 and R3300. Bookings can be made online, through hostels at the Baz office, 32 Burg St in the city centre or at the central tourist office in Cape Town.

South Africa's three established **intercity bus** companies are Greyhound (☎083 915 9000, ⓦgreyhound.co.za), Intercape (☎021 380 4400, ⓦintercape.co.za) and Translux (☎086 158 9282, ⓦtranslux.co.za); between them, they reach most towns in the country. Travel on these buses is safe, good value and very comfortable, the vehicles invariably equipped with air conditioning and toilets. Fares vary according to distances covered and the time of year, with peak fares corresponding approximately to school holidays; at other times you can expect about thirty percent off. As a rough indication you can expect to pay the following fares for single journeys from Cape Town: to Paarl, R270; Mossel Bay, R360; Port Elizabeth, R450.

Greyhound, Intercape and Translux intercity buses leave from around the interlinked complex in Cape Town's centre that includes the train station and **Golden Acre** shopping mall (see p.21). Note that Intercape and Translux arrive on the northeast side of the station, off Adderley Street, while Greyhound arrives on the northwest side in Adderley itself.

Translux and Greyhound also operate the no-frills budget bus lines **City to City** (ⓦcitytocity.co.za) and **Citiliner** (ⓦcitiliner.co.za) respectively, whose schedules and prices are listed on their websites. There is also a host of small private companies about which information is thin on the ground; your best bet is to enquire at the bus station the day before you travel.

Domestic flights

Driving the Garden Route in one direction – say out from Cape Town – and flying back from Port Elizabeth is a good (and popular) option, especially if time is short. Expect to pay at least R1400 each way for the flight, which takes just over an hour.

By far the biggest domestic airline is **South African Airways** (SAA; ☎0861 606 606, ⓦflysaa .com), with its associates **SA Airlink** and **SA Express** (reservations for the three are through SAA) with flights to **George** and **Port Elizabeth**, among other further-flung destinations. There are a number of smaller airlines that fly to **Port Elizabeth**, of which the most significant are **British Airways Comair** (☎086 043 5922, ⓦba.com) and its budget subsidiary **kulula.com** (☎086 158 5852, ⓦkulula.com); and Mango (☎086 100 1234, ⓦflymango.com). Cemair (☎011 395 4473, ⓦflyce mair.co.za) flies from Cape Town and Johannesburg to Plettenberg Bay in the heart of the Garden Route.

Driving and cycling

Cape Town has good roads and several fast freeways that, outside peak hours (7–9am & 4–6pm), can whisk you across town in next to no time. The obvious landmarks of Table Mountain and the two seaboards make orientation straightforward, particularly south of the centre, and some wonderful journeys are possible. The most notable are the drives along the Atlantic seaboard to Hout Bay and **Chapman's Peak Drive**, a narrow, winding, cliff-edge road with the Atlantic breaking hundreds of metres below; and around the **Cape Point** section of the Table Mountain National Park, via the False Bay seaboard.

National roads (with an "N" prefix) and **provincial roads** (with an "R" prefix) in the rest of the Western Cape are of a generally high standard. The only time you're likely to encounter adverse conditions is during school holidays, particularly the Easter and December breaks, when the N1 and N2 become fairly congested, nerves fray, alcohol is copiously consumed and drivers' behaviour deteriorates accordingly.

Petrol stations are frequent on the major routes of the country, and usually open 24 hours a day. Off the major routes, though, stations are less frequent, so fill up whenever you get the chance. Stations are rarely self-service; instead, attendants fill up your car, check oil, water and tyre pressure if you ask them to, and often clean your windscreen even if you don't. A tip of R5–10 is normal.

Regulations

You drive on the **left-hand side**, with **speed limits** ranging from 60kph in built-up areas to 100kph on rural roads and 120kph on highways and major arteries. In addition to roundabouts, which follow the British rule of giving way to the right, there are four-way stops, where the rule is that the person who got there first leaves first, and you are not expected to give way to the right. Note that traffic lights are often called **robots** in South Africa.

DRIVING TIPS

The only real challenge you'll face on the roads is **other drivers**. South Africa has among the world's worst road accident statistics – the result of reckless driving, drunken drivers (see p.33) or defective, overloaded vehicles. Keep your distance from cars in front, as domino-style pile-ups are common. Watch out also for **overtaking** traffic coming towards you. Overtakers often assume that you will head for the **hard shoulder** to avoid an accident (it is legal to drive on the hard shoulder, but be careful as people frequently walk on it). If you do pull into the hard shoulder to let a car overtake, the other driver will probably thank you by flashing the hazard lights. If oncoming cars **flash their headlights** at you, it probably means that there is a **speed trap** up ahead.

Driving in and around Cape Town presents a few peculiarities all of its own. An unwritten rule of the road on the peninsula is that **minibus taxis** have the right of way – and will push in front of you without compunction and will routinely run through amber lights as they change to red – as will many Capetonians.

Take care approaching a **freeway** in Cape Town: the slip roads frequently feed directly into the fast lane, and Capetonians routinely exceed the 100kph freeway and 120kph highway speed limits. Furthermore, there's often little warning of branches off to the suburbs, only the final destination of the freeway being signed. Your best bet is to plan your journey, and make sure you know exactly where you're going.

Foreign **driving licences** are valid in South Africa for up to six months, provided they are printed in English. If you don't have such a licence, you'll need to get an International Driving Permit before arriving in South Africa (available from national motoring organizations). When driving, make sure you have your driving licence and passport on you at all times.

Car and bike rental

Given Cape Town's scant public transport, **renting** a vehicle is the only convenient way of exploring the Cape Peninsula, and needn't break the bank. There are dozens of competing car rental companies to choose from (see below). To get the best deal, either pick up one of the brochures at the Cape Town Tourism office or book beforehand (often cheaper) with an international company which might offer particular deals tied in with your airline or credit card company. Many backpacker hostels have cheaper deals with agencies too.

For **motorbike rental**, Cape Town Scooter Hire, 255 Main Rd, Sea Point (9am–11pm; R220/day; ☎021 827 2828, ⓦcapetownscooter.co.za) will offer a 10 percent discount to the Rough Guides readers quoting this listing. For something more powerful, Cape Bike Travel, 125 Buitengracht (☎084 606 4449, ⓦcapebiketravel.com), rent out BMWs and Harley Davidsons along with full protective gear (BMW1200GS or Harley Heritage classic R R1200/day for seven days; scooters R150/day). Price includes comprehensive insurance and helmet.

For **cyclists**, one of the most popular – and hair-raising – road routes is along the narrow hairpins of Chapman's Peak Drive, which offer stupendous views of the Atlantic. There are also a number of dedicated mountain-biking routes in the peninsula's nature reserves. Mountain bikes are available from Downhill Adventures, Shop 10 Overbeek Building, corner of Kloof and Orange streets (☎021 422 0388, ⓦdownhilladventures.co.za), for R200 a day. They also offer organized cycle outings that include trips to Cape Point, the Winelands and a Table Mountain descent.

CAR RENTAL AGENCIES

Alamo ⓦ alamo.com
Auto Europe ⓦ autoeurope.com
Avis ⓦ avis.co.za
Budget ⓦ budget.com
Cheap Motorhome Rental ⓦ cheapmotorhomes.co.za
Dollar ⓦ dollar.com
Drive Africa ☎ 061 066 8578, ⓦ driveafrica.co.za
Europcar ⓦ europcar.com
Hertz ⓦ hertz.com
Holiday Autos ⓦ holidayautos.co.uk
National ⓦ nationalcar.com
SIXT ⓦ sixt.com
Tempest ☎ 11 552 3900, ⓦ tempestcarhire.co.za
Thrifty ⓦ thrifty.com
Vineyard Car Hire ⓦ vineyardcarhire.co.za

CAMPER VAN RENTAL AGENCIES

Kea Rentals ⓦ kea.co.za
Maui ⓦ maui.co.za

Tours

Cape Town is awash with tour packages, from standard, through-the-window outings that take you from one sight to the other, to really excellent specialist packages. For some depth, opt for one of the cultural tours, which cover all aspects of Cape Town life, or feel the exhilaration of the peninsula's environment on foot or from the saddle of a bike. Almost all these companies will pick you up from your accommodation and drop you off again at the end of the day.

WALKING TOURS

One of the best ways to orient yourself at the start of a visit is on a walking tour through central Cape Town. Tours run by these two companies depart mid-morning daily, except Sundays, from the Visitor Information Centre in Burg Street, lasting roughly three hours. You need to book in advance.

Footsteps to Freedom ☎ 083 452 1112, ⓦ footstepstofreedom .co.za; R220. Offers a tour that takes in historical sights and buildings with a conscious politico/socio slant.

Cape Town on Foot ☎ 021 462 4252, ⓦ wanderlust.co.za; R200. Run by an ex-teacher and writer, these tours take in the city centre as well as the Bo-Kaap, and can be taken in English or German.

CULTURAL TOURS

A smaller number of companies offer niche cultural tours; the most popular of these are township tours, the safest way to see the African and coloured areas that were created under apartheid.

Andulela Tours ☎ 021 418 3020, ⓦ andulela.com. Fabulous selection of under-the-skin tours which could get you drumming, bead-making or cooking in the African townships, visiting homes to hear music of well-known Cape Jazz musicians, cooking Cape Malay food in the Bo-Kaap, doing a soccer tour, visiting the Winelands, or learning more about baboons with a conservationist at Cape Point. They can also take you further afield to the Cederberg to look at rock art.

Bonani Our Pride ☎ 021 531 4291, ⓦ bonanitours.co.za. Recommended tours to meet people as well as to visit sights of political significance in the townships. They do township evening tours, gospel tours where you visit Xhosa churches on a Sunday morning and Xhosa folklore tours.

Coffeebeans Routes ☎ 021 424 3572, ⓦ coffeebeansroutes.com. Under the creative direction of Iain Harris, they are pioneers in creative tourism in the townships, and the people to go to for music and cultural journeys including the Cape Jazz Safari, cuisine, fashion or Township Futures tour.

GENERAL TOURS

If you want a trip that covers more distance – the major peninsula sights and beyond – there are a few excellent operators.

Cape Convoy ☎ 021 531 1928, ⓦ capeconvoy.com. Tours with popular, passionate and fun Brit Rob Salmon can be arranged to the Garden Route, the Winelands and Cape Point (R850, max 6 people per group, includes entrance fees).

Day Trippers ☎ 021 511 4766, ⓦ daytrippers.co.za. An excellent company if you want an active Peninsula and Cape Point day-tour that includes cycling and hiking. They also go further afield to hike and cycle in the Cederberg, Little Karoo and Winelands.

Discovery Tours ☎ 027 78 161 7818, ⓦ discoverytours.co.za. Specializing in private tours to the Peninsula, the Winelands and West Coast. Tours are tailored to each group by knowledgeable and friendly guides Tania and Yaseen but are the same price as groups open to the public (2 people R1250, 3 people R1000, entrance fees not included).

Health

You can put aside most of the health fears that may be justified in some parts of Africa; run-down hospitals and bizarre tropical diseases aren't typical of Cape Town and the Garden Route, and malaria isn't an issue here at all. All tourist areas enjoy generally high standards of hygiene and safe drinking water. The only hazard you're likely to encounter, and the one the majority of visitors are most blasé about, is the sun.

Public **hospitals** are fairly well equipped but are facing huge pressures, under which their attempts to maintain standards are unfortunately buckling. Expect long waits and frequently indifferent treatment. **Private hospitals** or clinics are usually a better option for travellers and are well up to British or North American standards. You'll get to see a doctor quickly and costs are not excessive, unless you require major surgery, in which case health insurance is a must.

Dental care in South Africa is well up to British and North American standards, and is generally less expensive. You'll find dentists in Cape Town and most smaller towns, listed under "Dentists" and doctors under "Medical" at the back of the *White Pages* telephone directory.

Inoculations

No specific inoculations are compulsory if you arrive in South Africa from the West, although the Hospital for Tropical Diseases in London advises that you ensure your polio and tetanus vaccinations are up to date. In addition, it recommends a course of shots against **typhoid** and an injection against **hepatitis A**, both of which can be caught from contaminated food or water – though this is extremely unlikely in the region covered by this guide. A **yellow fever** vaccination certificate is necessary if you've come from a country or region where the disease is endemic, such as Kenya, Tanzania or tropical South America.

If you decide to have an armful of jabs, start organizing them **six weeks** before departure. If you're going to another African country first and need the yellow fever jab, note that a yellow fever certificate only becomes valid ten days after you've had the shot.

MEDICAL RESOURCES FOR TRAVELLERS

Canadian Society for International Health ☎ 613 241 5785, Ⓦ csih.org. Extensive list of travel health centres.

CDC ☎ 1800 232 6348, Ⓦ cdc.gov/travel. Official US government travel health site.

Hospital for Tropical Diseases Travel Clinic Ⓦ thehtd.org /Travelclinic.aspx. Online destination health advice for travellers, inoculations, and an online shop selling goods such as first-aid kits, mosquito nets and suncream.

International Society for Travel Medicine ☎ 1 404 373 8282, Ⓦ istm.org. Has a full list of travel health clinics.

MASTA (Medical Advisory Service for Travellers Abroad) Ⓦ masta -travel-health.com. The website gives details of your nearest clinic.

The Travel Doctor ☎ 1300 658 844, Ⓦ tmvc.com.au. Lists travel clinics in Australia and New Zealand.

Travel Doctor ☎ 0861 300 911, Ⓦ traveldoctor.co.za. Lists travel clinics in South Africa.

Tropical Medical Bureau ☎ 1850 487 674, Ⓦ tmb.ie. Website offers extensive advice for travellers, with a number of clinics based in Ireland.

STATE HOSPITALS AND CLINICS IN CAPE TOWN

Groote Schuur Hospital Drive, Observatory ☎ 021 404 9111. Just off the M3, this is the largest state hospital in Cape Town.

New Somerset Hospital Cnr Beach Road and Lower Portwood Road, Green Point ☎ 021 402 6911. A state hospital with outpatient and emergency departments, although it's generally overcrowded, understaffed and under-equipped.

PRIVATE HOSPITALS, DOCTORS AND CLINICS

The two largest **private hospital groups** are **Netcare** (emergency response ☎ 082 911, Ⓦ netcare.co.za) and **Medi-Clinic** (emergency response operated by ER24 ☎ 084 124, Ⓦ mediclinic.co.za) chains, with hospitals all over the Cape Peninsula; in addition to the hospitals listed here, which are open 24 hours for emergencies, Netcare runs over two dozen **Medicross Medical Centres** (Ⓦ medicross.co.za) across the Western Cape, which are not open 24 hours, but do operate extended hours.

Cape Town Medi-Clinic 21 Hof St, Oranjezicht ☎ 021 464 5500; emergency ☎ 021 464 5555. Close to the city centre in the middle of the City Bowl.

Christiaan Barnard Memorial Hospital 181 Longmarket St ☎ 021 480 6111. Most central of the Netcare private hospitals is

convenient for the city centre, the V&A Waterfront, De Waterkant and the Atlantic seaboard.

Constantiaberg Medi-Clinic Burnham Road, Plumstead ☎ 021 799 2911; emergency ☎ 021 799 2196. In the southern suburbs, this is the closest private hospital to the False Bay seaboard.

UCT Private Academic Hospital Anzio Road, Observatory ☎ 021 442 1800. Netcare hospital adjacent to Groote Schuur in the heart of the southern suburbs.

Stomach upsets

Stomach upsets from food are rare. Salad and ice – the danger items in many other developing countries – are both perfectly safe. As with anywhere, though, don't keep food for too long, and be sure to wash fruit and vegetables as thoroughly as possible.

If you do get a **stomach bug**, the best cure is lots of water and rest. Papayas – the flesh as well as the pips – are a good tonic to offset the runs. Otherwise, most chemists should have nonprescription anti-diarrhoea remedies.

Avoid jumping for **antibiotics** at the first sign of illness. Instead keep them as a last resort – they don't work on viruses and they annihilate your gut flora (most of which you want to keep), making you more susceptible next time round. Most tummy upsets will resolve themselves if you adopt a sensible fat-free diet for a couple of days, but if they do persist without improvement (or are accompanied by other unusual symptoms), then see a doctor as soon as possible.

The sun

The **sun** is likely to be the worst hazard you'll encounter in South Africa, particularly, but not exclusively, if you're fair-skinned.

Short-term effects of **overexposure** to the sun include burning, nausea and headaches. This usually comes from overeager tanning, which can leave you looking like a lobster. The fairer your skin, the slower you should take tanning. Start with short periods of exposure and **high protection sunscreen** (at least SPF 15), gradually increasing your time in the sun and decreasing the factor of the sunscreen. Many people with fair skins, especially those who freckle easily, should take extra care, starting with a very high factor screen (SPF 25–30) and continue using at least SPF 15 for the rest of their stay.

Overexposure to the sun can cause sunburn to the surface of the eye, inflammation of the cornea and can result in serious short- and long-term damage. Good **sunglasses** can reduce ultraviolet (UV) light exposure to the eye by fifty percent. A **broad-brimmed hat** is also recommended.

The last few measures are especially necessary for **children**, who should ideally be kept well covered at the seaside. Don't be lulled into complacency on **cloudy days**, when UV levels can still be high. UV-protective clothing is available locally, but it's best to buy before you arrive. If you don't come with this gear, make sure children wear T-shirts at the beach, and use SPF 30 sunscreen liberally and often.

Bites and stings

Bites and stings in South Africa are comparatively rare. **Snakes** are present, but hardly ever seen as they move out of the way quickly. The sluggish puff and berg adders are the most dangerous, because they often lie in paths and don't move when humans approach. The best advice if you get bitten is to note what the snake looked like and get yourself to a clinic or hospital. Most bites are not fatal and the worst thing you can do is to panic: desperate measures with razor blades and tourniquets risk doing more harm than good.

Tick-bite fever is occasionally contracted from walking in the bush, long wet grass with the greatest prevalence of ticks in February and March at the end of summer. The offending ticks can be minute and you may not spot them. Symptoms appear a week later – swollen glands and severe aching of the joints, backache and fever. The disease will run its course in three or four days. Ticks you may find on yourself are not dangerous, just repulsive at first. Make sure you pull out the head as well as the body (it's not painful). A good way of removing small ones is to smear Vaseline or grease over them, making them release their hold.

Scorpion stings and **spider bites** are painful but almost never fatal, contrary to popular myth. Scorpions and spiders abound, but they're hardly ever seen unless you turn over logs and stones. If you're collecting wood for a campfire, knock or shake it before picking it up. Another simple precaution when camping is to shake out your shoes and clothes in the morning before you get dressed.

Rabies is present throughout southern Africa with dogs posing the greatest risk, although the disease can be carried by other animals. If you are bitten, you should go immediately to a clinic or hospital. Rabies can be treated effectively with a course of injections.

Sexually transmitted diseases

HIV/AIDS and venereal diseases are widespread in southern Africa among both men and women, and the danger of catching the virus through sexual contact is very real. Follow the usual precautions regarding safer sex; international brand condoms are widely available from pharmacies and supermarkets. There's no special risk from medical treatment in the country, but if you're travelling overland and you want to play it safe, take your own needle and transfusion kit.

The media

With two rather parochial daily English-language newspapers, plus a few magazines devoted mainly to entertainment and tourism, Cape Town's media are unlikely to blow anyone away. Radio and TV are dominated by South Africa's national broadcasters, with a few local radio offerings that include a talk station, a pioneering black community station and several others that play sounds from classical to pop.

Newspapers and magazines

Cape Town has two fairly uninspiring daily English **newspapers**, owned by the same company: the **Cape Times** broadsheet comes out on weekday mornings, while the tabloid-format **Cape Argus** also comes out during the week, but has Saturday and Sunday editions. Both are dominated by local news, with a smattering of national and international coverage. In addition there's the national **Business Day**, which is the best daily source of hard countrywide and international news.

Unquestionably the country's intellectual heavyweight ("heavy" being the operative word) is the **Mail & Guardian**, which comes out on Friday; it benefits enormously from its association with the London *Guardian* (from which it draws much of its international coverage). South Africa's **Sunday Times** can attribute the biggest circulation in the country – roughly half a million copies and over three million readers – to its well-calculated mix of solid investigative reporting, gossip, material from the British press and salacious rewrites of stories lifted from foreign tabloids. The **Sowetan**, targeted at a mainly black Jo'burg audience, is widely available across the country.

However, the liveliest of all South African news publications is the boundary-breaking, free online **Daily Maverick** (Ⓦdailymaverick.co.za), which is brimful of news and analysis with a stable of some of South Africa's most challenging and provocative columnists.

For **events listings** in Cape Town you could check out newspaper supplements and online sources. These include **Cape Town Magazine** (Ⓦcapetownmagazine.com) or **What's On in Cape Town** (Ⓦwhatsonincapetown.com).

Both local papers and international publications such as *Time*, *Newsweek*, *The Economist* and the weekly overseas editions of the British *Daily Mail*, the *Telegraph* and the *Express* are available from corner stores and newsagents.

Television

The South Africa Broadcasting Corporation's three TV channels churn out a mixed bag of domestic dramas, game shows, sport, soaps and documentaries, filled out with lashings of familiar imports. **SABC 1, 2 and 3** share the unenviable task of trying to deliver an integrated service, while having to split their time between the eleven official languages. English turns out to be most widely used, with SABC 3 broadcasting almost exclusively in the language, while SABC 2 and SABC 1 spread themselves thinly across the remaining ten languages, with a fair amount of English creeping in even here.

A selection of sports, movies, news and specialist channels are available to subscribers to the **M-Net** satellite service, which is piped into many hotels. South Africa's first and only free-to-air independent commercial channel **e.tv** won its franchise in 1998 on the promise of providing a showcase for local productions, a pledge it has signally failed to meet – its output has substantially consisted of imports.

There is no cable TV in South Africa, but **DSTV** (Ⓦdstv.co.za) offers a **satellite television** subscription service with a selection of sports, movies, news (including BBC, CNN and Al Jazeera) and specialist channels, some of which are available in hotels.

Radio

Given South Africa's low literacy rate and widespread poverty, it's no surprise that **radio** is a highly popular medium. The SABC operates a national radio station for each of the eleven official language groups. The English-language national service, **SAfm** (104–107FM, Ⓦsafm.co.za), is heavily laden with dull phone-in shows, but has two passable news programmes, one in the morning (5.30–8am) and the other in the evening (4–6pm).

Cape Town stations include **Cape Talk** (567AM, Ⓦcapetalk.co.za), which puts out wall-to-wall chatter consisting of news, reviews, discussions and phone-ins varying from first rate to brain-numbingly pedestrian, as well as wall-to-wall musical golden oldies during the daytime at weekends; and **Bush Radio** (89.5FM, Ⓦbushradio .co.za), one of South Africa's first community stations, which attempts to actively involve members of Cape Town's black community, who were denied a voice under apartheid. Apart from hosting debates about significant issues to the community and broadcasting informative social documentaries, Bush Radio also pumps out great local music. A number of other local stations are devoted to 24-hour music, the most successful being **Heart Radio** (109.4FM, Ⓦ1049.fm), which targets high-income black and coloured listeners in the Mother City with its mix of jazz fusion, funk, soul and R&B. Somewhat staid by comparison is **Fine Music Radio** (101 FM, Ⓦfmr.co.za), which politely delivers the classics and a smattering of respectable jazz.

Festivals

Many of the Western Cape's events take place outdoors in summer, and make full use of the city's wonderful setting. They include the **Cape Town Minstrel Carnival**, a unique event rooted in the city's coloured community, while the **Kirstenbosch Summer Sunset Concerts**, which run from late December to early April, are a must. Winter tends to be quiet, but it does herald the arrival of calving whales, and in their wake the **Hermanus Whale Festival** in September, which packs out this small southern Cape settlement.

Tickets for many of the events listed below are available from Computicket (☎083 915 8000, Ⓦcomputicket.co.za).

JANUARY

Cape Town Minstrels Carnival Jan 2. South Africa's longest and most raucous annual party, the carnival brings over ten thousand spectators to watch the parade through the city centre. It starts on Jan 2 for the Tweede Nuwe Jaar or "Second New Year" celebrations – an extension of New Year's Day unique to the Western Cape. Central to the festivities are the brightly decked-out coloured minstrel troupes that vie in singing and dancing contests. Tickets are best reserved through Computicket – you won't get such a good view if you buy tickets at the gate on the day.

Maynardville Shakespeare Festival Mid-Jan to mid-Feb; W maynardville.co.za. A usually imaginative production of one of the Bard's plays is staged each year in the beautiful setting of the Maynardville Open Air Theatre in Wynberg.

FEBRUARY

Cape Town Pride Pageant W capetownpride.co.za. Series of gay-themed events over two weeks, kicking off with a pageant at which Mr and Mrs Gay Pride are crowned, and taking in a bunch of parties and a street parade.

MARCH

Cape Argus Pick 'n Pay Cycle Tour First half of the month; W cycletour.org.za. The largest and arguably most spectacular, individually timed bike race in the world, with 35,000 participants on the 109km course – much of it along the ocean's edge – draws many thousands of spectators along the route. You can pick up entry forms from Pick 'n Pay supermarkets, cycle shops or enter online. Book early as it is heavily subscribed.

Cape Town Carnival Middle of the month; W capetowncarnival .com. A Rio-style street extravaganza that kicked off in 2010, the carnival is centred on Long Street with floats, parades and general euphoria intended to celebrate Cape Town's cultural diversity and richness. Festivities start at 3pm along the fan walk, and the parade at 7:30pm.

Cape Town International Jazz Festival Last weekend of the month; W capetownjazzfest.com. Initiated in 2000 as the Cape Town counterpart of the world-famous North Sea Jazz Festival, this event has now come of age and acquired a local identity. Notable past performers have included Courtney Pine, Herbie Hancock, and African greats such as Jimmy Dludlu, Moses Molelekwa, Youssou N'Dour, Miriam Makeba and Hugh Masakela.

APRIL

Klein Karoo Nasionale Kunstefees First week of the month; W kknk.co.za. South Africa's largest Afrikaans arts and culture festival packs out the Karoo *dorp* of Oudtshoorn with festival goers, turning the otherwise dozy town into one big jumping, jiving party. If you don't understand Afrikaans, you'll still find enough English offerings as well as dance, music and other performance to keep you busy.

Two Oceans Marathon Second half of the month; W twooceansmarathon.org.za. Another of the Cape's big sports events, this is in fact an ultra-marathon (56km), with huge crowds lining the route to cheer on the participants. A less scenic half-marathon is held at the same time.

Pink Loerie Mardi Gras End of the month; W pinkloerie.co.za. Five-day gay pride celebration of parties, contests, cabaret, drag shows and performance in Knysna, South Africa's oyster capital.

MAY

Franschhoek Literary Festival Middle of the month; W flf.co.za. Three-day celebration of books, writers and wine in the Winelands food capital, Franschhoek, featuring leading local and international writers, editors and cartoonists.

Good Food & Wine Show End of the month; W goodfoodand wineshow.co.za. Celebrity chefs from around the world is just one of the compelling attractions that make this Cape Town's foodie event of the year. There are also hands-on workshops, delicious nibbles and wine as well as kitchen implements and books for sale.

JUNE

Encounters South African International Documentary Film Festival Middle of the month; W encounters.co.za. Fortnight-long showcase of documentary film-making from South Africa and the world.

JULY

Franschhoek Bastille Festival Middle of the month; W franschhoekbastille.co.za. Celebrating centuries-old French Huguenot heritage in a splash of red, white and blue, this festival is centred around a marquee where you can sample wine and food from Franschhoek's acclaimed chefs and wine estates, while listening to live music and watching the boules and barrel-rolling competition.

Knysna Oyster Festival First ten days of the month; W oysterfestival.co.za. Just over a week of carousing and oyster-eating in all its forms along the Garden Route, kicked off with a road-bike race and closed with the Knysna Marathon.

AUGUST

Cape Town Comedy Festival First half of the month; W comedyfestival.co.za. Africa's biggest comedy festival brings the world's hottest acts to the Mother City for a week.

Cape Town Fashion Week Beginning of the month; W african fashioninternational.com Multiple catwalk shows over three days are aimed at showcasing new spring and summer collections from leading South African designers, including Thula Sindi, Craig Port, Rosenwerth and new talent like Mr Price & Elle and Anisa Malembo Mpungwe.

SEPTEMBER

Hermanus Whale Festival Towards the end of the month; W whalefestival.co.za. To coincide with peak whale-watching season, the Southern Cape town of Hermanus (see p.168) stages a week-long annual festival of arts and the environment. Activities include plays, a craft market, a children's festival and live music.

Out in Africa South African Gay & Lesbian Film Festival End of the month; W oia.co.za. Purportedly the most popular movie festival in the country, screening gay- and lesbian-themed international and local productions.

OCTOBER

Rocking the Daisies Beginning of the month; W rocking thedaisies.com. South Africa's premier and biggest youth music festival showcasing the biggest local and international acts. Held on Cloof Wine Estate in Darling, most people make the most of it, camping for all three days.

NOVEMBER

Cape Town International Kite Festival Beginning of the month; W capementalhealth.co.za/kite. This high-flying extravaganza attracts

20,000 visitors each year. Bring your own kite, buy one at the festival or join in a kite-making workshop. All proceeds go towards Cape Mental Health, providing services in resource-poor communities.

Kirstenbosch Summer Sunset Concerts Every Sun from end of the month to early April; ☎ 021 799 8783. Among the musical highlights of the Cape Town calendar are the popular concerts held on the magnificent lawns of the botanical gardens at the foot of Table Mountain. Performances begin at 5.30pm and cover a range of genres, from local jazz to classical music. Come early to find a parking place, bring a picnic and some Cape fizz – and enjoy. Tickets available at the gate.

DECEMBER

Carols by Candlelight at Kirstenbosch Thurs–Sun before Christmas; ☎ 021 799 8783. The botanical gardens' annual carol singing and nativity tableau is a Cape Town institution, drawing crowds of families with their picnic baskets. The gates open at 7pm and the singing kicks off at 8pm.

Franschhoek Cap Classique and Champagne Festival Beginning of the month; ⓦ franschhoekmcc.co.za. Popular three-day bacchanalia of bubbly sampling – a vast selection of local and French sparkling wine is on hand – and gourmandizing in the Cape Winelands.

Mother City Queer Projects Early in the month (see p.145). A hugely popular party attracting thousands of gay revellers, for which a vast venue is chartered. Outlandish get-ups, multiple dancefloors and a mood of sustained delirium make this event a real draw.

Spier Summer Festival December till March; ⓦ spier.co.za. Four months of major arts events, at the Spier wine estate, near Stellenbosch, which are increasingly taking on an African flavour, featuring music, opera, dance, stand-up comedy and theatre.

Parks, reserves and wilderness areas

The region covered by this guide is bookended by two major national parks: at the western extreme is the Table Mountain National Park, a patchwork of wilderness that covers the full extent of the Cape Peninsula; and at the eastern end is Addo Elephant National Park which, apart from the pachyderms, is also home to lions, buffalos, leopards and rhinos – the only such major game reserve in the southern half of the country.

Between the two lie a series of provincial reserves and national parks, many of which are worth incorporating into any journey across the Southern Cape. In addition to the aforementioned, among

the top wilderness areas in the country are **De Hoop Nature Reserve**, with its massive dunes and its status as one of the best places in the world for land-based whale-watching; and the **Tsitsikamma section** of the **Garden Route National Park**, which attracts large numbers of visitors for its ancient forests, cliff-faced oceans and the dramatic Storms River Mouth.

All the national parks covered in this guide fall under the aegis of **South African National Parks** (☎012 428 9111, ⓦsanparks.org). A few reserves mentioned, including De Hoop and Goukamma, are run by **CapeNature** (ⓦcapenature.org.za).

Entry fees and accommodation

National parks charge a **conservation fee**, which is usually **payable daily**. At most of the national parks covered by this guide this comes to between R80 and R220 per day for foreign visitors (half-price for children), though citizens of the Southern Africa Development Community (SADC: includes Angola, Botswana, Congo, Lesotho, Malawi, Mauritius, Mozambique, Namibia, South Africa, Swaziland, Tanzania, Zambia and Zimbabwe) pay half the adult foreigner's rate. South African residents pay a quarter of the adult foreigner's rate.

In the case of Table Mountain National Park Cape of Good Hope, there is a daily conservation fee of R110 (children R55), which applies to all visitors. Entry into CapeNature reserves generally costs around R40 (children R35) a day per person, irrespective of nationality.

Most national parks and some of the CapeNature Conservation reserves have **accommodation**, which generally has a pleasantly rustic atmosphere in keeping with the wilderness surrounds. Units vary from rondavels at De Hoop Nature Reserve that start at R400 per person a night (accommodation now privately managed by ⓦdehoopcollection.com), to pretty comfortable, fully equipped en-suite cottages and chalets at the Garden Route and Addo Elephant national parks that start at around R840 to R1180 a night for a couple. Some reserves have family units that sleep four or more, and you'll find **camping facilities** at virtually all the reserves.

You can **book** park accommodation in advance (to stay in high season, do so several months in advance) through SANParks if the park in question is managed by them or, in the case of a CapeNature site, through the park itself (details in the guide and on its website). Note that if you try booking for South African National Parks over the phone you

TOP PARKS AND WILDLIFE AREAS

PARK	PRINCIPAL FOCUS	DESCRIPTION & HIGHLIGHTS	DETAILS
Addo Elephant National Park	Endangered species	The only Big Five national park in the southern half of the country, known for its three-hundred-strong elephant herd.	p.244
Agulhas National Park	Marine and coastal ecology	Rugged southernmost tip of Africa with rich plant biodiversity and significant archeological sites.	p.176
De Hoop Nature Reserve	Marine mammals and coastal *fynbos*	A combination of whales, massive dunes, *fynbos* and spectacular coastline.	p.179
Garden Route National Park	Marine and coastal, and endangered species	Focused on three sections: • Wilderness and its lakes, rivers, lagoons, forest, *fynbos*, beaches and sea. • Knysna, a marine area that covers the lagoon and its dramatic headlands. The lagoon area protects the endangered Knysna sea horse. • Tsitsikamma, featuring cliffs, tidal pools, deep gorges and evergreen forests; offers snorkelling, scuba diving and forest trails.	Chapter 17
Goukamma Nature Reserve	Marine and coastal ecology	Comprises a river and estuary with some of the highest vegetated dunes in South Africa.	p.198
Robberg Marine and Nature Reserve	Rocky headland ecology	The promontory is a fine example of the interaction of plant and animal life on southern coastal headlands and a good place to spot seals at work; good hiking.	p.211
Table Mountain National Park	The natural areas of the peninsula	Famed for the extraordinary diversity of flora and fauna living in the wild areas within and around Cape Town. The area spans Table Mountain, the Boulders Beach penguin colony and the Cape of Good Hope reserve.	p.68

could well be in for a long wait; contacting them online is recommended.

Crime and personal safety

Despite horror stories of sky-high crime rates, most people visit South Africa without incident; be careful, but don't be paranoid. This is not to underestimate the issue – crime is probably the most serious problem facing the country. But some perspective is in order: crime is disproportionately concentrated in the townships rather than areas frequented by most visitors.

Protecting property and "security" are major national obsessions, and it's difficult to imagine what many South Africans would discuss at their dinner parties if the problem disappeared. A substantial percentage of middle-class homes subscribe to the services of armed private security firms. The other obvious manifestation of this obsession is the huge number of alarms, high walls and electronically controlled gates you'll find, not just in the suburbs, but even in less deprived areas of some townships.

Guns are openly carried by police – and often citizens. In many high streets you'll spot firearms shops rubbing shoulders with places selling clothes or books, and you'll come across notices asking you to deposit your weapon before entering the premises.

If you fall victim to a **mugging**, you should take very seriously the usual advice not to resist, and do as you're told. The chances of being mugged can be greatly minimized by using common sense and following a few simple rules (see box below).

Drugs

Alcohol is unquestionably the most widely used and abused drug in South Africa, followed by dagga (pronounced like "dugger" with the "gg" guttural, as in the Scottish pronunciation of "loch") or ca[...] in dried leaf form. Locally grown and produc[...], fairly easily available and the quality is generally good – but this doesn't alter the fact that it is illegal.

Alcohol and drink-driving

Strangely, for a country that sometimes seems to be on one massive binge, South Africa has laws that prohibit drinking in public – not that anyone pays any attention to them. The **drink-drive laws** are routinely and brazenly flouted, making the country's roads the one real danger you should be concerned about. People routinely stock up their cars with booze for long journeys and even at petrol stations you'll find places selling liquor. Levels of alcohol consumption go some way to explaining why,

---

SAFETY TIPS

IN GENERAL:

- don't openly display expensive watches, jewellery, cameras or video cameras in cities.
- if you are accosted, remain calm and cooperative.

WHEN ON FOOT:

- grasp bags firmly under your arm.
- don't carry excessive sums of money on you.
- always know where your valuables are.
- don't leave valuables exposed (on a seat or the ground) while having a meal or drink.
- don't let strangers get too close to you – especially people in groups.

ON THE ROAD:

- lock all your car doors, especially in cities.
- keep rear windows sufficiently rolled up to keep out opportunistic hands.
- never leave anything worth stealing in view when your car is unattended.

ON THE BEACH:

- take only the bare essentials.
- don't leave valuables, especially cameras, unattended.
- safeguard car keys by pinning them to your swimming gear, or putting them in a waterproof wallet or splash box and taking them into the water with you.

AT ATMS:

Cash machines are favourite hunting grounds for sophisticated con men, who use cunning rather than force to steal money. Never underestimate their ability and don't get drawn into any interaction at an ATM, no matter how well-spoken, friendly or distressed the other person appears. If they claim to have a problem with the machine, tell them to contact the bank. Don't let people crowd you or see your personal identification number (PIN) when you withdraw money; if in doubt, go to another machine. Finally, if your card gets swallowed, report it without delay.

WHEN PAYING WITH A CARD:

- never let your plastic out of your sight.
- at a restaurant, ask for a portable card reader to be brought to your table.
- at the till, keep an eye on your card.

during the Christmas holidays, over a thousand people die in an annual period of carnage on the roads. However, concerted attempts are being made to deal with the problem, including the widely publicized Arrive Alive campaign and the confiscation of the vehicles of drunk drivers and drivers travelling well over the speed limit.

Sexual harassment

South Africa's extremely high incidence of **rape** doesn't as a rule affect tourists. However, at heart the majority of the country's males, regardless of race, hold onto fairly sexist attitudes. Sometimes your eagerness to be friendly may be taken as a sexual overture – be sensitive to potential crossed wires and unintended signals.

Women should take care while travelling on their own, and should avoid hitchhiking or walking alone in deserted areas. This applies equally to Cape Town, the countryside or anywhere after dark. Minibus taxis should be ruled out as a means of transport after dark, especially if you're not exactly sure of local geography.

The police

For many black South Africans, the **South African National Police** (SANP) still carry strong associations of collaboration with apartheid and a lot of public relations work has still to be done to turn the police into a genuine people's law enforcement agency. Dismally paid, poorly trained, shot at (and frequently hit), underfunded, badly equipped, barely respected and demoralized, the police keep a low profile. If you ever get stopped, at a roadblock for example (one of the likeliest encounters), always be courteous. And if you're driving, note that under South African law you are required to carry your **driving licence** at all times.

If you are robbed, you will need to report the incident to the police, who should give you a case reference for insurance purposes – though don't expect too much crime-cracking enthusiasm, or to get your property back.

Travel essentials

Climate

As a winter rainfall area, Cape Town typically is at its coldest, wettest and stormiest from May to August. Having said that, it's not uncommon to have days or weeks of gloriously sunny days at this time of year. During the peak of the summer (November to February) you can expect long sunny days (and the blast of the seasonal southeasterly wind) with average temperatures peaking at 27ºC in February. In autumn and spring you can expect milder temperatures with occasional warm days without the summer wind and high UV index.

Costs

The most expensive thing about visiting South Africa is getting there. Once you've arrived, you're likely to find it a relatively inexpensive destination. How cheap you find South Africa will depend partly on exchange rates at the time of your visit – since becoming fully convertible (after the advent of democracy in South Africa) the rand has seen some massive fluctuations against sterling, the dollar and the euro.

When it comes to **daily budgets**, your biggest expense is likely to be **accommodation**. If you're willing to stay in backpacker dorms and self-cater, you should be able to sleep and eat for under £23/US$38/€28 per person per day. If you stay in B&Bs and guesthouses, eat out once a day, and have a

AVERAGE MONTHLY TEMPERATURES AND RAINFALL

	Jan	Feb	Mar	Apr	May	Jun	Jul	Aug	Sep	Oct	Nov	Dec
CAPE TOWN												
max/min (ºC)	26/16	27/16	25/14	23/12	20/9	18/8	18/7	18/8	19/9	21/11	24/13	25/15
max/min (ºF)	79/60	80/60	78/58	73/53	69 48	65/46	65/45	65/46	67/48	70/51	74/56	77/59
Rainfall (mm/inches)	15/0.6	17/0.7	20/0.8	41/1.6	69/2.7	93/3.7	82/3.2	77/3.0	40/1.6	30/1.2	14/0.6	17/0.7
GARDEN ROUTE NATIONAL PARK (TSITSIKAMMA)												
max/min (ºC)	23/17	22/17	21/16	20/14	19/12	18/10	17/10	17/10	17/11	19/13	20/14	22/16
max/min (ºF)	73/63	72/63	70/61	68/57	66/54	64/50	63/50	63/50	63/52	66/55	68/57	72/61
Rainfall (mm/inches)	77/3.0	70/2.8	81/3.2	80/3.1	86/3.4	75/3.0	78/3.1	111/4.4	66/2.6	83/3.3	78/3.1	60/2.4

snack or two you should budget for at least double that. In luxury hotels expect to pay upwards of £145/US$240/€175 a day, while luxury safari lodges in Addo and the private game reserves will set you back from £315/US$525/€380 a day to way beyond. **Extras** such as car rental, outdoor activities, horseriding and safaris will add to these figures substantially. While most museums and art galleries impose an **entry fee**, it's usually quite low: only the most sophisticated attractions charge more than £3/US$4.50/€3.

Electricity

South Africa's **electricity** supply runs at 220/230V, 50Hz AC. Sockets take unique round-pinned plugs; see Ⓦ kropla.com for details. Most hotel rooms have sockets that will take 110V electric shavers, but for other appliances US visitors will need an adaptor to make their appliances compatible with South Africa's 220V system.

Emergencies

Police Ⓣ 1011, state ambulance Ⓣ 10177, ER24 private ambulance and paramedic assistance Ⓣ 084 124.

Entry requirements

Nationals of the US, Canada, Australia, New Zealand, Japan, Argentina and Brazil don't require a **visa** to enter South Africa. Most EU nationals don't need a visa, with the exception of passport holders from the following countries who will need to obtain one at a South Africa Diplomatic mission in their home country: Bulgaria, Croatia, Estonia, Latvia, Lithuania, Romania and Slovenia.

As long as you carry a passport that is valid for at least six months and with at least two empty pages you will be granted a temporary visitor's permit, which allows you to stay in South Africa for up to ninety days for most nationals, and thirty days for EU passport holders from Cyprus, Hungary, Poland and Slovakia. All visitors should have proof of a valid return ticket; without one, you may be required to pay the authorities the equivalent of your fare home (the money will only be refunded through a lengthy process, after you have left the country). Visitors may also need to prove that they have sufficient funds to cover their stay.

Applications for visa extensions must be made at one of the main offices of the Department of Home Affairs, where you will be quizzed about your intentions and your funds. Their address in Cape Town is 56 Barrack St (Ⓣ 021 468 4500). The Department also has offices in a number of towns – check in the telephone directory or on its website (Ⓦ home-affairs.gov.za), and make sure that the office you're intending to visit is able to grant extensions.

Parents travelling with a child into or out of South Africa may be asked to show the child's unabridged (full) birth certificate, and where only one parent is accompanying, parental or legal consent for the child to travel (eg an affidavit from the other parent or a court order). There are other requirements for children travelling unaccompanied or with adults who are not their parents. For more information, see Ⓦ dha.gov.za.

SOUTH AFRICAN DIPLOMATIC MISSIONS ABROAD

Australia Corner State Circle and Rhodes Place, Yarralumla, Canberra, ACT 2600 Ⓣ 02 627 2 7300, Ⓦ sahc.org.au.
Canada 15 Sussex Drive, Ottawa, ON K1M 1M8 Ⓣ 613 744 0330, Ⓦ southafrica-canada.ca.
Netherlands 40 Wassenaarseweg 2596 CJ, The Hague Ⓣ 070 392 4501, Ⓦ zuidafrika.nl.
New Zealand c/o the High Commission in Australia, see above Ⓦ sahc.org.au/consular_new-zealand.htm.
UK Consular Section South Africa House, Trafalgar Square, London WC2N 5DP Ⓣ 021 7451 7299, Ⓦ southafricahouseuk.com.
US 3051 Massachusetts Ave NW, Washington, DC 20008 Ⓣ 202 232 4400, Ⓦ southafrica-newyork.net/homeaffairs/index.htm. Consulates: 333 E 38th St, 9th floor, New York, NY 10016 Ⓣ 212 213 4880; 6300 Wilshire Blvd, Suite 600, Los Angeles, CA 90048 Ⓣ 323 651 0902.

FOREIGN DIPLOMATIC MISSIONS IN CAPE TOWN

The embassies for most countries are in Pretoria, but the following have consulates in Cape Town.
Canada 19th Floor, South African Reserve Bank building, 60 St George's Mall Ⓣ 021 423 5240.
Netherlands 100 Strand St Ⓣ 021 421 5660.
UK 15th Floor, Southern Life Centre, 8 Riebeek St Ⓣ 021 405 2400.
US 2 Reddam Ave, Westlake Ⓣ 021 702 7300.

Insurance

It's wise to take out an **insurance policy** to cover against theft, loss and illness or injury prior to visiting South Africa. A typical travel insurance policy usually provides cover for the loss of baggage, tickets and – up to a certain limit – cash or cheques, as well as cancellation or curtailment of

---

ROUGH GUIDES TRAVEL INSURANCE

Rough Guides has teamed up with WorldNomads.com to offer great travel insurance deals. Policies are available to residents of over 150 countries, with cover for a wide range of adventure sports, 24hr emergency assistance, high levels of medical and evacuation cover and a stream of travel safety information. Roughguides.com users can take advantage of their policies online 24/7, from anywhere in the world – even if you're already travelling. And since plans often change when you're on the road, you can extend your policy and even claim online. Roughguides.com users who buy travel insurance with WorldNomads.com can also leave a positive footprint and donate to a community development project. For more information, go to ⓦ roughguides.com/travel-insurance.

---

your journey. Most of them exclude so-called **dangerous sports** unless an extra premium is paid: in South Africa this can mean scuba diving, whitewater rafting, windsurfing, horseriding, bungee jumping and paragliding. In addition to these it's well worth checking whether you are covered by your policy if you're hiking, kayaking, pony trekking or game viewing on safari, all activities people commonly take part in when visiting South Africa. Many policies can be chopped and changed to exclude coverage you don't need – for example, sickness and accident benefits can often be excluded or included at will. If you do take **medical coverage**, ascertain whether benefits will be paid as treatment proceeds or only after you return home, and if there is a 24-hour medical emergency number. When securing **baggage cover**, make sure that the per-article limit will cover your most valuable possession. If you need to make a claim, you should keep receipts for medicines and medical treatment, and in the event you have anything stolen, you must obtain an official statement from the police.

Internet

Finding somewhere to access the **internet** is easy in Cape Town and the Garden Route: internet cafés are found even in relatively small towns, and most backpacker hostels and hotels have internet and email facilities, albeit often too slow for Skype calls. Expect to pay R10–25 an hour for online access. If you are carrying your own device you'll also be able to take advantage of the paid wireless hotspots at a number of airports, cafés, malls and accommodation.

Mail

The deceptively familiar feel of South African post offices can lull you into expecting an efficient British- or US-style service. In fact, post within the country is slow and unreliable, and money and valuables frequently disappear en route. Expect domestic delivery times from one city to another of about a week – longer if a rural town is involved at either end. **International airmail** deliveries are often quicker, thanks to the city's direct flights to London. A letter or package sent by surface mail can take up to six weeks to get from South Africa to London.

Most towns of any size have a **post office**, generally open Monday to Friday 8.30am to 4.30pm and Saturday 8 to 11.30am (closing earlier in some places). The ubiquitous private **PostNet** outlets (ⓦ postnet.co.za) offer many of the same postal services as the post office and more, including **courier services**. Courier companies like FedEx (☏ 0800 033 339, ⓦ fedex.com/za) and DHL (☏ 086 034 5000, ⓦ dhl.co.za) are more expensive and available only in the larger towns, but they are far more reliable than the mail.

Stamps are available at post offices and also from newsagents, such as the CNA chain, as well as supermarkets. Postage is relatively inexpensive – it costs about R6 to send a postcard by airmail to anywhere in the world, while a small letter costs about R7 to send. You'll find **poste restante** facilities at the main post office in most larger centres, and in many backpacker hostels.

Maps

You'll find up-to-date maps of Cape Town, its suburbs, the Winelands and the Garden Route in the guide, but if you're looking for more substantial maps, make sure they're up to date as many **place names** in South Africa were changed after the 1994 elections – and changes are still being made. Bartholomew produces an excellent map of South Africa, including Lesotho and Swaziland (1:2,000,000), as part of its World Travel Map series.

South Africa's motoring organization, the **Automobile Association**, sells a wide selection of good regional maps (free to members) from its offices.

For travel around the **Western Cape** (including the Cape Peninsula and the Garden Route), the most accurate, up-to-date and attractive touring and hiking maps – the best bar none – are those produced by Cape Town cartographers Slingsby Maps (ⓦ slingsbymaps.com).

Money

South Africa's currency is the **rand** (R), often called the "buck", divided into 100 **cents**. Notes come in R10, R20, R50, R100 and R200 denominations and there are coins of 50 cents, and R1, 2, 5. At the time of writing, the **exchange rate** was fluctuating wildly – in favour of visitors, on average around R17 to the pound sterling, R10 to the US dollar, R13–14 to the euro and R9 to the Australian dollar.

All but the tiniest settlement will have a **bank** where you can **change money** swiftly and easily. **Banking hours** vary bank to bank, but at a minimum from Monday to Friday 9am to 3.30pm, and Saturday 8:30am to 11am; the banks in smaller towns usually close for lunch. In major cities, some banks operate **bureaux de change** that stay open until 7pm. Outside banking hours, some hotels will change money, although this entails a fairly hefty **commission**. You can also change money at branches of American Express and Rennies Travel.

Cards and travellers' cheques

Credit and debit cards are the most convenient way to access your funds in South Africa. Most international cards can be used to withdraw money at **ATMs**, open 24 hours a day in the cities and elsewhere. South African banks will usually charge a fee of R30–45 for withdrawal. Plastic can come in very handy for hotel bookings and for paying for more mainstream and upmarket tourist facilities, and is essential for car rental deposits. **Visa** and **MasterCard** are the cards most widely accepted in major cities.

Travellers' cheques make a useful backup as they can be replaced if lost or stolen. American Express, Visa and Thomas Cook are all widely recognized brands; both US dollar and sterling cheques are accepted in South Africa.

Travellers' cheques and plastic are useless if you're heading into remote areas, where you'll need to carry **cash**, preferably in a safe place, such as a leather pouch or waist-level money belt that you can keep under your clothes.

Opening hours and holidays

The **working day** starts and finishes early in South Africa: shops and businesses generally open on **weekdays** at 8.30 or 9am and close at 4.30 or 5pm. In small towns, many places close for an hour over **lunch**. Many **shops** and businesses close around noon on Saturdays, and most shops are closed on Sundays. However, in every neighbourhood, you'll find small shops and supermarkets where you can buy groceries and essentials after hours.

Some establishments have summer and winter opening times. In such situations, you can take **winter** to mean April to August or September, while **summer** constitutes the rest of the year.

School holidays in South Africa can disrupt your plans, especially if you want to camp, or stay in the national parks and the cheaper end of accommodation (self-catering, cheaper B&Bs, etc), all of which are likely to be booked solid during those periods. If you do travel to South Africa over the school holidays, book your accommodation well in advance, especially for the national parks.

The longest and busiest holiday period is **Christmas (summer)**, which for schools stretches over most of December and January. Flights and train berths can be hard to get from December 16 to January 2, when many businesses and offices close for their annual break. You should book your **flights** – long-haul and domestic – as early as six months in advance for the Christmas period. The inland and coastal provinces stagger their school

---

SOUTH AFRICAN PUBLIC HOLIDAYS

Many shops and tourist-related businesses remain open over public holidays, although often with shorter opening hours. Christmas Day and Good Friday, when most of the country shuts down, are the only exceptions. The main holidays are:

New Year's Day (Jan 1)
Human Rights Day (March 21)
Good Friday, Easter Monday (variable)
Freedom Day (April 27)
Workers' Day (May 1)
Youth Day (June 16)
National Women's Day (Aug 9)
Heritage Day (Sept 24)
Day of Reconciliation (Dec 16)
Christmas Day (Dec 25)
Day of Goodwill (Dec 26)

holidays, but as a general rule the remaining school holidays roughly cover the following periods: **Easter**, mid-March to mid-April; **winter**, mid-June to mid-July; and spring, late September to early October. Exact **dates** for each year are given on the government's information website: ⓦ info.gov.za /aboutsa/schoolcal.htm.

Phones

South Africa's **telephone** system, dominated by **Telkom**, generally works well. Public phone booths are found in every city and town, and are either coin- or card-operated. While **international calls** can be made from virtually any phone, it helps to have a **phonecard**, as you'll be lucky to stay on the line for more than a minute or two for R20. Phonecards come in R20, R50, R100 and R200 denominations, available at Telkom offices, post offices and newsagents.

Mobile phones (referred to locally as cell phones or simply cells) are extremely widely used in South Africa, with more mobile than land-line handsets in use. The competing networks – Vodacom, MTN, Cell C and VirginMobile – cover all the main areas and the national roads connecting them.

You can use a GSM/tri-band phone from outside the country in South Africa, but you will need to arrange a **roaming agreement** with your provider at home; be warned that this is likely to be expensive. A far cheaper alternative is to buy a very inexpensive **local SIM card** while you're in South Africa (for this to work, you'll need to make sure your phone has been "unblocked" to accept another network). The local SIM card (available in full size and micro-SIM from R10) contains your South African phone number, which you load with pre-paid airtime. These can be bought from the ubiquitous mobile phone shops and a number of other outlets, including supermarkets and the CNA chain of newsagents and supermarkets. Some will require your passport to purchase.

Another option is to **rent** just a South African SIM card or a phone and SIM card when you arrive. A phone with a SIM cards start at R7 a day for a basic handset, up to R35 for a smartphone.

PHONE RENTAL

Vodashop Renta Fone ⓦ rentafone.net. Vodacom's phone rental wing.

CALLING HOME FROM SOUTH AFRICA

To dial out of South Africa, the **international access code** is ☎ 00. Remember to omit any initial zero in the number of the place you're phoning.

Australia international access code + 61
Ireland international access code + 353
New Zealand international access code + 64
UK international access code + 44
US and Canada international access code + 1

Taxes

Value-added tax (VAT) of fourteen percent is levied on most goods and services, though it's usually already included in any quoted price. Foreign visitors older than seven can claim back VAT on goods over R250. To do this, you must present an official tax receipt with your name on it for the goods, a non-South African passport and the purchased goods themselves, at the **airport** just before you fly out. You need to complete a VAT refund control sheet (VAT 255), which can be obtained at international airports. For further information, contact the VAT Refund Administrator (☎ 011 394 1117, ⓦ taxrefunds.co.za).

Time

There is only one **time zone** throughout South Africa, two hours ahead of GMT year-round. If you're flying from anywhere in Europe, you shouldn't experience any jet lag.

Tipping

Ten to fifteen percent of the tab is the normal **tip** at restaurants and for taxis – but don't feel obliged to tip if service has been shoddy. Keep in mind that many of the people who'll be serving you rely on tips to supplement a meagre wage on which they support huge extended families. **Porters** at hotels normally get about R10 per bag. At South African garages and filling stations, someone will always be on hand to fill your vehicle and clean your windscreen, for which you should tip R5–10. It is also usual at **hotels** to leave some money for the person who services your room. Many establishments, especially private game lodges, take (voluntary) communal tips when you check out – by far the fairest system, which ensures that all the low-profile staff behind the scenes get their share.

Tourist information

There are several official **tourist information bureaus** in Cape Town and most towns have some sort of information office, but in this fast-changing country, the best way of finding out what's happening is often by word of mouth, and for this **backpacker hostels** are invaluable. If you're seeing South Africa on a budget, the useful notice boards, constant traveller traffic and largely helpful and friendly staff you'll encounter in backpacker hostels will greatly smooth your travels.

There are countless **guidebooks** on walks around Cape Town, hikes up Table Mountain, dive sites, fishing locations, surfing breaks and windsurfing spots (see p.261). For the best-stocked shelves, head to one of the Exclusive Books stores (see p.134). You'll also find useful books on all aspects of South Africa at the secondhand bookshops down Long Street.

To find out **what's on**, check out online listings such as *Cape Town Magazine* (Ⓦ capetown magazine.com), *What's On in Cape Town* (Ⓦ whats onincapetown.com), the entertainment pages of the daily newspapers or better still buy the *Mail & Guardian*, which comes out every Friday and lists the coming week's offerings in a comprehensive pull-out supplement.

TOURIST INFORMATION BUREAUS

Cape Town Tourism In the City Centre, The Pinnacle, Burg & Castle streets (Ⓣ 021 487 6800), open 8am–6pm; Cape Town Tourism also has a bureau at the airport (Ⓣ 021 934 1949), V&A Waterfront (Ⓣ 021 408 7600) and Table Mountain Lower Cableway (Ⓣ 021 422 1075); Ⓦ capetown.travel.

GOVERNMENT SITES

Australian Department of Foreign Affairs Ⓦ dfat.gov.au.
British Foreign & Commonwealth Office Ⓦ fco.gov.uk.
Canadian Department of Foreign Affairs Ⓦ international.gc.ca.
Irish Department of Foreign Affairs Ⓦ foreignaffairs.gov.ie.
New Zealand Ministry of Foreign Affairs Ⓦ mfat.govt.nz.
US State Department Ⓦ state.gov.

Travellers with disabilities

Facilities for **disabled travellers** in South Africa are not as sophisticated as those you might find in Europe and the US, but they're sufficient to ensure you have a satisfactory visit. By accident, often, rather than design, you'll find pretty good accessibility to many buildings, as South Africans tend to build low (single-storey bungalows are the norm), with the result that you'll have to deal with fewer stairs than you may be accustomed to. As the car is king, you'll frequently find that you can drive to, and park right outside, your destination.

There are **organized tours** and holidays specifically for people with disabilities, and **activity-based packages** are increasingly available. These offer the possibility for wheel-chair-bound visitors to take part in safaris, sport and a vast range of adventure activities, including whitewater rafting, horseriding, parasailing and zip-lining. Tours can either be taken as self-drive trips or as packages for large groups. The contacts below will be able to put you in touch with South Africa travel specialists.

If you want to be more independent on your travels, it's important to know where you can expect help and where you must be self-reliant, especially regarding transport and accommodation. It's also vital to know your limitations, and to make sure others know them. If you do not use a wheel-chair all the time but your walking capabilities are limited, remember that you are likely to need to cover greater distances while travelling (often over rougher terrain and in hotter temperatures) than you are used to. If you use a wheelchair, have it serviced before you go and take a repair kit with you.

USEFUL CONTACTS

Ⓦ **disabledtravel.co.za** Website of occupational therapist Karin Coetzee aimed at disabled travellers, with listings of accommodation, restaurants and attractions personally evaluated for accessibility as well as hugely useful links to everything from car rental and tours to orthopedic equipment.

Ⓦ **access-able.com** US-based website for travellers with disabilities that includes some useful information about South Africa.

Ⓦ **sanparks.org/groups/disabilities/general.php** Lists what wheelchair and mobility impaired access and facilities are available at South African National Parks.

Ⓦ **flamingotours.co.za** Flamingo tours and Disabled Ventures specializes in tours for tourists with special needs.

LONG STREET

The city centre

South Africa's oldest urban region pulses with the cultural fusion that has
been Cape Town's hallmark since its founding in 1652. The city centre is
spectacularly situated, dominated by Table Mountain to the southwest and
the pounding Atlantic to the northeast. Strand Street marks the edge of the
city's original beachfront (though you'd never guess it today), with the Lower
City Centre to the northeast and Upper City Centre to the southwest. The
obvious orientation axis, however, is Adderley Street, which connects the
main train station in the north with St George's Cathedral. Southwest of
here is Cape Town's symbolic heart, with the Houses of Parliament, museums,
historic buildings, archives and De Tuynhuys (the office of the president) all
arranged around the Company's Gardens.

1

Northwest of Adderley Street is the closest South Africa gets to a European quarter – a tight network of streets with cafés, buskers, bookstores, street stalls and antique shops congregating around the pedestrianized **St George's Mall** and **Greenmarket Square**.

Parallel to St George's Mall, **Long Street**, the quintessential Cape Town thoroughfare, is lined with colonial Victorian buildings which house pubs, bistros, nightclubs, backpacker lodges, bookshops and antique dealers, from whose wrought-iron balconies you can catch glimpses of Table Mountain and the ocean. Three blocks further west is **Bree Street**, which has established itself as a quieter and more relaxed alternative to Long Street, with an interesting choice of boutique stores and bars. The **Bo-Kaap**, or Muslim quarter, three blocks further northwest across Buitengragt, exudes a piquant contrast to this, with its minarets, spice shops and cafés selling curried snacks.

Southeast of Adderley Street lie three historically loaded sites. The **Castle of Good Hope** – the oldest building in South Africa – is an indelible symbol of Europe's colonization of South Africa (see p.252), a process whose death knell was struck from nearby **City Hall**, the attractive Edwardian building from which Nelson Mandela made his first speech after being released. South of the castle lie the poignantly desolate remains of **District Six**, the coloured inner-city suburb that was razed in the name of apartheid.

GETTING AROUND   CITY CENTRE

BY BUS

MyCiTi ☎0800 65 64 63, ⓦmyciti.org.za. The MyCiTi bus network emulates a rail system, with stations along dedicated trunk roads. Buses run from the Gardens at the edge of the City Bowl through the city centre to the Civic Centre and then on to the Waterfront. The Civic Centre is a central transport hub, where you can get buses to all areas served by MyCiTi buses. A number of buses run through the city centre, bringing you within a short walk of most of the central attractions. Buses #106 and #107 to Camps Bay via Waterfront go up Adderley St, Long St, Loop St and Kloof Nek; the #101 to Gardens goes via Loop St, while the #105 to Hout Bay crosses the centre at right angles to this, along Strand St.

City Sightseeing ☎021 511 6000, ⓦcitysightseeing .co.za. Hop-on, hop-off sightseeing buses also stop at all the major attractions in the city centre (see p.21).

Upper City Centre

Once *the* place to shop in Cape Town, **Adderley Street**, lined with handsome buildings spanning several centuries, is still worth a stroll today. Its attractive streetscape has been blemished by a series of large 1960s shopping centres, but just minutes away from these crowded malls, among the streets and alleys around Greenmarket Square, the area takes on a more human element and is full of historic texture.

Low-walled channels, ditches, bridges and sluices once ran through Cape Town, earning it the name **Little Amsterdam**. During the nineteenth century, the canals were buried underground, and, in 1850, Heerengracht (Gentlemen's Canal), formerly a waterway that ran from the Company's Gardens down to the sea, was renamed Adderley Street (see box, p.44). There's little evidence of the canals today, except in name – one section of the street is still called Heerengracht and a parallel street to its west is called Buitengragt (sometimes spelt Buitengracht after the Dutch style, and meaning the Outer Canal). The destruction of old Cape Town continued well into the twentieth century, with the razing of many of the older buildings.

Cape Town Station, at the junction of Adderley and Strand streets, is the city's commuting nexus; it has its own bustling life of hooting and hollering taxi drivers, buskers and stallholders hawking cheap Chinese goods. Between Strand and Darling streets lies the **Adderley Street Flower Market** (Mon–Sat 9am–4pm), a market run by members of the **Bo-Kaap** Muslim community for the past hundred years.

1

THE LANGUAGE OF COLOUR

It's striking just how un-African Cape Town looks and sounds. Halfway between East and West, this city drew its population from Africa, Asia and Europe, and traces of all three continents are found in the genes, language, culture, religion and cuisine of Cape Town's coloured population.

Afrikaans (a close relative of Dutch) is the mother tongue of a large proportion of the city's coloured residents, as well as many whites. However, a very substantial number of Capetonians are born English-speakers, and English punches well above its weight as the local lingua franca, which, in this multilingual society, virtually everyone can speak and understand.

The term "coloured" is contentious, but in South Africa it doesn't have the same tainted connotations as in Britain and the US; it refers to South Africans of mixed race. Most brown-skinned people in Cape Town (over fifty percent of Capetonians) are coloureds, with Asian, African and Khoikhoi ancestry.

In the late **nineteenth century**, Afrikaans-speaking whites, fighting for an identity, sought to create a "racially pure" culture by driving a wedge between themselves and coloured Afrikaans-speakers. They reinvented Afrikaans as a "white man's language", eradicating the supposed stigma of its coloured ties by substituting Dutch words for those with Asian or African roots. In 1925, the white dialect of Afrikaans became an official language alongside English, and the dialects spoken by coloureds were treated as inferior deviations from correct usage.

For Afrikaner nationalists this wasn't enough, and after the introduction of apartheid in 1948, they attempted to codify perceived racial differences. Under the **Population Registration Act**, all South Africans were classified as white, coloured or African. These classifications became fundamental to what kind of life you could expect. There are numerous cases of families in which one sibling was classified coloured with limited rights and another white with the right to live in comfortable white areas, enjoy superior job opportunities and be able to send their children to better schools and universities.

With the demise of **apartheid**, the make-up of residential areas is shifting – and so is the thinking on ethnic terminology. Some people now reject the term "coloured" because of its apartheid associations, and refuse any racial definitions; others, however, proudly embrace the term, as a means of acknowledging their distinct culture, with its slave and Khoikhoi roots.

Standard and First National banks

Adderley St • Mon–Fri 9am–3.30pm, Sat 8.30–11am • Ⓦ standardbank.co.za, Ⓦ fnb.co.za

Two grandiose bank buildings, still major working banks, stand on opposite sides of Adderley Street; the fussier of the two is the former **Standard Bank**, fronted by Corinthian columns and covered with a tall dome, and the **First National Bank**, completed in 1913, the last South African building designed by Sir Herbert Baker (see box, p.96). If you pop into the latter for a quick look, still in place inside the banking hall you'll find a solid-timber circular writing desk with the original inkwells, resembling an altar.

Groote Kerk

Adderley St • Daily 10am–2pm; services Sun 10am & 7pm • Free • Ⓦ grootekerk.org.za (Afrikaans only)

The **Groote Kerk** (Great Church), was the first church erected in South Africa, shortly after the arrival of the Dutch in 1652, who brought their rigorous Protestant beliefs with them. The current church replaces the earlier church that had become too small for the swelling ranks of the Dutch Reformed congregation at the Cape. The building is essentially classical, with Gothic and Egyptian elements, and was designed and built between 1836 and 1841 by Hermann Schutte, a German who became one of the Cape's leading early nineteenth-century architects. The beautiful freestanding clock tower adjacent to the newer building is a remnant of the original church.

The soaring space created by the vast vaulted ceiling and the magnificent pulpit, a masterpiece by sculptor Anton Anreith and carpenter Jan Jacob Graaff, are worth stepping inside for. The pulpit, supported on a pair of sculpted lions with gaping jaws, was carved by Anreith after his first proposal, featuring Faith, Hope and Charity, was

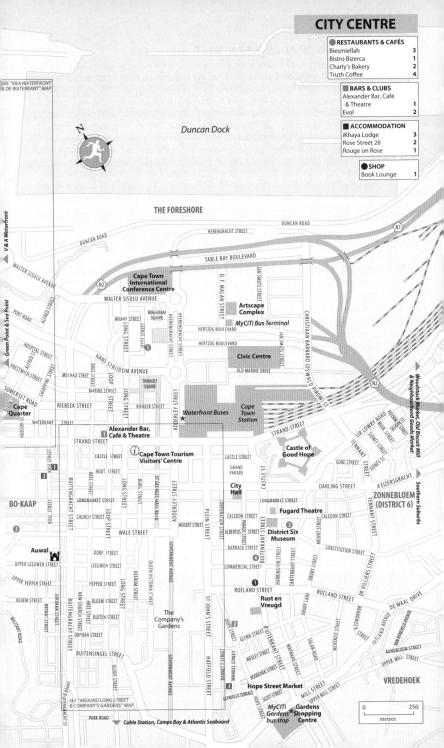

CITY CENTRE

SEE "V&A WATERFRONT
& DE WATERKANT" MAP

Duncan Dock

N

V & A Waterfront

Green Point & Sea Point

THE FORESHORE

DUNCAN ROAD

HERENGRACHT STREET

DUNCAN ROAD

N1

TABLE BAY BOULEVARD

WALTER SISULU AVENUE

N2

PORT ROAD

ALFRED STREET

Cape Town International Conference Centre

WALTER SISULU AVENUE

D. F. MALAN STREET

JAN SMUTS STREET

Artscape Complex

MyCiTi Bus Terminal

HERTZOG BOULEVARD

CHRISTIAAN BARNARD (OSWALD PIROW) ST

HOSPITAL STREET

ALFRED STREET

BREE STREET

LONG STREET

WHARF STREET

ROGGEBAAI SQUARE

JETTY STREET

HEERENGRACHT STREET

HERTZOG BOULEVARD

JAN SMUTS STREET

Civic Centre

PRESTWICH STREET

CHIAPPINI STREET

HANS STRIJDOM AVENUE

MECHAU STREET

BREE STREET

LOOP STREET

THIBAULT SQUARE

OLD MARINE DRIVE

N2

SOMERSET ROAD

MARINE STREET

Woodstock Market, Old Biscuit Mill
& Neighbourhood Goods Market

Cape Quarter

HUDSON ST

WATERKANT

RIEBEEK STREET

LONG STREET

RIEBEEK STREET

ADDERLEY STREET

Waterfront Buses

Cape Town Station

STRAND STREET

SIR LOWRY ROAD

REFORM ST

MUIR ST

SELKIRK ST

BLOEM STREET

BUITENGRACHT STREET

Alexander Bar, Café & Theatre

STRAND STREET

Castle of Good Hope

TENNANT STREET

SIDNEY STREET

SIDNEY ST

Southern Suburbs

CASTLE STREET

Cape Town Tourism Visitors' Centre

CASTLE STREET

GRAND PARADE

CASTLE ST

GORE STREET

BO-KAAP

HOUT STREET

BREE STREET

LONG STREET

BURG STREET

ST GEORGE'S MALL ROAD

ADDERLEY STREET

City Hall

DARLING STREET

K EIZERSGRACHT

ZONNEBLOEM (DISTRICT 6)

LONGMARKET STREET

CHURCH STREET

LOOP STREET

WALE STREET

MOSERT STREET

PLEIN STREET

CORPORATION STREET

LONGMARKET STREET

Fugard Theatre

CALEDON STREET

TENNANT STREET

MOUNT STREET

CONSTITUTION STREET

DE VILLIERS STREET

Auwal

DORP STREET

LEEUWEN STREET

KEEROM STREET

QUEEN VICTORIA STREET

CALEDON STREET

District Six Museum

PRINCE STREET

HARRINGTON STREET

CANTERBURY STREET

DRURY LANE

DRURY LANE

ROELAND STREET

DE WAAL DRIVE

UPPER LEEUWEN STREET

UPPER PEPPER STREET

BLOEM STREET

BREE STREET

NEW CHURCH STREET

PEPPER STREET

LONG STREET

BLOEM STREET

BUITEN STREET

ALBERTUS STREET

BARRACK STREET

COMMERCIAL STREET

ROELAND STREET

BUITENKANT STREET

SOLAN ROAD

MCKENZIE STREET

JUTLAND AVENUE

CHARLES STREET

Rust en Vreugd

MEULSTEL ROAD

JORDAAN STREET

BRYANT STREET

JORDAAN STREET

BUITENSINGEL STREET

ST JOHN'S STREET

GOVERNMENT AVENUE

HATFIELD STREET

The Company's Gardens

HOPE STREET

GLYNN STREET

WESLEY STREET

ROODEBEK STREET

BUITENKANT STREET

MANNING STREET

VREDEHOEK

AANDBLOEM STREET

UPPER MILL STREET

KLOOF STREET

UPPER BUITENGRACHT ST

PARK ROAD

SEE "AROUND LONG STREET
& COMPANY'S GARDENS" MAP

SCOTT STREET

OLYMPILLE TERRACE

HOPE STREET

Hope Street Market

MILL STREET

UPPER MILL STREET

MyCiTi Gardens Gardens
bus stop Shopping Centre

Cable Station, Camps Bay & Atlantic Seaboard

0   250
metres

1

THE NAMING OF ADDERLEY STREET

Although the Dutch used Robben Island (see p.63) as a political prison, in the 1800s the South African mainland only narrowly escaped becoming a second Australia, which at that time was a **penal colony** where British felons and enemies of the state could be dumped. In the 1840s, "respectable" Australians were lobbying for a ban on the transportation of criminals to the Antipodes, and the British authorities responded by trying to divert convicts to the Cape.

The British ship *Neptune* set sail from Bermuda for Cape Town in 1848, with a cargo of 282 prisoners. There was outrage when news of its departure reached Cape Town; five thousand citizens gathered on the Grand Parade the following year to hear prominent liberals denounce the British government, an event depicted in *The Great Meeting of the People at the Commercial Exchange* by Johan Marthinus Carstens Schonegevel, which hangs in the Rust-en-Vreugd Museum (see p.54). When the ship docked in September 1849, governor Sir Harry Smith forbade any criminal from landing; meanwhile, back in London, politician **Charles Adderley** successfully addressed the House of Commons in support of the Cape colonists. In February 1850, the *Neptune* set off for Tasmania with its full complement of convicts, and grateful Capetonians renamed the city's main thoroughfare **Adderley Street**.

rejected by the church council for being "too Popish". The Groote Kerk still has a keen family congregation, with a thundering organ and pealing bells.

Slave Lodge

Cnr Adderley and Wale sts • Mon–Sat 10am–5pm • R30 • ⓦ iziko.org.za/museums/slave-lodge

The **Slave Lodge**, which sits at the southern (confusingly referred to as the top) corner of Adderley Street, just as it veers sharply northwest into Wale Street, was built in 1679 to house the human chattels of the Dutch East India Company (VOC) – the Cape's largest single slaveholder.

For nearly two centuries – more than half the city's existence as an urban settlement – Cape Town's economic and social structures rested on slavery (see box opposite). By the 1770s, almost a thousand slaves were held at the lodge. Under VOC administration, the lodge also became the Cape Colony's main **brothel**, its doors thrown open to all comers for an hour each night. Following the British takeover and the auctioning of the slaves, the lodge became the **Supreme Court** in 1810, and remained so until 1914, after which the building was used as government offices.

The Slave Lodge has redefined itself as a museum of slavery as well as human rights, with displays showing the family roots, ancestry and peopling of South Africa, and changing exhibitions which have covered the likes of Steve Biko and slavery in Brazil. Taking an audio headset allows you to follow the footsteps of German salt trader Otto Menzl as he is taken on a tour of the lodge in the 1700s, and it gives you a good idea of the miserable conditions at the time. Of note is a scale model of the *Meermin*, one of several ships sent to Madagascar in the eighteenth century to bring men, women and children into slavery in the Cape. Another memorable stop is an alcove, lit by a column of light, where the names of slaves are marked on rings that resemble tree trunks, symbolic of the Slave Tree under which slaves were bought and sold. Though the actual **Old Slave Tree** is long gone, the spot is marked by a simple and inconspicuous plinth behind Slave Lodge, on the traffic island in Spin Street.

Long Street

Parallel to Adderley Street, buzzing one-way **Long Street** is one of Cape Town's most diverse thoroughfares, and is best known as the city's main nightlife strip. When Muslims first settled here some three hundred years ago, Long Street marked Cape Town's boundary; by the 1960s, the street had become a sleazy alley of drinking holes and whorehouses. Miraculously, it's all still here, but with a whiff of gentrification and a tedious section of discount furniture shops and fast-food joints. It deserves

1

exploration from the Wale Street intersection onwards. Mosques still coexist alongside bars, while antique dealers, craft shops, bookshops and cafés do a good trade. The street is packed with backpacker hostels and a couple of upmarket hotels, though the proliferation of nightclubs here means it can be very noisy into the early hours. At night, it's perfectly safe to pub or club crawl, and you'll always find taxis and some street food.

Long Street Baths

Cnr Long and Orange sts • **Pool** Daily 7am–7pm • R12 • **Turkish baths** Men Tues 1–7pm, Wed & Fri 8am–7pm, Sun 8am–noon; women Mon, Thurs & Sat 9am–6pm • R40/hr • 📞 021 400 3302

The **Long Street Baths** is an unpretentious and relaxing historic Cape Town institution, established in 1908 in an Edwardian building that occupies the top of Long Street, where it hits Buitensingel. Though shabby, it is a great place to do some lengths, and it's very cheap. The Turkish baths are open separately to men and women.

Palm Tree Mosque

185 Long St • Closed to the public

Further north of the Long Street Baths is the **Palm Tree Mosque**, an unmistakeable landmark which is fronted by a lone palm tree whose fronds caress the upper storey. Significant as the only surviving eighteenth-century building in the street, it was erected in 1780 by Carel Lodewijk Schot as a private dwelling. The house was bought in 1807 by Frans van Bengal, a member of the local Muslim community, and a freed slave, Jan van Boughies, who became its imam and turned the upper storey into a mosque, the lower into his living quarters.

Pan African Market

76 Long St • Summer Mon–Fri 8.30am–5.30pm, Sat 9am–3.30pm; winter Mon–Fri 9am–5pm, Sat 9am–3pm • 📞 021 426 4478

The inconspicuous frontage of the **Pan African Market**, one of Cape Town's most intriguing places for African crafts, belies the three-storey warren of passageways and rooms which bursts at the hinges with traders selling vast quantities of art and artefacts

SLAVERY AT THE CAPE

Slavery was officially **abolished** at the Cape in 1838, but its legacy lives on in South Africa. The country's **coloured inhabitants**, who make up fifty percent of Cape Town's population, are largely descendants of slaves, political prisoners from the East Indies and indigenous Khoisan people. Some historians argue that apartheid was a natural successor to slavery. Certainly, domestic service, still widespread throughout South Africa, and some labour practices such as the "dop system", in which workers on wine farms are sometimes partially paid in rations of cheap plonk, can be traced directly back to slavery.

By the end of the eighteenth century, the almost 26,000-strong **slave population** of the Cape exceeded that of the free burghers. Despite the profound impact this had on the development of social relations in South Africa, slavery remained one of the most neglected topics of the country's history, until the publication in the 1980s of a number of studies on slavery. There's still reluctance on the part of most coloureds to acknowledge their slave origins.

Few if any slaves were captured at the Cape for export, making the colony unique in the African trade. Paradoxically, while people were being captured elsewhere on the continent for export to the Americas, the Cape administration, forbidden by the VOC (see p.251) from enslaving the local indigenous population, had to look further afield. Of the 63,000 slaves imported to the Cape, most came from East Africa, Madagascar, India and Indonesia, representing one of the broadest cultural mixes of any slave society. This diversity initially worked against the establishment of a unified group identity, but eventually a **Creolized culture** emerged which, among other things, played a major role in the development of the **Afrikaans** language.

1

from all over the continent. The building is essentially classical, with Gothic and Egyptian elements, designed and built between 1836 and 1841 by Hermann Schutte, a German who became one of the Cape's leading early nineteenth-century architects. Hidden among less inspiring offerings you'll find terrific masks from West Africa, baskets from Zimbabwe, brass leopards from Benin and contemporary South African art textiles, as well as vendors selling CDs and musical instruments. This is also the place to get kitted out in African garb – in-house seamstresses are at the ready.

South African Missionary Meeting-House Museum

40 Long St • Mon–Fri 9am–4pm • Free • ☎ 021 423 6755

Towards the harbour end of Long Street, the **South African Missionary Meeting-House Museum** was the first missionary church in the country, where slaves were taught literacy and instructed in Christianity. This exceptional building, completed in 1804 by the South African Missionary Society, boasts one of the most beautiful frontages in Cape Town. Dominated by large windows, the facade is broken into three bays by four slender Corinthian pilasters surmounted by a gabled pediment. Inside, an impressive Neoclassical timber **pulpit** perches high above the congregation on a pair of columns and frames an inlaid image of an angel in flight.

Heritage Square

From Long Street, head northwest down Shortmarket Street to **Heritage Square**, the largest restoration project ever undertaken in Cape Town. The keystone of the 1771 complex is the *Cape Heritage Hotel*, one of the most stylish places to stay in the city (see p.107). It opens onto a cluster of restaurants and wine bars set around a tranquil courtyard, in which the oldest known (and still fruit-bearing) vine in South Africa continues to flourish. The square is worth visiting for the architecture and the general sense of tranquillity, best absorbed with a good glass of Cape wine under shady umbrellas.

Bo-Kaap

Minutes from Parliament, on the slopes of Signal Hill, is the **Bo-Kaap**, one of Cape Town's oldest and most fascinating residential areas. Its streets are characterized by brightly coloured nineteenth-century Dutch and Georgian terraces – an image that has become a bit of a tour-brochure cliché – which conceal a network of alleyways that are the arteries of its **Muslim community**. The Bo-Kaap harbours its own strong identity, made all the more unique by the destruction of District Six, with which it had much in common. A particular dialect of Afrikaans is spoken here, although it is steadily being eroded by English.

Bo-Kaap residents descend from slaves brought over by the Dutch in the sixteenth and seventeenth centuries. They were known collectively as "**Cape Malays**", still heard today, even though it's a misnomer: most originated from Africa, India, Madagascar and Sri Lanka, with fewer than one percent actually from what is now Malaysia.

SLAVERY AND SALVATION

The **South African Missionary Society** was founded in 1799 by the Reverend Vos, who was alarmed that many slaveholders neglected the religious education of their "property". The owners believed that once their slaves were baptized, their emancipation became obligatory – a misunderstanding of the law, which merely stated that Christian slaves couldn't be sold. Vos, himself a slaveholder, saw proselytization to those in bondage as a Christian duty, and even successfully campaigned to end the prohibition against selling Christian slaves, which he believed was "a great obstacle in this country to the progress of Christianity", because it encouraged owners to avoid baptizing their human possessions.

EXPLORING THE BO-KAAP

The easiest way to get to the Bo-Kaap is by foot along **Wale Street**, which trails up from the south end of Adderley Street and across Buitengragt, to become the main drag of the Bo-Kaap. The architectural charm of the colourful, protected historic core bounded by Dorp and Strand streets and Buitengragt and Pentz streets is undeniable. While there is still a solid **Muslim community** in the Bo-Kaap, it has become diluted by new residents who like the Muslim edginess of the area and value the central location and stunning views of Table Mountain. As such, in recent years a smattering of design studios, coffee shops and B&Bs have sprung up in the neighbourhood.

The best way to explore Bo-Kaap is by joining one of the **tours** that take in the Bo-Kaap Museum and walk you around the district. The most reliable is run by Bo-Kaap Guided Tours (meet at Bo-Kaap Museum; R350, including entrance to the museum; ☎ 021 422 1554, ⓦ bokaapcookingtour.co.za). It lasts two hours, includes **Cape Malay** snacks and is operated by residents of the area, whose knowledge goes beyond the standard tour-guide script. The same outfit also offers a similar tour for R600 that culminates at the house of a Bo-Kaap resident for lunch, and where you get to help prepare and cook a typical Cape Malay meal. For this, you need to book at least two days in advance, but for the delicious food, the forward planning is definitely worth it.

Bo-Kaap Museum

71 Wale St • Mon–Sat 10am–5pm • R20 • ⓦ iziko.org.za/museums/bo-kaap-museum

If you're exploring the Bo-Kaap on your own, a good place to head is the **Bo-Kaap Museum**, near the Buitengragt end. It consists mainly of the family house and possessions of **Abu Bakr Effendi**, a nineteenth-century religious leader brought out from Turkey by the British in 1862 as a mediator between feuding Muslim factions. He became an important member of the community, founded an Arabic school and wrote a book in the local vernacular – now regarded as possibly the first book to be published in what can be recognized as Afrikaans. The museum also has exhibits that explore the local brand of Islam, which has its own unique traditions and nearly two dozen *kramats* (shrines) dotted about the peninsula.

Auwal

43 Dorp St

The **Auwal** was South Africa's first official mosque, founded in 1797 by the highly influential Imam Abdullah ibn Qadi Abd al-Salam (commonly known as **Tuan Guru** or Master Teacher), a Moluccan prince and Muslim activist who was exiled to Robben Island in 1780 for opposing Dutch rule in the Indies. While on the island, he transcribed the Koran from memory and wrote several important Islamic commentaries, which provided a basis for the religion at the Cape for almost a century. On being released in 1792, he began offering religious instruction from his house in Dorp Street, before founding the Auwal nearby. Ten more mosques, whose minarets spice up the quarter's skyline, now serve the Bo-Kaap's Muslim residents.

Greenmarket Square

Cnr Shortmarket and Longmarket sts

Turning east from Long Street into Shortmarket Street, you'll skim the edge of **Greenmarket Square**, which is worth a little exploration to take in the cobbled streets, coffee shops and grand buildings. As its name implies, the square started as a vegetable market, though it spent many ignominious years as a car park. Human life has since returned, and it's now home to a flea market (see p.134), selling crafts, jewellery and hippie clobber. This is also one of the best places in Cape Town to buy from Congolese and Zimbabwean traders, who sell masks and malachite carvings that make great souvenirs.

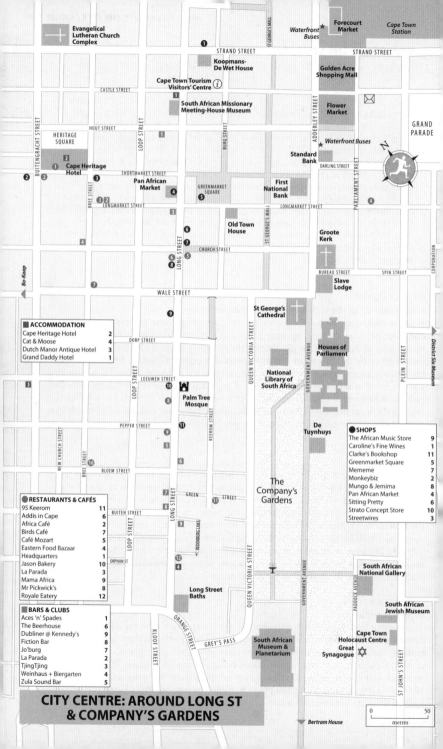

ELUTHERAN CHURCH COMPLEX

Evangelical
Lutheran Church
Complex

❶

STRAND STREET

ST GEORGE'S MALL

Waterfront
Buses

Forecourt
Market

Cape Town
Station

STRAND STREET

Koopmans-
De Wet House

Golden Acre
Shopping Mall

CASTLE STREET

Cape Town Tourism
Visitors' Centre ⓘ

❶

ADDERLEY STREET

South African Missionary
Meeting-House Museum

Flower
Market

HOUT STREET

❶

GRAND
PARADE

BUITENGRACHT STREET

LOOP STREET

BURG STREET

Waterfront Buses

HERITAGE
SQUARE

❷

Standard
Bank

DARLING STREET

PARLIAMENT STREET

❶ Cape Heritage
Hotel

SHORTMARKET STREET

❷

❸

Pan African
Market

GREENMARKET
SQUARE

First
National
Bank

BREE STREET

❸ ❷

LONGMARKET STREET

❹

❺

LONGMARKET STREET

❹

❹

❻

Old Town
House

Groote
Kerk

CHURCH STREET

LONG STREET

ST GEORGE'S MALL

❼

❺

BUREAU STREET

SPIN STREET

CORPORATION

❻ ❽

❼

WALE STREET

Slave
Lodge

Bo-Kaap

❾

St George's
Cathedral

District Six Museum

QUEEN VICTORIA STREET

GOVERNMENT AVENUE

Houses of
Parliament

PLEIN STREET

DORP STREET

LEEUWEN STREET

❶

National
Library of
South Africa

LOOP STREET

❿

❾

Palm Tree
Mosque

KEEROM STREET

De
Tuynhuys

PEPPER STREET

⓫

❾

NEW CHURCH STREET

BREE STREET

❺

BLOEM STREET

❻

The
Company's
Gardens

❼

GREEN   STREET

⓫

BUITEN STREET

LOOP STREET

❾

REDENBURG LANE

⓬

❹

ORPHAN ST

South African
National Gallery

PADDOCK AVENUE

South African
Jewish Museum

Long Street
Baths

ORANGE STREET

KLOOF STREET

GREY'S PASS

QUEEN VICTORIA STREET

GOVERNMENT AVENUE

South African
Museum &
Planetarium

Cape Town
Holocaust Centre

Great
Synagogue

ST JOHN'S STREET

CITY CENTRE: AROUND LONG ST
& COMPANY'S GARDENS

0   50
metres

Bertram House

Michaelis Collection

Old Town House, Greenmarket Square • Mon–Sat 10am–5pm • R20 • ☎ 021 481 3933, 🖰 iziko.org.za

On the western side of Greenmarket Square are the solid limewashed walls and small shuttered windows of the **Old Town House**, entered from Longmarket Street. Built in the mid-1700s, this beautiful example of Cape Dutch architecture, with a fine interior, has seen duty as a guardhouse, a police station and Cape Town's city hall. Today it houses the **Michaelis Collection** of minor but interesting seventeenth-century Dutch and Flemish landscape paintings.

The seventeenth century was one of great prosperity for the Netherlands and has been referred to as the Dutch "Golden Age", during which the nation threw off the yoke of its Spanish colonizers and sailed forth to establish colonies of its own in the East Indies and, of course, at the Cape. The wealth that trade brought to the Netherlands stimulated the development of the arts, and the paintings of the era reflect the values and experience of Dutch Calvinists. A notable example is **Frans Hals**' *Portrait of a Woman*, hanging in the upstairs gallery. Executed in shades of brown, relieved only by the merest hint of red, it reflects the Calvinist aversion to ostentation. The sitter for the picture, completed in 1644, would have been a contemporary of the settlers who arrived at the Cape some eight years later (see p.251). Less dour and showing off the wealth of a middle-class family is the beautiful *Couple with Two Children in a Park*, painted by **Dirck Dirckz Santvoort** in the late 1630s, in which the artist displays a remarkable facility for portraying sensuous fabrics which glow with reflected light; you can almost feel the texture of the lace trimming.

Other paintings, most of them quite sombre, depict mythological scenes, church interiors, still lifes, landscapes and seascapes, the latter being very close to the seventeenth-century Dutch heart, often illustrating vessels belonging to the Dutch East India Company or the drama of rough seas encountered by trade ships. A tiny **print room** on the ground floor has a small selection of works by Daumier, Gillray and Cruikshank, as well as one of **Goya**'s most famous works, *El Sueño de la Razón Produce Monstruos* (The Sleep of Reason Produces Monsters).

Small visiting exhibitions also find space here, and there are regular evening classical concerts in the Frans Hals room; the website lists forthcoming events.

St George's Mall

East of Greenmarket Square lies **St George's Mall**, a pedestrianized road that runs northeast from Wale Street to Thibault Square, near the train station. Coffee shops, snack bars and numerous street traders and buskers make this a more pleasant route between the station and the Company's Gardens than Adderley Street.

St George's Cathedral

5 Wale St • Daily 8.30am–4.30pm; services Mon–Fri 7.15am & 1.15pm, also Tues–Thurs 8am & 4pm, Wed 10am and Sat 8am; Sun Mass 9.30am • Free • ☎ 021 424 7360, 🖰 sgcathedral.co.za

St George's Cathedral, at the southern end of St George's Mall, is as interesting for its history as for its Herbert Baker Victorian-Gothic design. There are daily **services**, as well as the main Mass on Sunday mornings, and the cathedral hosts good classical, jazz and choral **concerts** (check website for details). The most famous archbishop of Cape Town is undoubtedly Nobel Peace Laureate **Desmond Tutu**, who hammered on the cathedral's doors symbolically on September 7, 1986, demanding to be enthroned as South Africa's first black archbishop. Three years later, he heralded the last days of apartheid by leading thirty thousand people from St George's to the City Hall, where he coined his now famous slogan for the new order: "We are the rainbow people!", and told the crowd, "We are the new people of South Africa!" In 2014, at the cathedral, Archbishop Tutu launched a book on a topic close to his heart, *The Book of Forgiving*, with his daughter, Reverend Mpho Tutu.

1

Church Street

Church Street, which crosses St George's Mall towards its southern end, and its surrounding area abound with antique dealers selling bric-a-brac and Africana. The pedestrianized section, where Church Street meets the perpendicular Burg Street, is a very pleasant little area, where art galleries mingle with the smell of coffee, and you can rest your legs at one of the outdoor tables at *Café Mozart* (see p.117).

Government Avenue

A stroll down **Government Avenue**, the southwest extension of Adderley Street, makes for one of the most serene walks in central Cape Town. This oak-lined, pedestrianized boulevard runs past the rear of Parliament through the Gardens, and its benches are frequently occupied by snoring *bergies* (homeless inhabitants of Cape Town).

Houses of Parliament

Parliament St • Hourly tours Mon–Fri 9am–noon, 1hr; question time Wed from 3pm • Free; book one week in advance for tours • ☎ 021 403 2001, ⓦ parliament.gov.za • For debating sessions day-tickets and tour entry, go to the Plein St entrance; bring ID

South Africa's **Houses of Parliament**, east of the north end of Government Avenue, are a complex of interlinking buildings, with labyrinthine corridors connecting hundreds of offices, debating chambers and miscellaneous other rooms. Many of these are relics of the 1980s reformist phase of apartheid when, in the interests of racial segregation, there were three distinct legislative complexes sited here to cater to people of different "race".

The original wing, completed in 1885, is an imposing Victorian Neoclassical building which first served as the legislative assembly of the Cape Colony. After the Boer republics and British colonies amalgamated in 1910, it became the parliament of the Union of South Africa. This is the old parliament, where over seven decades of repressive legislation, including apartheid laws, were passed. It's also where **Hendrik Verwoerd**, the arch-theorist of apartheid, met his bloody end at the hand of Dimitri Tsafendas, a parliamentary messenger who inexplicably went off the rails, committing the act because, as he told police, "a tapeworm ordered me to do it". Due to his mental state, the assassin escaped the gallows to outlive apartheid – albeit in an institution. Verwoerd's portrait, depicting him as a man of vision and gravitas, used to hang over the main entrance to the dining room. In 1996 it was removed "for cleaning", along with paintings of generations of white parliamentarians, and never returned.

The new chamber was built in 1983 as part of the **Tricameral Parliament**, P.W. Botha's attempt to avert majority rule by trying to co-opt Indians and coloureds – but in their own separate debating chambers. The "tricameral" chamber, where the three non-African "races" on occasions met together, is now the **National Assembly**, where you can watch sessions of parliament. One-hour **tours** take in the old and new debating chambers, the library and museum. You can also get day-tickets to the **debating sessions** – the most interesting of which is question time, when ministers are quizzed by MPs.

National Library of South Africa

5 Queen Victoria St • Mon–Fri 9am–5pm, Wed from 10am • Free • ⓦ nlsa.ac.za

If you head south from the top of Government Avenue, you'll soon come across the **National Library of South Africa** on your right. The building houses one of the country's best collections of antiquarian historical and natural history books, covering southern Africa. Built with the revenue from a tax on wine, it opened in 1822 as one of the first free libraries in the world.

Company's Gardens

19 Queen Victoria St • Daily: March–Nov 7am–9pm; Dec–Feb 7.30am–8.30pm • Free • ☎ 021 426 1357

The **Company's Gardens**, which stretch from the National Library of South Africa down to the South African Museum, were the *raison d'être* for the Dutch settlement at the

Cape. Established in 1652 to supply fresh greens to Dutch East India Company ships travelling between the Netherlands and the East, the gardens were initially worked by imported slave labour. This proved too expensive, as the slaves had to be shipped in, fed and housed, so the Company opted for outsourcing: it phased out its farming and granted the land to free burghers, from whom it bought fresh produce.

At the end of the seventeenth century, the gardens were turned over to botanical horticulture for Cape Town's growing colonial elite. Ponds, lawns, landscaping and a crisscross web of oak-shaded walkways were introduced. It was during a stroll in these gardens that **Cecil Rhodes** (a statue of whom you'll find here) first plotted the invasion of Matabeleland and Mashonaland (which together became Rhodesia and subsequently Zimbabwe). He also introduced an army of small, furry colonizers to the gardens – North American grey squirrels.

Today, alongside some small vegetable patches, the gardens are full of local plants, the result of long-standing European interest in **Cape botany**; experts have been sailing out since the seventeenth century to classify and name specimens. This is a pleasant place to meander, and features a good outdoor café situated under massive trees.

De Tuynhuys

Government Ave • Not open to the public

South of the National Library of South Africa, past the rear of Parliament, you can peer through an iron gate to see the grand buildings and tended flowerbeds of **De Tuynhuys**, the office (but not residence) of the president.

Under the governorship of **Lord Charles Somerset** (1814–26), an official process of Anglicization at the Cape included the enforcement of English as the sole language in the courts, but equally important was his private obsession with architecture, which saw the demolition of the two Dutch wings of **De Tuynhuys** in Government Avenue. Imposing contemporary English taste, Somerset reinvented the entire garden frontage with a Colonial Regency facade, characterized by a veranda sheltering under an elegantly curving canopy, supported on slender iron columns.

South African National Gallery

Government Ave, Company's Gardens • Daily 10am–5pm • R30 • ⓦ iziko.org.za/museums/south-african-national-gallery

The **South African National Gallery**, situated at the point where tiny Gallery Lane joins Government Avenue, is an essential port of call for anyone interested in the local art scene and includes a small but excellent permanent collection of contemporary South African art. Displays change every three months, as the number of items far exceeds the capacity of the exhibition space. However, one of the pieces that regularly makes an appearance is **Jane Alexander**'s powerfully ghoulish plaster, bone and horn sculpture, *The Butcher Boys* (1985–86), created at the height of apartheid repression. It features three life-size figures with distorted faces that exude a chilling passivity, expressing the artist's interest in the way violence is conveyed through the human figure. Alexander's work is representative of "**resistance art**", which exploded in the 1980s, broadly as a response to the growing repression of apartheid. The movement was inspired by the idea that artists had a responsibility to engage politically; it spanned a wide range of subject matter, styles and media.

Paul Stopforth's powerful graphite-and-wax triptych, *The Interrogators* (1979), featuring larger-than-life-size portraits of three notorious security policemen, is a work of monumental hyperrealism. Many other artists, unsurprisingly for a culturally diverse country, aren't easily categorized; while works have tended to borrow from Western traditions, their themes and execution are uniquely South African. The late **John Muafangelo** employed biblical imagery in works such as *The Pregnant Maria* (undated), producing highly stylized, almost naive black-and-white linocuts; while in *Challenges Facing the New South Africa* (1990), **Willie Bester** used paint and shantytown objects to depict the melting pot of the Cape Town squatter camps.

1

Since the 1990s, and especially in the post-apartheid period, the gallery has engaged in a process of redefining what constitutes contemporary **indigenous art** and has embarked on an acquisitions policy that "acknowledges and celebrates the expressive cultures of the African continent, particularly its southern regions". Material that would previously have been treated as ethnographic, such as a major **bead collection** as well as carvings and **craft objects**, is now finding a place alongside oil paintings and sculptures.

The only permanent collection consists of minor works by British artists, including George Romney, Thomas Gainsborough, Joshua Reynolds and some Pre-Raphaelites. The gallery also has an excellent shop with some local crafts.

South African Jewish Museum

Next to the South African National Gallery but accessed from 88 Hatfield St • Mon–Thurs & Sun 10am–5pm, Fri 10am–2pm • R50 • ⓦ sajewishmuseum.co.za

The **South African Jewish Museum** is partially housed in South Africa's first synagogue, built in 1863. One of Cape Town's most ambitious permanent exhibitions, it tells the story of South African Jewry from its beginnings, over 150 years ago, to the present – a narrative which starts in the Old Synagogue from which visitors cross, via a gangplank, to the upper level of a two-storey building, symbolically re-enacting the arrival by boat of the first Jewish immigrants at Table Bay harbour in the 1840s. Multimedia interactive displays, models and Judaica artefacts explore Judaism in South Africa, drawing parallels between Judaism and the ritual practices and beliefs of South Africa's other communities. The **basement** level houses a walk-through reconstruction of a Lithuanian *shtetl* or village (most South African Jews have their nineteenth-century roots in Lithuania). A restaurant, shop and auditorium are also housed in the museum complex.

Cape Town Holocaust Centre

88 Hatfield St • Mon–Thurs & Sun 10am–5pm, Fri 10am–2pm • Free • ⓦ ctholocaust.co.za

Opened in 1999, the **Holocaust Exhibition** is one of the city's most moving and brilliantly executed displays. Housed upstairs in the **Cape Town Holocaust Centre** (in the same complex as the Jewish Museum), it resonates sharply in a country that only recently emerged from an era of racial oppression – a connection that the exhibition makes explicitly.

Exhibits trace the history of anti-Semitism in Europe, culminating with the Nazis' Final Solution; they also look at South Africa's Greyshirts, who were motivated by Nazi propaganda during the 1930s and were later absorbed into the National Party. To conclude, a twenty-minute video tells the story of survivors who eventually settled in Cape Town.

Great Synagogue

88 Hatfield St • For access, ask at Cape Town Holocaust Centre; you may be asked to provide some form of identification • ⓦ gardensshul.org

The **Great Synagogue**, next door to the Holocaust Centre, is one of Cape Town's outstanding religious buildings. Designed by the Scottish architects Parker & Forsyth and completed in 1905, it features an impressive dome and two soaring towers after the style of Central-European Baroque churches. To see the arched interior and the alcove decorated with gilt mosaics, you need to ask at the Holocaust Centre.

South African Museum

25 Queen Victoria St • Daily 10am–5pm • R30 • ⓦ iziko.org.za/museums/south-african-museum

West of Government Avenue is the nation's premier museum of natural history and human sciences, the **South African Museum**. The museum is notable for its **ethnographic galleries** (which contain some good displays on the traditional arts and crafts of several African groups), some exceptional examples of rock art (entire chunks

FROM TOP THE BO-KAAP; STREET VENDORS ON LONG STREET >

1

of caves are in the display cases) and casts of the stone birds found at the archeological site of Great Zimbabwe, in southeastern Zimbabwe. Upstairs, the **natural history galleries** display mounted mammals, dioramas of prehistoric Karoo reptiles and Table Mountain flora and fauna. The highlight is the four-storey "whale well", in which a collection of beautiful whale skeletons hangs as if made up of massive mobiles, accompanied by the eerie strains of their song.

Planetarium

In the South African Museum, 25 Queen Victoria St • Shows daily: children Mon, Wed & Fri 2pm, Sat & Sun noon & 2.30pm; teens and adults Tues 8pm, Sat & Sun 1pm; closed first Mon of month outside school hols • R40 • ⓦ iziko.org.za/museums/planetarium

Housed in the South African Museum building is the **Planetarium**, in which you can see the constellations of the southern hemisphere, with an informed commentary, and a changing programme of shows covering topics such as San sky myths, with some programmes geared specially for children. You can also buy a monthly chart of the current night sky.

Bertram House

Government Ave, accessed from Orange St • Mon–Sat 10am–5pm • Donation • ⓦ iziko.org.za/museums/bertram-house

At the southernmost end of Government Avenue, you'll come upon **Bertram House**, whose beautiful two-storey brick facade looks out across a fragrant herb garden. Built in the 1840s, the museum is significant as the only surviving brick, Georgian-style house in Cape Town, and displays typical furniture and objects of a well-to-do colonial British family in the first half of the nineteenth century.

The site was bought in 1839 by John Barker, a Yorkshire attorney who came to the Cape in 1823. His wife, Ann Bertram Findlay, who died in 1838, was responsible for building it, and Barker bestowed her middle name on the house. Declared a National Monument in 1962, Bertram House was extensively restored in the 1980s (and again in 2010): imported face brick and Welsh slate were used to re-create the original facade, while the interior walls were redecorated in their earlier dark green and ochre, based on the evidence of paint scrapings. The reception rooms are decorated in the Regency style, while the porcelain is predominantly nineteenth-century English, although there are also some very fine Chinese pieces.

Rust en Vreugd

78 Buitenkant St • Mon–Fri 10am–5pm • Donation • ⓦ iziko.org.za/static/page/rust-en-vreugd

The most beautiful of Cape Town's house museums, **Rust en Vreugd**, a couple of blocks east of the Gardens, was built in 1778 for Willem Cornelis Boers, the colony's Fiscal (a powerful position akin to the police chief, public prosecutor and collector of taxes rolled into one), who was forced to resign in the 1780s following allegations of wheeler-dealing and extortion. Under the British occupation, it was the residence of Lord Charles Somerset during his governorship (1814–26).

The house was once surrounded by countryside, but now stands along a congested route that brushes past the edge of the central business district. Designed by architect Louis Michel Thibault and sculptor Anton Anreith, the two-storey facade features a pair of stacked balconies, the lower one forming a stunning portico fronted by four Corinthian columns carved from teak. The front door, framed by teak pilasters, is an impressive work of art, rated by architectural historian De Bosdari as "certainly the finest door at the Cape". Above the door, the fanlight is executed in elaborate Baroque style.

Inside, the William Fehr Collection of artworks on paper occupies two ground-floor rooms and includes illustrations by important documentarists such as **Thomas Baines**, who is represented by hand-coloured lithographs and a series of watercolours recording a nineteenth-century expedition up Table Mountain. The work of **Thomas Bowler**, another prolific recorder of Cape scenes, is also on display here, with his striking landscape painting of Cape Point from the sea in 1864, which shows dolphins frolicking in the foreground.

The property is defined by a boundary of bay trees. The **garden**, a tranquil escape from the busy street, is a reconstruction of the original eighteenth-century semiformal one, laid out with herbaceous hedges and gravel walkways, and features a spacious lawn with a quaint little gazebo.

Castle of Good Hope

Castle St · Daily 9am–4pm; tours 11am, noon & 2pm · R30 including tour · ⓦ castleofgoodhope.co.za

From the outside, South Africa's oldest official building looks somewhat miserable, and its position behind the train station and city-bus terminal does nothing to dispel this. Don't be put off by the off-putting exterior – the **Castle of Good Hope** is well worth a visit. Built in 1666, it still serves as a military barracks site (albeit significantly down scaled) and is considered the best-preserved example of a Dutch East India Company (VOC) fort. For a hundred and fifty years, this was the symbolic heart of the Cape administration, though in the last decade or so it has come to represent a place of reconciliation and healing.

Finished in 1679, complete with the essentials of a moat and torture chamber, the castle replaced Van Riebeeck's earlier mud-and-timber fort which stood on the site of the Grand Parade. The building was designed along seventeenth-century European principles of fortification, comprising strong bastions from which the outside walls could be protected by crossfire.

Moving boundaries

The original, seaward **entrance** had to be moved to its present position facing landward because the spring tide sometimes came crashing in – a remarkable thought given how far aground it is now, thanks to land reclamation. The entrance gate displays the coat of arms of the United Netherlands and those of the six Dutch cities in which the VOC chambers were situated. Still hanging from its original wooden beams in the tower above the entrance is the **bell**, cast in 1697 by Claude Fremy in Amsterdam; it was used variously as an alarm signal, which can be heard from 10km away, and as a summons to residents to receive pronouncements.

From castle to prison

The castle was the general and slave **prison** for the Cape Colony, and prisoners held here included indigenous Khoi people and slaves who were accused of transgressions against slave owners. As punishment could only be dealt once a confession was given, detainees were routinely questioned and tortured. Besides riveting stories about slavery, the free **tour** takes you to the dark, inconspicuous room where these acts took place, with the original iron chains that were used to bind the prisoner still firmly attached to the wall, as well as to the adjacent solitary-confinement room – the much feared *Donker Gat* (Dark Hole). In other prison cells and dungeons, you can still see the touching centuries-old poetry and graffiti painstakingly carved into the walls by prisoners.

The **inner courtyard** is home to the platform where families of slaves would stand as they were bought and sold. As no law existed to keep families together, a mother would watch her children being sold off individually to different farms and vineyards in the Western Cape.

The William Fehr Collection

Elaborately carved double doors at the rear of the *kat* balcony open onto four interlocking rooms that were once the heart of VOC government at the Cape and which now house the bulk of the **William Fehr Collection**, one of the country's most important exhibits of decorative arts. The contents, acquired by businessman William Fehr from the 1920s, were sold and donated to the government in the 1950s and

1

1960s and continue to be displayed informally, as Fehr preferred. The galleries are filled with items found in middle-class Cape households from the seventeenth to nineteenth centuries, with some fine examples of elegantly simple Cape furniture from the eighteenth century. Early colonial views of Table Bay appear in a number of paintings, including one by Aernot Smit that shows the Castle in the seventeenth century, right on the shoreline. Among the fascinating items of antique oriental ceramics are a blue-and-white Japanese porcelain plate from around 1660, which displays the VOC monogram, and a beautiful polychrome plate from China, which dates to around 1750 and depicts a fleet of Company ships in Table Bay against the backdrop of a very oriental-looking Table Mountain.

Grand Parade to City Hall

The **Grand Parade**, just northwest of the Castle of Good Hope, is a large open area where the residents of District Six used to come to trade. On Wednesdays and Saturdays it still transforms itself into a **market** (9am–4pm) where you can buy a whole array of bargains ranging from cheap clothes to spicy food.

The Grand Parade appeared on TV screens throughout the world on February 11, 1990, when 100,000 people gathered to hear **Nelson Mandela** make his first speech after being released from prison, from the balcony of the **City Hall**. It's also where an interfaith prayer was made upon his death, on December 6, 2013. The City Hall is a slightly fussy Edwardian building, dressed in Bath stone; it manages, despite its drab surroundings, to look impressive against the backdrop of Table Mountain.

District Six

South of the Castle of Good Hope, in the shadow of Devil's Peak, is a vacant lot shown on maps as the suburb of **Zonnebloem**. Before being demolished by the apartheid authorities, it was an inner-city slum known as **District Six**, an impoverished but lively community of fifty-five thousand predominantly coloured people. Once regarded as the soul of Cape Town, the district harboured a rich – and much mythologized – cultural life in its narrow alleys and crowded tenements: along the cobbled streets, hawkers rubbed shoulders with prostitutes, gangsters, drunks and gamblers, while craftsmen plied their trade in small workshops. This was a fertile place of the South African imagination, inspiring novels, poems and jazz, often with more than a hint of nostalgia, anger and pain of displacement.

In 1966, apartheid ideologues declared District Six a **White Group Area** and the bulldozers moved in, taking fifteen years to drive its presence from the skyline, leaving only the mosques and churches. But, in the wake of the demolition gangs, international and domestic outcry was so great that the area was never developed, apart from the addition of a few luxury townhouses on its fringes and the hefty **Cape Technikon**, a college that now occupies nearly a quarter of the former suburb. After years of negotiation, the original residents are moving back under a scheme to develop low-cost housing in the area.

District Six Museum

25A Buitenkant St • Mon–Sat 9am–4pm • R30 • ⓦ districtsix.co.za

Few places in Cape Town speak more eloquently of the effect of apartheid on the day-to-day lives of ordinary people than the compelling **District Six Museum**. On the northern boundary of District Six, on the corner of Buitenkant and Albertus streets, the museum occupies the former **Central Methodist Mission Church**, which offered solidarity and ministry to the victims of forced removals right up to the 1980s, and became a venue for anti-apartheid gatherings. Today, it houses a series of fascinating displays that include everyday household items and tools of trades, such as hairdressing implements, as well as documentary photographs, which evoke the lives

1

of the individuals who once lived here. Occupying most of the floor is a huge map of District Six as it was, annotated by former residents, who describe their memories, reflections and incidents associated with places and buildings that no longer exist. There's also an almost complete collection of original street signs, secretly retrieved at the time of demolition by the man entrusted with dumping them into Table Bay. Their **coffee shop** offers a variety of snacks, including traditional, syrupy *koeksisters*.

Strand Street

A major artery from the N2 freeway to the central business district, **Strand Street** neatly separates the Upper from the Lower city centre. Between the mid-eighteenth and mid-nineteenth centuries, this was one of the most fashionable streets in Cape Town, due to its proximity to the shore – it used to run along the beachfront, but now lies about a kilometre south of it. Its former cachet is now only discernible from the handful of quietly elegant national monuments left standing amid the roar of traffic.

Evangelical Lutheran Church

98 Strand St, at Buitengracht • Mon, Wed & Fri 9am–noon • Free • ☎ 021 886 9747

The **Evangelical Lutheran Church** was converted by Anton Anreith in 1785 from a barn. The establishment of a Lutheran church in Cape Town struck a significant blow against the extreme **religious intolerance** that pervaded under VOC rule. Before 1771 (when permission was granted for Lutherans to establish their own congregation), Protestantism was the only form of worship allowed, and the Dutch Reformed Church held an absolute monopoly over saving people's souls. The Lutheran Church's congregation was dominated by Germans, who at the time constituted 28 percent of the colony's free burgher population.

The facade of the Evangelical Lutheran Church includes classical details such as a broken pediment perforated by the clock tower, as well as Gothic features such as arched windows. Inside, the magnificent **pulpit**, supported on two life-size Herculean figures, is one of Anreith's masterpieces; the white swan perched on the canopy is a symbol of Lutheranism.

Koopmans-De Wet House

35 Strand St • Mon–Fri 10am–5pm • R20 • ⓦ iziko.org.za/museums/koopmans-de-wet-house

Sandwiched between two office blocks, **Koopmans-De Wet House** is an outstanding eighteenth-century pedimented Neoclassical townhouse and museum which accommodates a very fine collection of antique furniture and rare porcelain.

The earliest sections of the house were built in 1701 by **Reyner Smedinga**, a well-to-do goldsmith who imported the building materials from Holland. After changing hands more than a dozen times over the following two centuries, the building eventually fell into the hands of **Marie Koopmans-De Wet** (1834–1906), a prominent figure on the Cape social and political circuit.

The house represents a fine synthesis of Dutch elements with the demands of local conditions: typically Dutch sash windows and large entrances combine with huge rooms, lofty ceilings and shuttered windows, all installed with high summer temperatures in mind. The **lantern** in the fanlight of the entrance to the house was a feature of all Cape Town houses in the eighteenth and early nineteenth centuries, its purpose to shine light onto the street and thus hinder slaves from gathering at night to plot.

Bree Street

Dotted with design and boutique shops and humming with restaurants and bars, **Bree Street** has become the new stomping ground for hipsters and well-heeled Capetonians. The conversion of old buildings into new spaces enhances the lovely architecture that may have been overlooked in the past, and has sparked the reclamation of sidewalks by pedestrians. The intersection with Longmarket Street is your best bet to get a feel for this vibrant road.

Lower City Centre

In the mid-nineteenth century, the city's middle classes viewed the **Lower City Centre** and its low-life activities with a mixture of alarm and excitement – a tension that remains today. **Lower Long Street** divides the area just inland from the docklands into two. To the east is the **Foreshore**, an ugly post-World War II wasteland of grey corporate architecture, among which is the **Artscape Centre**, Cape Town's premier arts complex. The Foreshore is at last being redeveloped, its centrepiece being the successful **Cape Town International Convention Centre**, linked by a canal and pedestrian routes with the Waterfront.

The Foreshore

The Foreshore is an area of reclaimed land northeast of Strand Street which stretches to the docks and northwest of Lower Long Street. The area was developed in the late 1940s in a spirit of modernism – large, highly planned, urban spaces – that was sweeping the world. It was intended to turn Cape Town's harbour into a symbolic gateway to Africa; instead, all that emerged was a series of large concrete boxes surrounded by acres of windswept tarmac car parks. In 2013, the construction of the Portside Tower gave Cape Town its tallest building (139m), in the heart of a small financial and legal district, but there is still no street life at all in the area and no real reason to explore it (unless you're coming to see a performance at the Artscape Complex; see below).

Artscape Complex

D.F. Malan St, just east of Heerengracht • Performance times vary; visit website for listings • Ⓦ artscape.co.za

The only building worth visiting in the Foreshore – but only when there's something on – is the **Artscape Complex**, Cape Town's monumental performance venue with its huge theatre, an opera house and the compact Arena Theatre. Artscape is the home of Cape Town Opera, which features the best of South Africa's singers, and Jazzart, the Western Cape's longest-established contemporary dance company.

Duncan Dock

North of the Foreshore, **Duncan Dock** is Cape Town's working harbour. Work started on the dock in 1938, when the city beachfronts at Woodstock and Paarden Island were swallowed up to cater for the growing supertanker traffic that was outstripping the capacity of the Victoria and Alfred docks. Today, the dock is a forbidding industrial landscape of large ships and towering cranes cut off from the city by an enormous perimeter fence.

THE V&A WATERFRONT

V&A Waterfront, Robben Island and De Waterkant

The Victoria & Alfred Waterfront, known simply as the Waterfront, is Cape Town's original Victorian harbour, incorporating nineteenth-century buildings, shopping malls, waterside piers and a functioning harbour that all share a magnificent Table Mountain backdrop. Redeveloped in the 1990s, it is the city's most fashionable area for shopping, eating and drinking, and incorporates the Nelson Mandela Gateway – the embarkation point for unmissable trips to Robben Island. West of the Foreshore, with the Waterfront to its north, is De Waterkant, a once down-at-heel district that has gentrified at a cracking pace to become Cape Town's self-styled gay quarter and a significant draw for tourists, with plentiful accommodation, bars and shops.

By car If you have a car, you'll find yourself well catered for, as there are several car parks and garages in the area.

By taxi There are a number of taxi ranks dotted about, such as the one on Breakwater Boulevard.

By MyCiTi bus ☎ 0800 65 64 63, ⓦ myciti.org.za. This area is well served by public transport. Bus #104 to Seapoint or City Bowl runs directly past the Waterfront. The #106 or #107 go to Camps Bay via the Civic Centre and City Bowl (Adderley St, Long St, Kloof St and Kloof Nek). To get to the airport, take the #A01 from the Waterfront via the Civic Centre.

By sightseeing bus City Sightseeing buses link the Two Oceans Aquarium at the Waterfront with a number of major sights in the city centre and on the peninsula (☎ 086 173 3287, ⓦ citysightseeing.co.za; see p.21).

The V&A Waterfront

Throughout the first half of the nineteenth century, arguments raged in Cape Town over the need for a proper dock. The Cape was often known as the **Cape of Storms** because of its vicious weather, which left Table Bay littered with wrecks. Many makeshift attempts were made to improve this, including the construction of a lighthouse in 1823, and work began on a jetty at the bottom of Bree Street in 1832. With the increase in sea traffic arriving at the Cape in the 1850s, clamour for a harbour grew. It reached its peak in 1860, when the Lloyds insurance company refused the risk of covering ships dropping anchor in Table Bay.

The British colonial government dragged its heels due to the costs involved, but eventually conceded; on a suitably stormy September day in 1860, at a huge ceremony, the teenage Prince Alfred tipped the first batch of stones into Table Bay to begin the **breakwater**, the westernmost arm of the harbour. Convicts were enlisted to complete the job, and in 1869, the dock was completed, and the sea was allowed to pour in.

Victoria & Alfred Wharf

Red Shed • Daily 9am–9pm • ⓦ waterfront.co.za

The shopping focus of the Waterfront is **Victoria & Alfred Wharf**, an enormous flashy mall on two levels, extending along quays Five and Six. It's here that most visitors to the Waterfront arrive. The restaurants and cafés on the mall's east side, with their outdoor seating, have fabulous views of Table Mountain across the busy harbour. On the west side of the wharf and physically linked to it, the rather contrived **Red Shed Craft Workshop** (Mon–Sat 9am–9pm, Sun 10am–9pm; ☎ 021 408 7847) brings together craft workers such as glass-blowers, leatherworkers, township artists and jewellery-makers under one huge roof. Outdoor action is centred around **Market Square** and the **Agfa Amphitheatre**, where you can catch musical performances. Beyond Victoria Wharf is the Pierhead and, further on, the Marina.

Two Oceans Aquarium

Dock Rd • Daily 9.30am–6pm • Adults R125, children 14–17 R97, 4–13 R60, under-4s free • ⓦ aquarium.co.za

At the Marina's North Wharf, the **Two Oceans Aquarium** showcases the Cape's unique marine environment, where the warm Indian Ocean mingles with the cold Atlantic. Unfortunately, at the time of writing the biggest draws, the Predators and Kelp Forest displays, were being upgraded; these are due to reopen in early 2016.

The general route begins on the ground floor with the **Indian Ocean Gallery**, home to dazzling tropical fish, honeycomb eels and a coral exhibit as well as a display on one of the major currents affecting the east coast of South Africa, the Agulhas. The **Atlantic Ocean Gallery** contains an astonishing variety of strange marine creatures, including giant spider crabs, octopuses and seahorses, the primitive eyeless and jawless hagfish and a display featuring floating gossamer jellyfish. Also on this level is the interactive **Touch Pool**, where children can get their hands wet while inspecting animals such as anemones and crabs and ask questions to their hearts' content, and the **Microscope Exhibit** where, with the assistance of highly knowledgeable staff, you can observe tiny animals that would otherwise probably go unnoticed.

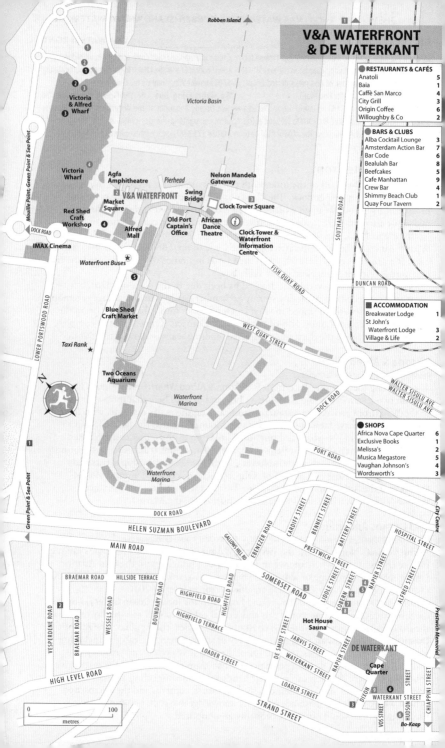

V&A WATERFRONT & DE WATERKANT

Robben Island

RESTAURANTS & CAFÉS
Anatoli	5
Baia	1
Caffè San Marco	4
City Grill	3
Origin Coffee	6
Willoughby & Co	2

BARS & CLUBS
Alba Cocktail Lounge	3
Amsterdam Action Bar	7
Bar Code	6
Bealulah Bar	8
Beefcakes	5
Cafe Manhattan	9
Crew Bar	4
Shimmy Beach Club	1
Quay Four Tavern	2

ACCOMMODATION
Breakwater Lodge	1
St John's Waterfront Lodge	3
Village & Life	2

SHOPS
Africa Nova Cape Quarter	6
Exclusive Books	1
Melissa's	2
Musica Megastore	5
Vaughan Johnson's	4
Wordsworth's	3

Victoria Basin

Victoria & Alfred Wharf

Victoria Wharf

Agfa Amphitheatre

Pierhead

Nelson Mandela Gateway

V&A WATERFRONT

Market Square

Swing Bridge

Clock Tower Square

Red Shed Craft Workshop

Alfred Mall

Old Port Captain's Office

African Dance Theatre

Clock Tower & Waterfront Information Centre

IMAX Cinema

Waterfront Buses

Blue Shed Craft Market

Taxi Rank

Two Oceans Aquarium

Waterfront Marina

Waterfront Marina

Moullie Point, Green Point & Sea Point

Dock Road

Lower Portswood Road

Green Point & Sea Point

Southarm Road

Duncan Road

West Quay Street

Walter Sisulu Ave

Dock Road

Port Road

Dock Road

Helen Suzman Boulevard

Main Road

Braemar Road

Hillside Terrace

Highfield Road

Highfield Road

Highfield Terrace

Vesperdene Road

Braemar Road

Wessels Road

Boundary Road

Gallows Hill Rd

Ebenezer Road

Cardiff Street

Bennett Street

Battery Street

Prestwich Street

Hospital Street

Somerset Road

Liddle Street

Cobern Street

Napier Street

Alfred Street

City Centre

Prestwich Memorial

Hot House Sauna

DE WATERKANT

Cape Quarter

De Smidt Street

Jarvis Street

Napier Street

Waterkant Street

Loader Street

Loader Street

High Level Road

Strand Street

Waterkant Street

Dixon Street

Vos Street

Hudson Street

Chiappini Street

Bo-Kaap

0   100
metres

The basement houses the **AfriSam Children's Play Centre**, a good place to keep the little ones occupied, with free organized activities such as puppet shows, face painting and arts and crafts. The centre is combined with an area where the resident rockhopper penguins can be observed frolicking underwater during the day.

The top floor, accessed via a ramp, accommodates the **Penguin Exhibit**, featuring a small breeding colony of endangered African penguins (which you can see in their natural habitat at Boulders Beach; see p.102).

Nelson Mandela Gateway

Clock Tower Precinct • Daily 7.30am–9pm • Free • ☎ 021 409 5100

2

The imposing **Clock Tower** by the Waterfront's swing bridge was built as the original Port Captain's office in 1882. Adjacent to this is the **Nelson Mandela Gateway**, the embarkation point for ferries to Robben Island (see below) and sometimes referred to as **Jetty 1**. Here, the Robben Island Museum has installed a number of exhibitions that are open to the public and free of charge. These include accounts of ex-political prisoners, ex-prison warders and the families of both, as well as posters of individual and collective struggles of those who went through this portal on their way to prison.

Robben Island

Flat and windswept **Robben Island**, only a few kilometres from the buzz and commerce of the Waterfront, is a symbol of the triumph of the human spirit over adversity. Suffused by a meditative, otherworldly silence, this key site of South Africa's liberation struggle was intended to silence apartheid's domestic critics, but instead became an international focus for opposition to the regime. The island was declared a National Monument and National Museum in 1996, and a World Heritage Site in 1999. From the seventeenth until the late twentieth centuries, the island was used at different times as a prison and leper colony, and as a military base during World War II (see box, p.66).

Allow more than half a day for the trip, and book as far in advance as possible.

ESSENTIALS ROBBEN ISLAND

Getting there The catamaran from the Waterfront (daily 9am, 11am, 1pm & 3pm) takes 30–45min to reach Robben Island, where ex-prisoners and ex-warders work as guides, sharing their experiences. A new boat, purchased in 2014, should (we hope) overcome the problem of tours sometimes being cancelled.

Tours Tours (total 3hr 30min) are of varying quality. After arrival at the tiny Murray's Bay harbour, you are taken on a bus tour around the island and on foot inside the prison.

Tickets Although a number of vendors sell tickets for cruises that may go close to Robben Island, the only ones that will get you onto it (R250, including voyage, entry and tour) must be bought from the Nelson Mandela Gateway (see above). Bookings must be made well in advance with a credit card, as the boats are often full, especially around Dec and Jan (☎ 021 413 4219, ⊛ robben-island.org.za). Be sure to present your booking reference number and arrive 30min before departure to collect your ticket.

The bus tour

The **bus tour** stops off at several historical landmarks, the first of which is the **kramat**, a beautiful shrine built in memory of Tuan Guru, a Muslim cleric from present-day Indonesia who was imprisoned here by the Dutch in the eighteenth century (see box, p.66). On his release, he helped to establish Islam among slaves in Cape Town, where it has flourished ever since. The tour also passes a leper graveyard and male leper church, built to a Sir Herbert Baker design in 1895. Both are quiet reminders that the island was a place of exile for leprosy sufferers up until 1931, when they were relocated to Pretoria, and sadly leprosy is not yet beaten in South Africa.

Robert Sobukwe's house

Robert Sobukwe's house seems to echo with loneliness and is perhaps the most affecting relic of incarceration on the island. It was here that Sobukwe, leader of the

Pan Africanist Congress (a radical offshoot of the ANC; see p.256), was held in solitary confinement for nine years. He was initially sentenced to three years, but was regarded as so dangerous by the authorities that they passed a special law – the "Sobukwe Clause" – to keep him on Robben Island for a further six years. No other political prisoners were allowed to speak to him, but he would sometimes gesture his solidarity with other sons of the African soil by letting sand trickle through his fingers as they walked past. After his release in 1969, Sobukwe was restricted to Kimberley under house arrest, until his death from cancer in 1978.

2

Lime quarry

Another stop is the **lime quarry** where Nelson Mandela and his fellow inmates spent countless hours of hard labour. The soft, pale stone is extremely bright under the summer sun, as a result of which Mandela and others have in later years suffered eye disorders. As the years passed, the lime quarry became a place of furtive study among the prisoners, with the help of sympathetic warders.

Wildlife spotting

The bus tour also takes in a stretch of coast dotted with shipwrecks and abundant sea birds and waterfowl including the elegant **sacred ibis**. You may also spot some of a recently expanded population of **antelope**: springbok, eland and bontebok.

The Maximum Security Prison

The **Maximum Security Prison**, a forbidding complex of unadorned H-blocks on the edge of the island, is introduced with a tour through the famous **B-Section**; you'll be guided by a former inmate, after which you're free to wander. B-Section is a small compound, full of tiny rooms, that has become legendary in South African history; initially a place of defeat for the resistance movement, ironically it came to incubate and concentrate the energies of liberation. **Mandela's cell** has been left exactly as it was, without embellishments or display, but the rest are locked and empty.

In the nearby **A-Section**, the "Cell Stories" exhibition skilfully suggests the sparseness of prison life. The tiny isolation cells feature personal artefacts loaned by former prisoners (including a functional saxophone made of found objects), plus boards bearing quotations, recordings and photographs.

Towards the end of the 1980s, cameras were sneaked onto the island, and inmates took snapshots of each other, which have been enlarged to almost life size and mounted as the **Smuggled Camera Exhibition** in the **D-Section** communal cells. The jovial demeanour of the prisoners indicates their realization that the end was within sight.

Another interesting part of the prison visit is the **Living Legacy** tour in **F-Section**, in which ex-political prisoner guides describe their lives here and answer visitors' questions.

De Waterkant

As an atmospheric central neighbourhood in easy striking distance of the city centre, the Waterfront and the Atlantic seaboard, **De Waterkant** has a lot going for it and is a decent place to base yourself. Its terraces, which date back to the mid-eighteenth century, line cobbled streets that trawl up the mountainside. The district plays up its assets for all they're worth, with a high number of its houses turned over to guesthouses and self-catering flats. Within easy wandering distance of everything are restaurants, delis, clubs, art dealers, interior design boutiques and a couple of very upmarket shopping malls – one of them the sizeable **Cape Quarter**. With a clutch of **gay-friendly nightclubs and pubs** (see p.143), the area officially just outside De Waterkant, on the east side of **Somerset Road**, which heads from the city centre into Green Point, is known as the **Pink Village**.

CLOCKWISE FROM TOP V&A WATERFRONT; STREET PERFORMER AT THE WATERFRONT; THE CLOCK TOWER (P.63) >

2

"WE SERVE WITH PRIDE": THE HISTORY OF ROBBEN ISLAND

Nelson Mandela may have been the most famous Robben Island prisoner, but he wasn't the first. In the seventeenth century, the island became a place of banishment for those who offended the political order. Initially that power lay in the hands of the Dutch, then the British, followed by the Afrikaner Nationalists. The island's first prisoner was the indigenous Khoikhoi leader **Autshumato**, who learnt English in the early seventeenth century and became an emissary of the British. After the Dutch settlement was established, he was jailed on the island by Jan van Riebeeck in 1658. The rest of the seventeenth century saw a succession of East Indies political prisoners and Muslim holy men exiled here for opposing Dutch colonial rule.

During the nineteenth century, the **British** used Robben Island as a dumping ground for deserters, criminals and political prisoners, in much the same way as they used Australia. Captured **Xhosa leaders** who defied the British Empire during the Frontier Wars of the early to mid-nineteenth century were transported by sea from the Eastern to the Western Cape to be imprisoned, and many ended up on Robben Island. In 1846, the island's brief was extended to include a whole range of the **socially marginalized**: criminals and political detainees were now joined by vagrants, prostitutes, lunatics and the chronically ill. All were victim to a regime of brutality and maltreatment, even in hospitals. In the 1890s, a leper colony existed alongside the social outcasts. Lunatics were removed in 1921 and the lepers in 1930. During World War II, the **Defence Force** took over the island to set up defensive guns against a feared Axis invasion, which never came.

Robben Island's greatest era of notoriety began in 1961, when it was taken over by the **Prisons Department**, under the control of the National Party government, who instigated apartheid. Prisoners arriving at the island prison were greeted by a slogan on the gate that read: "Welcome to Robben Island: We Serve with Pride." By 1963, when Nelson Mandela arrived, it had become a maximum-security prison. All the warders – but none of the prisoners – were white. Prisoners were only allowed to send and receive one letter every six months, and common-law criminals and political prisoners were housed together until 1971, when they were separated in an attempt to further isolate the political activists. Harsh conditions, including routine beatings and forced hard labour, were exacerbated by geographical location. There's nothing but sea between the island and the South Pole, so icy winds routinely blow in from across the Atlantic – and inmates were made to wear shorts and flimsy jerseys. Like every other prisoner, Mandela slept on a thin mat on the floor (until 1973, when he was given a bed because he was ill) and was kept in a solitary confinement cell, measuring two square metres, for sixteen hours a day.

Amazingly, the prisoners found ways of **protesting**, through hunger strikes, publicizing conditions when possible (by using visits from the International Committee of the Red Cross, for example) and, remarkably, by taking legal action against the prison authority to stop arbitrary punishments. They won improved conditions over the years, and the island also became a university behind bars, where people of different political views and generations met; it was not unknown for prisoners to give academic help to their warders.

The last political prisoners were **released** from Robben Island in 1991 and the remaining common-law prisoners transferred to the mainland in 1996. On January 1, 1997, control of Robben Island was transferred from the Department of Correctional Services to the Department of the Arts, Culture, Science and Technology, which established it as a **museum**. In December 1999 the entire island was declared a **UN World Heritage Site**.

Prestwich Memorial

Cnr Buitengracht St and Somerset Rd • Mon–Fri 8am–5pm, Sat & Sun till 3pm • Free • ☎ 021 487 2755

The **Prestwich Memorial**, housed in an elegant modernist structure, accommodates **2500 sets of human bones**, excavated in 2003, of forgotten and marginalized Capetonians – many of them slaves buried in the vicinity in the seventeenth and eighteenth centuries. A collection of interesting interpretation boards provides accounts of burial practices, historic hospitals in the vicinity and, across one wall, a reproduction of a beautiful panorama of Cape Town from the sea painted by Robert Gordon in 1778.

TABLE MOUNTAIN

Table Mountain and the City Bowl

Table Mountain, the icon that announced Cape Town to seafarers for centuries, dominates the peninsula, and its flat top can be recognized from many miles away. The 1087m-high massif, with dramatic cliffs and eroded gorges rising out of two oceans, is one of the world's great physical symbols and an icon for the Mother City. On the mountain slopes, encircling the city centre, lie the very desirable residential suburbs of Vredehoek, Gardens, Oranjezicht, Tamboerskloof and Bo-Kaap, which together make up the City Bowl. This is where most tourists stay, attracted by the harbour views, the city's greatest concentration of restaurants and cafés and the easy access to the city centre sights, the Waterfront and Table Mountain itself.

GETTING AROUND

TABLE MOUNTAIN AND THE CITY BOWL

BY BUS

MyCiTi ☎ 0800 65 64 63, ⓦ myciti.org.za. For the City Bowl suburbs of Gardens, Vredehoek and East City, take the #103, which runs from Oranjezicht to Civic Centre via Gardens and Buitenkant St, or the #101 from Vredehoek to Civic Centre via Gardens, Loop St, Orange St and Mill St.

Buses #106 and #107 go to the Table Mountain Lower Cable Station from the Waterfront (see p.61).

City Sightseeing ☎ 086 173 3287, ⓦ citysightseeing .co.za. The open-topped City Sightseeing bus stops at the Table Mountain Lower Cable Station.

Table Mountain

The north face of **Table Mountain** overlooks the city centre, flanked by the distinct formations of **Lion's Head** and **Signal Hill** to the west and **Devil's Peak** to the east. A series of gable-like formations known as the **Twelve Apostles** makes up the mountain's drier west face and the southwest face towers over Hout Bay. The forested east, looming over the southern suburbs, gets the most rain.

The mountain is a wilderness where you'll find wildlife and 1400 species of flora. Indigenous mammals include baboons, dassies (see box opposite) and porcupines. Getting up and down the mountain can be a doddle, via the highly popular **cable car**

DASSIES

The outsized fluffy guinea pigs you'll encounter at the top of Table Mountain are **dassies** or hyraxes (*Procavia capensis*) which, despite their appearance, aren't rodents at all, but the closest living relatives of elephants. Their name, which was given to them by the first Dutch settlers and is pronounced like "dusty" without the "t", is the Afrikaans version of *dasje*, which means "little badger". Dassies have poor body temperature control and, like reptiles, rely on shelter against both hot sunlight and the cold. They wake up sluggish and seek out rocks where they can catch the sun in the early morning – this is one of the best times to look out for them. One adult stands sentry against predators and issues a low-pitched warning cry in response to a threat.

Dassies are very widely distributed, having thrived in South Africa with the elimination of predators, and can be found in suitably **rocky habitats** all over the country. They live in colonies consisting of a dominant male and eight or more related females and their offspring.

at the western table, though **climbing** up will give you a greater sense of achievement; if you're up to the challenge it's best to go on a **guided hike** (see p.142).

3

Cable car

Lower Cable Station, Tafelberg Rd • Daily (every 10–15min): Jan & Dec 8am–9pm; Feb 8am–7.30pm; March 8am–6.30pm; April 8am–5.30pm; May–Sept 8am–5pm; Oct 8am–6pm; Nov 8am–7pm • R215 return • Operations can be disrupted by bad weather or maintenance work; for information on current schedules call ☎ 021 424 8181, or check ⓦ tablemountain.net

The highly popular **cable car** offers dizzying views across Table Bay and the Atlantic. The state-of-the-art Swiss system is designed to complete a 360-degree rotation on the way, which gives passengers a full panorama. You can make a real outing of it by going up for breakfast or a sunset drink and meal at the vamped-up **eco-restaurant**; the upper station is an incomparable spot from which to watch the sun go down. Note that people start queuing in summer very early and finish late, and Sundays and public holidays tend to be very busy.

ARRIVAL AND DEPARTURE   TABLE MOUNTAIN

By car If you're driving, you'll find parking along Tafelberg Rd, but you may be in for a bit of a walk in peak season – the stretch of parked cars can extend several hundred metres.

By bus Take MyCiTi bus #106 or #107 (Waterfront to Camps Bay via Adderley St) and get off at Kloof Nek, which is at the junction on Tafelberg Rd, from where it's a steep uphill 1km walk to the Lower Cable Station – the route is well signposted. The open-topped City Sightseeing bus also serves the cableway (see p.21).

By taxi You can get to the Lower Cable Station by *rikki*, metered taxi, or in one of the minibus taxis that ply the route here from Adderley St (10–15min).

HIKING AND CLIMBING

There are half-day or full-day guided hikes which are thoroughly recommended (see p.142). The hikes are tailored to hikers' individual levels of fitness. You can also abseil (see p.139) or paraglide (see p.140) off Table Mountain, while experienced rock climbers can find enough satisfying routes to last a lifetime, on either granite or Table Mountain sandstone; the climbs are of varying degrees of difficulty, and some are thrillingly exposed (see p.140).

Climbs and walks

Table Mountain offers gorgeous hikes. There are hundreds of possible **walks and climbs** on its slopes, but unless you're going with a knowledgeable guide, it's recommended that you attempt one of the **routes** outlined below, which are the simplest. Every year the mountain strikes back, taking its toll of lives; it may look sunny and clear when you leave, but conditions at the top could be very different – strong sun and violent winds can be brutal, and mists that obscure the path can sometimes descend very quickly. Plan well and keep safe (see box, p.70), and you will be rewarded with a very worthwhile hike that offers some spectacular views.

TABLE MOUNTAIN SAFETY

- Inform someone that you're going up the mountain; tell them your route, when you're leaving and when you expect to be back.
- Don't go up alone. As well as general mountain-safety issues (particularly for the less-experienced climbers), there have also been a number of tourist muggings over the past decade.
- Leave early enough to give yourself time to complete your route during daylight.
- Don't try to descend via an unknown route. If you get lost in poor weather, seek shelter, keep warm and wait for help.
- Never make fires. No cooking is allowed, even on portable stoves – mountain fires are a serious hazard in Cape Town, especially during the dry, hot summer months.
- Never leave even the tiniest scrap of litter on the mountain.

WEAR:

- Good footwear. Walking boots or sturdy running shoes are recommended.
- A broad-rimmed hat.
- Long trousers to protect you from the sun and scratchy shrubs.

TAKE:

- A backpack.
- A water bottle; allow two litres per person.
- Enough food for the trip.
- A warm top.
- A windbreaker.
- Sunglasses.
- High-factor sunscreen.
- A map (available from Cape Union Mart at the Waterfront, or Cavendish Square Shopping Centre in Claremont).
- A mobile phone with Table Mountain Rescue number saved (☎021 948 990).

Signal Hill and Lion's Head

From the roundabout at the top of **Kloof Nek** – the saddle between Table Mountain and Lion's Head, over which Kloof Nek Road runs to reach the Atlantic seaboard – the fairly steep 3.5km Signal Hill Road runs the length of **Signal Hill** to a car park and lookout at the northern end, with good views over Table Bay, the docks and the city. A cannon was formerly used for sending signals to ships at anchor in the bay, and the **Noon Gun**, still fired precisely at noon by the South African Navy, from its slopes daily, sends a thunderous rumble through the Bo-Kaap and city centre below. Halfway along the road, you'll see a sacred Islamic *kramat* (shrine), one of several dotted around the peninsula, which are said to protect the city (see box opposite).

You can also walk up **Lion's Head**, a hike that seems to bring out half the population of Cape Town every full moon. One of the attractions of this two-kilometre ascent is that, as you spiral around the mountain, there are constantly changing views of the city and the ocean. The route starts halfway along Signal Hill Road, at the *kramat*. The climb is relatively easy and manageable for all levels, as long as you leave enough time to descend, and it takes on average an hour to an hour and a half, one-way. The hike is mostly on a track, followed by a path with minor rock scrambling and a ladder at one point, as well as chains to assist hikers up a short vertical ascent (a longer diversion bypasses the chains).

Platteklip Gorge

The first recorded ascent to the summit of Table Mountain was by the Portuguese captain Antonio de Saldanha, in 1503. He wisely chose **Platteklip Gorge**, the gap visible from the front table (the north side), which, as it turned out, is the most accessible way up. A short and easy extension will get you to Maclear's Beacon; at

1086m, it is the **highest point** on the mountain. The Platteklip route starts out at the Lower Cable Station and has the added advantage of ending at the upper station, so aren't committed to walking back down.

From the lower station, walk east along Tafelberg Road until you see a high embankment built from stone and maintained with wire netting. Just beyond and to the left of a small dam is a sign pointing to Platteklip Gorge. A steep fifteen-minute climb brings you onto the **Upper Contour Path**. About 25m east along this, take the path indicated by a sign that says "Contour Path/Platteklip Gorge". The path zigzags from here onwards and is very easy to make out. The gorge is the biggest chasm on the whole mountain. It leads directly and safely to the top, but it's a very steep, three-hour slog, even if you're reasonably fit. Once on the top, turn right and ascend the last short section onto the **front table** for a breathtaking view of the city. A sign points the way to the upper cable station – a fifteen-minute walk along a concrete path thronging with visitors.

Maclear's Beacon

Maclear's Beacon is about 35 minutes from the top of the Platteklip Gorge, on a path that leads eastward, with white squares on little yellow footsteps guiding you all the way. The path crosses the front table with Maclear's Beacon visible at all times. From the top, you'll get views of False Bay to the south and the Hottentots Holland Mountains to the east.

Skeleton Gorge

This route allows you to combine a visit to the gardens at Kirstenbosch (see p.79) with an ascent up Table Mountain via one route and a descent down another, starting and ending at the gardens' **restaurant**. This entire walk lasts four to five hours. From the restaurant, follow the **Skeleton Gorge** signs that will lead you onto the **Contour Path**. At the Contour Path, a plaque indicates that this is **Smuts' Track**, the route favoured by Jan Smuts, Boer leader, former prime minister and international statesman, known for his love of the mountains. The plaque marks the start of a broad-stepped climb up Skeleton Gorge, involving both wooden and stone steps, wooden ladders and loose boulders. Be prepared for steep forested ravines and the odd rock scramble – and under no circumstances stray off the path. It requires reasonable fitness, and can take about two hours to ascend.

The Skeleton Gorge descent can be unpleasant, especially in the wet season when it gets slippery; a recommended alternative is **Nursery Ravine**. At the top of Skeleton Gorge, walk a few metres to your right to a sign indicating **Kasteelspoort**. It's just 35 minutes from the top of Skeleton Gorge, along the Kasteelsport path, to the head of Nursery Ravine. This descent returns you to the 310m Contour Path, which leads back to Kirstenbosch.

SACRED CIRCLE

A number of Muslim holy men and princes were exiled from the East Indies by the Dutch during the late seventeenth and early eighteenth centuries and brought to the Cape, where some became revered as **auliyah**, or muslim saints. The **kramats**, of which there are nearly two dozen in the province, are the *auliyah*'s burial sites, shrines and places of pilgrimage. The Signal Hill *kramat* is a shrine to Mohamed Gasan Galbie Shah, a follower of Sheik Yusuf, a Sufi scholar, who was deported to the Cape in 1694 with a 49-strong retinue. According to tradition, Yusuf conducted Muslim prayer meetings in private homes and slave quarters. Sheik Yusuf became the founder of Islam in South Africa, and his *kramat* on the Cape Flats is said to be one of a sacred circle of six *kramats* (including one on Robben Island; see p.63) that protect Cape Town from natural disasters.

CITY BOWL SUBURBS

City Bowl

The **City Bowl** suburbs, the residential areas south of Orange Street and the Company's Gardens, gently climb the lower slopes of Table Mountain. It is not so much a district to explore, as one in which to consume, with a high number of good restaurants (see p.118), bars (see p.126) and cafés (see p.118) to service the affluent residents, tourists and people working in the city centre.

A landmark of the district, as you arrive in the city along the M3, is the **Mount Nelson Hotel** (see p.108), on the south side of Orange Street in the suburb of **Gardens**, an area that takes its name from the historic gardens on the opposite side of the road. The grand hotel harks back to the heyday of British colonialism and is announced by a gigantic, white, pedimented gateway supported on nearly two dozen Corinthian columns. Almost next door to the *Mount Nelson Hotel* is the **Labia**, an inexpensive art-house cinema that attracts movie buffs from all over the peninsula (see p.131).

Kloof Street is the throbbing artery which links central Cape Town to Kloof Nek and the cable car, and is the only exit over the Table Mountain chain to the other side – the Atlantic seaboard. As you drive over the *nek* (neck), you are greeted by astounding vistas down through stone pines to the blue ocean beyond.

The **views** from the airy Victorian villas, modern houses, apartment blocks and stylish pieds-à-terre in the City Bowl get better the higher you go. From the more elevated buildings, you can see the harbour and Table Bay clearly, but from anywhere in the City Bowl, or indeed in the city itself, you can't help but see the massive rock faces of Table Mountain.

3

CAPE SUGARBIRD, KIRSTENBOSCH GARDENS

Southern suburbs and Cape Flats

The suburbs of Woodstock and Salt River, recently gentrified but still rough around the edges, begin where the city ends. The formerly whites-only residential areas of the southern suburbs stretch out down the east side of Table Mountain almost to the False Bay coast. Greener and more forested than the drier, hotter Atlantic Coast, this side of the peninsula is home to the sublime Kirstenbosch National Botanical Gardens. Further afield, in the Constantia winelands, lie South Africa's oldest wineries, and in the same vicinity is the dappled Tokai Forest, a relaxing refuge from the midsummer sun and the howling southeaster.

East of the **M5 highway**, which skirts through the margins of the southern suburbs as far as Muizenberg, lie the **Cape Flats** – the windswept flatlands that splay out towards the airport, and which became the apartheid dumping ground for Africans and coloureds.

ARRIVAL AND DEPARTURE

SOUTHERN SUBURBS AND CAPE FLATS

By car The quickest way of reaching the southern suburbs from the city centre, Waterfront or City Bowl suburbs is the M3 highway; outside rush hour, it takes about 30min to get from the centre to Tokai, where the highway ends. During the week, traffic is appalling – avoid the M3 southbound between 3.30pm and 6pm, and use it only after 9am from the south to reach the centre.

By train The Metrorail train line from Cape Town Station to Fish Hoek and Simon's Town runs through the southern suburbs and provides a handy means of getting to most of them. However, there are no stops near enough to Rhodes Memorial, Kirstenbosch, Constantia (and its winelands) and Tokai to be practical, and in these cases you'll have to rely on your own wheels, taxis or the Sightseeing bus (see below). Metrorail trains run to the Cape Flats and the townships, but we recommend you

avoid taking public transport to these areas and only make a journey there on a guided tour (see p.26).

By minibus No MyCiTi buses serve this route; instead, use (with caution) the informal shared-minibus taxis which run from above Cape Town Station to Wynberg via Main Rd, where they pass Woodstock, Observatory and University of Cape Town. You will see a fleet of minibuses and touts bawling "Wynberg, Wynberg", to urge you southwards. Stand anywhere on Main Rd to hail a minibus back to Cape Town Station. Minibus taxis also serve the Cape Flats and African townships, and most of the train stations (especially Cape Town, Mowbray and Wynberg) have crowds of shared taxis outside waiting to rush people home from work.

By bus The hop-on, hop-off City Sightseeing bus goes to Kirstenbosch and Groot Constantia (☎ 086 173 3287, ⊛ citysightseeing.co.za).

Woodstock and Salt River

4

Windblown and gritty, **Woodstock** and **Salt River** are the oldest of Cape Town's suburbs. These predominantly working-class coloured areas are being transformed into Cape Town's premier design district. Old folk conversing on their *stoeps*, keeping an eye on children running around the crumbling streets, gives a hint of what Cape Town must have been like before the forced evictions to the Cape Flats in the Seventies and Eighties. Slowly but surely, however, the area is gentrifying. Each block on Main and Albert roads which go through both suburbs brings a new cluster of design or artisan coffee shops, art galleries or custom-made furniture. Industrial architecture is juxtaposed with minimalist-chic interiors, where soaring ceilings house artists and designers. Woodstock blends imperceptibly with Salt River, but the latter remains

THE CHANGING CLOTHES OF CHANGING TIMES

Salt River was once the centre of South Africa's prosperous **clothing industry** and the main form of employment for Cape Coloureds. Apartheid laws made it difficult for black South Africans to be employed in urban areas, but these laws did not apply to the Cape's coloured population, so in the 1960s, much of South Africa's clothing industry moved to the Cape, with its high population of coloured people. After the end of apartheid, local clothing production collapsed rapidly, unable to compete with Chinese imports. In the first eleven years between 1994 and 2003, seventy thousand jobs (mostly held by women) in the Cape clothing sector were lost, affecting three hundred and fifty thousand dependents and at least ten percent of Cape Town's total population.

In recent years, **economic prosperity** has finally started to return to Salt River as the clothing industry reinvents itself with a niche design district (see p.132) that draws on its Cape Coloured culture roots. However, while the **job opportunities** for skilled labour have increased, the old semi- and unskilled clothing workers find it almost impossible to get employment, and many live below the poverty line. The economic benefits of the clothing industry resurgence are primarily enjoyed by a small percentage of the predominately white population in the Cape. The stallholders at the Neighbourhood Market in Woodstock (see p.136), for example, are mostly white, skilled designers selling their wares.

poorer and more industrial, and it lacks the pretty old Victorian houses that new arrivals in Woodstock have snapped up and renovated.

Albert Road

A visit to these outer city fringes should take in three main hubs, all along the Woodstock section of **Albert Road**: best known is the **Old Biscuit Mill**, with its terrific Saturday-morning organic and artisanal food market (see p.136), where you can eat yourself silly, wander about craft and design shops or visit art galleries. This is also where you'll find two of the best contemporary restaurants in town – *Test Kitchen* (see p.120) and *Pot Luck Club* (see p.120).

The **Woodstock Exchange** (66 Albert Rd; Mon–Fri 8am–5pm, Sat 8am–2pm; ☏021 486 5999, ⓦwoodstockexchange.co.za) with its creative collectives, beautiful leather workshops and work-friendly cafés for Capetonian freelancers is the next focus. **The Woodstock Foundry** (ⓦfacebook.com/WoodstockFoundry), in a renovated heritage building home to a mixture of shops and creative studio spaces, is the third stop-off.

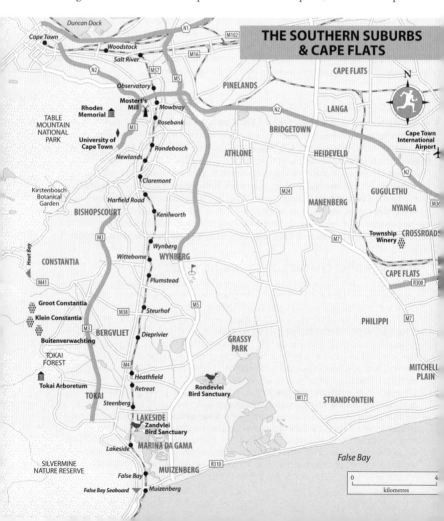

THE SOUTHERN SUBURBS & CAPE FLATS

For a further selection of the most interesting names in the area, see ⓦmondaydesign .co.za/Woodstock-design-district.

Observatory

Abutting the southern end of Woodstock, **Observatory** is generally regarded as Cape Town's bohemian hub, a reputation fuelled by its proximity to the University of Cape Town in Rondebosch and its large student population. Many of the houses here are student digs, but the narrow Victorian streets are also home to young professionals, hippies and arty types. The refreshingly dilapidated and peeling arcades on Observatory's Lower Main Road, and the streets off it, have some nice cafés and lively bars, as well as a wholefood shop, organic café, African fabrics shop and a couple of antiques emporiums.

Mowbray and Rosebank

South of Observatory is **Mowbray**, originally called Drie Koppen (Three Heads) after the heads of three murderers were impaled here in 1724, but its name was changed in the 1840s. In the nineteenth century, this was the home of philologist **Willem Bleek**, who lived with a group of San convicts given up by the colonial authorities so that he could study their languages and attitudes. Bleek's pioneering work still forms the basis of much of what we know about traditional Khoisan life. There isn't much to see here; there's just a small row of shops and some attractive Victorian buildings. **Rosebank**, to Mowbray's south, has a substantial student community, and university residences, blocks of flats and sports fields dominate the area. The only reason to visit is to take in the Irma Stern Museum.

Irma Stern Museum

Cecil Rd, Rosebank · Tues–Fri 10am–5pm, Sat 10am–2pm · R10 · ⓦ irmastern.co.za

Irma Stern is acknowledged as one of South Africa's pioneering artists, more for the fact that she brought modern European ideas to the colonies in the twentieth century than for any huge contribution she made to world art. The **Irma Stern Museum** was the artist's home for 38 years, until her death in 1966, and is definitely worth visiting for a look at Stern's collection of Iberian, African, oriental and ancient artefacts. The whole house, in fact, reflects the artist's fascination with exoticism, starting with her own Gauguinesque paintings of stereotyped African figures as well as the fantastic carved doors she brought back from Zanzibar, and the very untypical garden that brings a touch of the tropics to Cape Town, with its exuberant bamboo thickets and palm trees.

THE LIFE AND WORKS OF IRMA STERN

Born in a backwater town in South Africa in 1894 to German-Jewish parents, **Irma Stern** studied at Germany's Weimar Academy. In reaction to the academy's conservatism, she adopted **expressionist distortion** in her paintings, some of which were included in the 1918 Neue Sezession Exhibition in Berlin. Stern went on several expeditions into Zanzibar and the Congo in the 1940s and 1950s, where she found the source for her intensely sensuous paintings, which shocked South Africa at the time.

Although Stern's work was appreciated in Europe, when she returned to South Africa after World War II, critics claimed that her style was simply a cover for technical incompetence. South African art historians now regard her as the towering figure of her generation. One of her most famous works is the much reproduced *The Eternal Child* (1916), a simple but vibrant portrait of a young girl, while *The Wood Carriers* (1951) uses raw ochres, browns and oranges to create an exoticized portrayal of a pair of African women.

Rondebosch

South of Rosebank, neighbouring **Rondebosch** is home to the **University of Cape Town** (UCT), whose nineteenth-century buildings sit grandly on the mountainside, each handsomely festooned with creepers, overlooking the M3 highway. The city's best schools are here, as is one of Cape Town's premier arts complexes, the **Baxter Theatre** (see p.129). This is the heartland of liberal, educated, English-speaking Cape Town.

Groote Schuur

Rhodes Drive · Not open to the public

Cecil John Rhodes, prime minister of the Cape from 1890–1897, features big in this neck of the woods: if you head south from the Woolsack (see below) down the M3 (here known as Rhodes Drive), you'll pass **Groote Schuur**, another house built for him. Bordering on Main Road, Groote Schuur is one of Herbert Baker's most celebrated South African buildings, exemplifying the Cape Dutch Revival style. Rhodes' large estate here became the official prime-ministerial residence of the Cape, then of South Africa, and when the country switched to a presidential system it became the home of the president – though Nelson Mandela preferred to use a nearby residence named Genadendal.

The Woolsack

Woolsack Drive, UCT campus · Not open to the public

Of passing interest on the UCT campus is the **Woolsack**. This "cottage in the woods for poets and artists", just off Woolsack Road, was designed in 1900 by Sir Herbert Baker for Rhodes. Rhodes invited **Rudyard Kipling** to "hang up his hat there" whenever he visited the Cape. Taking his friend at his word, Kipling fled the English winter every year from 1900 to 1907, bringing his family to Cape Town and spending five to six months at the Woolsack, where he is said to have written his famous poem *If*. The house is now occupied by the university's architecture faculty.

Rhodes Memorial

Rhodes Ave · Restaurant and tea garden daily 9am–5pm · ⓦ rhodesmemorial.co.za · Reached via a signposted road that spurs northwest off the M3, just as Rhodes Drive becomes the Princess Anne Interchange

Just to the north of the UCT campus is the **Rhodes Memorial**. On a site chosen by Herbert Baker and Rudyard Kipling, the monument sits grandiosely conspicuous against the slopes of Devil's Peak as herds of wildebeest and zebra nonchalantly graze nearby.

Built in 1912 to resemble a Greek temple, the memorial celebrates Rhodes' energy with a sculpture of a wildly rearing horse. Carved in stone beneath the empire-builder's bust is a ponderous inscription by Kipling: "The immense and brooding spirit still shall order and control." Also on site is a relaxing **restaurant and tea garden** with terrific views of Cape Town.

Newlands and Claremont

If you continue south from Rondebosch along either the M3 or the more congested Main Road, you'll pass some of Cape Town's most prestigious suburbs. **Newlands**, almost merging with Claremont, is home to the city's famous rugby and cricket stadiums. Worth a stop here is the **Montebello Craft and Design Centre** (see p.133).

The well-heeled suburb of **Claremont**, south of Newlands, is an alternative focus to the city centre for shopping at **Cavendish Square Mall** (see p.137). Alongside the high-quality shops, hawkers sell clothes, vegetables and herbs; closer to Claremont station, you can buy tasty *boerewors* (spicy sausage) from women cooking them outdoors.

Bishopscourt

Southwest of Claremont, beyond the signpost to Kirstenbosch Garden, is **Bishopscourt**. As the name suggests, it's home to the Anglican bishop of Cape Town, and it was in a mansion here that Archbishop Desmond Tutu lived even in the years when blacks weren't supposed to live in whites-only suburbs. Partly because of its prime siting – some plots have views of both Newlands Forest and the sea – this is one of the poshest areas in Cape Town; a number of consuls live here in huge properties behind high walls, which are about all you see as you pass through the area.

Wynberg

Further down the train line from Claremont is **Wynberg**, known for its Maynardville Shakespearean **open-air theatre** (see p.129) and its quaint row of shops and restaurants in Wolfe Street. By contrast, Wynberg's Main Road offers a distinctly less genteel shopping experience: street vendors and fabric shops are intermingled with outlets catering to the large number of workers travelling between Wynberg and Khayelitsha in the Cape Flats.

Kirstenbosch National Botanical Garden

Rhodes Drive • Gardens daily 8am–6pm, Sept–March till 7pm; open-air concerts Sun evenings, late Nov to early April; coffee shop daily 7am–7pm; tea room daily 8.30am–5pm; restaurant Mon–Thurs & Sun 9am–6pm, Fri & Sat 9am–9pm • R47; concert prices vary • ☎ 021 799 8783, ⓦ sanbi.org/gardens/kirstenbosch • The City Sightseeing Bus stops at the garden several times a day; Golden Arrow buses run 6 buses a day from Mowbray to the garden (7am–4.30pm)

Thirteen kilometres from the city centre, and absolutely unmissable, is the **Kirstenbosch National Botanical Garden**. Established in 1913, this is one of the planet's great natural treasure houses, a status acknowledged in 2004 when it became part of South Africa's sixth UNESCO World Heritage Site – the first botanical garden in the world to achieve this. The listing recognizes the international significance of the *fynbos* (see box, p.104) vegetation and the Cape plant kingdom that predominates here, attracting botanists from all over the world. Little signboards and paved paths guide you through the highlights of the garden, with trees and plants identified to enhance the rambling. Allow a couple of hours to visit Kirstenbosch, in the shelter from the battering summer Cape Town winds.

An exciting feature of the garden is the **Tree Canopy Walkway**, a raised steel-and-timber path that snakes its way up and through the trees of the **Arboretum**, with panoramic views of the garden and surrounding mountains. Another interesting route is via the **Fragrance Garden** and adjacent **Braille Trail** created for blind visitors, with information signs in Braille and an abundance of aromatic and textured plants.

Walks

The garden trails off into **wild vegetation** which covers a huge expanse of the rugged eastern slopes and wooded ravines of Table Mountain – the setting is quite breathtaking. Two popular paths, starting from the **Contour Path** above Kirstenbosch, are Nursery Ravine and Skeleton Gorge (see p.71). While the garden is safe from crime, if you are hiking up the slopes, or onward to Constantia Neck or Newlands Forest and Rhodes Memorial, along the Contour Path, the usual safely precautions should be followed (see p.70).

Concerts

If you're visiting Kirstenbosch National Botanical Garden in **summer**, one of the undoubted delights is to bring a picnic for a Sunday evening **open-air concert**, where you can lie back on the lawn, sip Cape wine and savour the mountain air and sunsets. Otherwise, there's an outdoor **coffee shop**, open daily for breakfast, lunch and teas, a **tea room** and a **restaurant** with a fire going on winter days.

4

CAPE DUTCH ARCHITECTURE

Cape Dutch style, which developed in the Western Cape countryside from the seventeenth to the early nineteenth century, is so distinctively rooted in the Winelands that it has become an integral element of the landscape. The dazzling limewashed walls glisten in the midst of glowing green vineyards, while the thatched roofs and elaborate curvilinear gables mirror the undulations of the surrounding mountains. Although there were important developments in the internal organization of Cape houses during this period, their most obvious element is the **gable**. Central gables set into the long side of roofs were unusual in Europe, but became the quintessential feature of the Cape Dutch style.

In central Cape Town, the gable only survived until the 1830s, to be replaced by buildings with flush facades and flat roofs. **Arson** appears to be a major reason for this – fires, purportedly started by slaves, including one that razed Stellenbosch in 1710, and Cape Town's **great fires** of 1736 and 1798 led officials to ban thatched roofs and any protrusions on building exteriors. With the disappearance of pitched roofs, the urban gable withered away, surviving symbolically in some instances as minimal roof decoration; an example of this is the wavy parapet on the **Bo-Kaap Museum** in Wale Street (see p.47).

The threat of fire spreading from one building to another was a less serious consideration in the countryside. Consequently, VOC building regulations carried little weight and the pitched roof survived, as did gables, becoming the hallmark of country manors. From functional origins, gables evolved into **symbols of wealth**, with landowners vying to erect the biggest, most elaborate and most fashionable examples. Some fine ones can be found on the historic estates of the Winelands, as well as at Tokai Manor (see p.82), Groot Constantia (see opposite), Klein Constantia (see opposite) and Buitenverwachting (see p.82).

Constantia and its winelands

There is no public transport to this area, although several tours run from central Cape Town daily, and the City Sightseeing Bus stops at Groot Constantia; all estates listed here are clearly marked off the M3

South of Kirstenbosch lie the elegant suburbs of **Constantia** and the Cape's oldest **winelands**. Luxuriating on the lower slopes of Table Mountain and the Constantiaberg, with tantalizing views of False Bay, the winelands are an easy drive from town, not more than ten minutes off the M3 which runs between the centre and Muizenberg.

The winelands began cultivated life in 1685 as the farm of **Simon van der Stel**, the governor charged with opening up the fledgling Dutch colony to the interior. This area is now Cape Town's oldest and most prestigious residential area. Exuding the easy ambience of landed wealth, Constantia is a green and pleasant shaded valley, where the upper slopes are covered by vineyards.

Constantia grapes have been making wine since Van der Stel's first output in 1705. After his death in 1712, the estate was divided up and sold off as the modern **Groot Constantia**, **Klein Constantia** and **Buitenverwachting**. The wine estates are open to the public and offer tastings; they're definitely worth visiting if you aren't heading further afield to the winelands proper (see p.149).

Groot Constantia

Groot Constantia Rd • **Grounds** Daily 9am–6pm • Free • **Cellar tours** Daily on the hour 10am–4pm • R40 including five wines to taste and a souvenir glass; booking essential • **Wine tasting** Daily 9am–5.30pm • R30 • ☏ 021 794 5128, ⓦ grootconstantia.co.za

The largest Constantia estate and the one most geared to tourists is **Groot Constantia**, a terrific example of Cape Dutch grandeur reached along an oak-lined axis that passes through vineyards with the hazy blue Constantiaberg as its backdrop. It is restful and serene, and if you don't want to taste wines, or if you reach it after hours, you can simply walk around the vineyards and enjoy the architecture. Its big pull is that it retains the rump of Van der Stel's original estate, as well as the original buildings, though its portrayal of life in a seventeenth-century colonial chateau makes scant reference to the slave labour that underpinned its operations.

The interior of the **manor house**, a quintessential Cape Dutch building and Van der Stel's original home, forms part of the **museum** and is decorated in a style typical of eighteenth- and nineteenth-century Cape landowners, containing interesting Neoclassical as well as Louis XV and XVI furniture and Delft and Chinese ceramics.

If you walk straight through the house and down the ceremonial axis, you'll come to the so-called **cellar** (actually a two-storey building above ground), fronted by a brilliant relief pediment. Attributed to the sculptor Anton Anreith, it depicts a riotous bacchanalia, featuring Ganymede, a young man so handsome that Zeus, in the form of an eagle, carried him off to be the cup-bearer of the gods.

Klein Constantia

Klein Constantia Rd • Summer wine tasting Mon–Sat 10am–5pm, Sun 10am–4pm; for winter hours call or check website • R30 • ☏ 021 794 5188, ⓦ kleinconstantia.com

Smaller in scale than Groot Constantia, **Klein Constantia** offers wine tasting in less regimented conditions than at the bigger estate, and although the buildings are far humbler, the settings are equally beautiful. Klein Constantia has a friendly atmosphere and produces some fine wines, such as its Cabernet Sauvignon Reserve and a number of excellent whites, among which its Semillon really stands out. Something of a curiosity is its **Vin de Constance**, the re-creation of an eighteenth-century Constantia wine that was a favourite of Napoleon, Frederick the Great and Bismarck. It's a delicious dessert wine, packaged in a replica of the original bottle, and makes an original souvenir.

Look out for the **wildlife** here, notably the guinea fowls that roam the estate munching on beetles that attack young vine leaves; in summer, migrant steppe buzzards prey on unsuspecting starlings, which eat the grapes.

Buitenverwachting

Klein Constantia Rd · **Buildings** Mon–Fri 9am–5pm, Sat 10am–3pm · Free · **Picnic lunches** Late Nov to end March noon–4pm · R135 per head, booking essential · ☎ 021 794 5190, ⓦ buitenverwachting.co.za

Buitenverwachting (roughly pronounced "bay-tin-fur-vuch-ting", with the "ch" as in the Scottish rendition of loch) is a bucolic place in the middle of the suburbs, where sheep and cattle graze in the fields as you approach the main buildings. Despite deep historic roots, the estate now treats its employees much better than most.

The architecture and setting at the foot of the Constantiaberg are good reasons to come here, as are the top-ranking wines. Overlooking the vineyards and backing onto the garden, the **homestead** was built in 1794 (the 1769 on the gable appears to be wrong) by Arend Brink, and features an unusual gabled pediment broken with an urn motif. There is a fantastic **restaurant** here and, for a day out on the farm (they have cattle and horses, too), they also do luxury **picnic lunches**, which you can enjoy under the oaks.

Tokai

To drive to Tokai from the centre of Cape Town, head south along the M3 and exit north onto Ladies Mile Road; continue for 100m before turning south into Spaanschemat River Road (M42), signposted Tokai, which runs through the suburb

Effectively the southern extension of Constantia, forested **Tokai** is an excellent area for leafy recreation away from the city centre. It offers relaxed and child-friendly places for eating and drinking, and shelter from the strong southeastern wind. You can easily combine Tokai with a trip to the seaside, as the suburb is fifteen minutes' drive from the False Bay seaboard.

Tokai Forest

Most people come out to Tokai for the well-marked hiking paths and mountain-biking trails in the pine plantations of the **Tokai Forest**. You can get here from Spaanschemat River Road, turning west into Tokai Road, which heads straight to the forest. About 500m from Spaanschemat River Road, you'll pass through pine forests equipped with picnic tables, though you'd do well to carry on to the arboretum for the best eating spots. A little further along the road from the picnic sites, you can't fail to see the imposing **Tokai Manor House** (not open to the public). Designed by Louis Michel Thibault and built around 1795, this National Monument is an elegant gem of Cape Dutch architecture combined with the understated elegance of French Neoclassicism.

Tokai Arboretum

Tokai Rd · Daily dawn to dusk; café closed Mon · R10 donation · ☎ 021 712 7471

The historic tree plantation that constitutes the **Tokai Arboretum** is a National Monument. It's the work of Joseph Storr Lister, who was a nineteenth-century Conservator of Forests for the Cape Colony. In 1885, he experimented with planting 150 species of tree from temperate countries, including a large number of oak and eucalyptus, as well as some beautiful California redwoods. Storr discovered that conifers were best suited to the Cape, hence the plantation to the west of the arboretum, owned by the Safcol timber company, consists mainly of pines. The arboretum is the best place to begin rambling and an ideal place to bring **children**, with outdoor seating, plenty of shade and logs to jump on and over. There's also a car park and a thatched **café** close to the entrance gate.

The Cape Flats and the townships

East of the northern and southern suburbs, among the industrial smokestacks and the windswept **Cape Flats**, reaching well beyond the airport, is Cape Town's largest residential quarter, taking in the **coloured districts**, **African townships** and

THE HISTORY OF THE TOWNSHIPS

The African townships were historically set up as dormitories to provide labour for white Cape Town, not as places to build a life, which is why they had no facilities and no real hub. The **men-only hostels**, another apartheid relic, are at the root of many of the area's social problems. During the 1950s, the government set out a blueprint to turn the tide of Africans flooding into Cape Town. No African was permitted to settle permanently in the Cape west of a line near the Fish River, the old frontier over 1000km from Cape Town; women were entirely banned from seeking work in Cape Town and men prohibited from bringing their wives to join them. By 1970, there were ten men for every woman in Langa (see below).

In the end, apartheid failed to prevent the influx of work-seekers desperate to come to Cape Town. Where people couldn't find legal accommodation, they set up **squatter camps** of makeshift iron, cardboard and plastic sheeting. During the 1970s and 1980s, the government attempted to demolish these and destroy anything left inside – but no sooner had the police left than the camps reappeared, and they are now a permanent feature of the Cape Flats. One of the best known of all South Africa's squatter camps is **Crossroads**, whose inhabitants suffered campaigns of harassment that included killings by apartheid collaborators and police and continuous attempts to bulldoze it out of existence. Through sheer determination and desperation its residents hung on, eventually winning the right to stay, and now it is covered by tiny brick houses, with electricity supplies and running water, which improve quality of life.

shantytown **squatter camps**. The Cape Flats are exactly that: flat, barren and populous, exclusively inhabited by Africans and coloureds in separate areas, with the M5 acting as a dividing line between it and the largely white southern suburbs. This is still a divided city.

Several projects are under way to encourage tourists into the townships which highlight social and economic development initiatives (see p.84). The best way to visit these projects is on a **tour**; Coffeebeans Routes (☎021 424 3572, ⓦcoffeebeansroutes.com; see p.26), which safely navigates visitors through the sprawling and disorientating townships, is recommended. Visiting the townships under your own steam is unadvisable – besides the threat of possible opportunistic crime, road signage is very poor and opening and closing times erratic, so it's hard to find your own way around to the places listed. It's possible, too, to gain a deeper understanding of the daily lives of the majority of South Africans by **staying overnight** in a B&B at one of the townships (see box, p.109).

Besides the privately funded social and economic development projects, there are two memorials to visit in Gugulethu (Gugs) and a small museum in Langa.

Langa

Langa is the oldest and most central township; it lies east of the white suburb of Pinelands and north of the N2. In this relentlessly grey and littered place without the tiniest patch of green relief, you'll find a vibrant street life, with hairdressers galore and people selling sheep's and goats' heads. Several families live in smart suburban houses within Langa (some Africans who can afford to move out say they find the white suburbs sterile and unfriendly) while, not far away, there are former men-only hostels where as many as three families share one room.

Langa Heritage Museum

Washington St • Mon–Sat 9am–4pm • Free • ☎021 694 8320

The **Langa Heritage Museum** is the only museum in Cape Town's townships. It is dedicated to the "*dompas*" or pass system which, during apartheid years, required black citizens to carry a pass to enter "white-only" areas for work. The modest and rather austere museum is located in the Old Pass Court where people were tried for transgressing the pass laws.

TOWNSHIP HIGHLIGHTS

MEMORIALS

Gugulethu Seven Memorial and Amy Bielh Memorial, Gugulethu The Gugulethu Seven Memorial, which consists of seven solid and powerful granite statue-like constructions, is dedicated to the struggle and death of an anti-apartheid group who were shot and killed by members of the South African police force in 1986. The Amy Biehl Memorial, the site where Amy, a white American anti-apartheid activist was murdered by local residents in 1993, is a moving tribute to her courageous, all-too-short life (Ⓦ amybiehl.co.za).

WINERY

The Township Winery, Philippi This is Cape Town's first township- and black-owned winery, situated in an area where patches of farmland exist amid mass housing. The winery aims to increase community ownership by giving hundreds of individual homesteads Sauvignon Blanc vines to grow at their homes. Once harvested, they will go towards production of a wine called "Township Winery" (Ⓦ townshipwinery.com).

EATING AND DRINKING

Department of Coffee Next to Khayelitsha Station, Khayelitsha; ☎ 073 300 9519, Ⓦ twitter .com/Dpmofcoffee. Here, at the first artisan coffee house in a township, you can get real coffee, hot chocolate, orange juice or muffins for under R10, and sit at the outdoor seating under orange umbrellas. For the more intrepid traveller, this can be visited independently. Mon–Fri 6am–6pm, Sat 8am–3pm.

Mitchell's Plain

South of the African ghettoes is **Mitchell's Plain**. Populated by Cape Coloureds, the area stretches down to the False Bay coast (you'll skirt Mitchell's Plain if you take the M5 to Muizenberg). More salubrious than any of the African townships, Mitchell's Plain reflects how, under apartheid, lighter skins meant better conditions, even if you weren't quite white. But for coloureds, the forced removals were no less tragic, many being summarily forced to vacate family homes because their suburb had been declared a White Group Area. Many families were relocated here when District Six was razed (see p.56), and their communities never fully recovered – one of the symptoms of dislocation and poverty is the violent gangs that have become an everyday part of Mitchell's Plain youth culture.

NOORDHOEK BEACH

Atlantic Seaboard

The suburbs along the Atlantic Seaboard cling in a dramatic ribbon to the slopes of Table Mountain. Although the waters on this western flank can be very chilly, the Atlantic Seaboard offers mind-blowing views from some of the most incredible coastal roads in the world, particularly beyond Sea Point. The coast itself consists of a series of bays and white-sand beaches edged with smoothly sculpted, bleached rocks; inland, the Twelve Apostles, a series of rocky buttresses, gaze down onto the surf. The beaches are ideal for sunbathing, and it's from this side of the peninsula that you can watch the sun create fiery reflections on the sea and mountains behind as it sinks into the ocean. You'll find some of the city's trendiest outdoor cafés and bars here, where you can beautiful-people watch and make the most of the views.

5

BY BUS

MyCiTi ☎ 0800 65 64 63, ⊚ myciti.org.za. There is a good network of MyCiTi buses that serve the Atlantic Seaboard (as far south as Hout Bay). See individual accounts for details.

City Sightseeing ☎ 086 173 3287, ⊚ citysightseeing .co.za. A service runs from the Clock Tower at the Waterfront via Kirstenbosch and Constantia Nek to: World of Birds (1hr 15min), ImiZamo Yethu (1hr 20min), Hout Bay Harbour (1hr 30min) and Camps Bay (1hr 50min) returning

via Sea Point (mid-Sept to April every 35min, May to mid-Sept every 45min).

BY MINIBUS TAXI

Noordhoek, Kommetjie and Scarborough are not served by organized public transport; however, there are minibus taxis from Fishhoek Train Station to Noordhoek and Kommetjie, at various times during the day, but most frequently during the morning and evening rush hours.

Green Point and Mouille Point

Green Point's proximity to the Waterfront – from which it's an easy ten-minute amble – and to the coast, as well as to the centre of Cape Town, has turned this once-sleazy district into a desirable location with good accommodation (see p.112) and cafés (see p.120). The **Green Point Stadium and Park** (daily 7am–7pm; free; ☎ 021 417 0111) is the obvious focal point. Adjoining Green Point is **Mouille** ("moo-lee") **Point**, known for its squat, rectangular, red-and-white-striped Victorian lighthouse. From here, you can walk or jog a few kilometres south along the safe and much-used coastal promenade to Sea Point and Bantry Bay.

Sea Point

MyCiTi bus #104 (Sea Point to the Civic Centre via the Waterfront and Beach Rd); the City Sightseeing Bus also stops here

Nudging up to the western edge of Green Point, **Sea Point** is a cosmopolitan area crammed with apartment blocks, tourist accommodation (see p.112) and restaurants (see p.121). The Sea Point promenade is the best way to appreciate the rocky coastline and salty air, along with pram-pushing mothers, old ladies, power walkers and joggers. People picnic and play ball games on the grassy parkland beside the coastal walkway, while busy Main Road, a block nearer Lion's Head, is frequented by drunks, hookers and middle-class shoppers, creating an edgy mix of sleaze and respectability.

Sea Point Pavilion Swimming Pool

Lower Beach Rd • Daily: May–Nov 9am–5pm; Dec–April 7am–7pm • R20 • ☎ 021 434 3341

At the westernmost end of the Sea Point promenade is the **Sea Point Pavilion Swimming Pool**, a set of four unheated filtered saltwater pools, situated alongside the crashing surf, and which its fans breathlessly claim is the most beautifully located pool in the world. The largest of the four is Olympic-sized, making it a popular training tank for many of Cape Town's long-distance swimmers. There are also two children's splash pools and a fully equipped diving pool for the brave.

THE CAPE TOWN WORLD CUP STADIUM

Described by British architecture critic Jonathan Glancey as "a stunning white apparition … in a sublime setting", **Cape Town Stadium** was arguably the jewel in South Africa's 2010 World Cup crown. The towering, 68,000-seater stadium relies on natural light, and at night the open-meshed roof can blaze up to resemble an ethereal UFO. Controversy surrounded the high building costs, which were funded by taxpayers, and it was revealed that there had been **corruption** among the bidding construction companies in the tender process for the project.

While you may catch a **football match** in the stadium, it is seriously underutilized, and more often than not, the only way to fill the seats is with a **concert** given by a British or American rock or pop star, as if to make up for the many years when South Africa was a pariah and no international stars were ever seen.

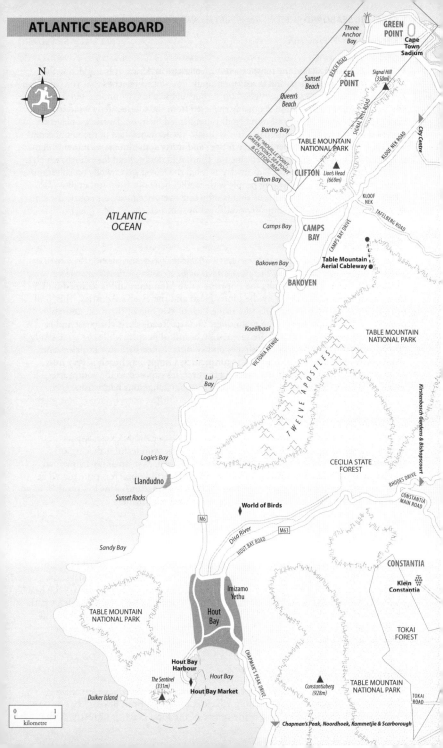

5

Clifton

MyCiTi bus #104 (Sea Point to the Civic Centre via the Waterfront and Beach Rd)

Fashionable **Clifton** sits on the most expensive real estate in Africa. It is studded with fabulous seaside apartments and boasts four sandy, interlinked **beaches** that you can reach via steep stairways. The sea here is good for surfing and safe for swimming, but bone-chillingly cold, though Clifton is notably sheltered from the southeasterly wind in summer. First Beach (they're all numbered) is frequented by muscular frisbee-players, surfers and their female counterparts, but is usually the least crowded of the four. Second and Third beaches are split between the teenies and thirty-somethings, with beautiful men sun-worshipping and sometimes cruising on Third; if in doubt, head for Fourth, which is favoured by families with small kids by day as it has the fewest steps, while on still summer evenings, mellow groups of young people with candles hang out from sunset onwards.

Bring your own **refreshments**, as there's only one overpriced café on Fourth Beach, and parking can be tricky along Victoria Road in summer.

Camps Bay

Several buses serve Camps Bay in all directions; for the most direct from the Waterfront or city centre, take MyCiTi #106 or #107 (Camps Bay to the Waterfront via Civic Centre, Adderley St, Long St, Kloof St and Kloof Nek Rd); the City Sightseeing Bus also stops here

The suburb of **Camps Bay** climbs the slopes of Table Mountain and is scooped into a small amphitheatre, bounded by the Lion's Head and the Twelve Apostles. This, and the airborne views across the Atlantic, make Camps Bay one of the most desirable places to live in Cape Town. The main drag, Victoria Road, skirts the coast and is packed with trendy restaurants, frequented by beautiful people, while the wide sandy beach is enjoyed by families of all shapes and colours. Lined by a row of palms and some grassy verges with welcome shade for picnics, Camps Bay beach is very busy around the Christmas and Easter breaks. However, it's exposed to the southeaster, and there's the usual Atlantic chill and the occasional dangerous backwash.

Llandudno

The Hout Bay buses #108 and #109 pass the entrance to Llandudno, from where it's a steep 20min walk down to the beach

There's little development between Camps Bay and the wonderful little cove of **Llandudno**, 20km from Cape Town along Victoria Road. A steep and narrow road winds down past smart homes to the shore, where the sandy beach is punctuated at either end by magnificent granite boulders and rock formations. This is a good sunbathing spot and a choice one for bring-your-own sundowners.

Sandy Bay

A 20min walk from Llandudno

Isolated **Sandy Bay**, Cape Town's main nudist beach and a popular gay and lesbian hangout, can only be reached on foot from Llandudno. In the apartheid days, the South African police went to ingenious lengths to trap nudists, but nowadays the beach is relaxed, so feel free to come as undressed – or dressed – as feels comfortable. A path leads from the south end of the Llandudno car park, through *fynbos* vegetation and across some rocks, to the beach. There are no facilities whatsoever here, so come prepared with supplies.

Hout Bay

MyCiTi bus #108 or #109 (Hout Bay to Civic Centre via Camps Bay and the Waterfront); the City Sightseeing Bus also stops here

Although no longer the quaint fishing village it once was, **Hout Bay** still has a functioning fishing harbour and is the centre of the local crayfish industry. Some

5

DUIKER ISLAND CRUISES

The best way to take in the Atlantic Seaboard landscape is on one of the short cruises just out of Hout Bay, from the harbour to **Duiker Island**, sometimes called "seal island" because it's home to a massive **seal colony**. It makes for a great trip, and the seals are delightful clowns, even if their fishy smell will make you wish you'd packed your nose plugs.

South African, or Cape, fur seals are the largest of the fur seals, which accounts for their popularity among hunters, who began harvesting them in the seventeenth century. By 1893, when restrictions were introduced, the seal population was severely depleted. Controlled **hunting** in South Africa continued till 1990 when it was finally suspended, with the exception of two culls on Malgas Island in 1999 and 2000 to protect gannet populations.

Of the operators that run 45-minute tours to seal island, **Nauticat** (8.45am, 9.45am, 11am, 12.45pm, 2.45pm & 3.45pm; R70; ☎ 021 790 7278, ⓦ nauticatcharters.co.za) and **Circe Launches** (8.45am, 9.30am, 10.15am & 11.10am; R55; ☎ 021 790 1040, ⓦ circelaunches.co.za) have glass-bottomed boats which allow you to see action under water, as well as kelp forests when conditions are clear. Apart from the seals, the outings also provide fabulous views from the water of the Sentinel, the distinctive formation on the promontory that guards one side of the bay.

20km from the centre, it's a favourite **day-trip**, and despite ugly modern developments and a growing shantytown, the natural setting is quite awesome, with the Sentinel and Chapman's Peak defining the entry to the bay. Here poor black areas nose right up to wealthy white ones – something very rarely seen in Cape Town, with its legacy of apartheid town planning. Away from the harbour, the village is just managing to hang onto a shred of its historic ambience; worth investigating is the lively **Hout Bay Market** (see p.136).

ImiZamo Yethu

Tours daily 10.30am, 1pm & 4pm • R75 • ☎ 083 719 4870, ⓦ suedafrika.net/imizamoyethu • Tours start and end from the police station at the entrance to the township, where there are reserved parking places for visitors driving there; the City Sightseeing Bus also stops here

As you approach Hout Bay from Constantia Nek, you come to the township of **ImiZamo Yethu**, a tightly packed shackland settlement crawling up the hillside, more or less in the middle of Hout Bay. The township was first settled during the late 1980s, in the dying days of apartheid, by Xhosa job-seekers from Willowvale in the rural Eastern Cape. Its population is now estimated at between twelve and thirty thousand. Although conditions are pretty dire (the highest levels of E. coli ever recorded in South Africa were found in the Disa River which flows through the settlement), there's a surprising amount of optimism here. One of the most positive recent developments has been the building of 450 brick houses with the help of Irish millionaire Niall Mellon, who was so appalled by the conditions he saw in ImiZamo Yethu during a visit in 2002, that he set up the Niall Mellon Township Trust (ⓦ nmtownshiptrust.com) dedicated to providing subsidized housing in townships across South Africa and which has now become the biggest housing charity in the country.

Although ImiZamo Yethu is unsafe to wander in by yourself, you can take a fun, two-hour **walking tour** with enthusiastic and accomplished guide **Afrika Moni**, who knows the place and its history inside out. He walks you through his home township, stopping to chat to proprietors of informal "spaza" shops, sipping traditional beer at a *shebeen*, as well as popping into shacks and brick houses.

World of Birds

Valley Rd • Daily 9am–5pm; monkey jungle daily 11.30am–1pm & 2–3.30pm; feeding times: penguins 11.30am & 3.30pm, pelicans 12.30pm, birds of prey 4.15pm • R85 • ⓦ worldofbirds.org.za • The City Sightseeing Bus stops here

If you like birds, you'll love **World of Birds**, Hout Bay's biggest institutional attraction, which accommodates more than three thousand birds, in surprisingly pleasant and peaceful walk-through aviaries, and four hundred small mammals. The setting, in lush

5

gardens with a mountainous backdrop, makes for a very tranquil outing; you'll need about two hours to get the most out of your visit.

The birds include **indigenous species** such as cranes, vultures, ostriches and pelicans, as well as a number of feathered **exotics**. A large walk-in **monkey jungle** counts cute squirrel monkeys among its inhabitants, which visitors are allowed to pet.

Chapman's Peak Drive

Toll charge R36 · ☎ 021 791 8222, Ⓦ chapmanspeakdrive.co.za

The thrilling **Chapman's Peak Drive**, which winds along a cliff-edge east of Hout Bay to Noordhoek, is one of the world's great ocean drives. There are a number of safe viewpoints along the route, some of which have picnic sites, so bring snacks and refreshments, and stop to enjoy the spectacular view. The road is occasionally closed due to rockfalls, so it's advisable to phone or visit their website to check out the current situation before setting off.

Noordhoek

Noordhoek, a desirable settlement at the southern end of the descent from Chapman's Peak Drive, 25km from the city centre, consists of smallholdings and riding stables in a gentle valley planted with oaks, the centre of which is the Farm Village. When Chapman's Peak is closed, Noordhoek is accessible via the M3 south over Ou Kaapse Weg.

Noordhoek Beach

On the left, if you're heading towards Chapman's Peak from the Noordhoek Farm Village (see opposite), is the unobtrusive sign for **Noordhoek Beach** – wind through a residential area until you reach a parking area from which you can walk 6km across the white, kelp-strewn sands towards Kommetjie. Each morning at 7.15am,

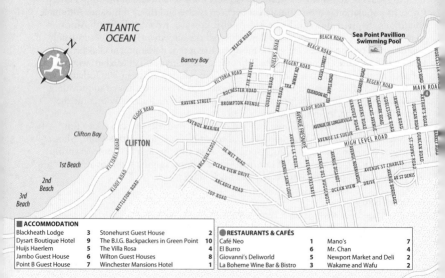

MOUILLE POINT, GREEN POINT, SEA POINT & CLIFTON

■ ACCOMMODATION			
Blackheath Lodge	3	Stonehurst Guest House	2
Dysart Boutique Hotel	9	The B.I.G. Backpackers in Green Point	10
Huijs Haerlem	5	The Villa Rosa	4
Jambo Guest House	6	Wilton Guest Houses	8
Point B Guest House	7	Winchester Mansions Hotel	1

● RESTAURANTS & CAFÉS			
Café Neo	1	Mano's	7
El Burro	6	Mr. Chan	4
Giovanni's Deliworld	5	Newport Market and Deli	2
La Boheme Wine Bar & Bistro	3	Wakame and Wafu	2

racehorses are galloped along the sand, and you will invariably see riders (see p.139) sharing the wide beach with local dog-walkers. The sea is cold, wild and spectacular to look at, framed by Chapman's Peak. Experienced **surfers** relish the area close to the rocks at the base of the peak.

Note that strong winds can sometimes turn the beach into a sandblaster. Signposted close by is the entrance to *Monkey Valley Resort* (see p.113), which welcomes non-guests for reasonably priced meals with great views, and its groves of milkwood trees offer shelter from the wind.

Noordhoek Farm Village

Daily 9am–5pm • Free • ☎ 021 789 2812, ⓦ noordhoekvillage.co.za

The **Noordhoek Farm Village**, close to the signposted entrance to Chapman's Peak Drive, is essentially a rural mall, but it's one of the pleasantest shopping venues on the Cape Peninsula and is an excellent choice if you're on holiday with children. It also has one of Cape Town's best restaurants, *The Foodbarn* (see p.121). The village is laid out like a Cape Dutch farm complex; the manor houses a hotel and has outbuildings arranged around a yard. There's also a sushi restaurant, a café, deli and pub, as well as a children's playground and several craft shops.

Cape Point Vineyards

Silvermine Rd • Tues–Sun 10am–6pm; Community market Thurs 4.30–8.30pm • Free; picnic basket for two R330 • ☎ 021 789 0900, ⓦ noordhoekvineyards.co.za

Cape Point Vineyards, known for its Savignon Blanc, is another excuse to sample Cape wines in a beautiful setting. The vineyard offers a lavish picnic basket which you can eat on slopes close to a lake, with views over the distant beach and mountains. Greatly popular is the community market on a Thursday evening, where locals browse through a selection of different food stalls, sit at the tables on the lawn and take in the sunset, wine in hand.

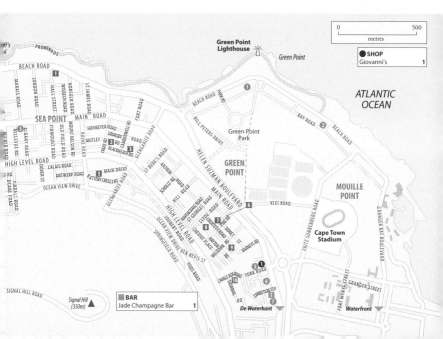

5

Kommetjie

Kommetjie (pronounced "cawm-ma-key"), halfway down the peninsula, and 31km from central Cape Town, is a small and very attractive seaside suburb, dominated by the Slangkop lighthouse, and a place you will most likely drive through on a Cape Point round-the-peninsula trip. It is built around a small rocky inlet, called **De Kom** (Afrikaans for basin), where you can walk around or take a dip in the water. Kommetjie is another favourite **surfing** spot for the very experienced; if you want to learn, though, Muizenberg is the place (see p.142). Kommetjie also has access to Noordhoek Beach, but the road between the two places goes inland to avoid the wetland area behind the beach.

Imhoff Farm Village

Kommetjie Rd, opposite the Ocean View turn-off · Free · Opening hours vary for the different establishments · ☎ 021 783 4545, ⓦ imhofffarm.co.za

Imhoff Farm Village, on Kommetjie Road, with camels kneeling at the entrance, is a favourite place for kids (see p.147) and, surprisingly enough, also has an excellent and well-priced restaurant in a Cape Dutch manor, **Blue Water Café** (see p.122), with matching wines and views onto the wetlands. It makes an inviting lunch stop on a peninsula tour. There are a couple of other eateries in the village and a deli, as well as farmyard delights for younger children.

Scarborough

The developing and idyllic village of **Scarborough**, almost 10km by road from Kommetjie, is the most far-flung settlement along the peninsula, with cold, turquoise water and white sands. It's a lovely, easy drive to Scarborough from Simon's Town, winding over the spine of the peninsula, and onto Cape Point. The only food in town can be found at the *Camel Rock* restaurant (see p.123).

BEACH HUTS, ST JAMES

The False Bay seaboard to Cape Point

In summer, the waters of False Bay are several degrees warmer than those on the Atlantic Seaboard, which is why Cape Town's oldest and most popular seaside developments are along this flank of the peninsula. A series of village-like suburbs, which back onto the mountains and are all served by Metrorail stations, is dotted all the way south from Muizenberg, through St James, Kalk Bay, Fish Hoek and down to Simon's Town. Each suburb has its own character and places to eat, drink and sleep, while Simon's Town, one of South Africa's oldest settlements, makes either a pleasant day-trip or useful base for visiting the African penguins at Boulders, just south of town, and Cape Point itself. This is the less fashionable, less glamorous and less moneyed side of the peninsula, but it is no less beautiful.

6

By car Driving here from central Cape Town, the best route is along the M3 south to Muizenberg. Boyes Drive, a high-level alternative to Main Rd, runs for about 5km between the suburbs of Lakeside at the southern end of the M3 and Kalk Bay, and offers spectacular views across to the Hottentots Holland Mountains on the east side of False Bay. The road is also one of several spots on the Cape Peninsula where, at the right time of year, you might spot whales (see box, p.97).

By train The train ride to Simon's Town is reason enough to visit, and from Muizenberg most stations are situated close

to the surf. From Cape Town there are roughly two trains an hour Mon–Fri to Simon's Town (5am–7pm; 1hr 15min; R13) and more frequently to Fish Hoek (58min; R10). Both of those routes run via Muizenberg (48min; R10), St James (51min; R10) and Kalk Bay (53min; R10); on Sat & Sun, services are reduced to roughly one an hour from Cape Town to Simon's Town. Metrorail (☎021 449 6478, ⓦ www.metrorail.co.za) provides telephonic timetable information, and downloadable PDFs are available from their website.

Muizenberg

Once boasting South Africa's most fashionable beachfront, **Muizenberg** (pronounced "mew-zin-burg"), 27km from the city centre, is now rather run-down but is attempting to re-create itself with a new beachfront housing development and a splurge of good coffee shops – and nothing can detract from its long, safe and fabulous **beach** where brightly coloured huts are cheerful reminders of a more elegant heyday. During the 1920s, it was visited by the likes of Agatha Christie, who enjoyed riding its waves while holidaying here: "Whenever we could steal time off," she wrote, "we got out our surf boards and went surfing." Today, the water is invariably bobbing with dozens of surfers; you can hire boards from the several surf schools at the beachfront (see p.142).

The beach

Super Tubes (waterslides) Daily 9.30–5.30pm, Mon–Fri during term time from 1.30pm; night slide Fri 6–9pm • R40/1hr, R75/day • ☎ 021 788 4759 • **Minigolf** Daily 10am–5pm • R9.50 • ☎ 021 788 8800

Muizenberg's gently shelving, sandy **beach** is the most popular along the peninsula for swimming, especially on Sundays in summer, though note that it can be very windy.

Three **waterslides** (Super Tubes) and a **minigolf** course at the northern end of the beach also help keep kids well occupied. Away from the shoreline, Muizenberg's shabby-chic village high street is worth a wander, frequented by the local artistic fraternity as well as a Congolese community.

The Historical Mile

A short stretch of the shore, starting at **Muizenberg Station**, is known as the **Historical Mile**, dotted with a run of notable buildings and easily explored on foot. The train station, an Edwardian-style edifice completed in 1913, is now a National Monument, while the **Posthuys** is a rugged whitewashed and thatched building dating from 1673 and a fine example of the Cape vernacular style.

Casa Labia

192 Main Rd • Tues–Sun 10am–4pm • Free • ☎ 021 788 6068, ⓦ casalabia.co.za

The most idiosyncratic of the buildings along the Historical Mile and closest to Muizenberg is **Casa Labia**. It was completed in 1930 as the residence of the Italian consul, Count Natale Labia. Built in the eighteenth-century Venetian style, it's a

---

BEACH SAFETY TIPS

Don't take anything **valuable** on the beach, and don't leave anything unguarded while you're there, as opportunist theft is rife. Guards are present at the car park, so preferably leave valuables in your car boot. Some of the beachfront establishments will look after car keys while you head for the water. False Bay is also home to **great white sharks**, and you will notice shark flags raised and a siren calling surfers and bathers out of the water on the odd occasion that a shark is spotted.

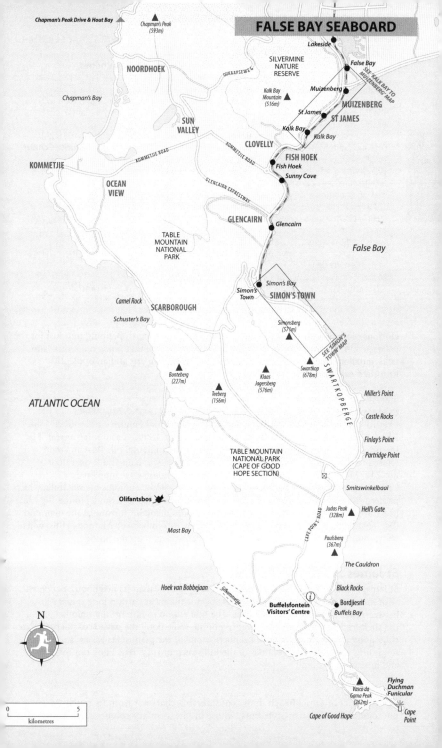

6

THE CAPE DUTCH REVIVAL

During the 1890s, millionaire tycoons like British expatriate **Cecil John Rhodes** found themselves at the top of the South African pecking order. These men saw themselves as an Anglo-African aristocracy lording it over the country much as the landed gentry did back in Britain. The so-called **Randlords** (Johannesburg mining magnates) and people like Rhodes in the Cape were among the biggest patrons of architecture, and they sought a language to express their new power and status.

Rhodes commissioned **Herbert Baker**, a young English architect schooled in the British Arts and Crafts Movement and who worked with Sir Edward Lutyens, to build **Groote Schuur** (1898), his home on Klipper Road in Rondebosch, which is now South Africa's official presidential residence (see p.78). In looking for precedents, Baker identified Cape Dutch architecture (see box, p.80) as a suitable model – it was old and it represented wealth, making it the closest equivalent in South Africa to the stately homes of England.

Baker used recognizable **Cape elements** such as gables, curving multi-paned windows and steeply pitched roofs. He also drew on English traditions, such as barley-sugar chimneys that hark back to Tudor architecture, while bird figures that Rhodes removed from Great Zimbabwe were used to suggest the gargoyles of Gothic architecture.

This style came to be known as **Cape Dutch Revival**, and was used again by the architect at **Rust en Vrede** (1902), Rhodes' seaside residence, adjacent to Rhodes' Cottage Museum in Muizenberg (see below). The Cape Dutch Revival has become well established in South African architectural parlance: the twentieth century saw the appearance of Cape Dutch features, particularly gables, in suburban houses, no matter how inappropriate the scale or context.

glorious piece of architectural bling on Main Road and worth popping into just for the palazzo's film-set interiors. It also houses a **cultural centre** that puts on concerts and talks, a **gallery** that features contemporary South African art, and an opulently furnished café plus craft shop.

Rhodes' Cottage Museum

246 Main Rd · Daily 10am–3pm, winter till 2pm · Free · ☎ 021 788 1816, ⓦ facebook.com/RhodesCottageMuseum

Controversial millionaire mining magnate, politician and empire builder Cecil John Rhodes bought his modest cottage in Muizenberg, in 1899, as a country retreat. His intention was to spend time here while his more monumental pile **Rust en Vrede** (closed to the public), designed by Sir Herbert Baker, was being built next door at no. 244. He died at the cottage in 1902, before the house was completed.

Now the **Rhodes' Cottage Museum**, the politician's home contains memorabilia which paints a distinctly rosy portrait of the man, with photographs, a model of the Big Hole in Kimberley in the Northern Cape (where Rhodes made his fortune at the diamond diggings) and a curious diorama of World's View in Zimbabwe's Matopos Hills, where he was buried. The cottage's lovely *fynbos* garden straggles up the hillside.

St James

St James, 2km south of Muizenberg, is more upmarket than its neighbour, peppered with mountainside homes that are accessible for the most part up long stairways between Main Road and Boyes Drive. The best reason to hop off the train here is for the **sheltered tidal pool** and the twenty-minute walk along the **paved coastal path** that runs along the rocky shore to Muizenberg – one of the peninsula's easiest and most rewarding walks, with panoramas of the full sweep of False Bay. Look out for seals, and in season, whales.

The beach

The compact St James **Beach** draws considerable character from its much-photographed Victorian-style huts, whose bright, primary colours catch your eye as you pass by road or rail. The beach tends to be overcrowded at weekends and during school holidays; far fewer visitors take the trouble to stroll along the short footpath that leads south along the lawned shore from St James to the adjacent sandy stretch of **Danger Beach**, an excellent spot for sunbathing and building sand castles. As the name suggests, its surf should be treated with respect, as there is a powerful undertow here.

Kalk Bay

6

One of the most southerly and smallest of Cape Town's suburbs, **Kalk Bay** centres around a lively working harbour with wooden fishing vessels, mountain views and a strip of shops brimming with collectables, antiques dealers and plenty of places to eat and drink. Kalk Bay somehow managed to slip through the net of the Group Areas Act (see p.256), making it one of the few places on the peninsula with an intact coloured community; Kalk Bay and the larger Hout Bay (see p.88) are the only harbour settlements still worked by coloured fishermen. Kalk Bay is also home to numerous artists and creative types who thrive on the village atmosphere and the natural beauty of the place.

The settlement is arranged around the small **docks**, where you can watch the boats come in; you can also buy fresh fish, which are flung onto the quayside and sold in a spirited fashion, though stocks are declining and fishing rights for many of the people here are being taken away. The harbour is busiest on Saturdays and Sundays when Capetonians descend to pick up something for a weekend braai or to have lunch at one of the several terrifically located **restaurants** in the area (see p.122), some within spitting distance of the breakers.

WHALE SPOTTING ON THE FALSE BAY SEABOARD

The most common whales you'll see off the Cape are **southern rights**, and the warmer **False Bay** side of the peninsula has the best **whale-watching spots** in season (roughly Aug–Nov). There is some chance of spotting them on the **Atlantic seaboard**, too (see p.85); whichever seaboard you're visiting, you should have binoculars handy. The months when you are more or less guaranteed sightings are September and October.

Boyes Drive, which runs along the mountainside behind Muizenberg and Kalk Bay, provides an outstanding vantage point. To get there by car, head out on the M3 from the city centre to Muizenberg; take a sharp, signposted right onto Boyes Drive, at Lakeside, from where the road begins to climb, descending finally to join Main Road between Kalk Bay and Fish Hoek.

Alternatively, if you stick close to the shore along Main Road, the stretch between **Fish Hoek** and **Simon's Town** is recommended, with a particularly nice spot above the rocks at the south end of Fish Hoek Beach, as you walk south towards Glencairn. **Boulders Beach**, at the southern end of Simon's Town, has a whale signboard and smooth rocky outcrops above the sea to sit on and gaze out over the water.

Without a car, you can get the train to Fish Hoek or Simon's Town and whale-spot from the **Jager's Walk** beach path that runs along the coast from Fish Hoek to Sunny Cove, just below the train line.

It's worth noting that there are more spectacular spotting opportunities further east, especially around **Hermanus** (see p.168) and **De Hoop** (see p.179).

Although False Bay is great for land-based whale watching, on a boat you get a different perspective: you're in the mammal's own element and you may just get a closer look. It also offers the chance to spot other whales such as Brydes, humpbacks and orcas, and other marine animals including dolphins and seals (which are visible any time of year). Simon's Town Boat Company (☏ 083 257 7760, ⊕ boatcompany.co.za), based at the Simon's Town pier, is the only outfit licensed to do False Bay boat-based **whale-watching trips** (daily 10.30am & 2pm; R850); they also do cruises around Cape Point (R550), to Seal Island (R400) and historic guided tours that include a visit to the Naval Dockyard (R50).

Silvermine Nature Reserve

Ou Kaapse Weg • May–Sept 8am–5pm; Oct–April 7am–6pm • R40 • ☎ 021 780 9002

Rising up behind Boyes Drive is the **Silvermine Nature Reserve** which runs across the peninsula's spine, almost stretching to the west side at Chapman's Peak. Comprising part of the Table Mountain chain of peaks, the **walks** here provide fabulous views of False Bay, the mountains and montane *fynbos*, and you can picnic next to an idyllic **lake**.

By car, take the Ou Kaapse Weg (the M64 to Noordhoek), signposted at the southern end of the M3. The entrance is at the top of the mountains on the right-hand side. The road from the entrance gate leads through areas of *fynbos* to **Silvermine Dam**, where you can swim in summer. Alternatively, you can park at the entrance gate and do the easy and rewarding one-hour **River Walk** to the dam, which has no steep gradients, is well shaded and offers protection from the wind in summer. The other popular walk, which starts from the car park at the dam and offers good views, is to **Elephant's Eye Cave**. Both walks are signposted.

It's also possible to get into the eastern half of the reserve for free via paths that strike up from Boyes Drive, including a set of stairs in Kalk Bay that heads up from Boyes Drive just as it makes a sharp turn down to the harbour. The climb is well worth the effort for the superb **aerial views** of the Indian Ocean.

The excellent Slingsby **map** of Silvermine is widely available at outdoor shops such as Cape Union Mart, with the hiking trails marked on; otherwise there is a sketchy one handed out as you enter the gate.

Fish Hoek

🌐 fishhoek.com

Fish Hoek, south of Kalk Bay, boasts one of the peninsula's finest family **beaches** along the False Bay coast. The best and safest swimming is at its southern end, where the surf is moderately warm, tame and much enjoyed by boogie boarders. Thanks to the beach, there's a fair amount of accommodation (see p.114), but this is otherwise one of the dreariest suburbs along the False Bay coast. An obscure by-law banning the sale of alcohol in supermarkets or bottle stores boosts the town's image as the Mother Grundy capital of the peninsula.

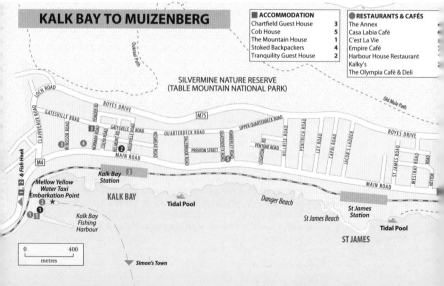

KALK BAY TO MUIZENBERG

◼ ACCOMMODATION	
Chartfield Guest House	3
Cob House	5
The Mountain House	1
Stoked Backpackers	4
Tranquility Guest House	2

● RESTAURANTS & CAFÉS
The Annex
Casa Labia Café
C'est La Vie
Empire Café
Harbour House Restaurant
Kalky's
The Olympia Café & Deli

SILVERMINE NATURE RESERVE
(TABLE MOUNTAIN NATIONAL PARK)

Facilities include a playground, changing rooms, toilets, fresh drinking water and the *Fish Hoek Galley Seafood Restaurant* right on the beach. From behind the restaurant, a picturesque concrete pathway called **Jager's Walk** provides a good vantage point for seeing whales. It skirts the rocky shoreline above the sea for 1km to Sunny Cove, from where it continues for 6km as an unpaved track to Simon's Town.

Simon's Town and around

Just 40km from Cape Town, roughly halfway down the coast to Cape Point, **Simon's Town** makes the perfect base for a mellow break along the peninsula and offers easy day-trips by train to Cape Town. Despite being South Africa's principal naval base, and incidentally the country's third-oldest European settlement, Simon's Town isn't the hard-drinking, raucous place you might expect. It's exceptionally pretty, with a preserved streetscape, slightly marred on the ocean side by the domineering **naval dockyard**, but this, and glimpses of naval squaddies square-bashing behind the high walls or strolling to the station in their crisp white uniforms, are what give the place its distinct character. A few kilometres to the south is the rock-strewn **Boulders Beach**, with its colony of nonchalant **African penguins** – reason enough to venture here.

Brief history

Founded in 1687 as the winter anchorage of the Dutch East India Company, Simon's Town was one of several places in and around Cape Town modestly named by **Governor Simon van der Stel** after himself. Its most celebrated visitor was Lord Nelson, who convalesced here as a midshipman en route to return home from the East in 1776. Nineteen years later, the British sailed into Simon's Town and occupied it as a bridgehead for their first invasion and occupation of the Cape. After just seven years, they left, only to return in 1806. Simon's Town remained a British base until 1957, when it was handed over to South Africa.

There are fleeting hints, such as the occasional mosque, that the town's predominantly white appearance isn't the whole story. In fact, the first **Muslims** arrived from the East Indies in the early eighteenth century, imported as slaves to build the Dutch naval base. After the British banned the slave trade in 1807, ships were compelled to disgorge their

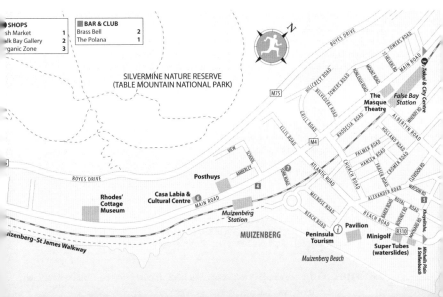

6

human cargo at Simon's Town, where one district became known as Black Town. In 1967, when Simon's Town was declared a White Group Area, there were 1200 well-established coloured families descended from these slaves. By the early 1970s, the majority had been forcibly removed under the Group Areas Act to the township of Ocean View, whose inspiring name belies its desolation.

ARRIVAL AND DEPARTURE | SIMON'S TOWN

By train If you're travelling by train to Simon's Town, you can arrange to be collected by HGTS Tours, who act as a taxi service and have an office on the station platform (☎ 021 786 5243); a one-way trip to Boulders costs R40; an excursion to Cape Point returning you to the station is R300, excluding entry fees.

Kalk Bay–Simon's Town water taxi Mellow Yellow Water Taxi runs an hourly service between Kalk Bay Harbour and Simon's Town public jetty at the marina (daily 9am–4pm, on the hour from Simon's Town, half past the hour from Kalk Bay; R100 one way, R150 return; ☎ 073 473 7684, ✉ bookings@watertaxi.co.za, ⓦ watertaxi.co.za). Although tickets can be bought on the boat, it's best to book ahead as the vessel takes a maximum of ten passengers and services are subject to the weather and whales crossing. The trip is highly recommended, and one of the few ways to get on the water in False Bay.

Simon's Town Museum

Court Rd • Mon–Fri 9am–4pm, Sat 10am–1pm • R10 • ☎ 021 786 3046, ⓦ simonstown.com/museum/stm_main.htm

The building now housing the **Simon's Town Museum** was once the Old Residency, built in 1772 for the Governor of the Dutch East India Company, and has also served as the slave quarters (the dungeons are in the basement) and town brothel. The museum's motley collection includes maritime material and an inordinate amount of information and exhibits on Able Seaman Just Nuisance, a much-celebrated seafaring **Great Dane**. He enjoyed drinking beer with the sailors he accompanied into Cape Town, and was adopted as a mascot by the South African Royal Navy in World War II.

The building also reputedly still houses the **ghost** of Eleanor, the 14-year-old daughter of Earl McCartney, who lived here in the closing years of the eighteenth century. Forbidden by her parents from playing on the sands with the children of coloured fishermen, Eleanor would escape to the beach through a secret tunnel she had discovered. The dankness of the tunnel supposedly gave her pneumonia, from which she tragically died.

South African Naval Museum

West Dockyard, accessed from St George's St • Daily 10am–4pm • Free • ☎ 021 787 4686, ⓦ simonstown.com/navalmuseum

At the **South African Naval Museum**, lively displays include the inside of a submarine, a ship's bridge that simulates rocking, and a lot of official portraits of South African naval commanders from 1922 to the present. Although much altered now, the museum is housed in the original Dutch East India Company magazine and storehouse, which was taken over by the Royal Navy when it installed its headquarters in Simon's Town in 1810.

SHARK COUNTRY

False Bay is one of the best places in the country to encounter **Great White sharks**. For one thing, the False Bay sharks are on average about a third bigger than their Gansbaai counterparts.

Apex Shark Expeditions (Quayside Building, Shop no. 5 Main Rd; ☎ 021 786 5717, ⓦ apex predators.com) is operated by naturalists Chris and Monique Fallows, who have worked with National Geographic and the BBC. They operate a range of marine trips in False Bay, among them shark-cage diving. Their emphasis is on observing shark behaviour – and that of other marine creatures you'll encounter on the trip out to Seal Island – rather than the adrenaline rush. Trips are in groups of a maximum twelve people, which means you have a pretty personalized experience and each person gets twenty to thirty minutes in the cage. Trips leave from the Simon's Town pier and prices vary according to season (and the corresponding likelihood of encountering a shark): Feb–April R1700, May R1950, June–Aug R2400.

Jubilee Square and the Marina

In the centre of Simon's Town, a little over 1km south of the station, lies **Jubilee Square**, a palm-shaded car park just off St George's Street. Flanked by some cafés and shops, the street has on its harbour-facing side a broad walkway with a statue of the ubiquitous Able Seaman Just Nuisance and a few stalls selling curios. A couple of sets of stairs lead down to the **Marina**, a modest development of shops and restaurants set right on the waterfront. The best **fish and chips** is to be had at the *Salty Seadog* (see p.123).

Seaforth Beach

Seaforth Beach is the closest access point to a large viewing platform where the greatest numbers of penguins in Simon's Town congregate. It also has one of the best beaches for swimming, where clear, deep waters lap around rocks. It's calm, protected and safe, but not pretty (it's bounded on one side by the looming grey mass of the naval base), though it does have plenty of lawn shaded by palm trees, and a **restaurant** with outdoor seating and fresh fish on the menu.

You can access the Boulders penguin reserve (see below) via a pathway leading from Seaforth, 2km east of Jubilee Square, as well as from the signposted car park at Boulders itself.

Boulders Beach and the penguin reserve

Penguin reserve Jan & Dec 7am–7.30pm; Feb, March, Oct & Nov 8am–6.30pm; April–Sept 8am–5pm • R53 • ☏ 021 786 2329

Boulders Beach, the most popular Simon's Town beach, takes its name from the huge rounded rocks that create a cluster of little coves with sandy beaches and clear, cold sea pools that make for wonderful swimming. However, the main reason people come here is for the **African penguins** in the Boulders section of the Table Mountain National

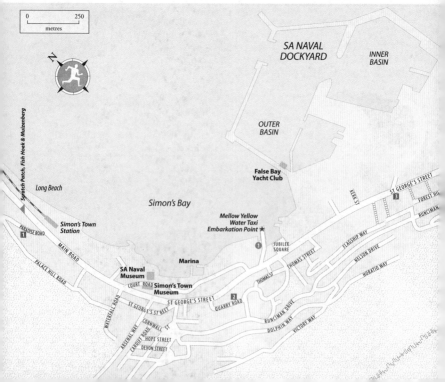

Park, a fenced **reserve** on Boulders Beach. African penguins usually live on islands off the west side of the South African coast; the Boulders birds form one of only two mainland colonies in the world. This is also the only place where the endangered species are actually increasing in numbers, and coming here will provide you with a rare opportunity to get a close look at them.

Miller's Point

Almost 5km to the south of Simon's Town is the popular **Miller's Point** resort, which has a number of small sandy beaches and a tidal pool protected from the southeaster. Along Main Road, the notable *Black Marlin* **restaurant** (see p.122) attracts busloads of tourists, while the boulders around the point attract rock agama, black zonure lizards and dassies.

6

Smitswinkelbaai

If you head south from Simon's Town, the last place you'll get to before the Cape of Good Hope section of the Table Mountain National Park is **Smitswinkelbaai** (pronounced "smits-vin-cull-buy"). This little cove has a small beach safe for swimming, but feels the full blast of the southeaster. It's not accessible **by car**, as local property-owners fiercely guard their privacy; to get there, you must park next to the road and walk down a seemingly endless succession of stairs.

Cape of Good Hope Nature Reserve

Cape Point Rd • Daily: April–Sept 7am–5pm; Oct–March 6am–6pm • R105 • ☎ 021 780 9526, ⓦ capepoint.co.za

Most people who visit the **Cape of Good Hope Nature Reserve**, which is part of Table Mountain National Park, are here to see the southernmost tip of Africa and the place

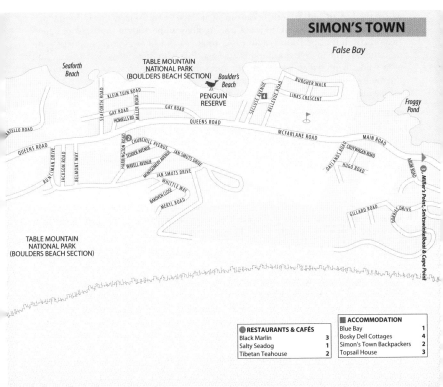

SIMON'S TOWN

● RESTAURANTS & CAFÉS	
Black Marlin	3
Salty Seadog	1
Tibetan Teahouse	2

■ ACCOMMODATION	
Blue Bay	1
Bosky Dell Cottages	4
Simon's Town Backpackers	2
Topsail House	3

6

FLORA, FAUNA AND FURRY FELONS

The majority of visitors to the Cape of Good Hope Nature Reserve make a beeline for Cape Point and take in the rest of the reserve through a vehicle window, but walking is really the best way to appreciate indigenous Cape **flora**. At first glance the landscape appears rocky and bleak, with short, wind-cropped plants, but the vegetation is surprisingly rich. Amazingly, many bright blooms in Britain and the US, including varieties of geraniums, freesias, gladioli, daisies, lilies and irises, are hybrids grown from indigenous Cape plants.

Along with indigenous plants and flowers, you may well spot some of the animals living in the reserve's **fynbos** habitat. **Ostriches** stride through the low *fynbos*, and occasionally **African penguins** come ashore. A distinctive bird on the rocky shores is the **black oystercatcher** which jabs limpets off the rocks with its bright red beak. You'll also see **Cape cormorants** in large flocks on the beach or rocks, often drying their outstretched wings. Running up and down the water's edge (where, as on any other beach walk in the Cape, you'll see piles of shiny brown *Ecklonia* kelp) are **white-fronted plovers** and **sanderlings**, probing for food left by the receding waves. As for mammals, **baboons** lope along the rocky shoreline, while **bontebok**, **eland** and **red hartebeest** graze along the heathery slopes, as do **Cape rhebok** and **grysbok**. If you're very lucky, you may even see some of the extremely rare **Cape mountain zebras**.

Baboons may look amusing, but be warned: they can be a menace. Keep your car windows closed, as it's not uncommon for them to invade vehicles, and they're adept at swiping picnics. You should lock your car doors even if you only plan to get out for a few minutes to admire the view, as there are growing reports of baboons opening unlocked doors while the vehicle owner's back is turned. Do not ever unwrap food or eat or drink anything if baboons are in the vicinity. Feeding them is illegal and provocative, and can incur a fine. There are authorized baboon-chasers, who ward off the baboons, in several places across the reserve.

where the Indian and Atlantic oceans meet at **Cape Point**. In fact, this is the site of neither: the continent's real tip is at Cape Agulhas, some 300km southeast of here (see p.176), but Cape Point is a lot easier to get to and an awesomely dramatic spot nonetheless. The reserve sits atop massive sea cliffs with huge views, strong seas, and an even wilder wind which whips off caps and sunglasses as visitors gaze southwards from the old lighthouse buttress. If you don't bring any food with you, you can take in the view while you eat at the decent enough restaurant here, *Two Oceans* (see p.123).

ARRIVAL AND INFORMATION   CAPE OF GOOD HOPE

However you get to the reserve, go as early as you can in the day to avoid tour buses and the likelihood of the wind gusting more strongly as the day progresses.

By car Most visitors see the Point as part of a circular driving trip, returning via Kommetjie and the especially scenic Chapman's Peak Drive (see p.90).

On a tour Numerous tours spend a day stopping off at the peninsula highlights; Day Trippers (📞 021 511 4766, 🌐 daytrippers.co.za) runs fun daily hiking tours for R630 (including a picnic lunch), which give you the option of cycling part of the way.

Information The Buffelsfontein Visitors' Centre (daily 7.30am–5pm; 📞 021 780 9204), 8km from the entrance gate, is worth a look, boasting attractive displays about the local fauna and flora as well as video screenings on the ecology of the area.

Flying Dutchman Funicular

Daily 9am–5.30pm • Single R42, return R53 • 📞 021 780 9010, 🌐 capepoint.co.za

From the nature reserve car park, it's a short, steep walk – one crawling with tourists – up to the famous viewpoint, the original lighthouse. The **Flying Dutchman Funicular** runs the less energetic to the top of the first lighthouse, where there's a shop selling knick-knacks. Built in 1860, the **lighthouse** was too often dangerously shrouded in cloud and failed to keep ships off the rocks, so in 1914 another was built lower down and closer to the Point. This second lighthouse, which you can walk to easily from the first, isn't always successful in averting disasters, but is still the most powerful light beaming onto the sea from South Africa.

Beaches
You'll find the **beaches** along signposted side roads branching out from the Cape Point road through the reserve. The sea here is too dangerous for swimming, but there are safe tidal pools at the adjacent **Buffels Bay** and **Bordjiesrif**, midway along the east shore. Both have braai stands, but more southerly Buffels Bay is the nicer, with big lawned areas and some sheltered spots to have a picnic, but don't produce any food if there are baboons in the vicinity.

Walks
There are several marked **walks** in the Cape of Good Hope reserve. If you're planning a big hike it's best to set out early, as shade is rare and the wind can be foul, especially during summer, and it often increases in intensity as the day goes on. One of the most straightforward **hiking routes** is the signposted forty-minute trek from the car park at Cape Point to the more westerly **Cape of Good Hope**. For exploring the shoreline, a clear path runs down the Atlantic side, which you can join at **Gifkommetjie**, signposted off Cape Point Road. From the car park, several sandy tracks drop quite steeply down the slope across rocks, and through bushes and milkwood trees to the shore, along which you can walk in either direction. Take plenty of **water** on any walk in the reserve, as there are no reliable fresh sources.

Navigators have been braving the rocks, winds and swells of Cape Point since the Portuguese first "rounded the Cape" in the fifteenth century. Several wrecks lie submerged off its coast, and at **Olifantsbos**, on the west side, you can walk to a US ship that sunk in 1942 and a South African coaster that ran aground in 1965.

6

CAPE HERITAGE HOTEL

Accommodation

Standards of accommodation are very high in Cape Town and cover an impressive range of options. In the city centre, you'll find outstanding boutique hotels, luxury guesthouses and welcoming hostels which often boast spectacular views of Table Mountain or the ocean. Stretch further along the Garden Route, and you'll discover country retreats in beautiful settings, ecolodges built within forests and sumptuous beds in grand Victorian townhouses – at prices that would only get you a good B&B back home. Other than in the cheapest rooms, you'll always get a private bath or shower, and you'll often have use of a garden and pool, or even your own private patio. One unusual prospect – and one of very few ways to experience black South Africa – is to stay in one of the African townships in Cape Town.

Although there's not much in the way of low-cost hotels, modest budgets are catered for by two main options. **Backpacker lodges** offer basic hostel accommodation in a dormitory, usually from around R135 per person. There's been a rise in **"boutique" backpackers**, which, as well as dorms, offer almost luxurious doubles, percale cotton sheets and feather duvets. Some backpacker places have family accommodation, some are quiet, but most, as is to be expected, are about socializing. They are independently run and listed in the free *Coast to Coast* booklet, which covers the whole country and is widely available in tourist information offices and hostels countrywide.

Self-catering apartments are especially good if you are travelling as a family. You can expect kitchens to come with crockery and cutlery, and for linen and towels to be provided. Nature-lovers who are after isolated splendour might want to stay at one of the National Parks self-catering cottages or glamping sites dotted about Table Mountain (book at the National Parks booking desk at Cape Town Tourism Office in Burg St, or on ☎021 712 7471, ⓦtmnp.co.za). A four-person hut near Platteklip on the top of Table Mountain costs R1750, while the largest, most luxurious houses on the beach at Cape Point and the top of Constantia Nek go for around R3500 for four people. Note that availability can be very limited at weekends.

Besides the many internet accommodation-booking services, the Cape Town Tourism website can help you find accommodation for all budgets (ⓦcapetown.travel).

ESSENTIALS

Rates In this guide (including the "Beyond the city" chapters), accommodation prices are, unless stated otherwise, quoted as the lowest price per double room for two people sharing in high season, though for backpacker hostels the rate for dorms is per person. Note, however, that on the ground many rates are quoted per person rather than per room – make sure which it is when you phone to book. An English breakfast is almost always included in the rate – if not, it should be available to order.

Seasons High season basically refers to the South African summer, when Cape Town is packed full to the brim – though note that prices rise again within this period, during Christmas and New Year and also over Easter. There's a lull in the midwinter low season (June–Aug), during which time you can find good-value places to stay, often with hefty discounts.

Booking If you want to stay in a particular guesthouse in a central location, in high season, it's strongly recommended that you book several months in advance.

CITY CENTRE

From **Long Street** and the surrounding area, you can walk to all the museums, trawl Cape Town's best bars and clubs, eat at numerous restaurants and easily find transport out of the centre or to the Waterfront. There are a number of backpacker lodges and a couple of hotels on Long Street itself, and you'll also find several places east of it, around the museum complex and the Company's Gardens. Expect rooms fronting Long Street to be noisy.

★ **Cape Heritage Hotel** 90 Bree St ☎021 424 4646, ⓦcapeheritage.co.za; map p.48. An exceptionally stylish, elegant and tastefully restored boutique hotel located in a row of houses dating back to 1771, in Cape Heritage Square, just below the Bo-Kaap. The rooms are spacious and decorated with contemporary handcrafted objects and original paintings. The service is charming. R2100

Cat & Moose 305 Long St ☎021 423 7638, ⓦcatandmoose.co.za; map p.48. The most stylish of the Long Street backpackers, housed in an eighteenth-century building a couple of doors from the steam baths at the south end of the city centre. Timber floors, rugs, earthy reds and ochres as well as some African masks imbue it with a warm ethnic feel, as do the humble communal cooking and eating areas. The rooms are arranged around a small leafy courtyard, which contains a small plunge pool. The double rooms are the most affordable in town. Dorm R140, double R410

Dutch Manor Antique Hotel 158 Buitengracht, Bo-Kaap ☎21 422 4767, ⓦdutchmanor.co.za; map p.48. Travel back in time to a townhouse meticulously filled with period furniture, lavish tapestries and four-poster beds. Bathrooms and breakfast room are spotless and modern, and there's a small balcony overlooking the street. Very central location in the City Bowl; off-street parking available. R1600

Grand Daddy Hotel 38 Long St ☎021 424 7247, ⓦgranddaddy.co.za; map p.48. The *Grand Daddy* features seven retro-cool American Airstream trailers, decorated by local artists, that sit on the roof and are linked by wooden walkways. You can stay in one of these snug trailers on the rooftop, or in one of the hotel's double rooms, which are also imaginative, colourful and funky, and have queen-size beds. R1910

iKhaya Lodge Wandel St, Dunkley Square ☎021 461 8880, ⓦikhayalodge.co.za; map p.43. This guesthouse is on a pretty square, right by the Company's Gardens and the museums, and close to trendy places to eat. En-suite rooms in the main lodge building have balconies overlooking the square, and a few luxury lofts boast ethnically inspired decor and separate double rooms. Offers 24hr reception, satellite TV and wi-fi throughout. Double **R995**, loft **R1900**

Rose Street 28 28 Rose St, Bo-Kaap ☎ 021 424 3813, ⓦ rosestreet28.co.za; map p.43. The most affordable and best value for money B&B in town. There are three jointly managed separate townhouses, centrally located on trendy Rose St, each containing three en-suite double rooms with shared kitchenette and courtyard. Houses vary slightly, though all bedrooms are compact, basic doubles. **R690**

Rouge on Rose 25 Rose St, at Hout St ☎ 021 426 0298, ⓦ rougeonrose.co.za; map p.43. Nine modern, comfortable suites in a Bo-Kaap guesthouse, on an increasingly gentrified street, with great views across to Signal Hill or the city. Convenient microwave and catering basics if you fancy a night in, and there's free wi-fi. **R1500**

V&A WATERFRONT AND DE WATERKANT

In keeping with the gentrified ambience of the **V&A Waterfront** (usually referred to simply as the Waterfront), accommodation here tends to be expensive; there are, however, a couple of more modestly priced places to stay. It's a good choice if you like shopping in a self-contained safe area and want to be able to walk to restaurants and cafés, and it boasts a pleasing harbour atmosphere. Nearby, **De Waterkant** is an area of pretty, cobbled streets and terraced houses, with some excellent, upmarket self-catering accommodation and good local restaurants within easy reach of the city's best nightlife.

Breakwater Lodge Portswood Rd, Waterfront ☎ 021 406 1911 (ask for Lodge Reservations), ⓦ breakwater lodge.co.za; map p.62. The most affordable place to stay in the Waterfront, this hotel is linked to Cape Town University's Graduate School of Business. It's pretty characterless and rates do not include breakfast; choose it only if the location is what matters most. **R1350**

St John's Waterfront Lodge 6 Braemar Rd ☎ 021 439 1404, ⓦ stjohns.co.za; map p.62. The closest hostel to the Waterfront (a 15min walk away), St John's is well run by friendly and helpful staff. Accommodation comes in dorms and private doubles, and communal facilities include a swimming pool, a great garden, an outdoor BBQ area, free wi-fi, a laundry service machine and a travel centre. Dorm **R150**, double **R550**

★**Village and Life** Reception at 1 Loader St, De Waterkant ☎ 021 409 2500, ⓦ villageandlife.com; map p.62. These attractively restored historic cottages are adjacent to the Bo-Kaap and less than 1km from the Waterfront, Green Point and city centre. The luxury cottages in Waterkant, Loader, Dixon and Napier streets have up to three bedrooms; some have garages, swimming pools and roof gardens with harbour or mountain views. The company also has self-catering apartments for rent in the Waterfront itself. 2-person apartment **R1950**

CITY BOWL SUBURBS

The **City Bowl suburbs** are popular for accommodation, and the most northerly sections are just a 5–10min walk from the Company's Gardens and the museums. A few backpacker lodges can be found along **Kloof Street**, the continuation of trendy Long Street, with some great cafés and restaurants. It's quieter and leafier than the city centre, especially the further up the mountainside you go, and you'll find gardens, good views and swimming pools at the more comfortable guesthouses. **New Church Street** is quieter traffic-wise than Long Street for backpacker accommodation, and several hostels there have comfortable en-suite doubles.

GARDENS

Ashanti Lodge 11 Hof St ☎ 021 423 8721, ⓦ ashanti .co.za; map p.72. This massive, refurbished two-storey Victorian mansion has marbling and ethnic decor, soaring ceilings, a nicely kept front garden and a swimming pool with sun terrace. The private rooms (with twin or double beds and shared bath) and dorms (sleeping 6–8) are furnished with custom-made wrought-iron bunks and beds. The bar is very lively, so if you are not a party animal, you might want to book in at their guesthouse, which offers en-suite private rooms, round the corner on Union St (R1000; check-in at the backpackers). Dorm **R190**, double **R650**

Mount Nelson Hotel 76 Orange St ☎ 021 483 1000, ⓦ mountnelson.co.za; map p.72. Cape Town's *grande dame*: a fine and famous high-colonial Victorian hotel, built in 1899 (and extended in the late 1990s). Perfectly located, the building is set in extensive established gardens, and the entrance is via a majestic palm-lined colonnade. *Mount Nelson* takes itself terribly seriously and charges accordingly. Rooms are not that large, but its location makes it a highly popular choice for internationals in the movie industry, parliamentarians or anyone whose work trip is being sponsored. **R7565**

Once 73 Kloof St ☎ 0214246169, ⓦ stayatonce.com; map p.72. This hostel is ideal for long-term volunteers or international students staying in Cape Town, who can get hefty discounts (R3800/month room only). Accommodation is in modern four-bed dorms, twins, doubles or family rooms, all of which have private en-suite bathrooms. Rates includes breakfast at the adjacent trendy coffee shop, whose outside benches are always filled with guests, social chatter, or those soaking up the Kloof St atmosphere and free wi-fi. Dorm R235, double R850

TAMBOERSKLOOF
★**Amber Tree Lodge** 10 Kloof Nek Rd ☎021 422 4126, ⓦambertreelodge.co.za; map p.72. A small owner-run backpacker lodge, with a peaceful lounge that's draped in warm tapestries and opens onto a peaceful courtyard. Four-bed dorm rooms are light, and wooden bunks are spacious and solid. Dorm R180, twin R750, family room R1200

★**The Backpack** 74 New Church St ☎021 423 4530, ⓦbackpackers.co.za; map p.72. An excellent back-packers made up of four interconnected houses, where the interior has a spacious maze-like effect. It's on the cusp of the City Bowl suburbs and the city centre, and walkable to both. *The Backpack* has the best communal and outdoor space in the area; it features pool terrace, lounge area, restaurant, bar and garden, all furnished with bold colours. Accommodation is in dorms (sleeping 4–8) and private rooms; some rooms are suitable for families. Dorm R240, double R1200
Blencathra 4 Cambridge Ave, at De Hoop ☎021 424 9571, ⓦwww.blencathra.co.za; map p.72. A large,

---

AFRICAN TOWNSHIP HOMESTAYS

7

One of the best ways to get a taste of the African townships is to spend a night there, which is made possible by the growing number of township residents offering **B&B accommodation**. You'll have a chance to encounter the warmth of **ubuntu** – traditional African hospitality – by staying with a family with whom you'll eat breakfast and dinner; they will often take you around their local area to **shebeens** (unlicensed bars), music venues, church, or just to meet the neighbours. **Prices** go from R480–600 per double, which is considerably cheaper than the centre of Cape Town, and you'll get to experience something a little different.

Some B&Bs will send someone to meet you at the airport; if you're driving, they'll give you detailed directions or meet you at a convenient and obvious landmark. Booking can also be made through Cape Tourism Centre in Langa (☎021 695 4981, ⓦcapetowntravel.co.za).

KHAYELITSHA

Kopanong B&B C329 Velani Crescent ☎021 517 4206 or ☎082 476 1278, ⓦkopanong-township .co.za. One of the most dynamic B&B operations in Khayelitsha, run by the tireless Thope Lekau, who is on a mission to replace gawping tourists in their buses with guests who engage with township life. This former NGO worker will treat you to a history of the township, introduce you to local music and dish up a traditional family breakfast. A traditional dinner is available on request, as is a guided tour.
Majoro's 69 Helena Crescent ☎082 537 6882, ⓦmycapetownstay.com/MajorosB. The charming Maria Maile hosts guests in her family home, which has three rooms that share a bath and toilet. Dinner includes traditional dishes such as *mielie pap* (maize

porridge), or you can choose to eat in a neighbouring restaurant after which you can watch TV with the family or visit the local tavern. The next day you'll be treated to an English breakfast of sorts, which may include bacon and egg alongside fish cakes, sausages and home-made steamed bread.
Malebo's 18 Mississippi Way ☎021 361 2391. This B&B consists of five rooms, which share bath and toilet facilities, in the welcoming home of Lydea Masoleng and her husband. In the morning you'll be served a continental breakfast; dinners, which combine Western dishes with traditional African food, are available on request. You're welcome to join your hosts on outings to a *shebeen* or, on Sunday, to church.

LANGA

Ma Neo's 30 Zone 7 St ☎021 694 2504, ✉maneo @absamail.co.za. Friendly hostess Thandiwe Peter offers accommodation in two rooms outside the house and one inside the family home, in Cape Town's oldest township, and the closest to the city centre; most guests drive here. She will take guests to some of the township highlights, including a local *shebeen*.
★**Nombulelo's Guesthouse** 9 Harlem St ☎072 827 5228, ✉sicamba.nombulelo@gmail.com.

Located in a very walkable neighbourhood within the Langa Quarter, this is a great place to stay, with friendly service courtesy of the lovely owner, Nombulelo. It's close to *Ace's* tavern and the ten homes collectively turned into Langa Township Arts Gallery. This is one of the cheapest of the homestays, as there are beds available in a shared dorm room, with breakfast included, for R200.

7

relaxed family house with stunning views on the slopes of Lion's Head, 2km from the city centre and 4km from the Atlantic. The self-catering rooms are peaceful and spacious; four are en suite, and there's also an en-suite four-person women's-only dorm. The garden has seating, a swimming pool and a cute twin-bed chalet. Dorm R180, double R900

Zebra Crossing 82 New Church St ☎021 422 1265, ⓦzebra-crossing.co.za; map p.72. A no-frills backpacker lodge, with a child-friendly attitude, wi-fi and off-street parking – perfect if you are looking for something affordable that's close to town. On the northern edge of the City Bowl suburbs, it's an easy walk to the Kloof St restaurants and pubs, as well as those in the city centre. The café-bar serves full meals and decent coffee, and there are two pleasant terraces under vines. Accommodation is in spacious dorms, a double and a few singles, with the best rooms taking in views of the mountain. Dorm R120, double R420

ORANJEZICHT

2Inn1 Kensington 21 Kensington Crescent ☎021 423 1707, ⓦ2inn1.com; map p.72. Entering from a broad, quiet street into two adjacent renovated houses with bright, sleek furnishings and quiet music drifting over the lounge and dining area gives a feel of a welcoming, private café. The building backs onto a 10m swimming pool and deck area with sunbeds, where guests can enjoy complimentary beer, wine, tea and coffee at sundowner time. Rooms have private terraces and are equipped with all the usual mod cons, plus there are spa treatments available on site. R1900

★ **Acorn House** 1 Montrose Ave ☎021 461 1782, ⓦacornhouse.co.za; map p.72. Set among a row of guesthouses high on the hill towards Table Mountain, this 100-year-old residence has maintained its grandeur with a sweeping lawn, colonial furnishings and a sun-filled lounge room, and added the comforts of a pool, breakfast room, courtyard and Nespresso machine. Each room is

unique; rooms at the front of the house offer great city views, while the back shows off Table Mountain. Family rooms have their own private courtyards. Excellent value for money, great service and small touches make a stay here personal and memorable. R1400

Conifer Guest House 1 Jagersfontein Lane ☎021 461 3762, ⓦconifer.co.za; map p.72. Situated on a leafy narrow street, this peaceful guesthouse is lovely and quiet, with a homely feel, wooden floors and white linen. There is also an outdoor breakfast area, gas BBQ and one excellent value-for-money family room (R1550). R1150

Lezard Bleu 30 Upper Orange St ☎021 461 4601, ⓦlezardbleu.co.za; map p.72. This guesthouse offers seven en-suite rooms, furnished with maple beds and cupboards in a spacious open-plan 1960s house. A cosy lounge is perfect for reading, and a wall of sliding doors opens onto an outside deck, plus each bedroom backs right onto the garden and swimming pool. It also boasts one of the best accommodation spaces in central Cape Town – a treehouse room. Double R1330

Redbourne Hilldrop 12 Roseberry Ave ☎021 461 1394, ⓦredbourne.co.za; map p.72. This small four-room B&B oozes hospitality and the quiet charm of being a guest in someone's home. It has a modern exterior, while the interior, with high ceilings and wooden floors, is appointed with antique furniture. There's an outside plunge pool and a small breakfast room with a panoramic view of the city. Hefty off-season discounts are available. R1375

VREDEHOEK

African Sun 3 Florida Rd ☎021 461 1601, ⓔafpress @iafrica.com; map p.72. A small self-catering apartment, attached to a family house a little over 1km from the city centre. Furnished with pared-back ethnic decor, it's run by friendly, well-informed owners, who are both well-known published writers. They also offer literary evenings and tours as an extra. Good value. R650

SOUTHERN SUBURBS

Cape Town's gracious southern suburbs – **Rosebank**, **Claremont**, **Newlands** and **Rondebosch**, on the forested side of the mountain – are home to Kirstenbosch Gardens as well as the fine Newlands cricket and rugby grounds, Groote Schuur hospital and the University of Cape Town. **Observatory** is a few minutes' drive from the city centre and offers buzzing cafés, a couple of backpacker lodges and reasonable nightlife.

African Heart 27 Station Rd, Observatory ☎0761183213, ⓦbackpackersincapetown.co.za. This uniquely designed hostel is set in a Victorian house with wooden floors, comfy couches and bold murals and mosaics. There's also several chillout areas and an outdoor braai area, and reduced rates for long-termers (R5200/month including meals). Great if you want to be in vibey Obs or are connected with the hospital, university or various humanitarian aid

projects in the area. Dorm R130, double R440

Carmichael House 11 Wolmunster Rd, Rosebank ☎021 689 8350, ⓦcarmichaelhouse.co.za. A two-storey guesthouse, close to the University of Cape Town, in a building that dates from the early twentieth century and contains six big rooms. There's a peaceful garden, a swimming pool and secure parking, plus wi-fi or the use of a laptop at reception to check your email. R1360

Elephant's Eye Lodge 9 Sunwood Drive, Tokai ☎021 715 2432, ⓦelephantseyelodge.co.za. This friendly B&B family home has half a dozen rooms in a converted Cape Dutch farmhouse. Set in its own large grounds with a pool, the lodge is minutes from Tokai Forest, a golf course and the wine estates of Constantia. It's a 30min drive or 40min train journey (to Retreat) from the centre, though. R1000

★**The Vineyard** Colinton Rd, at Protea Rd, Newlands ☎021 657 4500, ⓦvineyard.co.za. One of the city's top stays, where the rooms are luxurious and better value than the *Mount Nelson* (see p.108). It's in a restored 1799 country villa, decorated in a contemporary style. The extensive gardens are like those of a peaceful country estate, with an outstanding panorama of the forested slopes of Table Mountain. Has a spa and large heated swimming pool – a great choice for a pampered stay. R2550

ATLANTIC SEABOARD

Historically Cape Town's hotel and seafront apartment block area, you'll find a range of accommodation available in **Sea Point**, which makes it a good alternative to the City Bowl if you want to be close to both the city centre and the ocean. **Green Point** is another appealing choice, as it's the closest suburb to the Waterfront, city centre and Waterkant, though it's not directly on the water. The well-heeled mountainside suburb of **Camps Bay** offers soaring views over the Atlantic, an upmarket Californian feel to its laidback restaurants and bars, and it has the advantage of being a hop over Kloof Nek to the cable-car and city centre. Further south and isolated around a bay is **Llandudno**, which, although it lacks shops or restaurants, boasts some similar vistas and a supremely beautiful beach. **Hout Bay** is the main urban concentration along the lower half of the peninsula, with a harbour, pleasant waterfront development and the only public transport beyond Camps Bay.

GREEN POINT

★**The B.I.G. Backpackers in Green Point** 18 Thornhill Rd ☎021 434 0688, ⓦbigbackpackers.co.za; map pp.90–91. A backpacker lodge with a light, clean, modern, rustic feel and which caters for a quieter crowd looking for a short-term home away from home. It has a fully equipped self-catering kitchen, braai area, two comfy lounge rooms, a separate TV room and a sunny outside garden with a plunge pool. Four-bed dorms are light and spacious and have private balconies. Prices include breakfast and coffee. Dorm R200, double R800

Dysart Boutique Hotel 17 Dysart Rd ☎021 439 2832, ⓦdysart.de; map pp.90–91. This luxury boutique hotel is styled in Afro chic, with a polished yet natural-looking interior. Each of the six rooms boasts a private balcony, flat-screen TV and minibar. The real draw, however, is what lies outside: two infinity pools, and wooden decking with sunbeds, umbrellas and tables – perfect for relaxing with a cocktail. R2100

Jambo Guest House 1 Grove Rd ☎021 439 4219, ⓦjambo.co.za; map pp.90–91. In a quiet cul-de-sac off Main Rd, this small, atmospheric establishment offers four luxury en-suite rooms, each decorated in a unique style, and one garden suite. The lush, leafy exterior and enclosed garden with a pond are delightfully soothing, and the service is excellent. R1500

Point B Guest House 14 Pine Rd ☎021 434 0902, ⓦpointb.co.za; map pp.90–91. Set in a 1900s house, this guesthouse has slightly out-dated bright decor, wicker furniture and a comfortable lounge room overlooking the garden. Upstairs are two modern rooms with small balconies, and the inside rooms lead onto private patios. Outside is a communal, leafy garden courtyard, where guests are spoilt for choice for lounging away on the wooden decking, sunbeds, in the mosaic plunge pool or at the shady breakfast tables. Great personal service. R1300

Wilton Guest Houses 15 Croxteth Rd ☎021 434 7869, ⓦwiltonmanor.co.za; map pp.90–91. This beautifully renovated Victorian guesthouse is set on a quiet street, close to the city centre. Outside is a spacious and sunny decking area with a homely atmosphere, breakfast tables and a plunge pool to cool off in. R1500

SEA POINT

★**Blackheath Lodge** 6 Blackheath Rd ☎021 439 2541, ⓦblackheathlodge.co.za; map pp.90–91. Down a quiet backstreet, but close to the Sea Point action, this superb owner-run guesthouse just gets everything right. The sixteen rooms in the Victorian home are large and airy (some with views of Lion's Head and sea views), and the king-size beds are the most comfortable you'll find in Cape Town. Breakfast is served on a courtyard-garden deck overlooking the pool and bar. R1850

Huijs Haerlem 25 Main Drive ☎021 434 6434, ⓦhuijshaerlem.co.za; map pp.90–91. This elegant and friendly guesthouse is made up of two adjacent houses furnished with Dutch antiques. Each of its eight rooms has a sea view, a vista of Signal Hill or overlooks the lovely garden. R1450

★**Stonehurst Guest House** 3 Frere Rd ☎021 434 9670, ⓦstonehurst.co.za; map pp.90–91. An airy tin-roofed Victorian residence with original fittings and furnished with an attractive melange of antiques and collectables by the friendly antique-dealer owner, Jan. There's a pleasant front garden, a kitchen for self-catering and a guest lounge. Most rooms are en suite, and some have balconies. Great value and location, a couple of streets back from busy Main Rd. R850

7

The Villa Rosa 277 High Level Rd ☎021 434 2768, ☻villa-rosa.com; map pp.90–91. A friendly eight-room guesthouse in a brick-red two-storey Victorian house on the lower slopes of Signal Hill, two blocks from the beachfront promenade. Decorated with simplicity and style, all rooms have TVs, phones and safes, but only some, on the upper floor, have sea views. R975

★**Winchester Mansions Hotel** 221 Beach Rd ☎021 434 2351, ☻www.winchester.co.za; map pp.90–91. In a prime spot across the road from the seashore, this 1920s hotel has an atmosphere straight from the pages of Agatha Christie, though the best rooms are thoroughly fresh and contemporary. A cool Italianate courtyard restaurant is overlooked by balconies draped in luxuriant creepers. R2500

CAMPS BAY AND BAKOVEN

★**Boutique@10** 10 Medburn Rd, Camps Bay ☎021 438 1234, ☻boutique10.co.za. A stay here is as if you're a welcome guest at a friend's lavishly appointed house. Owner managed, it has only four rooms, each one supremely comfortable with unique decor. Restored with reclaimed timber from an old hotel, the light and airy open-plan lounge-and-kitchen opens through French doors onto the outside decking area, complete with sunbeds, plunge pool and a stunning view of the Atlantic Ocean and Lion's Head. R2200

Camps Bay Retreat 7 Chilworth Rd, Camps Bay ☎021 437 8300, ☻campsbayretreat.co.za. The secluded Earls Dyke mansion house, set on a four-acre nature reserve in the middle of Camps Bay, is located a 5min walk away from the beach. Rooms, which are situated in the mansion, Deck House and Villa, are spacious and appointed with plush colonial furnishings, as are the main hotel foyer, lounge, reading room and fine-dining restaurant and bar. The bar, on the veranda above a gentle sweeping lawn, has good views of the Atlantic. The estate has a spa, three swimming pools (including one made to look like a natural mountain pool) and tennis courts. R4000

Ocean View House 33 Victoria Rd, Bakoven ☎021 438 1982, ☻oceanview-house.com. A river runs through the grounds of this family-run, eccentrically blue-and-yellow boutique hotel, set in a gorgeous garden that borders a *fynbos* reserve. The fourteen spacious rooms are comfortably and stylishly furnished and have either mountain or sea views. R1950

HOUT BAY, LLANDUDNO AND NOORDHOEK

★**Hout Bay Hideaway** 37 Skaife St, Hout Bay ☎021 790 8040, ☻houtbay-hideaway.com. An outstanding guesthouse with genuine verve – Persian rugs, Art Deco armchairs, huge beds – and generally bursting with luxurious touches. Each of the four rooms has a mountain or sea view and outdoor decks where your private breakfast is served. At the back, there's a saltwater infinity pool in a *fynbos* garden that disappears onto the mountainside. R1650

★**Houtkappersspoort** Hout Bay Main Rd, around 5km from Hout Bay and 15km from the city centre ☎021 794 5216, ☻houtkappersspoortresort.co.za. These rustic one- and two-bedroom, stone-and-brick self-catering cottages are close to Constantia Nek, sit right by the Table Mountain Nature Reserve. You can take paths straight from the estate up the mountain slopes, play tennis or take a dip in the solar-heated pool. R1600

Monkey Valley Resort Mountain Rd, Noordhoek ☎021 789 8000, ☻monkeyvalleyresort.com. Spread over several acres of Chapman's Peak, some 40km south of the city centre, is this attractive group of mainly wooden-and-thatched chalets. Overlooking Noordhoek Beach, the site is surrounded by indigenous vegetation, though the only monkeys you'll find are in the name. You can eat in the restaurant, self-cater or stay on a B&B basis, in a variety of accommodation options, depending on the size of the group. Double R1500, self-catering cottage R2130

Sunbird Mountain Retreat & Lodge Boskykloof Rd, Hout Bay ☎021 790 7758, ☻sunbirdlodge.co.za. Four pleasant, spacious, self-catering apartments and a guesthouse that includes a family unit, all nestled in a forest high up on the mountainside. Every room has a great view, and there's a secluded swimming pool. Double R1200, apartment R800

★**Sunset on the Rocks** 11 Sunset Ave, Llandudno ☎021 790 2103, ☻sunsetontherocks.co.za. This is a magical hideaway on one of the loveliest coves on the peninsula; three compact, self-contained flats sit in the midst of a wonderful *fynbos* garden belonging to charming proprietors Brian and Helen Alcock. Llandudno itself is shy of any shops and restaurants, but Hout Bay is only 10min away by car. R800

Tintswalo Atlantic Chapmans Peak Drive, Hout Bay ☎011 300 8888, ☻tintswalo.com/atlantic. Perched on the rocks below Chapman's Peak, within Table Mountain Reserve and with a view of the dramatic Sentinel Peak and the Atlantic Ocean, is this stunning luxury lodge. The large bedrooms are hedonistically furnished, each with ocean views and unique in style. Two large meditative decking areas, with a heated jacuzzi and a separate heated saltwater pool, lounge, bar, restaurant and wine cellar are all at guests' disposal. Situated in a spectacular and isolated place, you need to be transported from Chapman's Peak Drive to the lodge by Land Rover. R8520

7

FALSE BAY SEABOARD

This is the area to look in if you want to swim every day, surf or walk on beaches, as well as enjoy eating in some excellent restaurants. Once hugely popular because of its stunning beach and bay views, **Muizenberg**, 25km from the centre, is now a bit run down, and its peeling beachfront hotels have been replaced with surf schools and a couple of cafés. To its south is salubrious **St James**, while the crown jewel is **Kalk Bay** which boasts a working harbour, antique shops and arty cafés. Accommodation is limited in Kalk Bay, but you have a good chance of finding a self-catering apartment, the best online source for which is ⓦ safarinow.com. **Fish Hoek**, further south, is recommended for its beach but not much else; while pretty **Simon's Town**, 40km from town, is still regarded by many as a separate village, although it's now technically part of the Cape Town metropolis.

MUIZENBERG TO FISH HOEK

★**Chartfield Guest House** 30 Gatesville Rd, Kalk Bay ⓣ 021 788 3793, ⓦ chartfield.co.za; map pp.98–99. This well-kept, rambling house sits halfway up the hill overlooking the harbour, with terrific sea views from some rooms and a hop and a skip down the cobbled road or steps to some of the city's finest restaurants. Double R900, 3-bed self-catering cottage R2000

★**Cob House** 13 Watson Rd, Muizenberg ⓣ 021 788 6613, ⓦ cobhouse.co.za; map pp.98–99. The greenest B&B in Cape Town, *Cob House* is run by an exceptionally friendly family and set just 200m from the beach. There is only one, comfy guest room, but it can sleep up to four, and the reasonable rate includes a room-service organic breakfast. The owner, Simric Yarrow (teacher, storyteller and musician) also runs excellent tours around the city (ⓦ offbeatcapetown.yolasite.com). Double R750, family R950

The Mountain House 7 Mountain Rd, Clovelly ⓣ 083 455 5664, ⓦ themountainhouse.co.za; map pp.98–99. Beautiful self-catering accommodation equidistant between Fish Hoek and Kalk Bay. Built in the garden of local architect Carin Hartford, the two-bedroom cottage has windows on all sides to capitalize on the incredible mountain setting, and the living space flows out to a timber deck. R1050

Stoked Backpackers 175 Main Rd, Muizenberg ⓣ 082 679 3651, ⓦ stokedbackpackers.com; map pp.98–99. Vibey, well-run backpackers next to the station, over the railway line from Surfers Corner. Surfing or kite-surfing lessons can be arranged for you, as well as Cape Point trips or wine tasting in Stellenbosch. The best en-suite rooms (worth the extra cost) are on the upper levels with sunrise sea views, and when there is no wind, the upstairs terrace area that overlooks the beach is stunning. Dorm R135, double R550

Tranquility Guest House 25 Peak Rd, Fish Hoek ⓣ 021 782 2060, ⓦ www.tranquil.co.za; map pp.98–99. This warm and welcoming place, walking distance to the beach, is situated on Fish Hoek mountainside and offers good ocean views. There are four cosy B&B en-suite rooms, plus a self-catering apartment with its own entrance for the same price. Guests can soak in the outdoor jacuzzi. R1200

SIMON'S TOWN AND AROUND

Blue Bay 48 Palace Hill Rd ⓣ 021 786 1700, ⓦ bbay .co.za; map pp.102–103. A luxurious self-catering house with stupendous ocean views and tranquil ambience, 1km from the centre of Simon's Town. Sleeping is in one double and two twin rooms, and the entire place is rented as a whole. 2–3 people R900, 6 people R1800

Bosky Dell Cottages 5 Grant Rd, Boulders Beach ⓣ 021 786 3906, ⓦ boskyonbouldersbeach.co.za; map pp.102–103. Once a farmhouse overlooking the granite rocks and coves of Boulders Beach, *Bosky Dell* offers five simple and comfortable self-catering cottages. A path runs down to the beach, and there are wide lawns from which to enjoy the stupendous views. R800

Simon's Town Backpackers 66 St George's St ⓣ 021 786 1964, ⓦ capepax.co.za; map pp.102–103. Conveniently located in the heart of Simon's Town, within walking distance of the station, this boutique backpacker joint offers bunk-bed dorms and fairly spacious doubles, plus there's a large balcony with a view of the waterfront. You can rent bicycles here and ride to Cape Point, or arrange a kayak tour to paddle past the penguin colony. Dorm R190, double R380

Topsail House 176 St George's St ⓣ 021 786 5537, ⓦ topsailhouse.co.za; map pp.102–103. An old convent converted into a backpacker lodge, with more space than average, though the place is a tad staid. There are various accommodation options including an extraordinary bedroom in a chapel, though the en-suite doubles upstairs are the nicest. R750

LUNCHTIME AT *KALKY'S*

Eating

Eating out is one of the highlights of visiting Cape Town. The city has a large number of relaxed and convivial restaurants and cafés which generally serve imaginative food of a high standard. Prices are inexpensive compared with much of the developed world, and you can eat innovative food by outstanding chefs in upmarket restaurants for the kind of money you'd spend on a pizza back home. One element that seems to unite the country is a love of meat, and Cape Town is an ideal place to try out all kinds of interesting varieties, such as ostrich and springbok. As for seafood, you can expect fresh fish at every good restaurant. Cape Town itself is a good source of cold-water fish such as hake, often served as English-style fish 'n' chips, and snoek, a delicious but bony fish.

You're often better off going for a chef and their reputation, rather than choosing a place for its cuisine type. Note that as a visitor, you might struggle to keep in check the locals' assumption that meat – and lots of it – is the ideal choice for your meals, but **vegetarians** need not despair, as there's always at least one concession to meatless food on menus. Even steakhouses will have a meat-free option and generally feature reasonable salad bars.

Cape Cuisine (see box, p.118) must be sampled at least once. It's the exclusive focus of some restaurants in the city, though many of the dishes considered as Cape Cuisine have actually crept into the staple South African diet and can be found on menus throughout Cape Town, and indeed the country.

The obvious accompaniment to your meals is locally produced **Cape wine**, costing R60 and up for a bottle of something quaffable, though **beer** is definitely the national drink, and there are some delicious craft beers to sample (see p.127). Note that Muslim establishments serving Cape Cuisine don't allow alcohol at all.

Dining is generally rather **early** – don't expect to walk into a restaurant at 10pm and get a full or decent meal. Booking is essential for top restaurants.

A great addition to eating out in Cape Town is the collection of **neighbourhood food markets**, located in different areas of the city, in interesting venues such as a warehouse, city farm, old fish factory and former aeroplane hangar. Whether you're after artisanal cheese, organic produce, scrumptious burgers, craft beer or a glass of bubbly, you'll be spoilt for choice. The markets are on specific days and times – a few of the best-known ones are a great attraction for breakfast on Saturday mornings (see box, p.136).

8

CITY CENTRE

95 Keerom 95 Keerom St ☎ 021 422 0765, ☷ 95keerom .com; map p.48. Flash, fabulous and expensive, *95 Keerom* offers fresh and light Italian nouvelle cuisine, with dishes such as grilled beef, butternut ravioli or seared tuna (average mains R220). In 2013, chef Giorgio Nava won gold in a Pasta World Championship in Italy with his broccoli and anchovy *pasta primi* (R70). Mon–Sat 6.30–9.30pm.

Addis in Cape 41 Church St ☎ 021 424 5722, ☷ addisincape.co.za; map p.48. This friendly restaurant has a lovely laidback atmosphere. You'll find delicious traditional Ethiopian dishes on the menu, such as spicy red lentils (R109), served on yummy *injera* (sourdough flatbread) to soak up the flavours and eat with your fingers (R110). Mon–Sat noon–10.30pm.

Africa Café 108 Shortmarket St, Cape Heritage Square ☎ 021 422 0221, ☷ africacafe.co.za; map p.48. Probably the best tourist restaurant in Cape Town for African cuisine, with a fantastic selection of dishes from across the continent. Given that you're served a communal feast of sixteen dishes, and that you can have

as many extra helpings as you like, the R250-per-head price tag is pretty reasonable. Booking essential. Mon–Sat 6–10.30pm.

Biesmiellah 2 Wale St, at Pentz St, Bo-Kaap ☎ 021 423 0850, ☷ biesmiellah.co.za; map p.43. This is one of the oldest restaurants for traditional Cape Cuisine; rather than a sit-down meal, join local residents in the queue for their takeaway samosas and delicious savoury wraps called *salomes* (R48). There are plain veg or bean ones for vegetarians, but the most popular remain prawn or mutton. Mon–Sat 7.30am–10pm.

Birds Café 127 Bree St ☎ 021 426 2534, ☷ facebook .com/BirdsCafe; map p.48. There are long communal tables in this airy, central venue, where you can happily check your emails over a cappuccino. The cakes – especially the carrot (R40) – are recommended, and everything is plated on local pottery. Pasta dishes (R70) change according to what is seasonally available, and there are plenty of vegetarian options. Mon–Fri 7am–5pm, Sat 8am–2pm.

ETHICAL EATING

It's a sad fact, but fish stocks are declining worldwide. If you want to do your bit and be ecologically responsible, go for a tasty Cape fish like **yellow tail**, which is not endangered and has a low carbon footprint, coming straight from the seas around the city. Although kingklip and Cape salmon are on many menus, these are ones to avoid ethically. The **Southern African Sustainable Seafood Initiative (SASSI)** can inform you about the conservation status of different kinds of seafood and other issues related to fishing (☷ wwfsassi.co.za).

★**Bistrot Bizerca** 98 Shortmarket St, Heritage Square ☎021 423 8888, ⍟bizerca.com; map p.43. A gourmet bistro with a modern, funky feel and consistently good reputation. The food, from French chef Laurent Deslandes, is light, elegant and creative, and made using local ingredients. The options are arrayed on a blackboard and include delightful meat and fish choices (mains R150) and impressive desserts. Not cheap, but you never feel ripped off, and the service is excellent. Booking essential. Mon–Fri noon–2.30pm & 6–10pm, Sat evening only.

★**Café Mozart** 37 Church St ☎021 424 3774, ⍟madamezingara.com; map p.48. Sit under trees in a handsome street, or in the colourful and attractive interior with quirky antique pieces, for hearty breakfasts, high teas or a good glass of wine. Their "table of love" (R45) is a mix of fresh salads and breads, which make up a delicious and healthy lunch. Mon–Fri 7am–4pm, Sat 9am–3.30pm.

Charly's Bakery 38 Canterbury St, District Six ☎021 461 5181, ⍟charlysbakery.co.za; map p.43. Do not be fooled by the plain decor here: these are the most spectacular and decorative Mucking Afazing cakes in Cape Town. The bakery is in a modest location, and there are often queues out of the door. Try the red velvet cupcakes or wheat- and gluten-free lemon meringue cupcakes (both R20). They also do breakfasts and light lunches (around R50), and this is a good refuelling spot if you're visiting Cape Town's best bookshop, the Book Lounge (see p.134). Tues–Fri 8am–5pm, Sat 8.30am–2pm.

Eastern Food Bazaar The Wellington, Darling St ☎021 461 2458, ⍟easternfoodbazaar.co.za; map p.48. Cheap, canteen-style restaurant with an Indian and Cape Malay menu (mains R30). You queue up to order, and there are often long waits at lunchtime. It is busy, lively and portions are huge; *faloodas* and *lassis* are made fresh on-site. No alcohol is permitted. Daily 11am–10pm.

Headquarters Heritage Square, 100 Shortmarket St ☎021 424 6373, ⍟hqrestaurant.co.za; map p.48. There is only one thing on the menu here – prime free-range Namibian sirloin steak and butter sauce with perfect matchstick chips and salad (R175). On Friday nights, they have a DJ with relaxing beats; things hot up around 10.30pm, when the tables are pushed back for dancing. Mon evenings you get two meals for the price of one, and there are two sittings at 6pm and 8.30pm. Booking always essential. Mon–Sat 12.30–10.30pm.

Jason Bakery 185 Bree St ☎021 021 424 5644, ⍟jasonbakery; map p.48. With an unswerving local

following, Jason is renowned for his pastries, pies and sourdough rye bread. A pie favourite at this fashionable spot is braised pork belly and apple (R40), and the other offerings can be very imaginative – bangers-and-mash pie sometimes features on the menu, which changes daily. While bacon croissants and excellent coffee are standard breakfast fare, Sat is the bonanza baking day, when Jason will tweet his specials. For lunch, the most popular sandwich is chicken Caesar on rye (R60). Mon–Fri 7am–3.30pm, Sat 8am–2pm.

La Parada 107 Bree St ☎021 426 0330, ⍟107bree .co.za; map p.48. This restaurant serves the most authentic tapas in South Africa. Food is served on long, wooden communal tables and is moderately priced (tapas R18–48). You'll also find craft beer, reasonable cocktails and a bustling, noisy atmosphere. There is an identical sister restaurant in Main Rd, Kalk Bay. Daily noon–2am.

Mama Africa 178 Long St ☎021 424 8634, ⍟mamaafricarestaurant.co.za; map p.48. With food from around the continent, the menu here includes a mixed grill of springbok, impala, kudu, ostrich and even crocodile (mains R170). You can also sit at the 12m-long bar – in the form of a green mamba – and listen to live marimba music. Mon–Sat 6.30–11pm, Tues–Fri also 11am–4pm.

Mr Pickwick's Café and Bar 2 Greenmarket Place, 54 Shortmarket St; map p.48. This is the number-one place to come for cheap, early breakfasts, or midnight munchies, every day of the year. Hearty and cheap "tin-plate" meals, including a challenging range of hot and cold foot-long sandwiches (R50) are dished out even after the pubs close, as are decadent milkshakes. Daily 7am–2am.

Royale Eatery 273 Long St ☎021 422 4536, ⍟royaleeatery.com; map p.48. A hip hangout serving inexpensive gourmet burgers, with unusual combinations in the bun such as brie or roasted vegetables. Choose from lamb, beef, chicken and seven vegetarian patties including tofu. The Miss Piggy burger with bacon and guacamole (R75) is a favourite. It's usually packed, so book ahead, especially if you would like a balcony seat with street views. Mon–Sat noon–10.30pm.

Truth Coffee 36 Buitenkant St ☎021 200 0440, ⍟truthcoffee.com; map p.43. Truth are artisan coffee roasters who supply some of the best restaurants in Cape Town, so you'll get a great cup of coffee (R18) here in a venue with a chic industrial design built around a cast-iron vintage roaster drum. It's worth going for the "steampunk" decor alone, but go somewhere else to eat. Mon–Fri 7am–6pm, Sat 8am–6pm, Sun 8am–2pm.

V&A WATERFRONT AND DE WATERKANT

The **Waterfront** offers a variety of food, from chain eateries and unimpressive quick eats after a bout of shopping or before you take in a movie, to outdoor people-watching cafés and smart fish restaurants. You'll also find some of the best sushi in town here. **De Waterkant** has some nice places to eat; head for the Cape Quarter building with its array of restaurants, delis and cafés.

CAPE CUISINE

Styles of cooking brought by Asian and Madagascan slaves have evolved into **Cape Cuisine** (sometimes known as **Cape Malay** food – a misnomer given that few slaves came from Malaysia). Associated with Cape Town's Muslim community, the food is characterized by mild, semisweet curries with a strong Indonesian influence, and though it doesn't offer that much variety, it can be delicious. Dishes include **bredie** (stew), of which **waterblommetjiebredie**, made using water hyacinths, is a speciality; **bobotie**, a spicy minced dish served under a savoury custard; and **sosaties**, a local version of kebab, made using minced meat. For dessert, dates stuffed with almonds make a light and delicious end to a meal, while **malva** pudding is a rich combination of milk, sugar, cream and apricot jam.

THE WATERFRONT

Baia Upper Level, Quay 6 ☎021 421 0933, ⓦbaiarestaurant.co.za; map p.62. Sit on the terraced balcony and take in the views of Table Mountain while dining on masterfully cooked fresh fish and seafood; there's line-fish papillote (baked in a parchment paper parcel with tomato, courgettes, fennel and thyme; R150), or grilled kingklip is recommended if you want something simpler (R170). Booking essential, especially for dinner. Daily noon–11pm.

Caffè San Marco Piazza level, Victoria Wharf ☎021 418 5434, ⓦsanmarco.co.za; map p.62. This coffee shop and bar with outdoor seating offers an all-day breakfast menu, good sandwiches on Italian breads, wraps and fresh salads. The grilled calamari with garlic and chilli is delicious (R90), and they sell eighteen flavours of ice cream and sorbet. Daily 8am–11pm.

City Grill Shop 155, Victoria Wharf ☎021 421 9820, ⓦcitygrill.co.za; map p.62. An excellent, if rather touristy and pricey steakhouse, celebrating the meaty heart of South African cuisine. Their ostrich kebab (R195) is recommended, and you can't go far wrong with a full-blooded rump steak (R150). As an appetizer, try a plate of biltong and dry sausage (R79). The wine list is excellent, with 150 vintage wines to choose from, and there are good sea views which you can enjoy from outdoor tables under umbrellas. Daily 9.30am–11pm.

CITY BOWL SUBURBS

GARDENS

Aubergine 39 Barnet St ☎021 465 4909, ⓦaubergine .co.za; map p.72. This is an unbeatable choice for a five-star elegant dinner, with a garden to sit in and enjoy the top-quality Afro-Asian cooking of chef Harald Bresselschmidt. Expensive, but memorable, with a strong emphasis on fresh and local foods. Vegetarians can also find an inspired selection. A three-course menu will set you back R435, or R600 with wine. Mon–Sat 6–10pm, Wed–Fri also noon–2pm.

Bacini's Ristorante & Pizzeria 177 Kloof St ☎021 423 6668, ⓦbacini.co.za; map p.72. A reliable, bustling Italian restaurant. The wood-fired ricotta, spinach, aubergine and sundried tomato pizza (R85) is delicious.

Willoughby & Co Shop 6182, Lower Level, Victoria Wharf ☎021 418 6115, ⓦwilloughbyandco.co.za; map p.62. Despite a lack of sea views, this is hands down the best fish restaurant at the Waterfront, serving fantastic sushi and seafood (mains around R160) in a lively atmosphere. Daily noon–11pm.

DE WATERKANT

★**Anatoli** 24 Napier St ☎021 419 2501, ⓦanatoli .co.za; map p.62. This Turkish restaurant, a little on the pricey side but bursting with personality, is set in an early twentieth-century warehouse. It's great for vegetarians, and the excellent meze includes exceptionally delicious Greek vine-wrapped *dolmades* (R40), and there are at least twenty others to choose from on a starters platter. For meat eaters, look no further than the kebabs and rice (R135). *Anatoli* also serves superb desserts, such as pressed dates topped with cream (R50). Mon–Sat 6.30–10.30pm.

★**Origin Coffee** 28 Hudson St ☎021 421 1000, ⓦoriginroasting.co.za; map p.62. These coffee devotees serve home-roasted beans from across Africa and beyond to Asia and Latin America, and their range of teas is equally appealing. Although you can complement your drink with a little something to eat, food is secondary to the quality of the drinks (R70). Mon & Wed–Fri 7am–5pm, Tues 7am–3pm, Sat & Sun 9am–2pm.

Daily noon–10.30pm.

★**Bombay Bicycle Club** 158 Kloof St ☎021 423 6805, ⓦthebombay.co.za; map p.72. Don't expect Indian cuisine here, but do expect a great place for a fun evening out. There are things to play with in every area, whether you're sitting at a table with swings, or wearing silly hats. Food includes grills, soups, pastas and carpaccios (average mains R150). Booking essential, as it's often full. Mon–Sat 6–11pm (bar from 4pm).

Carlyle's on Derry 17 Derry St ☎021 461 8787, ⓦcarlyles.co.za; map p.72. A friendly place where you'll need to book in advance for a table. From 6pm they serve a great selection of thin-based, gourmet pizzas such as fig and blue cheese, Thai chicken and coriander, or lemon-infused ham and rocket (R80). They also serve meat dishes (R95–130), pasta (R60–85) and salads (R45–85). Daily 5.30–10.30pm.

Hudson's The Burger Joint 69 Kloof St ☎021 426 5974, ⓦtheburgerjoint.co.za; map p.72. This is a good place to come for gourmet burgers (R38–88), with trendy young patrons, loud rock music, craft beer, home-made lemonade and Bar One milkshakes (R40). Besides a huge choice of burgers, there are also decent salads, such as "The Good Girl" – butternut squash with feta (R60). Daily noon–11pm.

Mount Nelson Hotel 76 Orange St ⓦmountnelson .co.za; map p.72. Colonial-style afternoon tea, with a smart-casual dress code, in Cape Town's oldest and most gracious hotel is a culinary highlight of the city. The large tea tables are piled high with hot and cold pastries, classic savouries like smoked salmon sandwiches and scrumptious cakes. You can skip dinner after the R235 feast you get here. Book in advance online. Tea at 1.30pm & 3.30pm.

★**Saigon** 72 Kloof St, at Camp St ☎021 424 7670; map p.72. Serving authentic Vietnamese food, as well as sushi, this is a good place to come if you like Asian food (mains around R90). The chicken with cashew nuts is very tasty, as is the duck curry. The best spot to sit is close to the large windows which frame Table Mountain. The service is impeccable. Daily noon–2.30pm & 6–10.30pm, Sat evening only.

★**Societi Bistro** 50 Orange St ☎021 424 2100, ⓦsocieti .co.za; map p.72. A little pricey, this friendly bistro offers good Italian-style food, in a lovely restored building and garden virtually opposite the *Mount Nelson* hotel (see p.108) and Labia cinema (see p.131), with a fireplace for winter evenings. The risotto here is always a hit (R112), and starters include ox tongue (R55), chicken liver parfait (R58) and beetroot carpaccio (R39). There is always a vegan dish on the menu, too, such as quinoa curry with seasonable vegetables, sambals and roti (R83). Mon–Sat noon–10pm.

TAMBOERSKLOOF

Miller's Thumb 10b Kloof Nek Rd ☎021 424 3838, ⓦmillersthumb.co.za; map p.72. In a house on a residential street, this restaurant serves consistently good seafood dishes, with a selection of line fish prepared in a variety of ways and served in a cheerful environment. If you're not into fish, you might want to try their juicy steaks (R120). Mon & Sat 6.30–10.30pm, Tues–Fri 12.30–2pm & 6.30–10pm.

VREDEHOEK

Deer Park Café 2 Deer Park Drive ☎021 462 6311; map p.72. On the lower slopes of Table Mountain and with an enclosed park sloping below outdoor tables, this is the best central place to take children. Besides plenty for the little ones on the menu, like French toast made with ciabatta (R56), it's a great place to come without a family, too – not only for the setting, but for fresh, well-priced food. For lunch, the toasted ciabatta with a selection of hummus, feta, roasted peppers, olive tapenade and basil pesto is a winner (R70). Daily 8am–8pm.

★**Sidewalk Café** 33 Derry St ☎021 461 2839, ⓦsidewalk.co.za; map p.72. This modern, funky café has large windows and an enticing and imaginative menu (mains around R110). Whether you're after healthy and fresh or decadent, you're sure to find something here to suit your mood for breakfast, lunch or dinner. Vegetarians can do well, too – the grilled field mushrooms, roasted aubergine, olives, halloumi and harissa-mayo sandwich with salad is a good choice for a light lunch. Free wi-fi. Mon–Sat 8am–10.30pm, Sun 9am–2pm.

SOUTHERN SUBURBS

Catharina's Steenberg Estate, Constantia ☎021 713 2222, ⓦsteenberghotel.com. This restaurant, on a lovely wine estate and serving beautifully plated food, is ideal for an elegant, special (though not stiflingly formal) occasion. The evenings here are cosy, and you can lounge on the comfy bar sofas while sipping champagne made on the

---

AFRICAN FOOD

Around the centre of Cape Town you will find a couple of restaurants offering African food, but these are geared towards tourists – you would never find a full-blooded Xhosa eating in Long Street. The best way to experience the African food in the **townships** is by staying over in one of the B&Bs (see box, p.109), or by taking a tour that incorporates an organized township meal or a drink in a *shebeen* (see p.26).

Mzoli's Shop 3, NY 115, Gugulethu ☎021 638 1355. In the closest township to the centre, *Mzoli's* is often full of tourists, but you will get the real thing food-wise. It's best at lunchtime, when you can devour tasty barbecued meat (*tshisanyama* – "chi-san-knee-yama") ranging from chops, *boerewors* sausage, cuts of beef and lamb served with *pap* dumplings (thick maize porridge), meat sauce and *chakalaka*, a tomato salad. A meal will set you back about R50, and you'll need to call up for reservations and directions. Not suitable for vegetarians or those with small appetites. Daily 9am–6.30pm, Fri–Sun till 8pm.

8

estate. During the day, there are views through large glass walls onto the vineyard. Seafood and venison regularly feature on the menu, but if meat is not your thing, try the rich potato gnocchi with asparagus, peas, artichokes and a creamy parmesan sauce (R105). Breakfasts and lunches are served here too. Daily 7–10am & 11am–11pm.

Chandani 85 Roodebloem Rd, Woodstock ☎021 447 7887, ⓦchandani.co.za. You are unlikely to do better in Cape Town for Indian dining than at *Chandani*, which specializes in North Indian food. Vegetarians can breathe a sigh of relief at the array. Paneer dishes abound, and their house speciality is a mashed version with onions, peas and spices (R80). The restaurant is set in a tastefully restored Victorian house, in a gritty neighbourhood. Mon–Sat noon–3.30pm & 7–10pm.

Common Ground Café 23 Milner Rd, Rondebosch ☎021 686 0154. Attached to a church, this is an unlikely contender for the best coffee in town, but the baristas are true artists who take their business seriously and go beyond the norm to decorate the foam of your cappuccino to order. They also offer among the most reasonably priced breakfasts in town (R43) and have a small sandwich menu and pay-by-weight lunchtime buffet. The atmosphere is relaxed – there are sofas to recline on – and the views of Devil's Peak across Rondebosch Common are lovely. Mon–Fri 7am–4pm, Sat 8am–2pm, Sun 8.30am–2pm & 5.30–8.30pm.

Kirstenbosch Tea Room Restaurant Rhodes Drive, Newlands ☎021 797 4883, ⓦktr.co.za. The gorgeous garden setting and the pleasing, Cape country food – particularly the pickled fish (R106) or home-made burgers (R95) – is the draw here. They have some good options for vegetarians and you can order a gourmet picnic (R160/person) and even rent a picnic blanket (R30). Daily 8.30am–5pm.

★**The Kitchen** 111 Sir Lowry Rd, Woodstock ☎021 462 2201. Run by Karen Dudley, *The Kitchen* only uses the freshest ingredients to create fabulous, inventive sandwiches. Karen's "love sandwiches" on artisanal bread (R45) are especially popular, and there is an ever-changing range of salads. This is one of the best and cheapest places in town, especially if you are vegetarian, for a casual, lively, good-value lunch. The service here is fast, efficient and the whole place buzzes; it's not a place to linger. Mon–Fri 8am–4pm.

★**Pot Luck Club** Top Floor, Silo Building, Old Biscuit Mill, Albert Rd, Woodstock ☎021 447 0804, ⓦthepotluckclub.co.za. Set in a remarkable venue, this place is all about inventive, expensive and tasty tapas dishes (around R80 each). The menu is arranged according to sweet, salty, bitter and *umami* flavours; order several, and share with friends. Sweet tapas, such as bean-paste-glazed beef short rib with a steamed bun and pickles (R95), is not to be confused with a "sweet ending", such as pot luck pecan pie with celeriac ice cream (R60). You'll need to book a few weeks in advance and will be allocated a seating time – whether you'd get in on the off-chance is certainly not a matter of pot luck. Mon–Sat noon–2.30pm & 6.30–10pm, Sun 11.30am–2.30pm.

★**Test Kitchen** Old Biscuit Mill, 375 Albert Rd, Woodstock ☎021 447 2337, ⓦthetestkitchen.co.za. At South Africa's top, award-winning fine-dining contemporary restaurant, you may need to book months in advance for a table. Should you manage to get one, be prepared to be overwhelmed by the sensual feast of tastes, smells and colours provided by the astonishing creative mastery and craft of chef Luke Dale Roberts. The food on the ever-changing menu, such as confit duck leg with mushroom and liver stuffing, assorted onions, truffle-and-*foie-gras* egg and duck liver jus (R160), is innovative, often with unusual ingredients and combinations of flavours that you can enjoy in an industrial-style setting with a casual ambience. Tues–Sat 12.30–2pm & 7–9pm.

ATLANTIC SEABOARD

GREEN POINT

El Burro 81 Main Rd, Green Point ☎021 433 2364, ⓦelburro.co.za; map pp.90–91. This fun, casual spot offers Mexican food without too much cheese and grease (mains R100), plus a good view from the balcony of Green Point Stadium. There are plenty of veggie options, and the butternut enchilada is delicious (R65). Mon–Sat noon–11.30pm.

★**Giovanni's Deliworld** 103 Main Rd ☎021 434 6893; map pp.90–91. With both indoor and pavement seating (good for people-watching), this lively Italian deli and coffee shop is right across from the stadium and has its own screen for watching sports. It offers delicious coffee, excellent made-to-order sandwiches, salads and dips and good prepackaged meals (R45–65). Daily 8am–9pm.

Mano's 39 Main Rd ☎021 434 1090, ⓦmano.co.za; map pp.90–91. Popular with model-types and generally beautiful people, this place serves seafood, grills and pasta from a curiously mixed menu where you could find fish 'n' chips, Prego rolls or *penne arrabiata* (all around R70), as well as exciting salads, and one of the best *crème brûlées* in town (R60). After dinner, the party continues in champagne bar *Jade*, upstairs (see p.127). Mon–Sat noon till late.

MOUILLE POINT

Café Neo 129 Beach Rd ☎021 433 0849; map pp.90–91. *Neo* serves up deli-style food with a Greek influence, where mains are around R50–70. There are tasty breakfast options, such as Greek yoghurt with nuts and honey, or milky porridge with berries, and at other times there are meze platters, salads and sandwiches. A big draw is the umbrella-shaded outdoor seating area that offers views of either Green Point stadium or the lighthouse. Vegetarians can do well here, too. Daily 7am–7pm.

★**Newport Market and Deli** 47 Beach Rd ☎021 439 1538, ⓦnewportdeli.co.za; map pp.90–91. This light, airy deli, with views onto Table Bay, serves coffee, excellent sandwiches such as gourmet smoked salmon (R60), tasty salads such as watermelon & feta (R60) and some hot dishes such as macaroni cheese (R56) or chicken burgers (R45–75). The smoothies are packed with interesting blends such as pawpaw, mixed berries and mango (R32), and they make a welcome change from breakfast fry-ups and toasted sandwiches – just right if you are walking or jogging along the Sea Point promenade. Daily 7am–10pm.

Wakame and Wafu 47 Beach Rd ☎021 433 2377, ⓦwakame.co.za; map pp.90–91. *Wakame* serves trendy Asian-fusion food with killer desserts – try the chocolate and banana spring rolls. Every table has a view of the ocean, and upstairs is *Wafu*, a popular contender for the sundowner spot, where you can soak up the best sea views in Cape Town, classic martinis in hand (R45). *Wafu* offers a tapas and dim sum menu, while *Wakame* does more formal meals – the sesame-crusted seared tuna is top-notch (R130). Each place has its own sushi bar too, where six salmon roses will set you back R75. Booking essential. Daily noon–3pm & 6–10pm.

SEA POINT

La Boheme Wine Bar & Bistro 341 Main Rd ☎021 434 6539, ⓦlabohemebistro.co.za; map pp.90–91. Come here for an enjoyable and inexpensive night out. The menu is full of interesting, well-presented rural French food and lovely wines by the glass – there are at least sixty to choose from. Dishes, which are around the R85 mark, include ostrich meatballs with tagliatelli, potato gnocchi and roasted pork belly. There's pavement seating for people-watching. Next door is their sister espresso and tapas bar – great for a small bite to eat, and the coffee is fantastic (R80). Daily 8.30am–9.30pm.

Mr Chan 178A Main Rd ☎021 439 2239, ⓦmrchan .co.za; map pp.90–91. Worthwhile Chinese restaurant, which has been serving happy customers for the last twenty years with excellent Hong Kong-style beef, prawns, roast duck and, for vegetarians, braised bean curd and mixed vegetables. Lunch specials are R65, dinner set menus R150. Daily noon–2.30pm & 6–10.30pm.

CAMPS BAY, HOUT BAY AND NOORDHOEK

Café Caprice 37 Victoria Rd, Camps Bay ☎021 438 8315, ⓦcafecaprice.co.za. Directly opposite Camps Bay Beach (though the tables are on the pavement, not on the beach itself), this lively, albeit pretentious, Mediterranean-style restaurant is a great place to soak up street life,

sunshine and sunsets. You can get nibbles like hummus and pitta (R42), or more substantial fish or meat dishes, or just a drink. Daily 9am–midnight.

Café Roux Noordhoek Farm Village ☎021 789 2538, ⓦcaferoux.co.za. This chilled-out café sells wholesome and healthy food with a contemporary feel, and live music on Sun afternoons and some weekday evenings. They offer breakfasts (from R45), gourmet sandwiches (from R70), burgers (from R75) and other simple fare, with a menu (and garden) that caters to children. Sit under umbrellas with your "crazy duck" salad (R92) or have tea after doing Chapman's Peak, and gaze at the surrounding mountains. Daily 8.30–11am & noon–5pm.

★**The Foodbarn** Noordhoek Farm Village ☎021 789 1390, ⓦthefoodbarn.co.za. Gourmet French food from an acclaimed chef, Franck Dangereux, is served at reasonable prices here, compared to the other top restaurants in the city centre. The food is excellent, and worth suffering the slow service. Children are welcome, and you can sit on a sunny veranda in beautiful rural Noordhoek surrounds. Starters such as spicy fish soup (R72) will get your senses humming, and there are some interesting meats on the menu, such as grilled springbok rump served with turnip tatin, wilted English spinach, poached quince and port jus (R165). Each dish is paired with a wine, so you may need to organize a taxi to take you home after a lingering lunch. Booking essential. Daily noon–3pm, Wed–Sat also 7–9.30pm.

★**Kitima** 140 Main Rd, Hout Bay ☎021 790 8004, ⓦkitima.co.za. Cape Town's best Asian-fusion restaurant, with a definite Thai slant, is situated in a lovely Cape Dutch manor house, where the food couldn't be fresher and is prepared in front of your eyes. There's sushi and sashimi, dim sum and a plethora of seafood and meat stir-fries and curries, such as salmon *panang* (R125) or ostrich with lemongrass (R125). *Kitima* is best known for its sumptuous Sunday buffets (R250), for which you'll definitely need to book. Tues–Sat noon–10.30pm, Sun noon–3pm.

La Cuccina Food Store Victoria Mall, Victoria Rd, Hout Bay ☎021 790 8008. This high-quality deli and café is set in pleasant surrounds, and the delicious food compensates for the lack of sea views. At lunchtime, *La Cuccina* has a tasty buffet of quiches, salads and lasagne, sold by weight (R16/100g). The breakfasts are great, too. Daily 7am–5pm.

Paranga's Shop 1, The Promenade, Victoria Rd, Camps Bay ☎021 438 0404, ⓦparanga.co.za. Popular hangout at the beach, a place to see and be seen while you pick at expensive salads, seafood, pasta or sushi. There's a variety of champagnes on offer (R60), plus all sorts of wines, whiskys and cocktails while you watch the sun sinking into the ocean. Daily 9 am–midnight.

Wharfette Bistro The Harbour, Hout Bay ☎021 790 1100, ⓦmarinerswharf.com. A relaxed, well-run and

8

popular seafood restaurant, decorated with nostalgic photographs and memorabilia from Cape Town's passenger liner days. The views from the terrace seating that overlooks the harbour outshine the food, but it's a fine spot to eat fish 'n' chips (R55) while sipping a cold beer. Daily 10am–9pm.

FALSE BAY SEABOARD

MUIZENBERG

Casa Labia Café 192 Main Rd ☎021 788 6068, ⓦcasalabia.co.za; map pp.98–99. At *Casa Labia*, you can expect contemporary Italian food and English-style high teas in seafront *palazzo* surroundings, furnished with oil paintings, antiques and beautiful table linen. Set breakfasts include pancakes, eggs, pancetta, beef sausages, mushrooms, cherry tomatoes, sweet potato toast with jam and coffee or tea, all for R155. There's usually a good art exhibition on upstairs, and the small craft shop sells carefully chosen pieces. Courtyard dining comes with mountain views, and you can soak up the historical experience of being inside the grandest house along Muizenberg's historical mile. Tues–Sun 10am–4pm.

Empire Café 11 York Rd ☎021 788 1250, ⓦempirecafe .co.za; map pp.98–99. Enjoy good coffee and munch on fresh pastries while you sit upstairs at *Empire* and gaze at passing trains and the blue ocean beyond, or work at your computer, use free wi-fi and wait for the surf to come up. Their tasty pastas (R50) make a wholesome lunch, and your waiter may slide down the banisters to despatch your order, though it's a rather slower process bringing the goods up. Daily 7am–4pm, Sun from 8am.

KALK BAY

★**The Annex** 124 Main Rd, above Kalk Bay Books ☎021 788 2453, ⓦtheannex.co.za; map pp.98–99. The best outdoor venue in Kalk Bay, this restaurant has tables under red umbrellas, on a terrace with superb views onto the harbour and bay beyond. Don't come here for the views alone though, as the food is simply terrific. The eggs Benedict on *The Annex*'s own home-baked ciabatta (R45) is a firm favourite, and you can leave with another loaf tucked under your arm from their downstairs deli. Since the owner is a wine maker, you can expect an informed and interesting selection of Cape wines at lunch or dinner. Daily 8am–9pm, Sat & Sun from 7am.

C'est La Vie 20 Main Rd, opposite Dale Brook Pool ☎083 676 7430; map pp.98–99. Unassuming and tiny French-styled bakery which offers pavement breakfasts (R45), real baguettes and orange juice, croissants and excellent coffee. Wed–Sun 7am–3pm.

Harbour House Restaurant On the harbour ☎021 788 4133, ⓦharbourhouse.co.za; map pp.98–99. This memorable venue serves seafood and Mediterranean food, in a spectacular setting on the breakwater of Kalk Bay harbour. Book a table with bay views or enjoy sundowners on the deck. There's a fireplace and comfortable sofas which comes in handy in winter. Seafood options are the obvious choice – the Mozambique tiger prawns (R195) are worth a try, but there is also lamb and beef on the menu, and there are some options for vegetarians. Portions are small, but rich and beautifully plated. Booking is essential and you'll have to choose one of two sitting times. Daily noon–4pm & 6–10pm.

Kalky's On the harbour ☎021 788 1726; map pp.98–99. For years, this totally unpretentious eatery has been serving the fishing community the best traditional fish 'n' chips on the peninsula and great-value seafood platters. Fish is hauled off the boats and straight into the frying pan; wait a bit longer and you can have your catch grilled. You sit at benches to eat, and fish 'n' chips will set you back R56. Daily 10am–7pm.

★**The Olympia Café & Deli** Main Rd ☎21 788 6396, ⓦfacebook.com/OlympiaCafeKalkBay; map pp.98–99. This is one of the few places that draws parochial uptown Capetonians down to the False Bay seaboard. Always buzzing, a tad scruffy and with views of the harbour, *Olympia* offers great coffee accompanied by their own freshly baked goods. Gourmet lunch menus are chalked up on a board, with local fish and mussels often featured (mains around R100). They don't take bookings, so arrive early for dinner or join the queue. Their bakery is round the corner, where you can get bread, pastries, excellent takeaway coffee and sandwiches. Daily 7am–9pm, bakery till 5pm.

SIMON'S TOWN AND THE DEEP SOUTH

Black Marlin Main Rd, south of Simon's Town ☎021 786 1621, ⓦblackmarlin.co.za; map pp.102–103. Every kind of sea denizen, apart from the restaurant's namesake, is on the menu at this popular place on the road to Cape Point. (Tour buses pull in here for lunch, but their passengers are corralled off into a separate section.) While there's nothing wrong with the food, don't expect pyrotechnics, although the clifftop views from the outdoor tables make up for any lack of culinary fireworks – especially when there are whale sightings. Catch of the day costs R119, and weekend breakfasts are very cheap – scrambled egg on toast is R25. Daily noon–10pm, Sat & Sun from 9am.

★**Blue Water Café** Imhoff Farm, Kommetjie Rd, opposite the Ocean View turn-off ☎021 783 2007, ⓦimhofffarm.co.za. This is the best restaurant to stop at if you are on a Cape Point round route – the menu offers surprisingly good fish (mussels R90), pasta (R86), wood-fired pizzas (R70) and wines, and they also do breakfasts and teas. Set in a handsome Cape Dutch homestead, there are good

8

views onto the wetlands and ocean beyond, and there's a fire to warm the place in winter. Service is attentive, and you can book a table outdoors next to a large lawn, where children can play – plus there's plenty at the farm to keep them occupied. Tues 9am–5pm, Wed–Sun 9am–9pm.

Camel Rock Main Rd, Scarborough ☎021 780 1122. A local hangout that makes scant effort to cater to tourists, this homely joint is notable more for the fact that it's the only place for a beer and bite in far-flung Scarborough, than for its unexceptional seafood dishes (R105). 11am–9pm; closed Tues.

Salty Sea Dog 2 Wharf St, Waterfront, Simon's Town ☎021 7861918, ⓦsaltyseadog.co.za; map pp.102–103. There's nothing fancy about this small restaurant on the wharf, but they do plain old fish 'n' chips (R40) extremely well, and they serve beer and wine. With indoors and alfresco seating, it makes a great lunch stop on an outing to Cape Point. Mon–Sat 8.30am–9pm, Sun (takeaways only) 8.30am–4.30pm.

Tibetan Teahouse 2 Harrington Rd, Seaforth Beach ☎021 786 1544; map pp.102–103. Traditional Tibetan recipes are served up here from a completely vegetarian menu, with offerings such as yak-free lentil stew (R60). You'll find the venue signalled by its prayer flags, close to Boulders Beach and on the way to Cape Point. Tues–Sun 10am–5pm.

Two Oceans Cape Point ☎021 702 0703, ⓦtwo -oceans.co.za. The real star of the show at this primarily seafood-focused restaurant is the sublime view from its alfresco deck that seems to float out a million miles above the ocean, taking in the whole of False Bay and its mountains – this is a great place to see whales in season. As well as a large fish and seafood menu including the "smack of sea" antipasti, with mackerel, prawns, cured trout, Cape yellowtail, crispy squid heads, pickled mussels and snoek pâté (R230), they also do sushi and some meaty options, plus there's a kids' menu and fried breakfasts (R60) till 11am. Daily 9am–4pm.

8

Drinking and nightlife

Being a hedonistic city – especially in the summer – Cape Town has plenty of great places to drink and party, especially on Long and Bree streets where it's safe and busy, and there are taxis to get you home. In the summer, the Atlantic Seaboard, notably Camps Bay, is a great option, where the party starts with the first sundowners. When it comes to live music, the best-known South African musicians are sadly better appreciated, and better remunerated, abroad than in their own country. But if you dig deeper you will find fine examples of South African jazz being played to a small, appreciative crowd. Whatever your scene, from rubbing shoulders with artists and actors in hip wine-bars to sweaty electronic music dancefloors, grungy nightclubs and open-air artisanal beer gardens, Cape Town has it all.

ESSENTIALS

Opening hours Most liquor licences stipulate that the last round is served at 2am, although recently some have been granted until 4am. Clubs get going after 10pm and are pretty international in flavour, with DJs mixing house hits you're bound to recognize. Laws prohibit bottle stores from selling liquor from 6pm on Sat and all day Sun.

Prices How much a drink costs obviously depends on the venue – a standard beer in a sports bar might set you back R18, with local craft brews costing upwards of R45. A smart bar will charge up to R65 for a cocktail, while glasses of

delicious Cape wine begin around R35. Some clubs may have a cover charge for live music or DJs, ranging from R20–100.

Food You'll find that many drinking places are also restaurants, and may be better known as the latter; in a city where wine is produced, food and wine definitely go together. Many bars and clubs offer food as well.

Safety It's really not a good idea to walk around late at night, not least because of dangerous drunk drivers on the road. Take a taxi number out with you to get from bar to bar, or back to your hotel (see box below).

LONG STREET AND BREE STREET

Aces 'N' Spades 62 Hout St ☎021 424 1620, ⓦacesnspades.com; map p.48. This place is usually jam-packed from the bar (bottled beers R20), where chic meets grunge, to the heaving dancefloor where rock 'n' roll music sets the tempo for enthusiastic dancing. A safe bet for a great night out, if you don't mind a mass of bodies and a croaky voice in the morning. Mon–Sat 7pm–2am.

The Beerhouse 223 Long St ☎021 424 3370, ⓦbeerhouse.co.za; map p.48. With a menu comprising 20 taps and 99 bottles, 75 percent of which are local craft brews, it's no wonder a whole day can go by at this modern "beer hall" without moving from the large balcony overlooking Long St. It's quite expensive (pint R40–70) and not conducive to thoughtful beer tasting, but the large tables are perfect for groups. Daily noon–late.

Dubliner @ Kennedy's 251 Long St ☎021 424 1212, ⓦdubliner.co.za; map p.48. Crammed, wildly popular traditional Irish pub with Guinness and Pilsner on tap (R28), pub meals from lunch until midnight daily, and live music from 10pm every night. Other features include flat screens for sporting events and a pool table. Cover charge R60–70 Fri & Sat. Daily 11am–4am.

Fiction Bar 226 Long St ⓦfictionbar.com; map p.48. *Fiction* hosts standout electronic music nights and never fails to bring in high-quality local and international DJs; the

likes of Skrillex, Diplo, Pendulum and Noisia have popped in for impromptu sideshows. Lose yourself on the energetic dancefloor, then head out to the balcony overlooking Long St to recover. Bottled beers R18; cover charge R30–60. Tues–Sat 10pm–4am.

Jo'burg 218 Long St ☎021 422 0142; map p.48. A good, if crowded, place to hang out, grooving to a fresh soundtrack or playing pool against one of the local patrons. Many people end up here at some point during a night out on Long St, and it's one of the few places open on Sun nights. Cool off on the open-air patio outside. Bottled beer R18. Mon–Sat noon–4am, Sun 6pm–4am.

★**La Parada** 107 Bree St ☎021 426 0330; map p.48. With its open windows, vibrant atmosphere and creative Spanish tapas menu, *La Parada* is a highlight of the hip bars on Bree and the long, sociable tables are filled with well-heeled Capetonians from lunch through to late. Cocktails range from R55–65, while a glass of wine will set you back R35. No bookings. Daily noon–2am.

★**TjingTjing** 165 Longmarket St ☎021 422 4374, ⓦtjingtjing.co.za; map p.48. This rooftop cocktail bar is a low-key favourite for young professionals with its upbeat soundtrack and mouthwatering cocktail menu (R50–65) – expect unusual ingredients like candyfloss vodka and balsamic vinegar. Tues–Fri 4pm–2am, Sat 6.30pm–2am.

GETTING HOME SAFELY

Most Capetonians you meet will tell you that walking around after dark, alone and inebriated, is to be avoided at all costs. Heed their words; even if you are in a group never carry your wallet or phone in your front or back pockets as you will be quickly relieved of your possessions by light-fingered thieves. There are many independent and official cabs roaming the streets, but we recommend the following for a prompt, reliable and safe service.

City Cabs ☎021 202 2222. Open 24hr and one of the best radio-controlled taxi services: fares are R12 a kilometre with a minimum fee if booked in advance (R16 for first 3km).

Excite Taxis ☎021 448 4444. Fares are R9 a kilometre within their normal operating area (city centre to southern suburbs; open 24hr), but there

may be an additional charge if your pick-up or drop-off point is further flung than this.

Rikkis ☎0861 745 547. Rikkis has one of the lowest fare-structures in town and operates in Hout Bay and the southern suburbs (Mon–Thurs 6.30am–2am, Fri–Sun 24hr) as well as the city centre (daily 24hr) and they also offer a cheaper option for shared rides.

9

TOP 5 BARS FOR MUSIC-LOVERS

Electronic dance Fiction; see p.125
Alternative rock Aces 'N' Spades; see p.125
Live bands The Dubliner; see p.125
Pop Tiger Tiger; see opposite
Smooth tunes Shimmy Beach Club; see below

Weinhaus + Biergarten 110 Bree St ☎ 021 422 2770, ⓦ biergarten.co.za; map p.48. For a great atmosphere and outdoor seating in the inner city, there is nowhere better: sample delicious craft beer (brewed in Europe; R45 a pint) in *Biergarten* or a wide selection of wines exclusive to their wine rooms, *Weinhaus*. Smack bang in the middle of the rejuvenated Bree St precinct, this is a popular place for after-work drinks with plenty more trendy wine bars in the vicinity. Tues–Thurs & Sat 3–11pm, Fri noon–11pm.

Zula Sound Bar 194 Long St ☎ 021 424 2442, ⓦ zulabar.co.za; map p.48. Live, local talent of variable quality (music, comedy and the odd poetry reading) is showcased here every night, while the well-priced restaurant serves-up nachos, salads, chicken wings and burgers alongside Cape wines and tap beers (R30). There's also a balcony and a games room. Cover charge R20–100. Tues–Sun 11am–4am.

ELSEWHERE IN THE CENTRE

Alexander Bar, Café & Theatre 76 Strand St ☎ 021 300 1088, ⓦ alexanderbar.co.za; map p.43. Handsomely furnished in old-world decor, this is a good spot for a quiet conversation or nightcap and a much needed addition to Cape Town's social scene. Old rotary phones in the bar even allow you to call the table next to you while sipping a single malt (R40). Upstairs is an intimate theatre space which hosts music, comedy and plays. Mon–Sat 11am–1am.

Evol 69 Hope St ☎ 021 465 4918; map p.43. Named after a Sonic Youth album, this is the best club in town to hear DJs mix alternative, electro, punk and particularly indie music for a committed crowd. Good dancing, open late into the night, but in a grungy and slightly dingy venue. Cover charge R20. Bottle beer 375ml/R18. Mon–Sat noon–4am.

The Power and The Glory 13d Kloof Nek Rd ☎ 021 422 2108; map p.72. On any night of the week "PnG's" is a magnet for hipsters sporting neatly trimmed beards, checked shirts, red lipstick and vintage dresses. The well-styled bistro, kitted out with old-school metal chairs and botanical drawing prints, serves coffee during the day then blends seamlessly with a smoking room and cosy bar serving craft beers (pint R45) at night. Mon–Sat 8am–2am.

Rafiki's 13B Kloof Nek Rd, Tamboerskloof ☎ 021 426 4731, ⓦ rafikis.co.za; map p.72. A laidback bar with a wraparound veranda where you can hang out all day slowly getting sozzled, cheering on sports teams on the big screen or making use of the free wi-fi. There are roaring fires during the winter months, and it's popular with students, backpackers and locals alike. Try their chilli-poppers, everything-on-it pizzas and a house cocktail (R45). Daily 11am–2am.

V&A WATERFRONT

The Waterfront is good for a quiet drink, boasting a couple of good bars in a triangle close to each other. The party heats up in Somerset Road and up into De Waterkant, and there are a couple of good spots in Green Point, near the Stadium. Most of the places in De Waterkant are listed in the "Gay Cape Town" chapter (see p.143).

Alba Cocktail Lounge Pierhead, above the Hilderbrand Restaurant ☎ 021 425 3385, ⓦ albalounge .co.za; map p.62. Cocktails and snacks in a stunning setting, equipped with sofas and fireplace for winter, looking out over the Waterfront. In summer, enjoy an Albatizer (made with JellyTots and Apple Sourz; R30) on the outdoor deck. Live music twice a week; DJ daily 5pm to closing. Daily 11am–1am.

Quay Four Tavern Quay Four ☎ 021 419 2008, ⓦ quay4.co.za; map p.62. Established nearly twenty years ago, the *Tavern* is an old favourite with tourists and locals alike. Watch the world go by with a drink on the terrace overlooking the V&A (pint tap beer R30), share a hearty pub meal with friends or catch the nightly free live music. Daily 11am–2am.

Shimmy Beach Club 12 South Arm Rd ⓦ shimmybeachclub.com; map p.62. With a private beach, outdoor deck and an infinity plunge pool to boot, it's no wonder the luxurious *Shimmy Beach Club* is draped with beautiful people day and night. Completing the flashy setup are an upmarket restaurant, indoor dancefloor, expensive cocktail menu (R40–60) and live local and international electronic-music acts every Sun during summer. Cover charge R100–250. Daily 11am–2am.

SOUTHERN SUBURBS & FALSE BAY SEABOARD

Brass Bell Kalk Bay Station, Main Rd, Kalk Bay ☎ 021 788 5455, ⓦ brassbell.co.za; map pp.98–99. The *Brass Bell* has arguably the best location on the peninsula, with False Bay's waves breaking against the wall of its outdoor terrace. It's a fantastic watering hole, with a range of wines by the glass (R30) and tap beers (pint R28–35), and decent fish and chips if liquid nourishment is not enough. *Daily 11am–10pm.*

Foresters' Arms 52 Newlands Ave, Newlands ☎021 689 5949, ⓦforries.co.za. Preppy students and professionals gather to quaff beer (bottles R18) at the very popular and busy "Forries" in the heart of leafy Newlands. A big wood-panelled pub, it boasts a beautiful hedged-in courtyard where you can grab a bench for a lazy afternoon pint. *Mon–Thurs & Sat 9am–11pm, Fri 9am–midnight, Sun 9am–9pm.*

The Polana Kalk Bay Harbour, off Main Rd, Kalk Bay ☎021788 7162, ⓦharbourhouse.co.za/polana; map pp.98–99. *The Polana* has a spectacular setting right on the rocks; in the summer you can nestle on battered couches and cushions by the open windows to watch the waves crashing in while a fire burns cheerily in winter. Local wines feature heavily on the drinks list (from R25 a glass) and there's also a short tapas menu; the only drawback is that smoking is allowed in the drinks/lounge area. There's often live music and dancing Sun evenings. *Daily 6–10:30pm.*

Tiger Tiger 103 Main Rd, Claremont ☎021 863 2220, ⓦtigertiger.co.za. *Tiger Tiger* is a reliable for parties, with six luxurious bars and a spacious dancefloor pumping commercial music out of a state-of-the-art sound system; Sat nights are especially good. Cover charge R50; bottled beers R18. *Thurs–Sat 8pm–4am.*

ATLANTIC SEABOARD

Café Caprice 37 Victoria Rd, Camps Bay ☎021 438 8315, ⓦcafecaprice.co.za. This beach-facing hangout, popular with tanned and gorgeous celebs and wannabes, is just right for cocktails (R55). Families are welcome during the day for breakfast and lunch, but the pace increases at sunset and pavement tables are like gold dust. *Daily 9am–late.*

Dunes 1 Beach Rd, Hout Bay ☎021 790 1876, ⓦdunesrestaurant.co.za. Right on Hout Bay beach, this is a popular hangout for families, especially on sunny weekend afternoons when kids roar about. Drinks include tap beer (R28) and cocktails (from R40). *Daily 9am–10pm.*

Jade Champagne Bar 39 Main Rd above Manos Restaurant, Green Point ☎021 439 4108, ⓦjadelounge.co.za. Classy lounge-bar with nightly DJs, plush sofas, chandeliers and a semi-enclosed balcony to relax on with a cocktail (R55). Over 23 only; reservations recommended. *Wed–Sat 8pm–2am.*

ALL ABOUT THE BEER

While the bulk of all **beer** production in the country is monopolized by the huge South African Breweries (SAB; tours Tues–Sat 10am–6pm; R75; ⓦnewlandsbrewery.co.za), one of the world's largest beer makers and the oldest brewery in Africa, South Africa's beer landscape has recently undergone a small transformation, propelled by a global **microbrew** renaissance in the USA, Australia, New Zealand and the UK. Dozens of microbreweries have popped up – including Jack Black, Boston, Darling Brew, Mitchell's and Cape Brewing Company – making excellent versions of popular American and European beer styles like weis, IPA, amber and pale ales. One interesting trend to watch out for is the beer-wine hybrids and experimental beers aged in wine barrels, currently produced by microbreweries such as Devil's Peak and Triggerfish who are taking cues from South Africa's booming winemaking industry.

You can take a dip into the world of craft beer in South Africa and find out about the latest festivals on ⓦthecraftbeerproject.co.za. Below are our top three places to sample **craft beer** in Cape Town:

★**Banana Jam Cafe** 157 2nd Avenue, Kenilworth ☎021 674 0186, ⓦbananajamcafe.co.za. Although not centrally located, this Caribbean-themed restaurant is the place to go for a relaxed introduction to the spectrum of South African beer. Their knowledgeable staff will talk you through their ever-increasing selection of local and imported beers, most of which are exclusive, plus weekly guest beers (pint R36–45) – try the six-sample tasting plate. *Daily 11am–late.*

Devil's Peak Taproom 95 Durham Ave, Salt River ☎021 200 5818, ⓦdevilspeakbrewing.co.za. Sample the entire Devil's Peak range in their chic, colonial-style bar-restaurant, directly adjacent to the brewery (pint R30–45), where the magic happens. As well as an excellent regular menu they also offer beer and food pairing. *Tues–Sat noon–10pm.*

The Wembley Tap 80 McKenzie St, Gardens ☎021 300 0946, ⓦwembleytap.co.za. Handily located in the city centre, offers thirty local and imported beers on tap (pint R38–45), and some exclusives, in minimal, industrial surroundings. There's also a large beer garden and menu of stomach-lining pizzas. *Mon 4–11pm, Tues & Wed noon–midnight, Thurs–Sat noon–1am.*

The arts and film

You'll find a satisfying and easily accessible range of dramatic and musical performances on offer in Cape Town, while the visual arts and design are thriving across the city. Theatres are scarcely full and tickets are a bargain compared to the prices you'd pay in London or New York. You are likely to find something appealing at the two major arts venues, the Baxter and Artscape, be it a play, a classical concert, some opera, contemporary dance or comedy, while the Fugard Theatre is also well worth investigating. Cape Town is known for its brand of Cape jazz, but there is nowhere regular to pick that up; the best jazz event of the year happens in late March at the annual Cape Town International Jazz Festival (see p.30).

ESSENTIALS

Listings Social media, websites of major ticket outlets, posters tied onto street lights and the daily *Cape Times* and *Argus*, which carry listings and reviews, are good for discovering what's on. The *021* listings magazine (ⓦ021cape.com) on sale at Vida e Caffè stores and bookshops, has a comprehensive selection of cultural listings.

Tickets Tickets for most of the venues and performances listed in this chapter are available from Computicket (ⓣ0861 915 8000, ⓦcomputicket.com) or Webtickets (ⓣ0861 22 5598, ⓦwebtickets.co.za). Most ticket prices are very reasonable at R90–200.

THEATRE AND MUSICALS

Cape Town's premier physical theatre company, **Magnet** (ⓦmagnettheatre.co.za), produces consistently excellent, politically conscious, non-didactic physical theatre. Some productions collaborate with **Jazzart** contemporary dance and theatre company (ⓦjazzart.co.za) where you'll see the finest black dancers in town, who have forged a fusion of Western and African dance in their work.

African Dance Theatre Moyo, Clock Tower, V&A Waterfront ⓣ021 424 9513, ⓦtheafricandancetheatre .co.za. Although distinctly for tourists, the African Dance Theatre gives a small snapshot of African dance culture with enthralling performances of warrior dances and township inventions like the gumboot dance, *pantsula* and *kwela*.

Alexander Bar, Café & Theatre 76 Strand St ⓣ021 300 1088, ⓦalexanderbar.co.za. An intimate 45-seat space which hosts music, comedy, play readings and theatre, many of which are written and performed by local playwrights, actors and artists, giving a real taste of the South African arts scene. From R40.

Artscape D.F. Malan St, Foreshore ⓣ021 410 9838, ⓦartscape.co.za. Cape Town's most central and largest arts venue, where major productions are staged. Catch some contemporary dance, ballet or opera, with some adventurous new dramas appearing periodically. Don't be intimidated by the monumental 1970s apartheid architecture.

Baxter Theatre Centre Main Rd, Rondebosch ⓣ021 685 7880, ⓦbaxter.co.za. This mammoth brick theatre complex – its design inspired by Soviet Moscow's central train station – is the cultural heart of Cape Town, mounting an eclectic programme of innovative plays, comedy festivals, jazz and classical concerts and kids' theatre. It's the first place to check out what's on when you hit town.

Fugard Theatre Caledon St, District Six ⓣ021 461 4554, ⓦthefugard.com. On the east side of central Cape Town in the old District Six, the Fugard Theatre runs a cross-section of interesting productions in a stylishly renovated church – it has a particularly nice ambience for a pre- or post-show drink.

Maynardville Open Air Theatre Piers/Wolfe St, Wynberg ⓦmaynardville.co.za. Every year for Jan and Feb only, an imaginative production of a Shakespeare play is staged by the cream of Cape Town's actors and designers under the summer stars in Maynardville Park.

Theatre On The Bay Camps Bay ⓦtheatreonthebay .co.za. Known for taking headline news from overseas and adapting them to the local stage using South African actors, Theatre On The Bay puts on Liberace-esque performances of drama, musicals, comedy, cabaret, music and dance.

CAPE TOWN'S FINEST

Athol Fugard is historically the best known of South African playwrights internationally, even producing fine work these days through a steady trickle of innovative plays. Concerned with forging a new African or fusion theatre, Fugard has long out-sped the days of didactic protest theatre – most critically acclaimed are *Bosman and Lena* and *Master Harold and the Boys*. More controversial is the brilliant **Brett Bailey**, a white man more "township" than many blacks, who creates electrifying, chaotic visual and physical theatre with his company **Third World Bunfight** (ⓦthirdworldbunfight.co.za). The company does theatre productions, installations, house music shows and opera, mostly concerned with the post-colonial landscape of Africa. You're as likely to catch his works in Europe as you are in Cape Town. Cape Town-born RSC actor **Sir Anthony Sher** is the city's most famous son, appearing every other year in the mother city in some fabulous productions.

As regards **musicals**, **David Kramer** and the late **Taliep Petersen** produced several hit shows, although Kramer is best known for his show *Kitaar Blues*, sung in Afrikaans with township and Cape rhythms. He doesn't perform often now (ⓦdavidkramer.co.za), but the soundtrack to *Kitaar Blues* is on sale from ⓦkalahari.net or the African Music Store, 134 Long St.

COMEDY

Comedy has a well-established following and is very popular, particularly with coloured Capetonians, making the mix of Afrikaans and cross-cultural inference potentially bewildering for outsiders. South Africa's best-known stage satirist is **Pieter Dirk Uys**, whose character **Evita Bezuidenhout**, South Africa's answer to Dame Edna Everidge, has relentlessly roasted South African society since apartheid days. He often performs in Cape Town, though the best place to catch him is over the weekend in Darling, an hour away. New generation home-grown comedians to look out for include **Marc Lottering**, a coloured Capetonian who derives his material from his own community; **Nik Rabinowitz**, an irreverent middle-class Jewish boy who uses his fluency in Xhosa to poke fun at cultural stereotypes; and **Riyaad Moosa**, a Muslim doctor-turned-comedian. If you can get a seat at one of his sold-out shows, **Trevor Noah** from Gauteng is one of the most talented young South African stand-ups, whose leading themes are often political and centred around his mixed-race heritage.

★ **Evita se Perron** Darling Station, Arcadia Rd, Darling ☎ 022 492 2831, ⊛ evita.co.za. An hour's drive north of Cape Town, on the R27, the town of Darling is well worth visiting for its camply converted train station, which plays host to the satirical shows of Pieter Dirk Uys. It makes for a great day out, and is a notable highlight of a stay in South Africa. Since it is dependent on Pieter Dirk Uys's schedule, check the website for dates.

Jou Ma Se Comedy Club The Pumphouse, V&A Waterfront ☎ 021 418 8880, ⊛ joumasecomedy.com. A dedicated comedy venue in Cape Town, run by comedian Kurt Skoonraad, which features up and coming South African comedians as well as established acts like Rob Van Vuuren. Their website also carries info about any other comedy events and clubs in the city. R95

On Broadway 44 Long St ☎ 021 424 1194, ⊛ onbroadway.co.za. One of the few venues committed to the city's small cabaret scene is this fun bar-restaurant with live performances, comedy and music for a big crowd every night of the week. Ticket prices are appealingly lower than mainstream venues. Daily 6.30pm–late.

CLASSICAL MUSIC

Classical music is thriving, albeit for small and elite audiences, and one of the best things you could take in on a visit to Cape Town is an **opera** (⊛ capetownopera.co.za). As in all areas of the arts, there is a quest for fusion, which has given rise to some fascinating performances, usually with an almost totally black cast boasting some of the most superb voices in the country, a great statement about opera crossing cultural barriers and centuries. **Symphony concerts** are usually held at the City Hall and Baxter Theatre, and there are free **lunchtime concerts**, often showcasing the work of students from Cape Town University's South African College of Music, on Thursdays at 1pm at the Baxter Theatre or at the college itself (☎ 021 650 2626, ⊛ web.uct.ac.za/depts/sacm). Recitals by visiting soloists and chamber ensembles are put on by an organization called **Cape Town Concert Series** (⊛ ctconcerts.co.za) and there are regular, excellent performances in different churches, by Cape Town's only baroque ensemble, Camerata Tinta Barocca (⊛ ctbmusic.co.za).

CINEMA

Despite the fact that Cape Town is booming as a film-production centre, local feature films are scarce, though some excellent documentaries are produced. There are several film festivals of note: the **South African International Documentary Festival** (⊛ encounters.co.za) in June or July features riveting South African documentaries as well as award-winning international films; the **TRI Continental Film Festival** (⊛ 3continentsfestival.co.za) in August or September has a strong developing world sociopolitical emphasis; each November South Africa's leading film school exhibits short films by graduates at the **AFDA Experimental Film Festival** (⊛ afda.co.za/festivals.php); and you can catch screenings of around thirty new South African short films and documentaries at the **Cape Town & Winelands Film Festival** (⊛ films-for-africa.co.za) in early November.

OPEN AIR CINEMAS

Galileo Open Air Cinema ⊛ thegalileo.co.za. Catch an all-time classic under the stars at three locations across the city: sunset over the Kirstenbosch Gardens or Waterfront are pretty spectacular backdrops. Nov–April; R70–100

Pink Flamingo Grand Daddy Hotel, 38 Long St ⊛ granddaddy.co.za/pinkflamingo. The urban rooftop setting, complete with vintage Airstream trailers, make this a great option for open air cinema. Mondays at sunset; R90

DESIGN ON THE EDGE OF AFRICA

Cape Town is becoming an increasingly important player in South African contemporary design. Winning the 2014 World Design Capital award injected a new enthusiasm into design and innovation across the city, with highlights ranging from sustainable development projects to graphics.

One of the best places to get a taste of the burgeoning design scene is **The Fringe** district (Ⓦ thefringe.org.za), a dedicated hub for creativity, entrepreneurship and innovation created by the City of Cape Town, Cape Peninsula University of Technology and Creative Cape Town (Ⓦ creativecapetown.com). Based on an "urban science park" model, the area is home to a host of design studios and institutes working to put Cape Town on the global design map. **Woodstock** (Ⓦ mondaydesign.co.za/Woodstock-design-district), meanwhile, has the highest concentration of design artists (see below) in South Africa.

Design-enthusiasts should also head to the City Bowl for **First Thursdays** (Ⓦ first-thursdays .co.za), on the first Thursday of every month, when galleries, exhibitions and shops stay open until 9pm. Started in a bid to get people walking on the streets at night, the event has taken a life of its own and been key in the rejuvenation of areas such as Bree and Harrington streets. If you're in Cape Town in March, keep an eye out for the **Design Indaba Conference** (Ⓦ designindaba.com), which hosts international and local speakers, and the smaller **Guild International Design Fair** (Ⓦ guilddesignfair.com) that showcases one-off projects from a range of designers and curators.

★**Labia** 69 Orange St ☎ 021 424 5927, Ⓦ labia.co.za. The retro Labia (Lah-bia) shows an intelligent mix of art films, cult classics and new releases, and is Cape Town's only independent cinema. R̄40

Ster-Kinekor Cinema Nouveau Waterfront ☎ 082 16789, Ⓦ sterkinekor.com. Reliable art-house cinema showing films three times a day. R̄65–90

CONTEMPORARY ART GALLERIES

All substantial collections of contemporary art are held in private and corporate collections and galleries in South Africa. From serious commercial players dealing at the highest level, to small galleries showcasing urban pop art, Cape Town has a small but passionate community of curators and art lovers.

Erdmann Contemporary and The Photographers Gallery 63 Shortmarket St Ⓦ erdmanncontemporary .co.za. Committed to promoting contemporary South African photography and fine art, with highly successful exhibitions including Roger Balen, David Lurie and Melanie Cleary. Mon–Fri 9am–4pm, Sat 11am–2pm.

Everard Read Portswood Rd, V&A Waterfront Ⓦ everard-read-capetown.co.za. First opened as a bric-a-brac shop in Johannesburg in 1912, this is one of the country's oldest and most prestigious galleries. It contains the work of international and local artists in a broad range of mediums including sculpture, painting, lithography, multimedia, craft and photography. Mon–Fri 9am–6pm, Sat 9am–1pm.

Goodman Gallery 176 Sir Lowry Rd, Woodstock Ⓦ goodman-gallery.com. Housed in an old textile factory, this industrial-chic gallery is at the forefront of contemporary art in South Africa, and houses an A-list of local artists, including William Kentridge and David Goldblatt, alongside emerging artists engaging with African issues. Tues–Fri 9.30am–5.30pm, Sat 10am–4pm.

Johans Borman Fine Art Gallery 16 Kildare Rd, Newlands Ⓦ johansborman.co.za. A small but satisfying collection of works by South African old masters like Sydney Kumalo and Neville Lewis, as well as contemporary artists, housed in a smart suburban home. Johans Borman has also written a couple of books on South African art with beautiful reproductions, which are on sale at the gallery. Mon–Fri 9.30am–5.30pm, Sat 10am–1pm.

The South African Print Gallery 109 Sir Lowry Rd, Woodstock Ⓦ printgallery.co.za. This small gallery is the only one that focuses solely on promoting South African work on paper, housing 1400 prints by artists including Alice Goldin and Anton Kannemeyer. Mon–Fri 9am–4pm, Sat 10am–1pm.

Stevenson 160 Sir Lowry Rd, Woodstock Ⓦ stevenson .info. With a focus on conceptual art and photography, Stevenson hosts solo and group exhibitions in its expansive, museum-like spaces: see the likes of internationally acclaimed photographer Pieter Hugo or sculptor Will Botha. Mon–Fri 9am–5pm, Sat 10am–1pm.

Whatiftheworld Gallery 1 Argyle St, Woodstock Ⓦ whatiftheworld.com. This tiny gallery has been gaining a reputation as a platform for a new generation of emerging artists, hosting group and solo exhibitions, workshops and art events. Watch out for Athi-Patra Ruga, Cameron Platter and Julia Rosa Clark to name a few. Mon–Fri 10am–5pm, Sat 10am–2pm.

10

TRADITIONAL AFRICAN BEADWORK

Shopping

The V&A Waterfront is the city's most popular shopping venue: it has a vast range of shops, the setting on the harbour is lovely and there's a huge choice of places to eat and drink. Nearby, the Cape Quarter, accessed off Somerset Road in Green Point, is smaller and more exclusive. The city centre itself offers variety: Long Street is good if you're looking for South African crafts, gifts, antiques and secondhand books, while Bree Street and Kloof Street are perfect for finding unique designer goods. For something edgier, the increasingly gentrified city-fringe suburbs of Woodstock and Salt River are destinations in their own right, with clusters of cutting-edge design shops, markets and some of the best restaurants and cafés in the city. Cape Town's Green Map (ⓦgreenmap.org) is a great source of information about ethical shopping, organic markets, delis and health shops.

ESSENTIALS

Opening hours Shops have traditionally opened from Mon–Fri 8.30am–5pm and Sat 8.30am–1pm, though lots of supermarkets, bookshops and other specialist outlets are now open beyond 5pm and also on Sun. That said, don't expect much to be open on Sun afternoon, except at the Waterfront or Cavendish Square, and no alcohol is sold in any shops on Sun in South Africa. The Waterfront has the latest opening hours, many shops open until 9pm.

FASHION, CRAFTS AND JEWELLERY

Designers abound in Cape Town, and with the added fillip of the city being crowned World Design Capital in 2014, you'll find plenty of interesting clothes and handmade objects to fill your luggage. Cape Town is not known for its indigenous arts and crafts, and apart from some beadwork and wirework, many of the goods you'll buy here are from elsewhere in Africa, especially Zimbabwe and Zambia. There are several crafts outlets in the city centre and the V&A Waterfront, but you'll often pick up the same wares for a lot less money at the pavement markets scattered around town. Don't expect exotic West African-style affairs, however: Cape Town's markets are more like European or North American flea markets. If you're after South African gold and diamonds, you'll find the V&A Waterfront is one of the best places to browse – but price tags are high.

FASHION

Hello Again 219 Long St ☎ 021 426 0242. Producing affordable menswear made in South Africa, Hello Again's designs are simple and have an urban, skate and streetwear feel, with printed T-shirts a speciality. Mon–Fri 10am–6pm, Sat 9am–5.30pm.

Mememe Cnr Church & Long sts ⓦ mememe.co.za; map p.48. A selection of somewhat edgy women's clothing and accessories characteristic of Capetonian style, such as sassy summer dresses, leather handbags and costume jewellery. Mon–Fri 9.30am–6pm, Sat 10am–4pm.

Mungo & Jemima 108 Long St ⓦ mungoandjemima .com; map p.48. Mungo & Jemima provides a platform for a variety of local designers producing small-run women's clothing collections including bikinis, soft cotton dresses and maxi-dresses. Mon–Fri 9.30am–5.30pm, Sat 10am–2pm.

Sitting Pretty 111 Long St ⓦ sittingpretty.co.za; map p.48. Perfect for those wanting to take a trip back to the Fifties and Sixties: local women's clothing labels like Silver Spoon, Fierce Couture and Hello Bebe hang here alongside vintage dresses. Mon–Sat 10am–6pm.

The Space Cavendish Square, Claremont ☎ 021 674 6643. A women's clothing store that draws on local influences past and present. Find a designer one- or two-piece swimsuit, handmade sandals or casual-chic afternoon wear. Mon–Sat 9am–7pm, Sun 10am–5pm.

Strato Concept Store 158 Long St ⓦ wearstrato.com; map p.48. The brainchild of Maloti Mothobi, a fashion designer from Lesotho, the unisex clothing here draws influences from Eighties streetwear; manufacturing is as local as it can be, occurring on site at the back of the store. Mon–Fri 7am–7pm, Sat 9am–3pm.

CRAFT SHOPS

Africa Nova Cape Quarter 72 Waterkant St, De Waterkant ⓦ africanova.co.za; map p.62. A better-than-average selection of ethnic crafts and curios as well as contemporary African textiles and artwork, with an emphasis on the individual and handmade. Mon–Fri 9am–5pm, Sat 10am–5pm, Sun 10am–2pm.

Ethno Bongo Mainstream Shopping Centre, Main Rd, Hout Bay ⓦ andbanana.com. A charming shop in the main shopping centre in Hout Bay, selling wonderful and well-priced crafts, jewellery and accessories made from recycled metal and wood, and also quirky kaftans and ethnic clothing – highly recommended for unique gifts and souvenirs. Mon–Fri 9.30am–5.30pm, Sat 9.30am–5pm, Sun 10am–4pm.

Kalk Bay Gallery 62 Main Rd, Kalk Bay; map pp.98–99. Graphics and engravings as well as African art and artefacts at reasonable prices, with the chance of picking up something very collectable. Daily 10am–5pm.

KEAG (Kommetjie Environmental Awareness Group Kommetjie) Imhoff Farm Village, Kommetjie Rd. Best known for fun jewellery and other objects created from recycled plastic, this shop is a great stop-off on a Cape Point tour. Daily 9am–5pm.

Monkeybiz 43 Rose St ⓦ monkeybiz.co.za; map p.48. A nonprofit income-generating project that produces unique and hand-signed items from 450 bead artists, aiming to create sustainable employment, particularly for women. Mon–Fri 9am–5pm, Sat 9am–1pm.

Montebello Craft & Design Centre 31 Newlands Ave, Newlands. A great selection of South African crafts – jewellery, beadwork, ceramics, woven goods and even musical instruments and garden items – are created here by people from townships being trained to become artisans. Besides watching the craftsmen at work, you can eat here at the restaurant under the oaks. Mon–Fri 9am–5pm, Sat 9am–4pm, Sun 9am–3pm.

Streetwires 77 Shortmarket St, Bo-Kaap ⓦ streetwires .co.za; map p.48. At this shop and working artists' studio you can try your hand at beading, purchase wire and bead craft artworks in any shape imaginable or even get something custom made. Mon–Fri 8.30am–5pm, Sat 9am–1pm.

11

MARKETS

Greenmarket Square Burg St; map p.48. City-centre open-air market on a cobbled square where you can pick up loads of presents to take home, from all over the continent. It's also the best place in town for colourful handmade Cape Town hippie gear and Tanzanian beach wraps. Mon–Sat 9am–4pm.

Pan African Market 76 Long St; map p.48. A multicultural hothouse of township and contemporary art, artefacts, curios and crafts. There's also a café specializing in African cuisine, a bookshop, a Cameroonian hairbraider and a West African tailor. Mon–Fri 9am–5pm, Sat 9am–3pm.

Victoria Road Market Camps Bay. Carvings, beads, fabrics and baskets sold from a roadside market spectacularly sited on a clifftop overlooking the Atlantic. No set times, but usually daily 9am–4pm.

Wola Nani 9 Drake St, Observatory ⓦ wolanani.co.za. A nonprofit organization established for fifteen years, Wola Nani supports crafters whose works include recycled papier-mâché bowls, jewellery, lampshades, designer light bulbs, beadwork and recycled-magazine mirrors. Mon–Fri 8.30am–4.30pm.

CERAMICS

Art In The Forest Off Constantia Nek Circle, Rhodes Drive, Constantia Nek ☎021 794 0291, ⓦ artintheforest.com. Perched within a hillside forest with sweeping views, this is a thriving ceramic centre and gallery. The studio, run by Anthony Shapiro, offers workshops and produces ceramics while the gallery hosts special exhibitions of leading South African ceramicists and showcases works by Ardmore from Kwa-Zulu Natal, Clementina van der Walt and Lisa Firer. All profits support their outreach programmes for vulnerable children. Mon–Fri 9am–4.30pm, Sat 10am–3pm.

Clementina Ceramics The Old Biscuit Mill, 375 Albert Rd, Woodstock ⓦ clementina.co.za. Specializing in ceramics by Clementina van der Walt and other leading South African ceramicists, with a shop stocking unusual cards and other designer crafts. Clementina's dinner sets and tableware, handcrafted in her Woodstock studio, deliberately subvert the sterility of mass production. Mon–Fri 9am–5pm, Sat 9am–3pm.

FURNITURE

Private Collections 66 Waterkant St, at Hudson St ⓦ privatecollections.co.za; map p.62. Among De Waterkant's dozens of upmarket arty shops, Private Collections is easy to miss yet possibly the most extraordinary. A massive warehouse on two levels, it's packed to the rafters with fantastic wooden architectural pieces, furniture and interior items from all over India, many of them antiques. Even if you're not planning on buying anything, just pop in and prepare to be awed. Mon–Fri 9am–5pm, Sat 8am–2pm.

BOOKS

South Africa has some very talented authors, and there are good, locally published novels as well as volumes on history, politics and natural history. Exclusive Books is the main chain you'll find in the airport and malls, while Upper Long St has several secondhand bookshops, specialist comic shops and a couple of notable independent bookshops.

★ **Book Lounge** 71 Roeland St ⓦ booklounge.co.za; map p.43. The most congenial central bookshop, with comfy sofas and a downstairs café, stocks an excellent selection of local books and imaginative list of imported titles, as well as running stimulating evening events with local intellectuals and writers. Mon–Fri 8.30am–7.30pm, Sat 9am–5pm, Sun 10am–4pm.

Clarke's Bookshop 199 Long St ⓦ clarkesbooks.co.za; map p.48. The best place in Cape Town for South African books has very well-informed staff who can help you find what you want among the huge selection of local titles covering literature, history, politics, natural history and the arts. It also deals in collectors' editions of South African books. Mon–Fri 9am–5pm, Sat 9.30am–1pm.

Exclusive Books Victoria Wharf, V&A Waterfront ⓦ exclus1ves.co.za; map p.62. Though small by British and American standards, Exclusive Books' reasonably well-stocked shelves include magazines and a wide choice of coffee-table books on Cape Town and South African topics. There are other branches at V&A, Cavendish Square and Constantia Village Shopping Centre, though their opening times may vary. Mon–Sat 9am–10.30pm, Sun 9am–9pm.

Kirstenbosch Shop Kirstenbosch National Botanical Gardens. A good selection of natural-history books, field guides and travel guides covering southern Africa, as well as a range of titles for kids. You don't need a Gardens ticket to browse. Daily 9am–6pm; open until 7pm in summer.

Wordsworth's Books V&A Waterfront ⓦ wordsworth.co.za; map p.62. A good general bookshop, with a specialist travel section with stores also in Gardens Shopping Centre and Sea Point. Daily 9am–9pm.

11

MUSIC

African Music Store 134 Long St ⓦafricanmusicstore.co.za; map p.48. Small, upbeat and centrally located shop specializing in African music from around the continent. It also has a modest collection of instruments, such as shakers and thumb pianos. Mon–Fri 9am–6pm, Sat 9am–2pm.

Mabu Vinyl 2 Rheede St, Gardens ⓦmabuvinyl.co.za; map p.72. The aficionado's choice for a great selection of secondhand CDs, vinyl and even cassettes, of many genres.

Since *Searching for Sugarman* won an Oscar, it has made a splash with tourists who pop by to see a part of Rodriguez history. Mon–Fri 9am–7pm, Sat 9am–6pm, Sun 11am–3pm.

Musica Megastore V&A Waterfront ⓦmusica.co.za; map p.62. A megastore by international standards, with one of the best ranges of African music in the city, plus classical and jazz, pop and rock, and DVDs and video games. Daily 9am–9pm.

FOOD AND PROVISIONS

Buying food from one of the weekly neighbourhood **markets** is always fun, while well-stocked delis provide more options. Of the two major **supermarket** chains, Pick n Pay and Woolworths, which you'll find all over the city, Woolworths is the more upmarket with good food, bread and wine for picnics or packaged salads and microwaveable meals to eat at your lodgings. The larger branches of the better supermarkets have fishmonger counters, though by far the most atmospheric places to buy **seafood** are the Hout Bay and Kalk Bay harbours. Cape Town also has a sprinkling of stores specializing in **health foods** and modest selections of organic fruit and vegetables, the best choice being at Woolworths. Supermarkets tend to have decent wine at competitive prices, but for more interesting labels, there are some first-rate specialist wine merchants. Otherwise, you can buy alcoholic beverages at **bottle stores** (the equivalent of the British off-licence), though they close at 6pm on Sat and all Sun, so plan ahead.

DELIS

Andiamo Cape Quarter Dixon St, De Waterkant ⓦandiamo.co.za; map p.62. Italian deli where you can select from meats, cheeses, salads, dips, meze and fresh breads to take on your mountain walk. Phone ahead and

they'll put the picnic together for you. Mon–Fri 7am–11pm, Sat & Sun 9am–11pm.

Giovanni's 103 Main Rd, Green Point; map pp.90–91. Excellent breads and Italian foods to take away and – if temptation overcomes you – there's always the option of

NEIGHBOURHOOD FOOD AND CRAFT MARKETS

Cape Town has a number of increasingly popular neighbourhood markets where you can browse interesting food and craft stalls, pick up a gourmet burger and often catch some live music. Below is our pick of the best.

Blue Bird Garage Market 39 Albertyn Rd, Muizenberg ☏082 331 2471. A lively Friday-night institution in the south, with stalls selling reasonably-priced food, wine and craft beer, often accompanied by live music, all in a former aeroplane hangar next to the railway line. Fri 4–10pm.

Hope Street (City Bowl) Market 14 Hope St ⓦcitybowlmarket.co.za. This weekly market is becoming a regular social affair for young locals. Entering the market hall is a sensory experience, with jam-packed stalls laden with everything from handmade jewellery and vintage clothing to curries, burgers and a live band creating a bubbly atmosphere. Take your pick from the mouthwatering options, then grab a spot at one of the communal tables. Thurs 4.30–8.30pm, Sat 9am–2pm.

Hout Bay Market Bay Harbour, 31 Harbour Rd, Hout Bay ☏082 570 5997, ⓦbayharbour.co.za. Situated in an old fish factory, this cavern-like hall might have humble beginnings but today it's a different picture.

Stalls sell African crafts and local designer clothes alongside a host of artisan food traders – some even offering oysters and champagne – and live acoustic acts. Fri 5–9pm, Sat & Sun 9.30am–4pm.

Neighbourgoods Market Old Biscuit Mill, 373–375 Albert Rd (off Lower Main Rd) ⓦneighbourgoodsmarket.co.za. This Victorian warehouse is one of the best places to head for a foodie experience: walk around marvelling at the array of artisanal cheese, wood-fired bread, coffee, beer, fresh flowers, fruit and veg. Not cheap, but it sells the best produce of its kind in the Cape, as well as exceptional local designer crafts, homewares and clothing. Sat 9am–2pm.

Oranjezicht City Farm Market Upper Orange St ⓦozcf.co.za. City Bowl locals get fabulously fresh organic produce, bread and coffee here on a Saturday morning. This thriving, nonprofit urban farm was started on disused ground that was once part of an eighteenth-century estate. Sat 9am–2pm, though produce sells out fast.

sitting down for a pavement coffee with a view onto Green Point Stadium. Daily 8.30am–9pm.

Melissa's Waterfront ⓦmelissas.co.za; map p.62. Highly delectable imported and local specialities at a popular and gourmet deli with the option of eating in. Branches on Kloof St, Gardens and in Constantia Village. Not cheap, but always worth it. Daily 7.30am–10pm, Sat & Sun 9am–10pm.

Organic Zone Lakeside Shopping Centre, Main Rd, Lakeside ⓦorganiczone.co.za; map pp.98–99. Always fresh and well-stocked organic fruit and veg, as well as grains, honey, breads and dairy products. Reasonably priced for quality. Mon–Fri 8.15am–6pm, Sat & Sun 8.15am–5pm.

FRESH FISH

Fish Market Mariner's Wharf, Hout Bay Harbour; map pp.98–99. Fresh seafood from South Africa's original Waterfront emporium, although it's slicker and less atmospheric than Kalk Bay Harbour. Daily 9am–5.30pm.

Kalk Bay Harbour Harbourside, Kalk Bay; map pp.98–99. Buy fresh fish directly from the fishermen and have it gutted and scaled on the spot. Your best bet is lunchtime, especially at weekends, though catches are dependent on several factors including the weather and rough seas, so you may not get any. Yellowtail fish are in good supply and excellent cooked on a braai. No set hours.

WINE

Caroline's Fine Wines 62 Strand St; King's Warehouse, V&A Waterfront ⓦcarolineswine.com; map p.48. Caroline Rillema has been in the wine business since 1979 and stocks the Cape's finest and most exclusive wines. Mon–Fri 9am–5.30pm, Waterfront also Sat 9am–1pm.

Vaughan Johnson's Dock Rd, V&A Waterfront ⓦvaughanjohnson.co.za; map p.62. One of Cape Town's best-known wine shops, which has a huge range of labels from all over the country, though it can be a bit pricey. Mon–Fri 9am–6pm, Sat 9am–5pm, Sun 10am–5pm.

Wine Concepts Gardens Lifestyle Centre, Kloof St ⓦwineconcepts.co.za; map p.72. An excellent selection of South African and foreign wines from a knowledgeable and helpful outfit. Mon–Fri 10am–6pm, Sat 9am–6pm.

MALLS AND SHOPPING CENTRES

South African shopping tends to follow the American model, with **malls** offering a sterile and safe indoor environment for browsing, banking and eating. The Waterfront however, offers waterside cafés and fabulous views.

Blue Route Mall Tokai Rd, Tokai. Major retailers and supermarkets are represented here, handy if you're staying in Constantia or along the False Bay. Mon–Sat 9am–7pm, Sun 9am–5pm.

Cavendish Square Mall Claremont Station, Vineyard Rd, Claremont. An upmarket multistorey complex, the major shopping focus for the southern suburbs. Mon–Sat 9am–7pm, Sun 10am–5pm.

Constantia Village Shopping Centre Main Rd, Constantia. A small, exclusive mall including two large supermarkets, post office and general, practical shopping facilities. Mon–Fri 9am–5pm, Sat 9am–5pm, Sun 9am–2pm.

Gardens Shopping Centre Mill St, Gardens; map p.72.

Very close to the Company's Gardens and city centre, this is a good-sized shopping mall with a selection of every shop you might need with two large supermarkets, bookstore, pharmacy, optometrist and surprisingly, local South African craft and fashion stores. Mon–Fri 9am–7pm, Sat 9am–5pm, Sun 9am–2pm.

V&A Waterfront map p.62. It would be possible to visit Cape Town and never leave the Waterfront complex, which has a vast range of upmarket shops packed into the Victoria Wharf Shopping Centre, including outlets of all the major South African chains, selling books, clothes, food and crafts, as well as two cinemas, one of them with art-house films. Daily 9am–9pm.

NEWLANDS CRICKET GROUND

Sports and outdoor activities

One of Cape Town's most remarkable features is the fact that it melds with Table Mountain National Park – a patchwork of mountains, forests and coastline – giving rise to myriad outdoor pursuits. In fact, there are few, if any, cities in the world where so many activities are so easily available and affordable. For land lovers, there's the obvious draw of hiking up the imposing faces of Table Mountain, as well as ubiquitous cycle paths and opportunities for horseriding. Surrounded by ocean coastline on all sides, it's not surprising that every watersport under the sun, from sea kayaking to surfing, is on offer, while true daredevils can marvel at the aerial views of the city by launching off the Lion's Head on a paraglider. Alternatively, just let everyone else get on with it while you sink a few beers and watch high-calibre cricket, rugby or football – no denying it, South Africa is a sports-mad country.

PARTICIPATION SPORTS AND OUTDOOR ACTIVITIES

ABSEILING

Abseil Africa ☎ 021 424 4760, ⓦ abseilafrica.co.za. You can abseil off Table Mountain for around R700. A guided summit walk up Platteklip Gorge goes for R250.

BIRDWATCHING

Although Cape Town has fewer species of birds compared to the east of the country, its pelagic population brings the number up to four hundred, including four species of the highly endangered albatross. Good places for birdwatching include Lion's Head, Kirstenbosch Gardens and the Cape of Good Hope Nature Reserve, as well as at Kommetjie and Hout Bay.

Anne Grey ☎ 083 311 1140, ⓦ annealbatross.org. Runs pelagic trips by boat if you're after the albatross and other rarities off the Cape coast.

Birding Africa ☎ 021 531 9148, ⓦ birdingafrica.com. Has a wealth of information on birding trips in Cape Town.

World of Birds Hout Bay ⓦ worldofbirds.org.za. The largest bird park in Africa with three thousand birds and four hundred species (R85). Daily 9am–5pm.

CYCLING

Cycling is very popular and a great way to take in the scenery, though you have to be very vigilant about intolerant car drivers – cyclists are frequently knocked down.

Moonlight Mass ⓦ moonlightmass.co.za. A casual night bicycle ride once a month, starting at 9pm at the Green Point Circle. It began as a social experiment on Twitter to promote non-motorized transport, and has been gaining popularity since to become Africa's biggest social ride.

Pedal Power Associates ☎ 021 689 8420, ⓦ cycletour .co.za. Organizes fun rides from Sept–May. Also has information on the annual, spectacular Argus Cycle Tour that takes place in March, 109km right around the peninsula, with forty thousand riders from all over the country as well as international entrants.

GOLF

Cape Town has several well-maintained golf courses, all with relevant dress code and caddies. You can play for a fraction of what you might pay back home, in far better weather conditions.

Milnerton Golf Course Bridge Rd, Milnerton ☎ 021 552 3108, ⓦ milnertongolf.co.za. Tucked in between a lagoon and Table Bay, and boasts classic views of Table Mountain.

Westlake Golf Club Westlake Ave, Lakeside ☎ 021 788 2020, ⓦ westlakegolfclub.co.za. Situated at the southern end of the Constantia valley where the M3 south ends, with a mountainous backdrop, Westlake is one of the nicest courses to play on, with visitors always welcome.

GYMS

Virgin Active ☎ 086 020 0911, ⓦ virginactive.co.za. These gyms are upmarket, well-appointed and dotted conveniently around the peninsula, all with large swimming pools and spotless changing rooms. Contact their call centre for current visitor rates, starting from R175 per day.

HEALTH SPAS

Most of Cape Town's luxury hotels have spas attached, which you can use as a day visitor, even if you are not staying there.

Twelve Apostles Hotel and Spa Victoria Rd, Camps Bay ☎ 021 437 9060, ⓦ 12apostleshotel.com. Cape Town's most lavish spa in the most beautiful setting imaginable with mountain and ocean views. There are hot and cold plunge pools as well as all the usual treatments. They offer massage in the open air too. Daily 8am–8pm.

The Vineyard Hotel Colinton Rd ☎ 021 674 5005, ⓦ vineyard.co.za. A gorgeous garden setting with mountain backdrop and zen-style decor make this a truly serene spot. The treatment rooms are decorated in silks and everything at the spa, like the rest of the hotel, is utterly elegant and pleasing. Daily 10am–8pm.

HORSERIDING

Prices usually run at around R450 for a two-hour outride for all levels.

Horse Trail Safaris Ottery ☎ 021 704 6908, ⓦ horsetrailsafaris.co.za. Offers riding through the dunes to the coast, though you are only on the actual beach for ten minutes.

Sleepy Hollow Horse Riding Noordhoek ☎ 021 789 2341, ⓦ sleepyhollowhorseriding.co.za. Covers the spectacular Noordhoek Beach.

KAYAKING

Downhill Adventures ☎ 021 422 0388, ⓦ downhilladventures.co.za. Offers trips from Mouille Point or Simon's Town from R500 per half-day.

Real Cape Adventures ☎ 021 790 5611, ⓦ seakayak .co.za. Runs a range of half- or full-day sea-kayaking packages that include trips around Cape Point, to the penguin colony at Boulders Beach and around Hout Bay.

KITEBOARDING

Kiteboarding has taken off in a big way in Cape Town and many companies offer lessons in Langebaan, a 75min drive north. This enormous lagoon is one of the best spots for kiteboarding, offering better conditions than the ocean around Cape Town, which has a bigger swell and is choppier. Closer to the city, Blouberg, which hosts the Red Bull King of the Year competition, is well set up to cater for

12

beginners and the more advanced. For more tips and wind reports see w kitespotters.co.za.

The Cabrinha shop Blouberg ☎021 554 1729, w cabrinha.co.za. Gear rental, repairs, lessons for kiteboarding as well as windsurfing, surfing and stand-up paddleboarding.

Cape Sport Centre Langebaan ☎022 772 1114, w capesport.co.za. Offers a variety of watersports and has accommodation along the same street. A two-day kitesurfing package costs from R2400, including gear and instruction.

Surfstore Africa Muizenberg ☎021 788 5055, w surfstore.co.za. While not as good as options further afield, Surfstore Africa is easily accessible and great for beginners. A full-day lesson costs R1290. They also offer stand-up paddleboarding lessons.

MOUNTAIN BIKING

Day Trippers ☎021 511 4766, w daytrippers.co.za. Offers expert mountain-bike tours, including one from Scarborough to Cape Point. Downhill Adventures (see opposite) offers similar tours, including Tokai Forest.

PARAGLIDING

Cape Town has great air thermals for paragliding: the usual spot is from Lion's Head, drifting down to Camps Bay.

Cape Town Tandem Paragliding ☎076 892 2283, w paraglide.co.za. Tandem jumps R950.

Wallend-Air School ☎021 762 2441, w wallendair .com. Peter Wallend, one of SA's paragliding champs, offers courses to get your paragliding licence.

ROCK CLIMBING

Table Mountain has fantastic rock-climbing routes for all abilities and there are some excellent guides. The cable car makes access to some pitches relatively easy.

City Rock Indoor Climbing Centre 21 Anson Rd, Observatory ☎021 447 1326, w cityrock.co.za. For practice walls, you'll find serious climbers at City Rock, which has good facilities, including a small wall for children, and more challenging surfaces for teenagers.

Guided by Mike ☎083 402 0288, w guidedbymike .co.za. Experienced and very personable mountaineer Mike Wakeford offers climbs on Table Mountain and other locations such as the Kalk Bay Mountains and Silvermine (half-day R950; full day R1600).

High Adventure ☎021 422 1234, w highadventure .co.za. This outfit, run by a well-known city rock-climber, Ross Suter, will take you to unusual and unique locations depending on your ability. Packages are tailor-made, with a minimum of two people.

RUNNING

Two of the best places to jog are Newlands Forest up the mountain tracks, and along the Sea Point Promenade. The Two Oceans Marathon, every Easter Saturday (w twooceansmarathon.org.za), is one of the world's most exciting runs – athletes descend on the city from all corners of the globe to run the arduous 56km ultra-marathon around the peninsula.

SAILING

Tigresse Catamaran w tigresse.co.za. Runs catamaran cruises taking in Table and Granger bays, Clifton beaches and Robben Island. Scheduled twice daily, weather permitting, plus champagne sunset cruises (R150–240).

Yachtmaster Sailing School ☎21 788 1009, w yachtmaster.co.za. Offers a wide range of weekend and week-long courses from beginner (R1800/2-day) to skipper to professional yachting career courses.

SANDBOARDING

Downhill Adventures ☎021 422 0388, w downhilladventures.com. The pioneers of this ski-related adventure sport. Boards, boots and bindings are provided, as well as expert instruction for beginners. Full day/R850.

Sunscene Outdoor Adventures ☎021 783 0203, w sunscene.co.za. For extreme junkies, Sunscene offers a full day sandboarding (R650) and combinations with paragliding (R2000), surfing (R900) or sky diving (R3000).

SCUBA DIVING

While the Cape waters are cold, they're also good for seeing wrecks, reefs and magnificent kelp forests.

Down South Scuba Muizenberg ☎021 788 7616, w downsouthscuba.co.za. Offering PADI courses and dive trips to observe cow sharks for those with a diving licence.

The Scuba Shack Cape Town ☎021 424 9368, w scubashack.co.za. Land and boat dives, from R520 for the dive and equipment, as well as dives in the Aquarium shark tank or kelp forest, which teems with non-biting fish. You can also take an internationally recognized PADI Open Water diving qualification. If you don't want to dive, you can snorkel with Cape fur seals off the coast.

SKYDIVING

The ultimate way to see Table Mountain and Robben Island is from a tandem jump 3000m up.

Skydive Cape Town ☎082 800 6290, w skydive capetown.za.net. Situated 30min from Cape Town, this is a long-established business offering reliable and good-quality dives for R1550.

SURFING

Cape Town and its surrounding coastline is host to a range of world-class waves including Dungeons, one of the top five biggest waves in the world, and Jeffery's Bay further afield along the east coast. For those with slightly humbler surf ambitions, the stretch between the city and Cape Point offers a host of point and beach breaks which cater to all skill levels. Top surfing spots include Big Bay at Blouberg, Llandudno, and Long Beach near Kommetjie and Noordhoek. Muizenberg is the best place for beginners, with a strip of surf shops and schools along the beachfront. Check out ⓦ wavescape.co.za for more information.

Gary's Surf School ☎ 021 788 9839, ⓦ garysurf.com. A surfing school which has been there forever, offering a 2hr lesson including gear rental for R380, which guarantees to get you up and moving on the board in your first lesson.

Surf Shack ☎ 021 788 9286, ⓦ surfshack.co.za. Various lesson packages available or just board and wetsuit rental R100 for 90min.

SWIMMING

Sea swimming is best in False Bay, as it is far warmer than the Atlantic side, especially at Muizenberg and Fish Hoek beaches, as well as St James Pool. For swimming pools, try:

Long Street Baths Long St ☎ 021 400 3302. Cape Town's only public heated indoor pool, with steam and sauna facilities to warm up on winter days (R5). Daily 7am–7pm.

Newlands Swimming Pool Cnr Main and San Souci rds, Newlands ☎ 0021 671 2729. An Olympic-sized chlorinated pool with trees, lawns, mountain views and a paddling pool for children (R15). Winter 9am–5pm; summer 10am–6pm.

Sea Point Swimming Pool Beach Rd ☎ 021 434 3341. An Olympic-sized chlorinated seawater pool, right on the edge of the ocean with lovely lawns to laze on, and watch the ships go by (R20). Winter (unheated) 9am–5pm; summer 7am–7pm.

HIKING

The best places for easy walks are Kirstenbosch Gardens, Newlands Forest, along the Sea Point Promenade and the beaches. If you want to hike, there are limitless opportunities; however, a Table Mountain hike is to be taken seriously so be prepared with a good map and adverse weather gear even in the height of summer. Less experienced hikers can take a guided tour.

Guided by Mike ☎ 083 402 0288, ⓦ guidedbymike .co.za. Experienced and very personable mountaineer, rock climber Mike Wakeford leads hikes up Table Mountain, Silvermine Reserve and Southern peninsula (half day- R950; full day R1600).

Table Mountain Walks ☎ 021 715 6136, ⓦ tablemountainwalks.co.za. A registered Table Mountain Guide, as well as offering other routes along the peninsula, Margie provides free pick-up from your accommodation, refreshments and lunch. Classic Table Mountain hike R800/pp.

YOGA AND PILATES

Cape Town is full of high-quality yoga and pilates studios, with internationally trained instructors who charge around half what you might pay back home.

Wynberg Pilates Studio 18 Mortimer Rd, Wynberg ☎ 021 797 2351, ⓦ pilatesafrica.co.za. The city's most experienced trainers for classes or individual tuition in a tranquil studio with a beautiful garden setting. The studio also offers Feldenkrais Method® and Gyrotonics®.

Karma Shala Yoga 117 Hatfield St, Gardens ⓦ karmacalmer.co.za. Jim Harrington is one of the best-regarded teachers in Cape Town, with classes at the centrally located studio above, as well as in Hout Bay and Noordhoek.

SPECTATOR SPORTS

CRICKET

Newlands Cricket Ground 61 Campground Rd, Newlands ☎ 021 657 2003, ⓦ cricket.co.za. This is the city's cricketing heart. One of the most beautiful grounds in the world, Newlands nestles beneath venerable oaks and the elegant profile of Devil's Peak, and plays host to provincial, test and one-day international matches.

RUGBY

The Western Cape is one of the world's rugby heartlands, and the game is followed religiously here.

Newlands Rugby Stadium Boundary Rd, Newlands ☎ 021 659 4600, ⓦ wprugby.co.za. Provincial, international and Super 12 Rugby contests are fought on this hallowed turf.

FOOTBALL

Though football matches aren't as well attended as cricket or rugby, Cape Town football is burgeoning and received a huge boost post the 2010 FIFA World Cup. The dusty streets of the Cape Flats have produced superb young footballers such as Benni McCarthy (Porto, Ajax, Amsterdam, Celta Vigo) and Quinton Fortune (Atlético Madrid, Manchester United). The most ambitious and professional club in the city is Ajax Cape Town (ⓦ ajaxct.com), jointly owned by its Amsterdam namesake, while the most exciting games to attend are those between a local outfit and one of the Soweto glamour teams, Orlando Pirates and Kaizer Chiefs. Matches take place at Green Point Stadium, off Beach Rd, and Cape Town Stadium off Klipfontein Rd, Athlone. For fixtures and results go to ⓦ beezsports.com or ⓦ psl.co.za.

12

THE CAPE TOWN GAY PRIDE FESTIVAL

Gay and lesbian Cape Town

South Africa has the continent's most developed and diverse gay and
lesbian scene – and Cape Town is its gay capital, on its way to becoming an
African Sydney, attracting gay travellers from across the country and the
globe. Cape Town is the only city in South Africa that is known to have a
gay-friendly district, De Waterkant, very centrally located with great cafés,
accommodation and nightlife. Walk around the gay village and you'll always
find a choice of places to drink or party. Furthermore, the country has one
of the world's first pro-homosexual constitutions: homosexuality is legal in
South Africa between consenting adults of 18 or over and has set a global
example in legalizing same-sex marriage.

13

Outside the big cities, however, and even in Cape Town's townships, attitudes remain pretty conservative and homophobic, and open displays of affection by gays and lesbians are unlikely to go down well; many whites will find it un-Christian, while blacks will think it un-African. It's still especially hard for African and coloured gay men and women to come out. Homophobic attacks are still a threat whatever your ethnicity, so take care when venturing beyond the centre of Cape Town. As you'd expect in a city where the great outdoors figures so prominently, there are a number of beaches popular with men, including **Clifton's Third Beach** (not Fourth Beach, which is family orientated; see p.148), and the nudist **Sandy Bay**, accessed from Llandudno Beach (see p.88).

RESOURCES AND CONTACTS

Information The website ⓦ gaynetcapetown.co.za is aimed specifically at gay and lesbian travellers, with restaurants and accommodation listings, as well as information about HIV and IDS. Health4Men, 24 Napier St (ⓦ health4men.co.za), provides advice on how to access ARV treatment for men living with HIV.

Listings The best listings magazine is *Out Africa*, available from the bars and restaurants in De Waterkant, and from GAP Leisure, on the corner of Napier and Waterkant streets

(ⓦ gapleisure.com), an agency that specializes in finding gay holiday accommodation in both the Waterkant and countrywide.

Advice The Triangle Project (☎ 021 712 6699, daily 1–9pm; ⓦ triangle.org.za) is the longest established organization offering care and support for gay, lesbian, bisexual and transgender people including HIV testing, ARV advice and other medical services.

BARS AND CLUBS

Amsterdam Action Bar 12 Cobern St, off Somerset Rd, De Waterkant ⓦ amsterdambar.co.za; map p.62. Old-school gay bar (men only) with a more mature crowd, keen on full leathers. There's no disco but they have a pool table. Daily 4pm till late.

Bar Code 18 Cobern St, De Waterkant ☎ 021 013 0031, ⓦ leatherbar.co.za; map p.62. A leather, uniform and jeans bar with darkrooms and an outdoor deck. It's worth finding out what the evening's dress code is beforehand, in case they're having a themed night. Bouncers and a R50 entrance fee ensure it stays men only. Sun–Thurs 10pm–2am, Fri & Sat 10pm–4am.

Bealulah Bar Cnr Somerset & Cobern sts, De Waterkant ☎ 072 557 4678; map p.62. One of the few and therefore most popular lesbian clubs in town, *Bealulah Bar* has all the frills with disco lights, a dancefloor, screens showing VH1 music videos and a DJ playing all the latest tracks. You will find a good mixture of couples and ladies, with the crowd usually migrating to *Crew Bar* next door for an after-party.

Cover charge from R30. Fri & Sat 9pm–4am.

Beefcakes 40 Somerset Rd, De Waterkant ☎ 021 425 9019, ⓦ beefcakes.co.za; map p.62. This is one seriously camp burger bar, with pink flamingo wallpaper and feathers, where you can build your own juicy burger, and wear a sequinned cowboy hat if you so wish. There is a range of live entertainment from Drag Divas to "Bitchy Bingo", on varying nights, which go down as well as their delicious cocktails. Mon–Sat noon till late.

Café Manhattan 74 Waterkant St, De Waterkant; 247 Main Rd, Sea Point; ☎ 021 421 6666, ⓦ manhattan .co.za; map p.62. A buzzing bar-restaurant chain with an affordable and largely meat orientated menu. The De Waterkant branch has an attractive terrace under oak trees, while the Sea Point branch is ideal for people-watching on a busy street. Always bustling and lively, especially when the weather is good. Patrons of all genders and orientation will feel comfortable, though it is primarily a gay venue. Daily 10am–2am.

CAPE TOWN PARTIES FOR LADIES WHO LOVE LADIES

For the newcomer, the gay scene in Cape Town is accessible: parties, clubs and bars geared towards men abound. But the **lesbian scene**, which is relatively tight knit and more elusive, is only recently starting to find its feet. Following a global trend in the lesbian scene to use burlesque performance as a way of embracing female sexuality, a selection of new events has emerged throughout the city. The event company **MISS** (Make It Sexy Sisters; ☎ 0837608499, ⓦ facebook.com/MISSmakeitsexysisters.com) is fast becoming the best platform for lesbian DJs and performers. Parties are themed, there are prizes for the best costumes and anyone is welcome. Tickets can be purchased online or at the door from R80 up and parties are held every two months.

13

PILLOW TALK

Although most establishments in the city, especially in De Waterkant, have a relaxed attitude towards same-sex couples, a good number of hotels in Cape Town are particularly accommodating.

4 on Varneys 4 Varneys Rd, Green Point ☎ 021 434 7167, ⓦ 4onvarneys.co.za. A little less extravagant than the other hotels recommended here, but still warm, welcoming and very comfortable, this guesthouse boasts a gorgeous plunge pool and wildflower terrace, not to mention big, soft beds, that offer some respite from the bustle of town. Decadent decorative flourishes, such as floor-to-ceiling windows, huge beds and marble baths, are complemented with unwavering service.

Cactus House Guesthouse 4 Molteno Rd, Gardens ☎ 021 422 5966, ⓦ cactushouse.co.za; map p.72. Centrally located, this gay male guesthouse has just six relaxing suites. They also offer a pool, terrace and mountain views.

Glen Boutique Hotel 3 The Glen, Sea Point ☎ 021 439 0086, ⓦ glenhotel.co.za. This gay-friendly hotel is located right on popular Camps Bay beachfront; there are 24 en-suite rooms each with private garden or en-suite terrace.

Guesthouse One Belvedere 1 Belvedere Ave, Oranjezicht ☎ 021 461 2442, ⓦ onebelvedere.co.za. A gay-friendly guesthouse in a lovely, two-storey colonial house with views of Table Mountain. Rooms come with wi-fi, TV, DVDs, safe, and an entrance to the all-round veranda, plus there's a pool, jacuzzi, steam room and off-street parking.

Crew Bar 30 Napier St, De Waterkant ⓦ facebook.com /CrewBarCapeTown; map p.62. This stylish bar's topless barmen and sexy go-go dancers keep the place packed every weekend, with music starting off chilled and getting hotter and hotter as the night goes on – the verandas above are the place to see and be seen in the summer. Daily 7pm–4am.

SAUNA

The Hothouse 18 Jarvis St, De Waterkant ☎ 021 418 3888, ⓦ hothouse.co.za; map p.62. A luxurious, men-only pleasure and total relaxation complex, and the only one of its kind in Cape Town, with all manner of jacuzzis and steam rooms, as well as a sundeck boasting superb views. There's also a bar, complete with fireplace and an adult store. Entrance R110–140 depending on days and times. Mon–Wed noon–2am, Thurs noon–4am, Fri–Sun noon–6am.

FESTIVALS

Gay and Lesbian Film Festival October ⓦ oia.co.za. The Gay and Lesbian Film Festival is a great exhibition of the latest in cinema.

Gay Pride Festival Late Feb ⓦ capetownpride.co.za. The annual Gay Pride Festival, running for ten days starting late February, has a small street parade in the city, but it's best to look out for a number of fun events and parties, with some seminars on gay issues too.

Mother City Queer Projects Party December ⓦ mcqp.co.za. Cape Town's most famous festival, this hugely popular annual event is one of the biggest parties of the year and attended by all orientations. A cousin of Sydney's Mardi Gras festival, people dress as outrageously as possible according to the official yearly theme (past ones have included "Space Cowboys" and "Made in China").

Pink Loerie Festival Late April ⓦ pinkloerie.co.za. This festival in Knysna is a good excuse to load up your car with pink accessories and bumble on down to the Garden Route to spend a weekend dancing in the streets.

THE ROCK POOLS, DE HOOP NATURE RESERVE

Cape Town for kids

Cape Town is an excellent place to travel with children. A love of the outdoors is inherent in most Capetonians and, as such, you'll find a multitude of activities and gardens to be enjoyed by the whole family, not to mention child-friendly restaurants and a couple of decent rainy-day options. See who can shriek the loudest as you descend into Crocodile Gorge at the Ratanga Junction theme park, or marvel at the jaw-dropping array of sea monsters at the Two Oceans Aquarium. Cape Town's beaches are a classic and easy summer-weekend family destination outing, while older children may want to learn to surf, sand board, rock climb or horse ride (see p.139).

ESSENTIALS

Entrance fees Activities are either free or around half the cost of an adult ticket: children's prices in this chapter apply to under-12s, unless otherwise stated.

Car rental Companies will give you child seats if you ask for them in advance.

Resources A good website for finding out what's on is ⓦ capetownkids.co.za. For reputable babysitters or even nannies to accompany you on road trips, try Sitters4U (☏ 083 691 2009, ⓦ sitters4u.co.za) or Super Sitters (☏ 021 552 1220, ⓦ supersitters.net).

MUSEUMS AND THEME PARKS

Cape Town Science Centre for Kids 370B Main Rd, Observatory ☏ 021 300 3200, ⓦ ctsc.org.za. Kids will love the interactive displays on science, new technologies and inventions here, which appeal to their innate sense of curiosity with things to touch, push and create. Highlights include a miniature train, a Lego room and a life-size space shuttle. R40. Mon–Sat 9am–4.30pm, Sun 10am–4.30pm.

Iziko South African Museum and Planetarium See p.54. Great for rainy days, especially for 5- to 12-year-olds, who'll enjoy the four-storey whale well and African animal dioramas, as well as the dinosaur displays. The Discovery Room features live ants, massive spiders and a crocodile display. The planetarium has special children's shows over weekends and in school holidays. Daily 10am–5pm.

Planet Kids 3 Wherry Rd, Muizenberg ☏ 021 788 3070, ⓦ planetkids.co.za. A great indoor play centre for kids up to 12, designed by an occupational therapist, which is loads of fun, as well as offering healthy snacks and a calmer environment than the usual plastic, sugar-crazed scene (R30/hr, parents free entry). With good assistants on hand, you can drop off your child for an hour, or have tea and a home-bake while you wait. All abilities welcome, with facilities for kids with special needs. Wed–Sun 10am–6pm.

Ratanga Junction Century City, signposted off N1 ☏ 021 550 8504, ⓦ ratanga.co.za. Popular and safe theme park with such thrilling rides as the Cobra, Crocodile Gorge and Monkey Falls. An easy and fun day out for parents as well as kids. Don't bring your own food – everything must be purchased on site. It's only open during Cape school holidays, so call beforehand. The entry price gives you unlimited rides (R172, younger kids R85, R60 for non-riders). Sat & Sun 10am–5pm.

Scratch Patch and Mineral World Dido Valley Rd, off Main Rd, Simon's Town ☏ 021 786 2020, and V&A Waterfront ☏ 021 419 9429. Over-3s can search for jewels, filling a bag with the reject polished gemstones that literally cover the floor. At the Simon's Town venue you can also see one of the world's biggest gemstone tumbling plants in operation (Mon–Fri only). Simon's Town daily 8.30am–4.45pm; V&A daily 9am–6pm.

Two Oceans Aquarium See p.61. One of Cape Town's most rewarding museums, the aquarium features loads of interest to a wide range of ages. Apart from the excitement of just looking at the weird and wonderful sea creatures, kids can actually handle a few species in the touch pool – sometimes this includes a small shark or sea urchins – while the Alpha Activity Centre usually has puppet shows or face painting, as well as computer terminals where older kids can learn about marine ecology. Daily 9.30am–6pm.

OUTDOOR AND PICNIC SPOTS

The Deer Park Cafe 2 Deerpark Drive, Vredehoek ☏ 021 462 6311. The most central outdoor family venue, on the edge of a small park (sadly no deer) with swings and slides, and views across the suburb to Table Bay. While there is a kids' menu, the food for adults is thankfully imaginative, with plenty of fresh stuff. Daily 8am–8pm.

Imhoff Farm Village Kommetjie Rd, opposite the Ocean View turn-off ☏ 021 783 4545, ⓦ imhofffarm .co.za. Activities here include camel rides, horseriding on the beach, paintball, a farmyard petting zoo and reptile park. There's also a good café, restaurant and farmers' shop with fabulous cheeses. Daily 9am–5pm.

Green Point Urban Park Beach Rd, Mouille Point. Offering vistas over the city and stadium, this grassy park has an educational biodiversity garden, tracks for jogging and cycling, a play park for small children and an outdoor gym for those a little older. Trees offer shade for picnics. Free entry. Daily 7am–7pm.

Kirstenbosch National Botanical Gardens See p.79.

Top of the list for a family outing, with extensive lawns for running about, trees and rocks to climb and streams to paddle in. There's no litter, no dogs, it's extremely safe and you can push a pram all over the walkways; it's also great for picnics or to have tea outdoors at the café. For older kids there are short waymarked walks.

Noordhoek Farm Village Village Lane, Noordhoek ☏ 021 789 2812. A small, grassy green, surrounded by cafés, a bakery, crafts stores and a gift shop, with gentle country charm. On weekends you can grab a coffee and listen to live music at Café Roux while kids run around in the adjacent play park. Daily 9am–5pm.

Oude Molen Eco Village Alexandra Rd, Pinelands ☏ 21 447 8226. A working model of a sustainable eco-village in a suburban area. You can sample home-grown organic produce and wood-fired bread at the Millstone Farmstall and Café before taking the kids to play in the garden tree house, swing and play area. Children are also encouraged to feed the horses and pigs nearby. Tues–Sun 8am–5pm.

14

14

Blue Train Park Beach Rd, Mouille Point ☎084 314 9200, ⓦthebluetrainpark.com. Take a trip on Cape Town's only miniature train for a view of the sea, passing ships and Robben Island. There's also plenty to wear kids out afterwards in the park with a jungle gym, a climbing rock, outdoor obstacles, basketball court, mini oval cement track and toddler push-bike track. Tues–Sun 9.30am–6pm.

Silvermine Nature Reserve See p.98. A good place to see *fynbos* vegetation at close quarters and stroll around the lake and picnic with small children; however, it is exposed, and not recommended in heavy winds or mist. For older children there are some mountaintop walks with relatively gentle gradients, which give spectacular views over both sides of the peninsula – try the hike to Elephant's Eye cave on Constantiaberg.

Tokai Forest Arboretum See p.82. The arboretum has good walks and mountain-biking trails, and a thatched teashop with outdoor seating. It's also a great place for young children to explore, with logs to jump off and a gentle walk to a stream; but best of all it is sheltered from the wind.

BEACHES AND SWIMMING POOLS

Most of Cape Town's sandy **beaches** are pretty undeveloped, so it's best to take what you need in the way of food and drink with you. Get to the beach as early as possible so you can leave by 11am before the sun gets too strong, and to avoid the wind, which often gusts up in the late morning in summer.

On the False Bay seaboard, **Boulders Beach** (see p.102) is one of the few beaches to visit when the southeaster is blowing. It has safe, flat water, making it ideal for kids – and its resident penguin-breeding colony is an added attraction. **Fish Hoek** (see p.98) is one of the best peninsula beaches, with gentle waves that are warm in summer, a long stretch of sand and a playground. The paved Jager's Walk, which runs along the rocky coast here, is suitable for pushchairs and offers beautiful views of the Hottentots Holland Mountains. **St James** (see p.96) boasts a safe tidal pool with a small sandy beach and photogenic, if run-down bathing boxes, but gets seriously overcrowded on the weekend. From here you can walk to **Muizenberg** along a pushchair-friendly coastal pathway, with more views of distant mountains across the water.

The **Atlantic seaboard** is too cold for serious swimming, but does have some lovely stretches of sand, boulders and rock pools – and astonishing scenery. The beaches here are excellent for picnics, and on calm summer evenings idyllic for sundowners and sunsets. In the summer they're less windy than the False Bay beaches, but the afternoons are often baking hot. The closest stretch of coast to the centre ideal for prams – and rollerblading – is the paved **Sea Point Promenade**, stretching 3km from the lighthouse in Mouille Point to Sea Point Pavilion, with the draw of playgrounds and ice-cream sellers en route. The tidal pool and small rock pools of **Camps Bay** (see p.88) make this popular beach very child-friendly, and it's easily reachable from the centre by car or bus. Finally, the six-kilometre stretch of white sand from **Noordhoek to Kommetjie** (see p.90) provides fine walking, kite-flying and horseriding opportunities, with stupendous views of Chapman's Peak. If you're heading for Kommetjie, consider a spot of camel-riding at Imhoff Farm Village (see p.92).

As regards child-friendly swimming pools, **Newlands Pool** (see p.142) has a toddlers' pool and little playground in the large grounds, while the marvelous **Sea Point Pool** at Sea Point Pavilion (see p.142) has two paddling pools for children and lawns to laze on, but is overcrowded on weekends, unless you go early or late in the day.

The Winelands

An hour from Cape Town, the Winelands is all about indulgence – eating, drinking and relaxing. Each of the Western Cape's earliest European settlements, at Stellenbosch, Paarl, Franschhoek and Somerset West, has its own established wine route, packed with picture-perfect Dutch colonial heritage in the form of shimmering white, gabled homesteads, surrounded by vineyards and tall, slatey crags. To top it all off, the area has a disproportionate concentration of South Africa's stellar restaurants. Franschhoek is the smallest of the towns: a centre of culinary excellence draped in heavily cultivated Provençal character. In a region of stunning settings, it has the best – at the head of a narrow valley. This is where you should go if you're principally after a great lunch and a beautiful drive out of Cape Town.

Stellenbosch, by contrast, has some attractive historical streetscapes, a couple of decent museums, cafés and shops and, as far as great restaurants go, it gives Franschhoek stiff competition. One of the region's scenic highlights is the drive along the **R310** across the heady **Helshoogte Pass** between Stellenbosch and the R45 Franschhoek–Paarl road. **Paarl**, also a pretty drive from Stellenbosch, is a workaday farming town set in a fertile valley overlooked by stunning granite rock formations. Beyond, head to the sprawling town of **Somerset West** for its one simply outstanding drawing card: **Vergelegen**, one of the most stunning of all the Wineland estates.

GETTING AROUND   THE WINELANDS

By car All the wineries are an easy drive from Cape Town; if you're not staying overnight, you can visit up to three or four in a day.

By train Use the train line from Cape Town via Stellenbosch and Paarl with caution, as trains pass through rough areas of the Cape Flats, and it is slow and unreliable.

On a tour Organized tours are operated from Stellenbosch (see p.154) and Cape Town, with many backpacker hostels and guesthouses running excursions. Stellenbosch's tourism office is also a good source of information.

15

INFORMATION

When to go Summer is the best time to visit, when days are longer (as are opening hours), the vines are in leaf and there's activity at the wineries. In winter the wine has been made and there are fewer cellar tours, though the landscape is still gorgeous, and many of the region's upmarket guesthouses let their rooms at half-price.

Wine tasting Wine tasting and buying are supposed to be fun, so don't take them too seriously. If you aren't a wine buff, you'll often find staff at tasting rooms are happy to talk you through a wine. Most estates charge a fee for a wine-tasting session (anywhere up to R40) and some only have tastings at specific times; see the individual accounts for more details. Note also that some wineries are closed on Sundays.

TASTING THE FORBIDDEN FRUIT: SOUTH AFRICA'S WINES

Despite South Africa having the longest-established **New World** winemaking tradition (going back more than 350 years), its rapid growth in wine production is remarkable for having taken place within the past two post-apartheid decades. Before that, South Africa's isolation had led to a stagnant and inbred industry that produced heavy Bordeaux-style wines. After the arrival of democracy in 1994, winemakers began producing fresher, fruitier wines, but many drinkers still turned their wine-tasting noses up at them. It's over the last ten years that things have really started to rev up and some South African winemakers are finding their feet in wines that combine the best of Old and New World styles. New wineries are opening up all the time, and more and more farms are planting vines.

South Africa produces wines from a whole gamut of major cultivars. Of the **whites**, the top South African Sauvignon Blancs can stand up with the best the New World has to offer; among the **reds**, it's the blends, created from Cabernet Sauvignon, Merlot and Shiraz that really shine. Also look out for red wine made from Pinotage grapes – a somewhat controversial curiosity unique to South Africa – which its detractors feel should stay on the vine. **Port** is also made, and the best vintages come from the Little Karoo town of Calitzdorp along the R62 (see p.235). There are also a handful of excellent **sparkling wines**, including Champagne-style, fermented-in-the-bottle bubbly, known locally as **méthode cap classique** (MCC).

The most enjoyable way to sample wines is by visiting wineries. The oldest and most rewarding wine-producing regions to tour are the **Constantia** estates in Cape Town (see p.81) and the **Winelands**; other wine-producing areas covered by this guide include **Walker Bay** around Hermanus (see p.168) and the **Little Karoo** along the R62 (see p.223). If you're serious about your wine tasting, think about buying the authoritative and annually updated *John Platter's South African Wine Guide* (also available as an iPhone app), which rates wines from virtually every producer in the country. *Wine* magazine (🌐winemag.co.za), published every month, has useful features on wineries, places to eat, wine reviews, information on latest bottlings, and a diary of events and wine festivals.

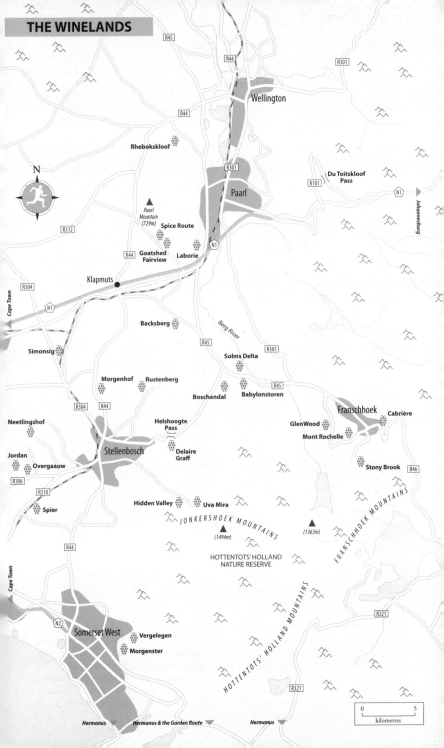

Stellenbosch

Dappled avenues of three-century-old oaks are the defining feature of **STELLENBOSCH**, 46km east of Cape Town – a fact reflected in its Afrikaans nickname Die Eikestad (the oak city). Stellenbosch's attractions lie principally in its setting and architecture, rooted in the seventeenth century, which make it a lovely place to simply wander around and one that's safe at night. Besides the designated historical and architectural sights, you'll find some good-quality galleries and arts and crafts shops down Church and Dorp streets, along with pavement cafés.

Stellenbosch today is the heart of the Winelands, having more urban attractions than either Paarl or Franschhoek, while at the same time being at the hub of the largest and oldest of the Cape **wine routes**. The city is also home to Stellenbosch University, Afrikanerdom's most prestigious educational institution, which does something to enliven the atmosphere. But even the heady promise of plentiful alcohol and thousands of students haven't changed the fact that at heart this is a conservative place, which was once the intellectual engine room of apartheid, and fostered the likes of Dr Hendrik Verwoerd, the prime minister who dreamed up the system (see p.255).

The tourist office is a good place to start your explorations. Heading east up this road, you'll soon reach a whitewashed block that was the **VOC Kruithuis**, the Dutch East India Company's powder magazine. From here, a right turn south down the side of the **Braak**, the large green occupying the centre of town, will take you past the **Rhenish Church** in Bloem Street, built in 1823 as a school for slaves and coloured people.

The Village Museum

18 Ryneveld St • Mon–Sat 9am–5pm, Sun 10am–4pm • R25

Stellenbosch's highlight, the extremely enjoyable **Village Museum**, cuts a cross section through the town's architectural and social heritage by means of four fortuitously adjacent historical dwellings from different periods. They're beautifully conserved and furnished in period style, and you'll meet the odd worker dressed in period costume.

Earliest of the houses is the homely **Shreuderhuis**, a vernacular cottage built in 1709, with a small courtyard garden filled with aromatic herbs, pomegranate bushes and vine-draped pergolas – bearing more resemblance to the early Cape settlement's European aesthetics than to modern South Africa.

Across the garden, **Blettermanhuis**, built in 1789 for the last Dutch East India Company-appointed magistrate of Stellenbosch, is an archetypal eighteenth-century Cape Dutch house, built on an H-plan with six gables. **Grosvenor House**, opposite, was altered to its current form in 1803, reflecting the growing influence of English taste after the 1795 British occupation of the Cape. The Neoclassical facade, with fluted pilasters supporting a pedimented entrance, borrows from high fashion then current at the heart of the growing empire. The more modest **O.M. Bergh House**, across the road, is a typical Victorian dwelling that was once similar to Blettermanhuis, but was "modernized" in the mid-nineteenth century on a rectangular plan, with a simplified facade without gables.

Dorp Street

Stellenbosch's best-preserved historic axis, **Dorp Street** lies south of the museum and is well worth a slow stroll just to soak in the ambience of buildings, gables, oaks and roadside irrigation furrows. Look out for **Krige's Cottages**, nos. 37–51 between Aan-de-Wagenweg and Krige streets, an unusual terrace of historic townhouses. The houses were built as Cape Dutch cottages in the first half of the nineteenth century; Victorian features were added later, resulting in an interesting hybrid, with gables housing Victorian attic windows and decorative Victorian verandas with filigree ironwork fronting the elegantly simple Cape Dutch facades.

15

STELLENBOSCH

▲ Franschhoek

Jan S. Marais Park

N

ACCOMMODATION
Banghoek Place	3
De Oude Meul	8
Glenconner	5
Knorhoek Country Guest House	2
Natte Vallej	1
Ryneveld Country Lodge	4
Stumble Inn	7
Ten Alexander	6
Villa Merwe	9

● EATING AND DRINKING
Jordan Restaurant	3
Katjiepiering	1
Overture	6
Schoon de Companje	2
Terroir	5
Volkskombuis	4

Danie Craven Stadium

Coetzenburg Stadium

0   250
metres

CLUVER RD

MARAIS ROAD

MERRIMAN AVENUE

SOETEWEIDE ROAD

VICTORIA STREET

DE WAAL ROAD

HOFMEYR ROAD

CLAASEN ROAD

VAN RIEBEECK STREET

COETZENBURG ROAD

JONKERSHOEK RD

VAN REEN PEL RD

BOSMAN ROAD

DIE LAAN

RATTRAY AVENUE

NOORDWAL-OOS ROAD

BANGHOEK ROAD

UNIVERSITY

VICTORIA STREET

MURRAY ROAD

NEETHLING STREET

Stellenbosch University Botanical Garden

MINISERIE ROAD

VAN RIEBEECK STREET

THE AVENUE

SUIDWAL

JOUBERT ROAD

MERRIMAN AVENUE

SMUTS ROAD

DE VILLIERS ROAD

RYNEVELD STREET

RYNEVELD STREET

DROSTDY ROAD

Village Museum

DORP STREET

CROZIER ROAD

VICTORIA STREET

City Hall

PLEIN STREET

CHURCH/KERK STREET

HELDERBERG ROAD

NOORDWAL-WES ROAD

SUIDWAL

BANGHOEK ROAD

BORCHERD ROAD

ANDRINGA STREET

ANDRINGA STREET

LOUW STREET

BIRD STREET

PIET RETIEF STREET

BIRD STREET

BIRD STREET

MILL

DU TOIT ROAD

DENNESIG ROAD

The Braak

Rhenish Church

BLOEM

DORP STREET

HAMMAN ROAD

MERRIMAN AVENUE

HOFMAN ROAD

PAUL KRUGER ROAD

MOLTENO ROAD

KOETSIEF

ALEXANDER ROAD

VOC Kruithuis

MARKET

KRIGE ROAD

BERGZICHT ROAD

HERTE ROAD

Oom Samie se Winkel

Stadium

DU TOIT ROAD

MARKET

PAPEGAAI ROAD

ADAM TAS

DU TOIT ROAD

HEROLD ROAD

AAN-DE-WAGENWEG

DENNESIG ROAD

Kleine Zalze Wine Esate & Somerset West

Stellenbosch Station

STRAND ROAD

WEIDENHOF STREET

ADAM TAS

Eerste River

Oude Libertas Estate, Airport & Cape Town

ARRIVAL AND INFORMATION

By train Metrorail trains (☎ 0800 65 64 63, ⓦ capemetrorail.co.za) travel between Cape Town and Stellenbosch roughly every ninety minutes during the day and take about an hour, but use this line with caution.

By bus The Baz Bus runs daily from Cape Town to Somerset West, where it drops passengers off at the BP filling station next to the *Lord Charles Hotel*. Some hostels operate shuttle services from there, but you need to arrange this beforehand.

Tourist information The busy tourist office about 1km from the station at 36 Market St (Mon–Fri 8am–5pm, Sat & Sun 9am–2pm; ☎ 021 883 3584, ⓦ stellenbosch.travel), provides information on local attractions and a comprehensive accommodation booking service.

TOURS

WALKING TOURS

Walking tours leave the tourist office in the morning and afternoon, and are a great way to see the architectural highlights and get a feel of the town (by appointment with Sandra ☎ 021 887 9150; R100 per person; minimum of six in a group).

WINE TOURS

If you want to get out of town and visit the vineyards, the tourism office represents a number of wine tour operators and can steer you towards the right one, depending on your time and budget. Expect to pay a minimum of R350 for a half-day tour and R550 for a full-day, inclusive of tasting fees. Recommended companies include:

Bikes n Wines ☎ 074 186 0418, ⓦ bikesnwines.com. If you are feeling energetic, you can tour the vineyards by bicycle with Bikes n Wines, who do a half-day tour (R550) and an overnight mountain-bike-trail option (R1950).

Easy Rider Wine Tours ☎ 021 886 4651, ⓦ winetour .co.za. Based at *Stumble Inn* backpacker lodge (see below), Easy Rider Wine Tours offer packages to four wineries (R500), with lunch at Franschhoek thrown in.

Equine Sport Centre ☎ 071 597 2546, ⓦ equinesportcentre.co.za. If you fancy exploring the vineyards on horseback, the Equine Sport Centre offers rides at Morgenhof, Knorhoek and Remhoogte wine estates. They can cater for beginners or experienced riders on well-schooled horses, with capable lead riders. Shorter rides cover one wine estate (R220), half-day rides cover two (R600) and full-day outings (R600) visit all three estates – there are stop-offs for tastings and great views of the sea and Table Mountain on some rides.

The Vine Hopper ☎ 084 492 4992, ⓦ vinehopper.co.za. A convenient hop-on, hop-off bus, which goes to a dozen wineries, including the Van Ryn's Brandy Cellar. Call in advance for their days and routes, which will vary depending on the season and tourism demand (day-ticket R240).

ACCOMMODATION

Accommodation can be difficult to find in Stellenbosch in the summer months: expect to find many places full and book well in advance. The tourist office can be helpful in finding you a place.

Banghoek Place 193 Banghoek Rd ☎ 021 887 0048, ⓦ banghoek.co.za. Slightly more upmarket sister hostel to *Stumble Inn* (see opposite), with mostly en-suite double, twin and triple rooms that offer terrific value, and three small dorms. Discount packages available include two nights' accommodation plus a wine tour. Dorm R150, double R500

De Oude Meul 10A Mill St (off Dorp St) ☎ 021 887 7085, ⓦ deoudemeul.com. Located in the middle of town on a fairly busy street, above an antique shop, these pleasant rooms are good value. Ask for one at the back to ensure a quiet night's sleep. R1000

Glenconner Jonkershoek Rd, 4km from the centre ☎ 021 886 5120 or ☎ 082 354 3510, ⓔ glenconner @icon.co.za. Both self-catering and B&B options are available at these pretty farm cottages with grazing horses in the fields below. The tranquil valley setting is spectacular, close to the walks in the Jonkershoek Nature Reserve. Breakfast can be taken under an old oak tree. R750

Knorhoek Country Guest House Knorhoek Wine Estate, off the R44, 7km north of town ☎ 021 865 2114, ⓦ knorhoek.co.za. With a bucolic setting in a snug valley, these old farm buildings have been turned into modern guest rooms and cottages. Each has a sunny patio, lawn and a feeling of calm luxury, plus guests can wander the gardens and vineyard. Double R900, cottage R1250

Natte Valleij On the R44, 12km north of town ☎ 021 875 5171, ⓦ nattevalleij.co.za. Guests have a choice of a large cottage sleeping six, a smaller one-bedroom unit attached to an old wine cellar or an en-suite room with its own entrance. There's a swimming pool, and breakfast (included) is served on the veranda. R720

Ryneveld Country Lodge 67 Ryneveld St ☎ 021 887 4469, ⓦ ryneveldlodge.co.za. Gracious late-nineteenth-century building, now a National Monument and furnished with Victorian antiques. The rooms are spotless, with the two best rooms upstairs leading onto a wooden deck. There are also two family cottages, which sleep up to four, and a pool. R1400

Stumble Inn 12 Market St ☎ 021 887 4049, ⓦ stumble innstellenbosch.hostel.com. The town's best and longest-standing hostel, spread across two houses that date from the turn of the last century and run by friendly, switched-on staff. Just down the road from the tourist office, the hostel is also noted for its good-value tours. Dorm R130, double R370

Ten Alexander 10 Alexander St ☎021 887 4414, ⓦ10alexander.co.za. This guesthouse is functional, quiet and pleasant, and very well run by the chatty owner. Rooms are small and spotless, plus there's a nice garden

and pool. There are also facilities for self-catering for those trying to keep down costs. R1120

Villa Merwe 6 Cynaroides Rd, Paradyskloof ☎021 880 1185, ⓦvillamerwe.co.za. Two immaculate and comfortable rooms in the owner's modern house, each with its own entrance and bathroom, with a lounge, pool and garden. It's a 5min drive from the centre. R900

EATING AND DRINKING

A meal on a **vineyard** is one of the top eating experiences in South Africa and several restaurants near Stellenbosch regularly make the *Eat Out* Top 10 (see box below). You'll need to reserve a table weeks or months in advance, particularly in the summer. In **Stellenbosch** itself there are some appealing pavement cafés, especially down Church Street, while in the evenings the student presence ensures a relaxed (and occasionally) raucous drinking culture. On Saturday mornings it's worth visiting the fabulous and very popular farmers' market in the Oude Libertas Estate grounds, off the R310 just south of the centre (ⓦslowmarket.co.za; 9am–2pm). You'll find a range of locally produced and organic food to eat and take away, including breads, cheeses, meats, vegetables, fruit, beers and estate wines.

15

Katjiepiering Botanical Gardens, cnr Neetling & Van Riebeeck sts ☎021 808 3054. Set beneath shady trees in a tranquil garden, this café offers a wonderful respite on a baking day. Reasonably priced dishes include an excellent *bobotie* (R60) and the salads are generous. Daily 8am–5pm.

★**Schoon de Companje** Cnr Bird & Church sts ☎021 883 2187, ⓦdecompanje.co.za. A café combined with a deli, with various nooks to settle down in with some good coffee and croissants. The pavement seating is one of the

big draws in summer, as are the artisan ice creams and locally brewed Stellenbrau craft beer. Tues–Sat 7.30am–7pm, Sun 8am–3pm.

Volkskombuis Aan-de-Wagenweg Off Dorp St ☎021 887 2121, ⓦvolkskombuis.co.za. Popular spot on the banks of the Eerste River, in a beautiful seventeenth-century Cape Dutch house. If you want to sample traditional Cape Cuisine then this is the place to head, with dishes including *bobotie* and braised oxtail (R140). Daily noon–3pm & 6pm onwards.

THE WINERIES

Stellenbosch was the first locality in the country to wake up to the marketing potential of a **wine route**. It launched its wine route in 1971, a tactic that has been hugely successful; today tens of thousands of visitors from all over the world are drawn here annually, making this the most toured area in the Winelands. Although the region accounts for only a fraction

TOP THREE STELLENBOSCH WINE ESTATE RESTAURANTS

Jordan Restaurant Jordan Wine Estate, 11.5km west of Stellenbosch, off the R310 ☎021 881 3612, ⓦjordanwines.com. One of the country's top chefs rules the roost here and never fails to please. Expect exquisite food, service and wines, which can be enjoyed on a deck overlooking a lake and distant mountains. The reasonably-priced set menu is based on seasonal ingredients (R275 for two courses, R320 for three) and you can even toddle off to their cheese tasting room in-between courses. Next to the restaurant is the *Bakery at Jordan* (ⓦthebakery.co.za), which does interesting breakfasts, lighter meals and cheese and charcuterie platters (R120). Jordan Restaurant summer Sun–Wed noon–3pm, Thurs–Sat noon–3pm & 6.30pm onwards; winter Wed, Sat & Sun noon–3pm, Thurs & Fri noon–3pm & 6.30pm onwards; Bakery at Jordan daily 8.30am–3.30pm.

Overture Hidden Valley Wine Estate, Annandale Rd ☎021 880 2646, ⓦdineatoverture.co.za. Top of the

town in more ways than one, *Overture* looks down magnificently from the hills into the Annandale Valley – and it consistently wins awards as one of the country's top ten restaurants. Based on classical French cuisine, with fresh ingredients and everything made from scratch, the dishes throw up interesting contemporary twists. Select three courses (R370) or sample the works with the six-course tasting menu (R600). Book way in advance. Wed & Sun noon–3pm, Thurs–Sat noon–3pm & 7–10.30pm.

Terroir Kleine Zalze Wine Estate, Strand Rd (R44) ☎021 880 8167, ⓦkleinezalze.com. Some 8km from Stellenbosch on a wine and golf estate, *Terroir* has a surprisingly relaxed dining room (for a nationally fêted restaurant) and tables outside under shady oaks. The expensive French-inspired menu is based as far as possible on local seasonal produce, with signature dishes that include a prawn risotto starter (R115) and kingklip with squid and mussels (R195). Mon–Sat noon–2.30pm & 6.30–9.30pm, Sun noon–2.30pm.

of South Africa's land under vine, its wine route is the most extensive in the country, approaching three hundred establishments; apart from the selection here (all of which produce creditable wines and are along a series of roads that radiate out from Stellenbosch) there are scores of other excellent places, which taken together would occupy months of exploration. If you're planning your own route, all the wineries are clearly signposted off the main arteries, or you can take a tour from Stellenbosch (see p.154). Several vineyards offer sit-down luxury meals (see box, p.155) or picnic baskets (reserve in advance), but many only lay on tastings. Opening hours may be shorter in the winter.

Delaire Graff Estate On the Helshoogte Pass, 6km east of Stellenbosch along the R310 to Franschhoek ☎ 021 885 8160, ⓦ delairewinery.co.za. The highly regarded *Delaire Graff* restaurant has possibly the best views in the Winelands, looking through pin oaks across the Groot Drakenstein and Simonsig mountains and down into the valley. Outstanding wines aren't hard to find here as most of their output delivers the goods: the majority are whites, but they also produce a great red blend. A tasting of three wines costs R50, or you can go for a food and wine pairing class with a tutor (book in advance; R150). Mon–Sat 10am–5pm, Sun 10am–4pm; restaurant Wed–Sat & Mon noon–2.15pm & 6.30–9pm, Tues & Sun noon–2.15pm.

Jordan Vineyards 11.5km west of Stellenbosch off the R310 ☎ 021 881 3612, ⓦ jordanwines.com. A pioneer among the new-wave Cape wineries, Jordan's high-tech cellar and modern tasting room is complemented by its friendly service. The drive there is half the fun, taking you into a *kloof* bounded by vineyards that get a whiff of the sea from both False Bay and Table Bay, which has clearly done something for its output – it has a list of outstanding wines as long as your arm and a highly rated restaurant (see box, p.155). Tasting R35 for six wines, refundable with purchases. Daily 9.30am–4.30pm.

Morgenhof 4km north of Stellenbosch on the R44 ☎ 021 889 551, ⓦ morgenhof.com. French-owned chateau-style complex on the slopes of the vine-covered Simonsberg, owned by Anne Cointreau-Huchon (granddaughter of the founder of Remy Martin cognac). Morgenhof has a light and airy tasting room with a bar, and delicious light lunches are served outside, topped off with ice cream on the lawns. They produce the excellent Morgenhof Estate red blend and a couple of brilliant whites (including a Chenin Blanc, Chardonnay and Sauvignon Blanc) under the same label, while the Fantail range is their second, more affordable label. Tasting R25 for five wines. Daily 9am–5.30pm; restaurant daily 9am–4pm.

Neethlingshof 6.5km west of Stellenbosch on Polkadraai Rd (the R306) ☎ 021 883 8988, ⓦ neethlingshof.co.za. Centred around a beautifully restored Cape Dutch manor dating back to 1814, reached down a kilometre-long avenue of stone pines, Neethlingshof's first vines were planted in 1692. There's a restaurant, and for R70 you can try their "flash food" light lunch – pairings of five wines with bite-sized delicacies (booking essential). The estate has two labels: Premium and Short Story reserve range, which consists of a Pinotage, a red blend and a flagship Noble

Late Harvest white. Tasting R30 for six wines. Mon–Fri 9am–5pm, Sat & Sun 9am–3.30pm; restaurant Mon–Sat 9am–8.30pm, Sun 9am–3.30pm.

Overgaauw 6.5km west of Stellenbosch, off the M12 ☎ 021 881 3815, ⓦ overgaauw.co.za. Notable for its elegant Victorian tasting room, this pioneering estate was the first winery in the country to produce Merlots, and it's still the only one to make a wine with Sylvaner, a well-priced, easy-drinking dry white. Tasting R20 for six wines, refundable upon purchase. Mon–Fri 9am–noon & 1–4pm, Sat 10am–2pm.

Rustenberg Wines Off Lelie Rd, Ida's Valley ☎ 021 809 1200, ⓦ rustenberg.co.za. One of the closest estates to Stellenbosch, Rustenberg is also one of the most alluring, reached after a drive through orchards, sheep pastures and tree-lined avenues. An unassuming working farm, it has a romantic pastoral atmosphere, in contrast to its architecturally stunning tasting room in the former stables; the first vines were planted here in 1692, but the viniculture looks to the future. Their high-flyers include the Peter Barlow Cabernet Sauvignon, John X Merriman red blend and Five Soldiers Chardonnay. Tasting R25 for six wines, refundable upon wine purchase. Mon–Fri 9am–4.30pm, Sat 10am–3.30pm.

Simonsig Estate 9.5km north of Stellenbosch, off Kromme Rhee Rd, which runs between the R44 and the R304 ☎ 021 888 4900, ⓦ simonsig.co.za. This winery has a relaxed outdoor tasting area under vine-covered pergolas, offering majestic views back to Stellenbosch of hazy stone-blue mountains and vineyards. The first estate in the country to produce a bottle-fermented bubbly some three decades back, it also produces a vast range of first-class still wines. Tasting R30 for five wines and a bubbly. Mon–Fri 8.30am–5pm, Sat 8.30am–4pm, Sun 10am–3pm.

★**Uva Mira** About 8km south of Stellenbosch, off Annandale Rd, which spurs off the R44 ☎ 021 880 1683, ⓦ uvamira.co.za. Enchanting boutique winery that punches well above its weight, but worth visiting just for the winding drive halfway up the Helderberg. The highly original tasting room, despite being fairly recently built, gives the appearance of a gently decaying historic structure, and there are unsurpassed views from the deck across mountainside vineyards to False Bay some 50km away – on a clear day you can even see Robben Island. Their 2005 Chardonnay stands out as an international winner and their flagship Bordeaux-style red blend is also noteworthy. Tasting R30 for three wines. Daily 10am–4.30pm, Sat & Sun 10am–4pm.

THE HISTORY OF VERGELEGEN

Vergelegen represents a notorious episode of corruption and the arbitrary abuse of power at the Cape in the early years of Dutch East India Company rule. Built by Willem Adriaan van der Stel, who became governor in 1699 after the retirement of his father, Simon, the estate formed a grand Renaissance complex in the middle of the wild backwater that was the Cape at the beginning of the eighteenth century. Van der Stel acquired the land illegally and used Dutch East India Company slaves to build Vergelegen, as well as company resources to farm vast tracts of land in the surrounding areas. At the same time he abused his power as governor to corner most of the significant markets at the Cape. When this was brought to the notice of the bosses in the Netherlands, they sacked Van der Stel and ordered the destruction of Vergelegen to discourage future miscreant governors. It's believed that the destruction was never fully carried out and the current building is thought to stand on the foundations of the original.

Somerset West

15

The only compelling reasons to trawl out to the unpromising town of **SOMERSET WEST**, 50km east of Cape Town along the N2, are for **Vergelegen** on Lourensford Road, and its immediate neighbour **Morgenster**, which are officially part of the Helderberg wine route, but can easily be included as an extension to a visit to Stellenbosch, just 14km to the north.

Vergelegen

Daily 9.30am–4pm • R10 • Wine tasting R30 for six wines • ☎ 021 847 1346, ⓦ vergelegen.co.za

An architectural treasure as well as an estate producing a stunning range of wines, Vergelegen was the only wine estate visited by the British queen during her 1995 state visit to South Africa – a good choice, as there's enough here to occupy even a monarch for an easy couple of hours.

The **interpretive centre**, just across the courtyard from the shop at the building entrance, provides a useful history and background to the estate. Next door, the **wine-tasting centre** offers a professionally run sampling with a brief talk through each label. They produce a vast range of wines, almost every one of which is excellent.

The **homestead**, which was restored in 1917 to its current state by Lady Florence Phillips, wife of a Johannesburg mining magnate, can also be visited. Its pale facade, reached along an axis through an octagonal garden that flits with butterflies in summer, has a classical triangular gable and pilaster-decorated doorways. Extensive grounds planted with chestnuts and camphor trees and ponds around every corner make this one of the most serene places in the Cape.

EATING AND DRINKING   VERGELEGEN

Vergelegen ☎ 021 847 1346, ⓦ vergelegen.co.za. Food options at Vergelegen are varied. One of the best ways to enjoy the surrounds is to order a gourmet picnic basket (R195 per person; summer only), which will be laid-out under the camphor trees, complete with checked table cloth and wicker basket. *The Stables* offers breakfast, lunch and coffees in a bistro environment, while *Camphors Restaurant* is one of the top Winelands eating experiences – the seasonal menu might include steak tartare from their own Nguni cattle (R375 for three courses, and R275 for two). The Stables daily 9.30am–4pm; Camphors Restaurant Wed, Thurs & Sun noon–2.30pm, Fri & Sat noon–2.30pm & 6.30–9.30pm.

Morgenster

Mon–Sun 10am–5pm • Olive oil tastings R20; wine tastings R45 • ⓦ morgenster.co.za

Apart from its exquisite rustic setting, the tasting room at **Morgenster**, Vergelegen's immediate neighbour, has a veranda that looks onto a lovely lake with hazy mountains in the distance. Its two stellar blended reds aside, the estate offers the unusual addition of olive tasting, with several types of olive and oil (including an award-winning cold-pressed extra virgin olive oil) and some delicious olive paste.

Paarl

Although **PAARL** is attractively ensconced in a fertile valley brimming with historical monuments, at heart it's a parochial *dorp*, lacking the sophistication of Stellenbosch or the striking setting and trendiness of Franschhoek. It is, however, a prosperous farming centre that earns its keep from the agricultural light industries – grain silos, canneries and flour mills – on the north side of town, and the cornucopia of grapes, guavas, olives, oranges and maize grown on the surrounding farms. Despite its small-town feel, Paarl has the largest municipality in the Winelands, with its most exclusive areas on the vined slopes of **Paarl Mountain** overlooking the town.

Brief history

In 1657, just five years after the establishment of the Dutch East India Company refreshment station on the Cape Peninsula, a party under Abraham Gabbema arrived in the Berg River Valley to look for trading opportunities with the Khoikhoi, and search for the legendary gold of Monomotapa. With treasure on the brain, they woke after a rainy night to see the glistening dome of granite dominating the valley, which they named **Peerlbergh** (pearl mountain), which in its modified form, Paarl, became the name of the town. Thirty years later, the commander of the Cape, Simon van der Stel, granted strips of the Khoikhoi lands on the slopes of Paarl Mountain to French Huguenot and Dutch settlers. By the time Paarl was officially granted town status in 1840, it was still an outpost

15

THE HISTORY OF AFRIKAANS

Afrikaans is South Africa's third mother tongue, spoken by fifteen percent of the population and outstripped only by Zulu and Xhosa. English, by contrast, is the mother tongue of only nine percent of South Africans, and ranks fifth in the league of the eleven official languages.

Signs of the emergence of a new southern-African dialect appeared as early as 1685, when a VOC official from the Netherlands, complained about a "distorted and incomprehensible" Dutch being spoken around modern-day Paarl. By absorbing English, French, German, Malay and indigenous words and expressions, the language continued to diverge from mainstream Dutch, and by the nineteenth century was widely used in the Cape by both white and coloured speakers, but was regarded by the elite as an inferior creole, unsuitable for literary or official communication.

Ironically, it was the British defeat of the Afrikaner republics in the second Anglo-Boer War at the turn of the twentieth century that provided the catalyst for a mass white Afrikaans movement. The official British policy of anglicizing South Africa helped unite a demoralized white Afrikaner proletariat and elite against the common English enemy.

In 1905, **Gustav Preller**, a young journalist from a working-class Boer background, set about reinventing Afrikaans as a "white man's language". Substituting Dutch words for those with non-European origins, Preller began publishing the first of a series of populist magazines written in Afrikaans and glorifying Boer history and culture. In 1925 Afrikaans became recognized as an official language.

When the National Party took power in 1948, its apartheid policy went hand in hand with promoting the interests of white Afrikaners, which they did through a programme of **uplifting poor whites**. Despite there being more coloured than white Afrikaans speakers, the language became associated with the **apartheid** establishment. When the government tried to enforce Afrikaans as the sole medium of instruction in African schools, the policy led directly to the **Soweto uprising** in 1976, which marked the beginning of the end for Afrikaner hegemony in South Africa. The repression of the 1970s and 1980s and the forced removals of coloureds and blacks led many coloured Afrikaans-speakers to adopt English in preference to their tainted mother tongue.

There are few signs, though, that Afrikaans will die out. Under the new constitution, language rights are protected, which means that Afrikaans will continue to be almost as widely used as before, except now it is as much with coloured as white people that the future of the *taal* (language) rests.

at the edge of the Drakenstein Mountains, a flourishing wagon-making and last-stop provisioning centre. This status was enhanced when the first **rail line** in the Cape connected it to the peninsula in 1863. Following in the spirit of the first Dutch adventurers of 1657, thousands of treasure-seekers brought custom to Paarl as the gateway to the interior during the diamond rush of the 1870s and the gold fever of the 1880s.

The town holds deep historical significance for the two competing political forces that forged modern South Africa. **Afrikanerdom** regards Paarl as the hallowed ground on which their language movement was born in 1875 (see box opposite), while for the **ANC** (and the international community), Paarl will be remembered as the place from which Nelson Mandela made the final steps of his long walk to freedom, when he walked out of **Groot Drakenstein Prison** (then called Victor Verster) in 1990.

Paarl's best-preserved historical frontage is along oak-lined **Main Street**, which stretches for some 2km – not ideal for strolling, especially on a hot day.

Paarl Museum

303 Main St • Mon–Fri 9am–4pm, Sat 9am–1pm • R5

Housed in a handsome, thatched Cape Dutch building with one of the earliest surviving gables (1787) in the "new style", characterized by triangular caps, the contents of the **Paarl Museum** don't quite match up to its exterior. It does include some reasonably enlightening panels on the architecture of the town, and several eccentric glass display cases of Victorian bric-a-brac. Post-apartheid transformation

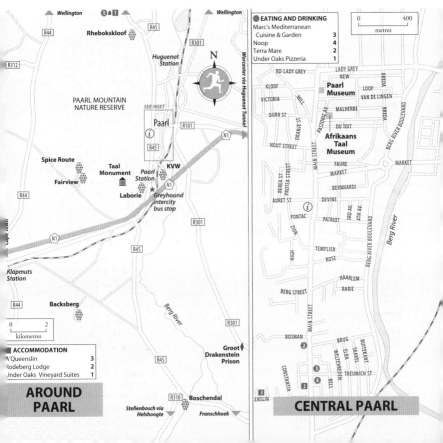

has introduced some coverage of the indigenous Khoisan populations of the area and the changes that came with European colonization, including slavery.

Taal Monument

South along Main St past the head office of the KWV; follow signs to the right up the slope of the mountain • Daily 9am–5pm • Free

The only other sight of any interest in Paarl itself is the grandiose **Taal Monument**, the controversial memorial to the Afrikaans language, standing just outside the centre on the top of Paarl Mountain. The monument used to be as important a place of pilgrimage for Afrikaners as the Voortrekker Monument in Pretoria, although when it was erected in 1973 detractors joked that monuments were usually erected to the dead. From the coffee and curio shop you can admire a truly magnificent panorama across to the Cape Peninsula and False Bay in one direction and the Winelands ranges in the other.

Groot Drakenstein (Victor Verster) Prison

Roughly 9km south of the N1 as it cuts through Paarl, along the R301 (the southern extension of Jan van Riebeeck St)

The **Victor Verster Prison**, renamed **Groot Drakenstein** in 2000, was Nelson Mandela's last place of incarceration. It was through the gates at Victor Verster that Mandela walked to his freedom on February 11, 1990, and it was here that the first images of him in 27 years were bounced around the world (under the Prisons Act, not even old pictures of him could be published during his imprisonment). The working jail looks rather like a boys' school fronted by rugby fields beneath hazy mountains, and there's something bizarre about seeing a prison sign nonchalantly slipped in among all the vineyard and wine-route pointers.

15

ARRIVAL AND INFORMATION   PAARL

By bus Daily Greyhound intercity buses from Cape Town (1hr) stop at the Monument Shell Garage, on the corner of Main Road and South Street, about 2km from the tourist office.
By train Metrorail and Spoornet services from Cape Town (18 daily; 1hr 15min) pull in at Huguenot Station in Lady Grey Street at the north end of town, near to the central shops.

Tourist information The tourist office, cnr Main and Plantasie sts (Mon–Fri 8am–5pm, Sat 9am–1pm & Sun 10am–1pm; ☎ 021 872 4842, ⓦ paarlonline.com), has a good selection of maps, including the wine routes, and can help with booking accommodation.

ACCOMMODATION

A'Queenslin 2 Queen St ☎ 021 863 1160, ⓔ aqueenslin @telkomsa.net. Two en-suite rooms with their own entrances and garden spaces, and three doubles that share a bathroom, in a split-level family home set in a quiet part of town, bounded on one side by vineyards and towered over by Paarl Rock. The rooms are large, each with a deck or patio and private and limited self-catering is possible – there's a fridge and microwave. A full English breakfast is an extra R65. **R700**
Rodeberg Lodge 74 Main St ☎ 021 863 3202, ⓦ rodeberglodge.co.za. Plain period furnishings give the en-suite rooms in this huge, centrally located and well-run

Victorian townhouse a cool, spacious feel. Ask for a room at the back if traffic noise bothers you. **R850**
Under Oaks Vineyard Suites Off R45, 8km north of Paarl ☎ 021 869 8535, ⓦ underoaks.co.za. Good-value-for-money luxury rooms, with ultra-comfy beds and linen, in a purpose-built, modern guesthouse on a vineyard overlooking the wide, fertile valley towards Wellington. Breakfast is served in a historic wine-estate dining room overlooking pastures, while dinner is at their pizzeria. You can try their flagship Sauvignon Blanc or Cabernet Sauvignon at the adjoining boutique winery. **R1200**

EATING AND DRINKING

A working town, Paarl has none of the Winelands foodie pretensions of Franschhoek or Stellenbosch, but you'll find a number of places along the main street for a decent coffee or a meal, as well as a couple of outstanding places on the surrounding vineyards.

Marc's Mediterranean Cuisine & Garden 129 Main St ☎ 021 863 3980, ⓦ marcsrestaurant.co.za. One of Paarl's most popular casual restaurants, *Marc's* dishes up a moderately priced, simple but tasty menu that includes

paella, Lebanese meze (R120), couscous, seafood and lamb, served in a converted historic house with a large outdoor area dotted with sun umbrellas and lemon trees. Mon–Sat 10am–2.30pm & 6.30–9.30pm.

Noop 127 Main St ☎ 021 863 3925, ⓦ noop.co.za. This super-cool pavement wine bar has a dauntingly long menu and equally extensive list of wines by the glass. They have some great takes on simple favourites such as burgers, pasta, pizza and steaks (R95) inspired, says the owner, by the old French stockpot. Mon–Sat 11am–9.30pm.

★ **Terra Mare** 90A Main St ☎ 021 863 4805. Italian- and Mediterranean-influenced dishes, such as three-mushroom risotto for starters (R85) and limoncello sorbet for dessert (R45), using local ingredients and infused with considerable flair. The glass and steel restaurant has great sweeping views of the Paarl Valley. Mon–Sun 11am–2pm & 6–10pm.

Under Oaks Pizzeria Paarl Main Rd, 8km from centre ☎ 021 869 8962. The best thing about eating a delicious wood-fired pizza here, and drinking wine from grapes grown on the farm, is the setting beneath majestic oak and the relaxed vibe, with children running about on the lawns; it is very popular with local families. Tues–Sat 11.30am–8.30pm, Sun noon–3.30pm.

THE WINERIES

There are a couple of notable wineries in Paarl itself, but most are on farms in the surrounding countryside. Boschendal, one of the most popular of these, is officially on the Franschhoek wine route (see p.166), but is in easy striking distance of Paarl. Most of the wineries have a restaurant, generally of a high standard, and some have beautiful rooms for staying over, more appealing than staying in central Paarl.

15

Backsberg Estate 22km south of Paarl on Simondium Rd (WR1) ☎ 021 875 5141, ⓦ backsberg.co.za; map p.159. Notable as the first carbon-neutral wine estate in South Africa, Backsberg produces some top-ranking red blends, and a delicious Chardonnay, in its Babylons Toren and Black Label ranges. Outdoor seating, with views of the rose garden and vineyard on the slopes of the Simonsberg, makes this busy estate a nice place to while away some time. There's also a restaurant and a maze to get lost in. Tasting R15 for five wines. Tasting and restaurant Mon–Fri 9am–3.30pm, Sat & Sun 9am–3.30pm.

The Goatshed Fairview Estate Suid Agter Paarl Rd, on the southern fringes of town ☎ 021 863 2450, ⓦ fairview.co.za; map p.159. One of the most fun of all the Paarl estates (especially for families), with a resident population of goats who clamber up the spiral tower, featured in the estate's emblem, at the entrance. A deli sells breads and preserves, and you can also sample and buy the goats', sheep's and cows' cheeses made on the estate (R15). As far as wine-tasting goes (six wines and cheese selection R25), Fairview is an innovative, family-run place, but it can get a bit hectic when the tour buses roll in. The restaurant, no surprises here, offers a cheese platter (R65) and they are well known for their Sunday lunches. Tasting and restaurant daily 9am–5pm.

Laborie Taillefert St ⓦ laboriewines.co.za; map p.159. One of the most impressive Paarl wineries, all the more remarkable for being right in town. The beautiful manor is fronted by a rose garden, acres of close-cropped lawns, historic buildings and oak trees – all towered over by the Taal Monument. There's a truly wonderful tasting room with a balcony that jetties out over the vineyards trailing up Paarl Mountain, as well as a great restaurant with terrace seating offering good views of the town vineyards and mountains. Their flagship is the Jean Taillefert Shiraz, while the Pineau de Laborie, a dessert wine made from Pinotage grapes laced with Pinotage brandy, is also worth a try. Tasting R25. Mon–Sat 9am–5pm, Sun 11am–5pm.

Rhebokskloof Signposted off the R45, 11.5km northwest of Paarl ☎ 021 869 8386, ⓦ rhebokskloof .co.za; map p.159. A highly photogenic wine estate, and a popular wedding venue and a great place to bring kids, Rhebokskloof sits at the foot of sculptural granite *koppies* overlooking a lake with a a shaded terrace for summer lunches and gourmet meals. Meat is the house speciality, with exciting combinations of flavours, both Cape and international. It's also a good place for morning or afternoon teas, and they can prepare picnics on the lawns outside (R295 for two). Their Sunday lunch buffets (R185) are tremendously popular. In terms of wine, Shiraz is

---

HORSE AND QUAD-BIKE TRAILS

Hopping into the saddle and trotting off through the countryside offers a great alternative to seeing the Winelands from behind a restaurant table. At Rhebokskloof, 11.5km northwest of Paarl, you can do both.

Wine Valley Horse Trails ☎ 083 226 8735, ⓦ horsetrails-sa.co.za. This company, based at Rhebokskloof, offers one- to four-hour equestrian trails for novices and experts through the surrounding countryside – a choice spot for some riding. Prices start from R300 for a one-hour trail. Longer trails are restricted to experienced riders, but a four-hour package of a ride plus a conducted wine tasting at the estate is available for novices. They also do quad-bike trails which start at R250 for a half-hour.

where they make their mark. Wine tasting R15 for five wines. Mon–Fri 9am–5pm, Sat & Sun 9am–3pm; restaurant daily 9am–5pm, dinner by reservation only Friday 6pm onwards.

Spice Route Suid Agter Paarl Rd ☎ 021 863 5222, ⓦ spiceroute.co.za; map p.159. The Spice Route farm offers unusual tastings drawn from several artisanal producers who have grouped together in different buildings on the same premises. You can try beer and biltong at the *Cape Brewing Company*, hand-made chocolate and wine pairing at the *DV Artisan Chocolate, Roastery and Expresso Bar* (R100), or local grappa at *La Grapperia Pizza and Tapas Bar*, the only place open in the evening after 5pm. Other residents include an art gallery, glass blowers and farm shop. Like nearby Fairview, it is favoured by groups, so book for tastings in advance. Daily 11am–5pm.

Franschhoek

If indulgence is what the Winelands is really about, then **Franschhoek** is the place that does it best. Despite being a fairly small *dorp*, it has managed to establish itself as the culinary capital of the Western Cape, if not the whole country. Its late Victorian and more recent Frenchified rustic architecture, the terrific setting (it's hemmed in on three sides by mountains), the vineyards down every other backstreet and some vigorous myth-making have created a place you can really lose yourself in, a set piece that unashamedly draws its inspiration from Provence.

Brief history

Between 1688 and 1700 about two hundred French Huguenots, desperate to escape religious persecution in France, accepted a Dutch East India Company offer of passage to the Cape and the grant of lands. They made contact with the area's earliest settlers, groups of Khoikhoi herders. Conflict between the French newcomers and the Khoikhoi followed familiar lines, with the white settlers gradually dispossessing the herdsmen, forcing them either further into the hinterland or into servitude on their farms. The establishment of white hegemony was swift and by 1713 the area was known as *de france hoek*. Though French-speaking died out within a generation because of explicit Company policy, many of the estates hereabouts are still known by their original French names. **Franschhoek** itself, 33km from Stellenbosch and 29km from Paarl, occupies parts of the original farms of La Cotte and Cabrière and is relatively young, having been established around a church built in 1833.

The Huguenot Museum and the monument

Mon–Sat 9am–5pm & Sun 2–5pm • R10

Driving through Franschhoek, you can't fail to miss the **Huguenot Memorial Museum**, thanks to its location next to the town's most obvious landmark, the **Huguenot Monument**. Set in a prime position at the head of Huguenot Road, where it forms a T-junction with Lambrecht Street, the monument consists of three skinny interlocking arches, symbolizing the Holy Trinity. The museum gives comprehensive coverage of Huguenot history and culture, and of their contribution to modern South Africa.

Museum van de Caab

Sun–Thurs 9am–5pm, Fri & Sat 9am–6pm • Free • ⓦ solms-delta.co.za

Twelve kilometres north of Franschhoek along the R45, at the Solms Delta Wine Estate, the highly recommended **Museum van de Caab** gives a condensed and riveting slice through South African vernacular history as it happened on the farm and its surrounds. Housed alongside the atmospherically understated tasting room in the original 1740s gabled Cape Dutch cellar, the display begins with Stone Age artefacts found on the site and goes on to trace the arrival of the aboriginal Khoisan people, their colonization by Europeans, the introduction of slavery and how this eventually evolved into the apartheid system and its eventual demise.

ARRIVAL AND INFORMATION

FRANSCHHOEK

By car There's no public transport to Franschhoek or in the town itself. From Stellenbosch take the R310 heading north, then east out of town. The route winds through the beautiful Helshoogte Pass, with a bunch of first-class wineries lining the mountainside along the way. Roughly 16km from Stellenbosch the R310 hits a T-junction with the R45, where you should turn east (right) and take the road for 18km to Franschhoek.

Tourist office Just north of the junction with Kruger St the tourist office at 62 Huguenot Rd (Mon–Fri 8am–5pm, Sat 9am–5pm, Sun 9am–4pm; ☎ 021 876 2861, ⓦ franschhoek.org.za) has some excellent maps of the village and its winelands.

ACTIVITIES

HIKING

The best hike in the vicinity is the Cat se Pad (Cat's Path), which starts as you head out of town up the Franschhoek Pass. The walk leads into *fynbos* with proteas, and gives instant access to the mountains surrounding the valley, with good views. The first two-kilometre section gets you to the top of the pass, and you can keep going for another 10km in the direction of Villiersdorp (though you don't actually reach it).

EQUESTRIAN WINE TOURS

Paradise Stables Roberstsvlei Rd ☎ 021 876 2160 or ☎ 084 586 2160, ⓦ paradisestables.co.za. Paradise Stables visits Rickety Bridge and Mont Rochelle wineries: wine tasting is included in the price, though lunch is not (2hr 30min in the saddle, 30–45min stop at each winery; R700; Mon–Sat 8.45am and 1.15pm). If you want to simply ride, they have outrides for R200 an hour (Mon–Sat at 7.30am and 5.45pm). Their Arabian horses, ridden with halters, are as good as gold, and beginners can be accommodated. The farm itself where you start the ride, has a couple of reasonably priced cottages for rent (R400).

ACCOMMODATION

On the whole, guesthouse accommodation here is pricey, but the rooms are of high quality and frequently in unparalleled settings; budget accommodation is hard to find, but there are a couple of reasonably priced self-catering cottages and a backpackers. It can be hard to find a bed in Franschhoek during the summer, so book as far ahead as possible. Some of the wine estates outside town also offer luxury rooms.

★**Akademie Street Boutique Hotel** 5 Akademie St ☎ 082 517 0405, ⓦ aka.co.za. Luxury guesthouse offering total privacy in each of its tastefully decorated and spacious suites set in beautiful gardens. Facilities include free wi-fi access, DVDs, a fridge stocked with free drinks and a long, saltwater swimming pool. Gourmet breakfasts with regional specialities are served poolside by the charming hosts who'll happily recommend a restaurant for dinner and book a table for you. R4100

Avondrood Guest House 39 Hugenot St ☎ 021 876 2881, ⓦ avondrood.com. A guesthouse with six rooms in a beautifully restored home, which gets accolade after accolade for the level of comfort and aesthetic experience offered. There are extensive lawns, a manicured garden and a pool. R2500

Bird Cottage and Frog Lodge Verdun Rd, 4.5km from

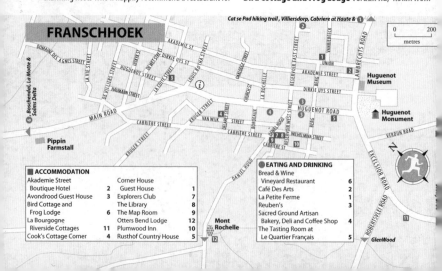

FRANSCHHOEK

Cat se Pad hiking trail , Villiersdorp, Cabriere at Haute & ▲

0   200
metres

■ ACCOMMODATION			
Akademie Street		Corner House	
Boutique Hotel	2	Guest House	1
Avondrood Guest House	3	Explorers Club	7
Bird Cottage and		The Library	8
Frog Lodge	6	The Map Room	9
La Bourgogne		Otters Bend Lodge	12
Riverside Cottages	11	Plumwood Inn	10
Cook's Cottage Corner	4	Rusthof Country House	5

● EATING AND DRINKING	
Bread & Wine	
Vineyard Restaurant	6
Café Des Arts	2
La Petite Ferme	1
Reuben's	3
Sacred Ground Artisan	
Bakery, Deli and Coffee Shop	4
The Tasting Room at	
Le Quartier Français	

town ☎021 876 2136, ✉grahamh@radionet.co.za. Two artistically furnished cottages that each sleep four, surrounded by beautiful indigenous gardens close to the mountains. This is about as remote as you'll find this close to Franschhoek as well as being thoroughly laidback and exceptional value. **R700**

Corner House Guest House Cnr Riebeeck & Union sts ☎021 876 4729, ⊚thecornerhouse.co.za. One of the few moderately-priced guesthouses, Dutch-run *Corner House* offers six bright and spotless rooms, and a pretty garden with pool. It's a good base from which to explore the area. They're especially pet-friendly. **R800**

★**Explorers Club, Cook's Cottage Corner, The Map Room and The Library** ☎021 876 4229, ⊚explorersclub.co.za. A quartet of centrally located self-catering houses – all luxurious, modern and tasteful. Each house sleeps 2–10 people. *The Map Room* is best suited to couples, with a living space upstairs and folding glass doors opening onto a terrace with vineyard and mountain views, while families and groups will be delighted with *The Library*'s gracious ambience. All the properties are in a great party of Franschhoek, close to vineyards and restaurants. **R2500**

La Bourgogne Riverside Cottages Excelsior Rd ☎021 876 3245, ⊚labourgogne.co.za. Six simply but very tastefully furnished converted labourers' cottages set in gardens along a river. The working farm presses their own oil and produces wines, including the highly rated Progeny Sémillon; wine tasting is offered for free when you stay here. **R900**

Otters Bend Lodge Dassenberg Rd ☎021 876 3200, ⊚ottersbendlodge.co.za. Rustic lodge with double and twin-bedded cabins, dorms and camping on the lawn, five minutes' drive from town and surrounded by orchards and vineyards. There is an inviting communal area, complete with a roaring fire in winter, a well-equipped kitchen and an outside braai area. Dorm/camping **R150**, double **R450**

Plumwood Inn 11 Cabrière St ☎021 876 3883, ⊚plumwoodinn.com. Unfailingly excellent boutique guesthouse with smart, clean and modern furnishings. They've paid close attention to detail throughout – from the custom-made cotton tablecloths to the luxurious beds and bathrooms, and the impeccable service. **R1400**

Rusthof Country House 12 Huguenot St ☎021 876 3762, ⊚rusthof.com. Modern eight-roomed guesthouse along the main drag (although it doesn't feel like it) within spitting distance of some of Franschhoek's top restaurants. Rooms open onto a rose garden, and the service is good. Besides double rooms, there are a couple available for families. **R2060**

EATING AND DRINKING

Eating and drinking is what Franschhoek is all about, so plan on sampling at least one or two of its excellent **restaurants**, some of which rate among the country's best. Franschhoek's cuisine tends to be French-inspired, but with an emphasis on local ingredients. Restaurants in town are concentrated along Huguenot Rd, but there are a number of excellent alternatives in the more rustic environment of the surrounding wine estates, several of which do picnics in their beautiful grounds. Booking is essential, particularly for the most flash of the restaurants, and winter opening hours may be reduced. Every Saturday (9am–2pm) there is a Farmers' Market in the churchyard on Main Rd.

Bread & Wine Vineyard Restaurant Moreson Farm, Happy Valley Rd ☎021 876 3692, ⊚moreson.co.za. Signposted off the R45 and surrounded by lemon orchards and vineyards, this is a genial and child-friendly venue, consistently in the top twenty in the country, specializing in home-cured charcuterie (R75) and the estate's own wines. Daily noon–3pm.

Café Des Arts 7 Reservoir St, next to the library ☎021 876 2952, ⊚cafedesarts.co.za. Service and food are consistently good here, with unfussy but flavoursome dishes; their teriyaki pork belly with stir-fried noodles is recommended (R110). It's a relaxed spot, also good for a coffee and something delicious from their small bakery. Mon–Sat 8am–3pm & 6.30–10pm.

La Petite Ferme Franschhoek Pass Rd ☎021 876 3016, ⊚lapetiteferme.co.za. With gorgeous views across a vineyard-covered valley, this restaurant has won awards galore – slow roasted lamb has been on the menu for thirty years and never fails to please (R162). Lunches are served with wines from the restaurant's cellar (R130). Friday night sundowners are a summer highlight, when there's often live music to accompany local wines on the lawn. Dinner Fri in summer only from 6.30pm. Daily noon–4pm.

Reuben's 19 Huguenot Rd ☎021 876 3772, ⊚reubens .co.za. Centrally situated restaurant with a modern interior, shady courtyard and trendy bar area with an old Dakota wing as the counter. Good for a lazy lunch in the summer under the cooling mist spray. The menu is modern French cuisine with cosmopolitan influences: venison features big and there's always poultry, lamb, pork, seafood and a vegetarian option such as potato gnocchi (R110). Daily noon–3pm & 7–9pm.

★**Sacred Ground Artisan Bakery, Deli and Coffee Shop** 36 Hugenot St ☎021 876 2759. An affordable place to have an excellent sandwich, such as the "veg patch" with mushrooms, olives, pesto and cheese (R50) or fresh pastries, pies and coffee. Mon–Sun 7am–6pm.

★**The Tasting Room at Le Quartier Français** 16 Huguenot Rd ☎021 876 2151, ⊚lqf.co.za. The place that made Franschhoek synonymous with food yonks ago, and has never put a foot wrong since, is irrepressibly one of South Africa's very best restaurants, skippered by Margot Janse – Africa's only female Grand Chef. Formal evening meals have a contemporary, global flavour and you need to book months in advance (R850 for a surprise eight-course menu). If you don't make it into the inner sanctum, there is an appealing lounge bar serving breakfast, craft beer, local wines and exceptionally good tapas, with dishes like prawn popcorn, wildebeest doughnuts and Gruyère Oreos. Restaurant Tues–Sat 7–10pm; bar daily 7am–11pm.

THE WINERIES

Franschhoek's wineries are small enough and sufficiently close together to make it a breeze to visit two or three in a morning. Heading north through town from the Huguenot Monument, you'll find most of the wineries signposted off Huguenot Rd and its extension, Main Rd; the rest are off Excelsior Rd and the Franschhoek Pass Rd.

★**Babylonstoren** Simondium Rd ☎021 863 3852, ⓦbabylonstoren. There are tourists aplenty here, but for good reason. Babylonstoren is a less traditional estate, beautifully set against the high Drakenstein mountains, with beautiful, extensive gardens, a shop (look for South African cookery books and upmarket crafts), ducks, chickens and olive trees as well as many acres under vine. They're the new kid on the block in terms of wine, but are already accruing a reputation for their red blend, Babel, and their Viognier. Of the two restaurants, the *Green House* is less formal while *Babel* is known for more traditional South African food. Entry to the estate costs R10. Estate daily 9am–5pm; Green House daily 10am–4pm; Babel Wed–Sun noon–4pm, Fri &Sat 6.30–8.30pm.

Boschendal Pniel Rd, just after the junction of the R45 and R310 to Stellenbosch ⓦboschendalwines.com. One of the world's longest-established New World wineries, Boschendal draws busloads of tourists – around 200,000 visitors a year – with its impressive Cape Dutch buildings, tree-lined avenues, beautiful gardens, restaurants and cafés and, of course, its wines. Of their six labels the Pavilion range delivers high-class, well-priced plonk (Shiraz–Cabernet Sauvignon, Rosé and a white blend); but their top ranges consistently deliver with classy wines like the Cecil John Reserve Shiraz and Sauvignon Blanc, and their Reserve range Cabernet Sauvignon, Shiraz and Bordeaux-blend Grande Reserve. Tasting R30. Try their famous "pique nique" basket (R165 per person; kids' option available) on the extensive lawns. Daily 9am–4.30pm.

Cabrière at Haute Cabrière About 2km from town along the Franschhoek Pass Rd ☎021 876 8500, ⓦcabriere.co.za. Atmospheric winery notable for its Pinot Noirs and colourful wine-maker Achim von Arnim, whose presence guarantees an eventful visit; try to catch him or, more commonly now, his son Takuan, when they demonstrate *sabrage* – slicing off the upper neck of a bubbly bottle with a French cavalry sabre. Cabrière is noted for its top-notch Pierre Jourdan range of sparkling wines and it specializes in Pinot Noir and blends made with the cultivar. Tasting R30 for five wines and R60 for five bubblies. Mon–Fri 9am–5pm, Sat 10am–4pm, Sun 11am–4pm.

GlenWood Robertsvlei Rd, signposted off the R45 ☎021 876 2044, ⓦglenwoodvineyards.co.za. Small winery in a beautiful setting that produces outstanding wines year after year. Although only ten-or-so minutes' drive from the village throng, it feels surprisingly remote, and vineyard and cellar tours are frequently conducted by the owner. Their flagship is the Grand Duc Chardonnay and Grand Duc Syrah. Tasting R30. The restaurant, *Le Bon Vivant @ Glenwood*, is good too, serving simple bistro food in a dramatic setting, but must be booked in advance. Estate Mon–Fri 11am–4pm plus Sept–April Sat & Sun 11am–3pm; restaurant Thurs–Tues noon–3pm.

★**Mont Rochelle** Dassenberg Rd ☎021 876 2770, ⓦmontrochelle.co.za. Set against the Klein Dassenberg, Mont Rochelle has one of the most stunning settings in Franschhoek and an unusual cellar in a converted nineteenth-century fruit-packing shed, edged by eaves decorated with fretwork, stained-glass windows and chandeliers. Chardonnay is what they do best here, but don't overlook their also stellar Sauvignon Blanc and Syrah. Tasting R30. They also offer very comfortable accommodation and have two restaurants and picnics available (R290 for two). Daily 10am–6pm.

★**Solms Delta** 13km north of Franschhoek along the R45 ☎021 874 3937, ⓦsolms-delta.co.za. Pleasantly bucolic Solms Delta produces unusual and consistently outstanding wines, which, on a summer's day, you can taste under ancient oaks at the edge of the vineyards with a picnic (R290 for two people). Half the profits from the wines produced go into a trust that benefits residents of the farm and the Franschhoek Valley. The Solms-Wijn de Caab range includes the excellent Hiervandaan (an unusual blend dominated by Shiraz, and including Carignan, Mourvèdre and Viognier grapes) and the even more highly rated Amalie (vine-dried Grenache Blanc and Viognier). Tasting R20 for six wines. Daily 9am–5pm.

Stony Brook Vineyards About 4km from Franschhoek, off Excelsior Rd ☎021 876 2182, ⓦstonybrook.co.za. Family-run boutique winery, with just 140,000 square metres under vine, that produces first-rate wines, including its acclaimed flagship Ghost Gum Cabernet Sauvignon, which takes its name from a magnificent old tree outside the house and informal tasting room. Tastings are convivial affairs conducted by the owners and are by appointment only (R35). Mon–Fri 10am–5pm, Sat 10am–1pm.

TRADITIONAL FISHERMAN HUTS, ARNISTON

The Whale Coast and Overberg Interior

From roughly July to November, southern right whales can be seen in the warm, sheltered bays of the Western Cape, and the southern Cape coast is prime territory for sightings. The Whale Coast, as the section from roughly Kleinmond to De Hoop has come to be known, is close enough for an easy outing from Cape Town, and yet is surprisingly undeveloped, with the exception of popular Hermanus. The Overberg Interior – the stretch as far as Swellendam, along the N2 towards the Garden Route – is dominated by the towns of Greyton, a peaceful, oak-lined country town 35km off the main road, and Swellendam itself, brimming with historical guesthouses and decent restaurants, as well as the Bontebok National Park.

Hermanus

On the edge of rocky cliffs and backed by mountains 112km east of Cape Town, **HERMANUS** sits at the northernmost end of **Walker Bay**, an inlet whose protective curve attracts calving whales as it slides south to the promontory of Danger Point. The town trumpets itself as the whale capital of South Africa, and to prove it, an official whale crier (purportedly the world's only one) struts around armed with a mobile phone and a dried kelp horn through which he yells the latest sightings. The hype aside, the bay on which Hermanus sits does provide some of the finest shore-based whale-watching in the world and, even if there are better spots nearby, the town is the best geared-up for tourists to enjoy it. There is still the barest trace of a once-quiet cliff-edge fishing village around the historic harbour and in some understated seaside cottages, but for the most part the town has gorged itself on its whale-generated income, which has produced modern shopping malls, supermarkets and craft shops.

Main Road, the continuation of the R43, meanders through Hermanus, briefly becoming Seventh Street. **Market Square**, just above the old harbour and to the south of Main Street, is the closest thing to a centre, and it's here you'll find the heaviest concentration of restaurants, craft shops and flea markets – the principal forms of entertainment in town when the whales are taking time out.

Apart from whales, Hermanus is also known for its wines, grown in the nearby Hemel en Aarde Valley, which sits inland from the R43. In the valley you'll also find some sensational eating and drinking experiences (see box, p.173).

16

The Old Harbour Museum

The Old Harbour • Mon–Sat 9am–4.30pm, Sun noon–4pm • R25

Just below Market Square is the **Old Harbour Museum** where, among the uncompelling displays, you'll find lots of fishing tackle and some sharks' jaws. Outside, a few colourful boats, used by local fishermen from the mid-eighteenth to mid-nineteenth centuries, create a photogenic vignette in the tiny harbour.

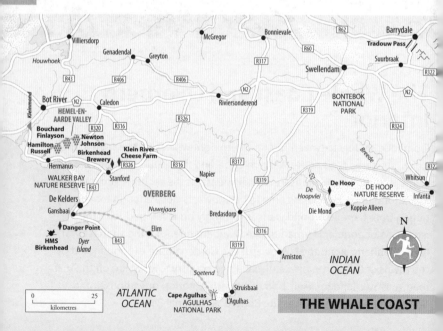

SWIMMING AND BEACHES

East of the Old Harbour, just below the *Marine Hotel*, a beautiful tidal pool offers the only **sea swimming** around the town centre's craggy coast; it's big enough to do laps. For **beaches**, you have to head out east across the Mossel River to the suburbs, where you'll find a decent choice, starting with secluded **Langbaai**, closest to town, a cove beneath cliffs at the bottom of Sixth Avenue that has a narrow strip of beach and is excellent for swimming. **Voelklip**, at the bottom of Eighth Avenue, has grassed terraces, toilets, a nearby café for tea and is great for picnics if you prefer your sandwiches unseasoned with sand. Adjacent is **Kammabaai**, with the best surfing break around Hermanus, and 1km further east, **Grotto Beach** (which despite its name is not a rocky cove), marking the start of a twelve-kilometre curve of dazzlingly white sand that stretches all the way to De Kelders.

The Cliff Path

An almost continuous five-kilometre cliff path through coastal *fynbos* hugs the rocky coastline from the Old Harbour to Grotto Beach in the eastern suburbs. For one short stretch, the path heads away from the coast and follows Main Road before returning to the shore. This path makes an excellent place to spot whales, and you can do as little or as much of the walk as you like.

Fernkloof Nature Reserve

Theron St • Dawn–dusk • Free

On the east side of town, off Main Road, the **Fernkloof Nature Reserve** encompasses fifteen square kilometres of mountainous terrain and offers sweeping views of Walker Bay. This highly recommended wilderness area is more than just another nature reserve on the edge of town – it has some 40km of **waymarked footpaths**, including a 4.5km circular nature trail. Visiting is an excellent way to get close to the astonishing variety of delicate montane coastal *fynbos* (over a thousand species have been identified in the reserve), much of it flowering species that attract scores of birds, including brightly coloured sunbirds and sugarbirds endemic to the area.

New Harbour

A couple of kilometres west of town along Westcliff, the **New Harbour** is a working fishing harbour, dramatically surrounded by steep cliffs, projecting a gutsy counterpoint to the more manicured central area. Whales sometimes enter the harbour – and there's nowhere better to watch them than from the *Harbour Rock* (see p.172).

Rotary Way

On the eastern edge of Hermanus, **Rotary Way** is a fantastic ten-kilometre drive that follows the mountain spine through beautiful montane *fynbos*, offering sweeping views of the town, the Hemel-en-Aarde Valley and Walker Bay from Kleinmond to Danger Point. To get there from town, turn right just after the sports ground, and take a track straddled by a pair of white gateposts labelled "Rotary Way". The road is tarred for part of the way, then becomes a dirt track, eventually petering out altogether, which means you have to return the same way.

Wine Village

Hemel-en-Aarde Village, at the junction of R43 and R320 • Mon–Fri 9am–6pm, Sat 9am–5pm, Sun 10am–3pm • ☎ 028 316 3988, ⊕ winevillage.co.za

Hermanus is home to possibly the best wine shop in South Africa, the **Wine Village**, with a staggering selection of labels from all of the country's various wine-producing districts, covering a vast price range. There are usually at least six bottles open for free wine-tasting and the staff are very knowledgeable. This is the place to stock up just before flying out – or have some cases shipped.

16

ARRIVAL AND DEPARTURE

By car There are two routes to Hermanus, 125km from Cape Town. It's more direct to take the N2 and head south onto the R43 at Bot River (a 1hr 30min drive), but the winding road that hugs the coast from Strand, leaving the N2 just before Sir Lowry's Pass, is the more scenic and one of the best coastal drives in South Africa (2hr).

By bus The Baz Bus (☎021 422 5202, ⊛bazbus.com) drops off at Bot River, 34km northeast of Hermanus on the

R43, where you can arrange to be collected by your hostel. Two shuttles – Bernadus (☎028 316 1093 or ☎083 658 7848) and Splash (☎028 316 4004) – ply the route between Hermanus and Cape Town (1hr 30min). They are effectively a taxi service, operating on demand, so you need to book in advance, though it is conveniently door to door. The journey one way costs from R400 per person to the centre of Cape Town.

INFORMATION

Tourist information The tourist office at the old station building in Mitchell Street (Mon–Sat: Sept–April 8am–6pm; May–Aug 9am–5pm & Sun 9am–2pm; ☎028 312 2629, ⊛hermanus.co.za) is a helpful place, with maps, useful brochures about the area and a free accommodation-finding

service. They can take bookings for boat-based and aerial whale-watching, as well as shark-cage diving trips.

Whale festival During the last week in September, the town puts on a fun show of anything that's got a whale connection – check ⊛whalefestival.co.za.

ACCOMMODATION

The most popular coastal destination outside Cape Town, Hermanus is awash with accommodation. If you want something a little more countrified, head off to Stanford, twenty minutes' drive away around the curve of the bay, though there are no beaches. Alternatively, head further along the coast to Gansbaai (see p.175), home to ugly holiday houses, but with great whale-viewing in season from the windows of any sea-facing room.

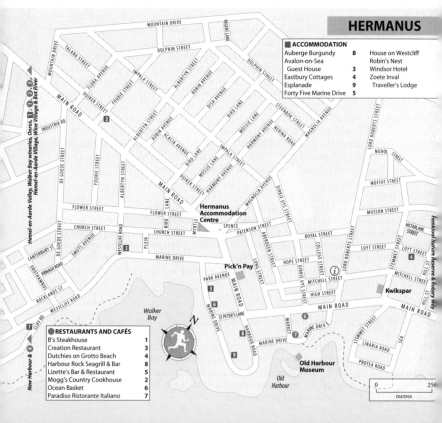

HERMANUS

■ **ACCOMMODATION**
Auberge Burgundy	8	House on Westcliff	
Avalon-on-Sea		Robin's Nest	
Guest House	3	Windsor Hotel	
Eastbury Cottages	4	Zoete Inval	
Esplanade	9	Traveller's Lodge	
Forty Five Marine Drive	5		

● **RESTAURANTS AND CAFÉS**
B's Steakhouse	1
Creation Restaurant	3
Dutchies on Grotto Beach	4
Harbour Rock Seagrill & Bar	8
Lizette's Bar & Restaurant	5
Mogg's Country Cookhouse	2
Ocean Basket	6
Paradiso Ristorante Italiano	7

Auberge Burgundy 16 Harbour Rd ☎028 313 1201, ⓦauberge.co.za. A Provençal-style country house in the town centre, close to the water, projecting a stylish Mediterranean feel. The rooms are light and airy with imported French fabrics, and a lavender garden. R1400

Avalon-on-Sea Guest House 1 Marine Drive ☎028 312 1258, ⓦavalononsea.co.za. Family seafront house within walking distance of the centre, with three sea-facing rooms and two without the view. Expect comfort but not masses of style. R900

Eastbury Cottages 36 Luyt St ☎028 312 1258, ⓦeastburycottage.co.za. Four fully equipped self-catering cottages close to the *Marine Hotel*. Prices vary depending on group size, and breakfast is available for R70. R580

WHALE-WATCHING

The Southern Cape, including Cape Town, provides some of the easiest and best places in the world for **whale-watching**. You don't need to rent a boat or take a pricey tour to get out to sea; if you come at the right time of year, whales are often visible from the shore, although a good pair of binoculars will come in useful for when they are far out.

All nine of the great whale species of the southern hemisphere pass by South Africa's shores, but the most commonly seen off Cape Town are **southern right whales** (their name derives from being the "right" one to kill because of their high oil and bone yields and the fact that they float when dead). Southern right whales are black and easily recognized from their pale, brownish **callosities**. These unappealing patches of raised, roughened skin on their snouts and heads have a distinct pattern on each animal, which helps scientists keep track of them.

Female whales come inshore to calve in sheltered bays, and stay to nurse their young for up to three months. **July to October** is the best time to see them, although they start appearing in June and some stay around until December. When the calves are big enough, the whales head off south again, to colder, stormy waters, where they feed on enormous quantities of plankton, making up for the nursing months when the females don't eat at all. Though you're most likely to see females and young, you may see **males** early in the season boisterously flopping about the females, though they neither help rear the calves nor form lasting bonds with females.

What gives away the presence of a whale is the blow or spout, a tall smoky plume which disperses after a few seconds and is actually the whale breathing out before it surfaces. If luck is on your side, you may see whales **breaching** – the movement when they thrust high out of the water and fall back with a great splash.

THE WHALE COAST'S HOTTEST WHALE SPOTS

In **Hermanus**, the best vantage points are the concrete cliff paths that ring the rocky shore from New Harbour to Grotto Beach. There are interpretation boards at three of the popular vantage points (Gearing's Point, Die Gang and Bientang's Cave). These are, however, the most congested venues during the whale season – at worst, the paths can be lined two or three deep with people – though there are equally good spots elsewhere along the Walker Bay coast. Aficionados claim that **De Kelders** (see p.175), some 39km east of Hermanus, is even better, while **De Hoop Nature Reserve** (see p.179), east of Arniston, is reckoned by some to be the ultimate place along the entire southern-African coast for whale-watching.

Several **operators** offer boat trips from Hermanus, all essentially offering the same service. For starters, try Hermanus Whale Cruises (☎028 313 2722, ⓦhermanus-whale-cruises.co.za), which is a coloured fishing village community project. A boat for 87 passengers goes out four times daily from the New Harbour, for the two-hour trip (June–Dec; R650). Boats must give a fifty-metre berth to whales, but if a whale approaches a boat, the boat may stop and watch it for up to twenty minutes.

Further around Walker Bay, close to Gansbaai, **Marine Dynamics and Dyer Island Cruises** (Geelbek St, Kleinbaai; ☎028 384 0406, ⓦwhalewatchsa.com) does whale cruises during whale season in the Dyer Island area, and on each trip there is a marine biologist on hand to answer questions. Whale-watching trips depart daily from Kleinbaai at 9.15am, 11.45am and 2.15pm (2hr 30min; R900).

Perhaps the ultimate way to see whales is from the air. Evan Austin, based in Hermanus (African Wings; ☎028 312 2701, ⓦafricanwings.co.za), flies a maximum of three people in a small plane over the bay to see whales, dolphins, sharks and other sea life. Flights range from thirty minutes (R3200) to an hour (R6000), all of which guarantee whale-spotting in season, and offer the opportunity to observe mothers and baby whales interacting.

16

Forty Five Marine Drive 45 Marine Drive ☎ 028 312 3610, ⓦ 45marinehermanus.com. Cliffside self-catering apartments of varying sizes, with terrific views across the bay. A more affordable and child-friendly option is available at the *Esplanade* (ⓦ hermanusesplanade.com; R250), also on the seafront at Marine Drive, in backpacker apartments, duplex units or cottages. December, in both, is booked out months in advance. R̲9̲0̲0̲

House on Westcliff 96 Westcliff Rd ☎ 028 313 2388, ⓦ westcliffhouse.co.za. This homely B&B is situated just out of the centre near the new harbour and boasts six bedrooms in a classic Cape-style house with a protected, tranquil garden and a solar-heated pool and jacuzzi. All rooms are en suite and have their own entrance off the garden, and there is also a three-bed family room. R̲9̲0̲0̲

Robin's Nest 10 Meadow Ave ☎ 028 316 1597, ⓔ leonie.b@telkomsa.net. Three fully equipped, but plain, self-catering studio flats above a garage in a garden,

4km west of the centre. Reached through the Hemel-en-Aarde shopping village, these purpose-built, two-storey flats sleep two and have good mountain views. R̲5̲0̲0̲

Windsor Hotel 49 Marine Drive ☎ 028 312 3727, ⓦ windsorhotel.co.za. This old, but popular, seafront hotel offers a full range of accommodation right on the cliff edge. It's ideally situated in the centre of Hermanus and guests can enjoy sea views from the dining room, lounges and almost half of the bedrooms. R̲1̲3̲6̲0̲

Zoete Inval Traveller's Lodge 23 Main Rd ☎ 028 312 1242, ⓦ zoeteinval.co.za. A quiet and relaxing hostel, with a distinct lack of party vibe, comprising dorms, doubles and family suites, with extras like good coffee, a jacuzzi (nice even in the rain!) and fireplace. If you're travelling with a baby, there is a baby bed that can be moved into your room. They'll organize all tours and outings, and arrange transport to and from the Baz Bus drop-off in Bot River. Dorm R̲1̲2̲0̲, double R̲4̲0̲0̲, family room R̲7̲5̲0̲

EATING AND DRINKING

Seafood is the obvious thing to eat in Hermanus – and you'll find plenty of restaurants serving it – though the views are generally better than the food. There are a couple of excellent restaurants in the wine estate valley of Hemel en Aarde (see p.168), west of town, and further afield in Stanford. **Book well ahead** at weekends and in summer; without a booking, you can always get fish and chips at the harbour, while grub features large at the **market** held every Saturday morning at the Hermanus Cricket Grounds (Sat 8am–noon; ⓦ hermanus.co.za/hermanus-market). Here you'll find excellent cheeses from Bot River as well as fresh pasta, pesto, muffins, hummus and baked goods.

B's Steakhouse Hemel-en-Aarde Village ☎ 028 316 3625. A friendly and buzzing independent steakhouse serving brilliantly prepared, reasonably priced, slabs of beef (R130). Its formidable wine list and child-friendliness make it an obvious choice for families, and they get endless repeat visits. Tues–Sun 6.30pm–10pm.

★**Creation Restaurant Hemel-en-Aarde Valley** ☎ 028 212 1107, ⓦ creationwines.com. A fabulous place to eat and drink, in a contemporary and elegant – yet informal – setting. Tables, both inside and out, look onto the *fynbos*-clad mountains. The antipasto dishes and canapés are sublime, and the food is created to complement the wines, rather than the other way around (food and wine pairing R125). Children are well catered for, with their own tasting menu of five pairings of food with five surprise drinks (R75). Daily 11am–4pm.

Dutchies on Grotto Beach 10th Avenue, Grotto Beach, Voelklip ☎ 028 314 1392, ⓦ dutchies.co.za. The only place to eat on the beach, and a good one at that. There isn't much of a Dutch character in the menu, but the management and service sparkle. Prices are reasonable – a health breakfast (hot drink, fresh orange juice, fruit salad, Greek yoghurt and muesli) will set you back just R50, while a Dutch cheese sandwich is R52. Book ahead, especially to get outdoor seating. Daily 8am–9pm.

Harbour Rock Seagrill & Bar New Harbour ☎ 028 312 2920. This busy and fairly upmarket restaurant

serves up seafood dishes with stunning views. Two favourite dishes are the seafood risotto and the local kabeljou fish (both R135). Part of the same establishment, but in a separate space, is a large, noisy bar, *The Gecko*, with the same views, and where smoking is permitted. If you don't mind that, it makes an excellent place for cocktails (R30–50), pizzas and burgers. It's always packed and has occasional live music. Daily: restaurant 12.30–3pm & 6.30–10pm; bar 12.30pm till late.

★**Lizette's Bar & Restaurant** 20 8th Street, Voelklip ☎ 028 314 0308, ⓦ lizetteskitchen.com. Well-known chef Lizette Crabtree cooks up a storm in this spacious restored house, which has plenty of outdoor seating, a play area for kids, water bowls for dogs and a cosy interior. With her experience of cooking in the East, you can expect some flavoursome noodles, and broths such as Vietnamese *pho bo* (R60), as well as Moroccan dishes, some South African favourites with a twist, and burgers. Takeaway available, too. Mon–Thurs 9am–10pm, Fri & Sat 9am–11pm, Sun 9am–4pm.

★**Mogg's Country Cookhouse** Hemel-en-Aarde Valley, 12km from Hermanus along the R320 to Caledon ☎ 076 314 0671, ⓦ moggscookhouse.com. A most unlikely location for one of Hermanus's most successful restaurants – a farm cottage – with superb views across the valley. *Mogg's* is an intimate place that's always full and unfailingly excellent, serving whatever

WALKER BAY WINERIES

Some of South Africa's top **wines** come from the **Hemel-en-Aarde (heaven and earth) Valley** along the **R320** to Caledon, which branches off the main road to Cape Town, 2km west of Hermanus. Several small **wineries** are dotted along the same road and are worth popping into for their intimate tasting rooms and first-class wines, with views of the stark, scrubby mountains just inland. The whole route is 20km, and some wineries also offer meals, notably Creation and Newton Johnson.

Hamilton Russell Winery (Off R320, Hemel-en-Aarde Road; Mon–Fri 9am–5pm, Sat 9am–1pm; ☎ 028 312 3595, ⓦ hamiltonrussellvineyards.com) is the longest established of the Walker Bay wineries and produces some of South Africa's priciest wines. They are especially known for their Pinot Noir and Chardonnay. Adjacent to Hamilton Russell, towards Caledon, **Bouchard Finlayson** (Mon–Fri 9.30am–5pm, Sat 9.30am–12.30pm; ☎ 028 312 3515, ⓦ bouchardfinlayson .co.za) is another establishment with a formidable reputation, and a wider range of wines than its neighbour. Their flagship and award-winning wine is the Galpin Peak Pinot Noir, grown on the slopes of Galpin peak. Their dry white blend, Blanc de Mer, alludes to the fact that these wines are hugely influenced by their proximity to the cool ocean. Two-thirds of the way down the route is **Newton Johnson** (Mon–Fri 9am–5pm, Sat & Sun 10am–1pm; ☎ 028 312 3862, ⓦ newton johnson.com); its estate restaurant is rated for lunch. Getting towards the top of the valley, Ataraxia Wines (Mon–Fri 9am–4pm, Sat 10am–5pm; ☎ 028 212 2007, ⓦ ataraxiawines.co.za) is a newer kid on the block; contemporary and stylish, it offers mountain views from its wine-tasting lounge which is built like a chapel to contemplate the heavenly wines. At the end of the line, and keeping the best till last, Creation (daily 10am–5pm; ☎ 028 212 1107, ⓦ creationwines.com) has fabulous wines and is known for its gourmet food and wine pairings (daily 11am–4pm), as well as chocolate- and tea-tasting. Book well in advance at weekends.

16

takes the fancy of chefs Jenny Mogg and her daughter Julia. Mains might include pan fried line fish on red pepper risotto with a mushroom sauce or chicken breast topped with marinated mozzarella, cherry tomatoes and pesto (R90–125) Booking is essential and kids are welcome. Wed–Sun noon–2.30pm.

Ocean Basket Fashion Square, 137 Main Rd ☎ 028 312 1313. As part of a reasonably priced and consistently reliable seafood chain, this restaurant is popular thanks in no small part to its fabulous setting, serving up fish and chips and a seafood platter for two (R220). Daily 11.30am–2.30pm & 6–9pm.

Paradiso Ristorante Italiano 83 Marine Drive ☎ 028 313 1153. Situated behind the village square, near the water in a zone of tourist restaurants, this reliable Italian place does seafood dishes and chicken, alongside delicious pizza (R80) and pasta. Lunchtime pizzas, with just two toppings, are cheaper (R60). Mon–Sun 11am–9pm.

Stanford

East of Hermanus, the R43 takes a detour inland around the attractive Klein River Lagoon, past the village of **STANFORD**, 155km from Cape Town. This historic village, established in 1857, has become something of a refuge for arty types seeking a tranquil escape from the urban rat race. To keep visitors racing around Stanford, the hamlet's residents have created an **arts and crafts route** that takes in over a dozen artists' studios. But apart from the town's excellent microbrewery and some wine estates, Stanford's principal attraction is its travel-brochure streetscape of simple **Victorian architecture** that includes limewashed houses and sandstone cottages – as well as an Anglican church – with thatched roofs that glow under the late afternoon sun.

The Klein River

The town's northern boundary is the attractive Klein River, which can be explored on a boat trip or by yourself in a kayak (for both, contact Ernie ☎ 083 310 0952; boat trip R100; canoe and kayak rental R100). There's rich birdlife in and among the rustling reed beds lining the riverbanks where you stand a chance of spotting the flashy malachite kingfisher.

STANFORD CHEESE AND WINE

Two kilometres beyond Birkenhead Brewery, and 7km from Stanford on the R326, is the **Klein River Cheese Farm** (Mon–Fri 9am–5pm, Sat 9am–1pm; ☎028 41 0693, ⓦkleinrivercheese .co.za), which offers tastings of its famous Gruyère, Leiden, Colby and Dando cheeses. Buy one of their picnic baskets (available Sept 15 to May 15 daily 11am–3pm; reserve ahead) to have under the trees next to the river.

As everywhere else in the Cape, more and more vineyards are opening, *fynbos* giving way to grapes, but possibly Stanford's best wine is sold from **Raka** (Mon–Fri 9am–4.30pm, Sat 10am–2.30pm; ☎028 341 0676, ⓦrakawine.co.za), 17km from town along the R326.

Walker Bay Estate and Birkenhead Brewery

Just across the R43 from Stanford along the R326 • Beer and wine tasting daily 11am–5pm; Lunch Wed–Sun 11am–4pm • ☎ 028 341 0013, ⓦ walkerbayestate.com

Although **Birkenhead Brewery** bills itself as a "craft brewery estate", the gleaming stainless-steel pipes and equipment inside soon dispel any images of bloodshot hillbillies knocking up a bit of moonshine on the quiet. This is a slick operation and a great place to go for a pub lunch or to buy craft beers, which put those of SAB, South Africa's big brewing near-monopoly, in their place. They have also added winemaking to their talents, so you can try both wine and beer.

ARRIVAL AND INFORMATION   STANFORD

By car Stanford is 155km from Cape Town. Take the Hermanus off-ramp from the N2 (about 90km from Cape Town), and follow the R43 for another 65km through Hermanus to Stanford.
Tourist office Main Road (Mon–Thurs 8.30am–4.30pm, Fri 8.30am–5pm, Sat 9am–4pm, Sun 9am–1pm;

☎028 341 0340, ⓦstanfordtourism.co.za). Can help with booking accommodation, and there is also a brochure for a walkabout you can do, taking in the various historical houses in the village. They can provide information on wineries to visit and other activities, as well as the arts and crafts route.

ACCOMMODATION

B's Cottage 17 Morton St ☎028 341 0430, ⓦstanford -accommodation.co.za. A small, open-plan, self-catering thatched house, sleeping two upstairs, with a sleeper couch in the downstairs living room, with an English-style country garden. It's popular and central, so book well ahead. **R600**
Klein River Cottage On the R326, 7km from Stanford ☎028 341 0693, ⓦkleinrivercheese.co.za/cottage.php. A charming three-bedroomed/two-bathroomed Victorian cottage on the river, complete with a fireplace for the winter, situated on the Klein River Cheese Farm (see box above). There's a minimum stay of two nights. **R600**
Mosaic Farm 10km from the centre, exit from Queen Victoria St ☎028 313 2814, ⓦmosaicfarm.net. Stone, canvas and thatch self-catering chalets on the river here,

with 4km of lagoon frontage. Chalets can sleep a couple or a group. Cruises, nature walks, canoeing and 4WD excursions to the beach are available. At the luxury end, the full-board *Lagoon Lodge* on the same site (R4800) is a lagoon-side safari camp. The natural setting of the farm and access to a wild part of the lagoon and coast is fabulous. **R800**
★ **Stanford River Lodge** 4km from the centre, exit from Queen Victoria St ☎028 341 0444 or ☎082 378 1935, ⓦstanfordriverlodge.co.za. Sunny, spacious and modern self-catering cottages with river and mountain views. It's a lovely, upmarket place with river swimming and canoeing in summer. Owners John and Valda Finch will show you a good time, and provide a breakfast basket for a bit extra. **R750**

EATING

In addition to the restaurants listed below, Stanford is also home to a number of lovely coffee shops, along the quiet main road.

★ **Madres Ktchen** Robert Stanford Estate, 1km west of Stanford ☎028 341 0647. The best place to have breakfast out, and the lunches, with platters of home-made bread, pâtés and cheeses, plus herbs and veggies from the garden, complemented with wines from their own estate, are also fabulous (R105). It is great for children, with lawns, a jungle

gym and ducks to feed. Thurs–Tues 8am–4pm.
★ **Mariana's Bistro and Home Deli** Du Toit St ☎028 341 0272. The innovative and reasonably-priced country food served at this Victorian cottage is good enough to draw Cape Town gourmands out for the day. Food and wines are local, and many of the vegetables are picked

from the owners' garden, who host in a warm and engaged way, and advise on food and wine choice (mains average R110). You'll need to book a couple of months beforehand, though cancellations are always a possibility. Try for a table on the *stoep* for a long lazy lunch. No children under 10. Thurs–Sun noon–4pm.

Gansbaai

GANSBAAI, 175km from Cape Town, is a workaday place, economically dependent on its fishing industry and the seafood canning factory at the harbour. This gives the place a more gutsy feel than the surrounding holiday lands, but there's little reason to spend time here unless you want to engage in **great white shark safaris**, Gansbaai's other major industry. It is an appropriately competitive and cut-throat business with operators engaged in a blind feeding frenzy to attract punters. Boats set out from Gansbaai to **Dyer Island** (see box, p.177), east of Danger Point, where great white sharks come to feed on the resident colony of seals.

De Kelders

A suburb of Gansbaai, **DE KELDERS** is a treeless blob of bland holiday homes and ostentatious seafront mansions on the cliffs staring across Walker Bay to Hermanus. Its rocky coast, though, provides outstanding whale-watching and there is access to a beautiful, long sandy beach at the Walker Bay Nature Reserve.

Walker Bay Nature Reserve and the Klipgat Strandloper Caves
Access is at the end of Cliff Rd • R25

You can clamber over rocky sections and walk for miles along the beach at the **Walker Bay Nature Reserve**, known by everyone as "Die Plat". Swimming is very dangerous though, and it's best not to venture in more than knee-high. From the car park, a path leads down to the **Klipgat Strandloper Caves**, excavated in the early 1990s, when evidence was unearthed of modern human habitation from 80,000 years ago. The caves became unoccupied for a few thousand years, after which they were used again by Khoisan people 20,000 years ago. Shells, middens, tools and bones were uncovered; some of these are now displayed in the South African Museum in Cape Town (see p.52). From the caves, the waymarked **Duiwelsgats hiking trail** goes east for 7km as far as Gansbaai and is a good way to explore the coastline, which can also be accessed at a number of other points.

16

ARRIVAL AND INFORMATION

GANSBAAI

By car Gansbaai is 175km from Cape Town. Take the Hermanus off-ramp from the N2 (about 90km from Cape Town), and follow the R43 for another 85km through Hermanus, Stanford, De Kelders and Gansbaai.

Tourist office Great White Junction, Kapokblom St (Mon–Fri 8.30am–5pm, Sat 9am–4pm, Sun 10am–2pm; ☎028 384 1439, ⓦ gansbaaiinfo.com).

ACCOMMODATION

Ama-Krokka 28 Vyfer St ☎028 384 2776, ⓦama -krokka.co.za. This homely B&B boasts a pool and the two suites have their own patio, and there's a microwave in the kitchen nook so you can have a stab at self-catering. While there are no sea views from the rooms, you are just 500m away from the shoreline. R1100

GROOTBOS PRIVATE NATURE RESERVE

Set among the hills 6km before De Kelders, *Grootbos Private Nature Reserve* (☎028 384 8000, ⓦgrootbos.com) is an exceedingly tasteful, luxurious ecolodge that offers whale-watching safaris, horseriding and *fynbos* tours. Even if you can't stay – and it is undoubtedly the top stay along the Whale Coast – you can visit for the day and enjoy superb gourmet meals at surprisingly reasonable rates, though you'll need to book ahead. Full board including all activities starts at R3760 per person per night in high season, dropping as low as R1992 per person per night during low season; note that there's a minimum stay of two nights.

Cliff Lodge 6 Cliff St ☎ 028 384 0983, ⓦ clifflodge .co.za. A stylish seafront guesthouse, perched on the cliffs of De Kelders, with breathtaking views from all four luxurious bedrooms and the spacious penthouse suite, plus a deck for whale-watching and a pool for your own splashing. **R2200**

★**Crayfish Lodge** Killarney St ☎ 028 384 1898,

ⓦ crayfishlodge.net. This is the top stay in town; a palatial guesthouse with sea views and an individual patio or courtyard for all five rooms. If you're treating yourself, go for the upstairs suites with jacuzzis. A path leads down to a rocky beach with a channel for bathing or there's a heated swimming pool. Double **R2200**, suite **R3000**

EATING AND DRINKING

Benguela Cnr Church & Harbour sts ☎ 028 384 2120. A smart restaurant in a harbour setting, offering a range of specialities – seafood, meat and vegetarian (R90) – with every plate picture-perfect. Surprisingly, the meat dishes surpass the fish. The desserts are recommended, prices reasonable and the host, Jonathan, is welcoming and friendly. Daily 11am–2pm & 7–10pm.

Coffee on the Rocks Cliff St ☎ 028 384 2017. A small bistro that does great coffee, cakes and light meals, with a deck in an unsurpassed position for whale-watching; also a good choice for leisurely Sunday roasts (R85). Booking is

essential. Wed–Sun 10am–5pm.

Gansbaai Fisheries Gansbaai Harbour. Over-the-counter traditional fresh fish and chips, while you watch the fishing boats come in (R50). Daily 9am–5pm.

★**Grootbos Nature Reserve** ☎ 028 384 8008. This delightful ecolodge is one of the culinary highlights of the area – offering fine-dining traditional cuisine with a modern twist. What's more, it's extremely reasonable for the quality of food you receive. They run a set menu only; a three-course lunch will set you back R235, while the six-course dinner is R395. Daily 1–3pm & 6.30–9pm.

Danger Point

Danger Point, the southernmost point of Walker Bay, is where British naval history was allegedly made. True to its name, the Point lured the ill-fated HMS *Birkenhead* onto its hidden rocks on February 26, 1852. As was the custom, the captain of the troopship gave the order "Every man for himself". Displaying true British pluck, the soldiers are said to have lined up in their ranks on deck where they stood stock-still, knowing that if one man broke ranks it would lead to a rush that might overwhelm the lifeboats carrying women and children to safety. The precedent of "women and children first", which became known as the **Birkenhead Drill**, was thus established, even though 445 lives were lost in the disaster.

Cape Agulhas and around

Along the east flank of the Danger Point promontory, the rocky and shallow coastline with heavy swells and strong currents makes this one of South Africa's most treacherous stretches of coast – one that has claimed over 250 wrecks and around 2500 lives. Its rocky terrain also accounts for the lack of a coastal road from Gansbaai and Danger Point to **Cape Agulhas**, the southernmost tip of Africa.

The plain around the southern tip of South Africa has been declared the **Agulhas National Park** to conserve its estimated two thousand species of indigenous plant, marine and intertidal life as well as a cultural heritage which includes shipwrecks, archeological sites – stone hearths, pottery and shell middens have been discovered here.

The actual tip of the continent is marked by a rock and plaque about 1km from the landmark of Agulhas Lighthouse, towards Suiderstrand. Following the dirt road to **Suiderstrand** itself takes you to some beautiful, undeveloped beaches with rock pools to explore, and is definitely the best part of Agulhas.

L'AGULHAS, the rather windblown settlement associated with the southern tip, consists of a small collection of holiday houses and a few shops. It's a much quieter coastal destination than anywhere along the Garden Route. The centre of Agulhas, if you can call it a centre, is along Main Road, where you'll find a couple of restaurants, small supermarket and a craft shop.

DYER ISLAND AND SHARK ALLEY

How a black American came to be living on an island off South Africa in the early nineteenth century is something of a mystery. But, according to records, **Samson Dyer** arrived here in 1806 and made a living collecting guano on the island that subsequently took his name.

Dyer Island is home to substantial **African penguin and seal breeding colonies**, both of which are prized morsels among great white sharks. So shark-infested is the channel between the island and the mainland at some times of year that it is known as **Shark Alley**, and these waters are used extensively by operators of great-white viewing trips. If you go on a trip, you'll be safely contained within a sturdy boat or cage. This is a luxury that a group of West African castaways could not afford when, in 1996, they found themselves washed up here as the Taiwanese merchant vessel they were riding on sank en route to the Far East. One of them drowned, but the rest (amazingly) survived five days at sea, including a stint down Shark Alley, clinging to pieces of timber and barrels.

Agulhas Lighthouse

Daily 9am–4.30pm • R25

The red-and-white Agulhas Lighthouse, commissioned in 1849, offers vertiginous views from its top, reached by a series of steep ladders. The appeal of lonely lighthouses on rocky edges beaming out signals to ships at night is explored here through interesting exhibits about lighthouses around South Africa.

Struisbaai

East of Agulhas is Struisbaai (pronounced strace-bye), notable for its endless white-sand beach. The further away you walk from the uninspiring holiday homes and camping site, the better it gets, and you could literally walk the whole day on the beach. Swimming is fantastic too, and safe for being in a bay, with the typically dark turquoise-coloured water of these parts.

16

ARRIVAL AND INFORMATION
AGULHAS

By car Agulhas is 230km from Cape Town. Take the N2 to Caledon (115km), then the R316 to Bredasdorp; here, the westerly branch of the R319 will take you down to Agulhas (43km). The drive takes you through rolling farmlands where you are almost certain to see South Africa's national bird, the elegant and endangered blue crane, feeding in the fields. Both the small towns of Napier and Bredasdorp en route have appealing cafés and restaurants to tempt you to break the journey.

Tours There's no public transport here, but Derek Burger of Tip of Africa Safaris (☎ 082 774 4448, ⊛ tipofafricasafaris .com) offers a reliable touring service in his comfortable Land Cruiser to visit De Hoop (R1000) and other remote parts of the coast.

Tourist information At Agulhas Lighthouse (Mon–Sun 9am–5pm; ☎ 028 435 7185, ⊛ discovercapeagulhas .co.za). They produce an excellent guidebook *Discover Cape Agulhas* (free) which is useful if you want a map to explore several new vineyards and wineries that have opened up in the area, as well as the comprehensive *Overberg Wine* (free), which covers Elim, Greyton, Stanford, Napier and Hermanus. The excellent Wine Boutique (☎ 082 567 7858) on the Main Road, next to *Seagulls Pub and Restaurant*, stocks wines of the region, and has regular tastings.

ACCOMMODATION

Agulhas Ocean Art House Main Rd ☎ 028 435 7503, ⊛ capeagulhas-arthouse.com. Six rooms, furnished in a contemporary style, each with a balcony with either sea or mountain views. The striking modern building also houses a café and an art gallery that displays local paintings, photography and sculpture. R2000

Cape Agulhas Backpackers Corner of Duiker & Main rds ☎ 082 372 3354, ⊛ capeagulhasbackpackers.com. The only budget place around Agulhas has camping, dorms and doubles, all with good bedding, plus a pool and garden. It's run by a couple who are big on helping you enjoy the outdoors and will organize boating, surfing lessons, kiteboarding, horseriding and other activities around Struisbaai. Pick-ups from Botrivier or Swellendam can be arranged. Camping R70, dorm R120, double R350

★ **Pebble Beach** Suiderstrand; follow signs to the Southern Tip of Africa and then the signs for Suiderstrand, 4km beyond the Tip ☎ 028 435 7270 or ☎ 082 774 5008, ⊛ pebble-beach.co.za. Uniquely positioned on the edge of Agulhas National Park, with kilometres of undeveloped beach

ELIM MISSION STATION

ELIM, a Moravian mission station 40km northwest of Agulhas, founded in 1824, has streets lined with thatched, whitewashed houses and fig trees, though feels rather run-down and forsaken. Tours, arranged by the tourist office in Church Street (Mon–Sat 9am–12.30pm & 1.30–5pm; ☎028 482 1806) take in the oldest house in the settlement, the church, the restored water mill where wheat is still ground, and the pottery studio. This central area is the most attractive part of the village. There's also a memorial commemorating the **emancipation of slaves** in 1834, the only such monument in South Africa; its presence reflects the fact that numerous freed slaves found refuge in mission stations like Elim. The Mission is best visited on a day-drive if you are exploring the area or visiting wine farms.

to explore to the west, and the scent of *fynbos* wafting in from the dunes. A modern, thatched house, this sea-facing guesthouse has two en-suite rooms, plus a special upstairs bedroom that features a bath and a large balcony, all of which have white beds and wooden floors. **R1050**

Southermost B&B On the corner of Van Breda and Lighthouse sts ☎028 435 6565, ⓦsouthermost.co.za. A well-loved and rather dilapidated historic beach cottage, run by the welcoming Meg, opposite the tidal pool with an indigenous garden sloping down to the water's edge. It is an easy walk from here to the centre to get an evening meal. Closed in winter. **R700**

EATING

Agulhas Seafoods Main Rd ☎028 435 7207. The fish and chips at *Agulhas Seafoods* are so succulent and delicious that Capetonians have been known to travel all the way out here to enjoy them (R55). As well as local fish, they also serve calamari. Mon–Sat 10am–7pm, Sun 10am–3pm.

Twisted Fork Restaurant and Bar 184 Main Rd ☎028 435 6291. This is the place to go for a night out at the pub, and the food is not bad either. The Thai chicken and prawn curry is recommended (R95), and the catch of the day is served with excellent chips. Daily 11am–2am.

Zuidste Kaap 99 Main Rd ☎028 435 7838. Straightforward, no-frills cooking in this elegant thatched restaurant. It has a lovely ambience with an airy, open feel, but sadly no sea views. Recommended dishes include stuffed chicken breasts and locally-caught line fish (R135). Mon–Fri noon–10pm, Sat & Sun 11am–9pm.

Arniston

After the cool deep blues of the Atlantic to the west, the azure of the Indian Ocean at **ARNISTON** is startling, made all the more dazzling by the white dunes interspersed with rocky ledges. Situated 220km from Cape Town, this is one of the best places to stay in the Overberg – if you want nothing more than the sea. The colours may be tropical, but the wind can howl unpredictably here, as anywhere else along the Cape coast, and when it does, there's nothing much to do. The village is known to locals by its Afrikaans name, Waenhuiskrans ("wagon-house cliff"), after a cliff containing a huge cave 1500m south of town (see opposite), which trekboers reckoned was spacious enough for a wagon and span of oxen (the largest thing they could think of). The English name derives from a British ship, the *Arniston*, which hit the rocks here in 1815.

The shallow seas, so treacherous for vessels, provide Arniston with safe swimming waters. You can swim next to the slipway or at **Roman Beach**, the main swimming beach, just along the coast as you head south from the harbour.

Kassiesbaai

A principal attraction of Arniston is **Kassiesbaai**, a district of starkly beautiful, limewashed cottages, now declared a National Monument and home to coloured fishing families who have for generations made their living here. But Kassiesbaai sits a little uneasily as a living community, as it's also a bit of a theme park for visitors stalking the streets with their cameras. Heading north through Kassiesbaai at low tide, you can walk 5km along an unspoilt beach unmarred by buildings until you reach an unassuming fence – resist the temptation to climb over this, as it marks the boundary of the local testing range for military material and missiles.

Arniston Caves

Heading south of the harbour for 1500m along spectacular cliffs, you'll reach the vast **cave** after which the town is named. The walk is worth doing simply for the *fynbos*-covered dunes you'll cross on the way. From the car park right by the cave, it's a short signposted walk down to the dunes and the cave, which can only be reached at low tide. The rocks can be slippery and have sharp sections, so be sure to wear shoes with tough soles and a good grip.

ARRIVAL AND INFORMATION   ARNISTON

By car From Cape Town (225km), take the N2 to Caledon (115km), then the R316 to Bredasdorp, continuing along the R316 afterwards for 25km to Arniston. There is no

public transport to Arniston.

Tourist office There is no tourist office in Arniston, but the one in Agulhas covers the area (see p.177).

ACCOMMODATION

The holiday accommodation is in the new section of town, adjacent to the traditional fishing village quarter of Kassiesbaai. You won't find pumping nightlife or adrenaline-packed attractions here, only azure sea, and peace and quiet.

Arniston Lodge 23 Main Rd ☎028 445 9175, ⓦ arnistonlodge.co.za. In the residential area, this B&B offers four rooms in a two-storey thatched home with a pool. The upstairs rooms have views and better bathrooms than those downstairs. **R1190**

Arniston Resort Signposted 300m from the centre along the main road into Arniston ☎028 445 9620. You can pitch your own tent or stay in one of the rather plain and functional bungalows here, which have four or six beds. The cheaper, older ones don't provide linen, and you'll pay a bit more to have all the mod cons including TV. The place can get crowded and very noisy over weekends and during peak season. **R480**

Arniston Seaside Cottages Huxham St, signposted as you arrive from Bredasdorp ☎028 445 9772,

ⓦ arnistonseasidecottages.co.za. A series of attractive and modern self-catering establishments built in the style of traditional fisherman's cottages with limewashed walls and thatched roofs. Clean and bright, they're in a good position just a few minutes' walk from the beach and come fully equipped. **R640**

★ **Arniston Spa Hotel** Beach Rd ☎028 445 9000, ⓦ arnistonhotel.com. Dominating the seafront, this luxurious spa hotel boasts every comfort, including a spa with massage and beauty treatments. The best rooms have a fireplace, or a balcony with sea views. If it's way out of your budget, go during the week or in winter when prices drop. It is one of the best-set beach hotels in the country, and the only one in town. **R2150**

EATING AND DRINKING

Arniston Hotel Beach Rd. Pleasing fresh fish dinners (R120), with outdoor seating to take in the sea views. It also holds the town's only bistro bar, which serves burgers and the like and has sport on TV. Daily 11am–9.30pm.

Willeen's Meals Arts and Crafts House C26, Kassiesbaai ☎028 445 9995. An authentic fisherman's cottage where

you'll be served traditional Cape Malay meals by family members. You can try *bobotie*, a seafood platter (R150) or fried fish. They have a BYO booze policy, though soft drinks are available. You can also just have tea and scones in the garden that boasts sea views. Daily 8am–10pm.

De Hoop Nature Reserve

Daily 7am–6pm • R40

De Hoop is the wilderness highlight of the Western Cape and one of the best places in the world for land-based whale-watching. July to October is the best time for this, with the highest number of whales in August and September, but you stand a very good chance of a sighting from June through to November. There's no need to take a boat or use binoculars – in season you'll see whales blowing or breaching – leaping clear of the water, or perhaps slapping a giant tail. Although the reserve could technically be done as a day-trip from Agulhas, Arniston or Swellendam, you'll find it far more rewarding to come here for a night or more. The Whale Trail hike is one of South Africa's best walks and among the finest wildlife experiences in the world (see box, p.180).

The breathtaking coastline is edged by bleached sand dunes standing 90m high in places, and rocky formations that at one point open to the sea in a massive craggy arch.

The flora and fauna are impressive, too, encompassing 86 species of mammal, 260 different birds and 1500 varieties of plants. Inland, rare **Cape mountain zebra**, **bontebok** and other **antelope** congregate on a plain near the reserve accommodation.

ARRIVAL AND TOURS
DE HOOP NATURE RESERVE

By car De Hoop is signposted off the N2, 13km west of Swellendam, the quickest route from Cape Town. Alternatively, if you are in the Overberg, take the signposted dirt road that spurs off the R319 as it heads out of Bredasdorp, 50km to its west.

Tours You can take a full-day tour from Agulhas or Arniston with Derek Burger of Tip of Africa Safaris (R1000; ☎082 774 4448, ⓦtipofafricasafaris.com) who will take you on the dirt roads in his comfortable Land Cruiser.

ACCOMMODATION AND EATING

Accommodation within the National Park is available through the De Hoop Collection (ⓦdehoopcollection.co.za), and varies from camping to luxurious cottages. There are a couple of options outside of the park, but if you can get a place inside, it is preferable as the journey to the coastline is shorter. There are a couple of different locations within the park, the most convenient are at De Opstel, where the information office restaurant is located, a twenty-minute drive from the coast.

There are **no food supplies** at De Hoop, bar a small shop selling basics, so be sure to stock up with everything you need before you arrive, in Swellendam or Bredasdorp.

★ **De Hoop Cottages** De Hoop Nature Reserve ☎021 422 4522, ⓦdehoopcollection.co.za. You'll find an array of accommodation here, none of them especially cheap, but all appealing and comfortable. Camping is the cheapest way to visit the reserve, and there are a number of appealing self-catering properties of varying sizes. Camping R295, cottage R800

Fig Tree On the reserve, close to reception ☎028 542 1254. De Hoop's only restaurant uses local ingredients complementing the Elim wines, with good-value set-menu dinners, often including fish (R200), plus a children's menu. Reservations are required, especially in quiet times during the winter months when the restaurant may be closed for

lack of trade. Picnics can be ordered, and there is a lovely spot outside that's perfect for sundowners after a good day at the beach. Daily 8–11am, noon–3pm & 7–9pm.

Verfheuwel Farm Potberg Road, in the direction of Malgas ☎028 542 1038 or ☎082 767 0148, ⓦverfheuwelguestfarm.co.za. This cottage accommodation, attached to the main farmhouse, is run by hospitable Afrikaner farming folk who can bring dinner to your cottage if you ask in advance. It sleeps a couple, with beds in the living area for children. The garden is beautiful and has a swimming pool. If *Verfheuwel* is full, owner Matti can direct you to other friends and relatives in the area with farm accommodation. R700

The Overberg Interior

Just off the N2, **Caledon** merits a quick visit for its refreshing hot springs, while a few towns are worth visiting for a night or two. Closer to Cape Town, **Greyton** makes a perfect weekend break, with enough good food, walks and lounging in garden cafés to occupy you for a couple of nights. Nearby, South Africa's oldest mission station, **Genadendal**, 6km west of Greyton, is also worth a look around. **Swellendam**, further

ON THE WHALE TRAIL

Only moderately difficult, the five-day, four-night, self-guided **Whale Trail** (☎0861 227 362 8873, ⓦcapenature.co.za) is one of South Africa's most desirable hikes and follows a spectacularly beautiful 55km route from the Potberg Mountains along the deserted coast to Koppie Alleen. To walk in whale season, however, you'll need to book a year in advance and take any date offered. Bookings are for a minimum of six and maximum of twelve people (with no children under 8), and you pay for six even if there are just two of you. Prices are about R1700 per person and include porterage of your supplies, clothes and bedding to each night's accommodation – comfortable cottages, each in splendid isolation. For the duration of the trail you see only your own group, and no other people or signs of habitation at all.

along the N2, is often treated as the first night stop along the Garden Route, but makes a good base for visiting **De Hoop Nature Reserve** (see p.179), or to see some antelope and ostriches in the **Bontebok National Park**, a few kilometres away.

Greyton

GREYTON, a tranquil village 46km north of Caledon, is a favourite weekend destination for Capetonians. Based around a core of Georgian and Victorian buildings, shaded by grand old oaks and tucked away at the edge of the Riviersonderend (meaning "river with no end") Mountains, it is a great place to unwind, stroll and potter about the handful of galleries, antique shops and cafés, with good accommodation and excellent food on offer. It also boasts some great hikes, most notably the superb **Boesmanskloof Traverse** trail, which crosses the mountains to a point 14km from McGregor.

ARRIVAL AND INFORMATION   GREYTON

By car Greyton is 145km from Cape Town. The best route is to take the signposted, sealed R406 from the N2, just west of Caledon and 105km from Cape Town. Follow the R406 for 30km – ignore any other signs to Greyton on the N2 as they are for unsealed, difficult roads. Allow two to two and a half hours for the journey.

Tourist office 29 Main St, along the main road as you come into town (Mon–Fri 8am–5pm, Sat 9am–2pm; ☎ 028 254 9414, ⓦ greytontourism.com).
Horseriding Graeme (☎ 083 631 9533) has three, well-schooled competition ponies (R200/hr).

ACCOMMODATION

Definitely stay somewhere with a fireplace if you're here in winter, as it can be cold in this mountainous terrain, and conversely look for a pool or shady gardens in summer. Greyton is awash with self-catering cottages, of which the tourism office has lists and pictures.

Anna's Cottages 1 Market St ☎ 084 764 6012, ⓦ greyton -accommodation.com. A treehouse with an oak tree growing though it, complete with bath, and three lovely self-catering garden cottages, all attractively and eclectically furnished. Mark Cottage is a large space with two double bed alcoves, indoor and outdoor cooking facilities, fairy lights and fireplaces. Cottage R600, treehouse R800

High Hopes 89 Main Rd ☎ 028 254 9898, ⓦ highhopes .co.za. One of the best B&Bs in town, in a beautiful country-style home set in large gardens with a swimming pool. Besides four rooms, there's a self-contained unit with a kitchen, which can be taken on a B&B or self-catering basis. They have a variety of therapies, including massage, on offer, and bikes for hire, too. Substantial midweek discounts. R1100

EATING AND DRINKING

The town has a short Saturday **market** at the corner of Main Road and Cross Market Street, opposite the church (10am–noon), to which locals bring their produce: organic vegetables, fabulous and well-priced cheeses, decadent cakes, breads, biscuits and preserves.

Abbey Rose Main Rd ☎ 028 254 9470. A nice garden and street-side setting, with the delightful rose garden that the name suggests, and hearty but uncomplicated

food; try the oxtail stew (R120) and the malva pudding (R36). Tues 4–10pm, Thurs 11.30am–3pm, Fri & Sat 11.30am–3pm & 6–10pm, Sun 9am–3pm.

CALEDON SPA

The thermal springs at **Caledon Spa** (Tues–Sun 10am–7pm; R150; ☎ 028 214 5100, ⓦ thecaledoncasino.co.za/caledon_spa) make a fun day-trip out of Cape Town (111km away), or a restorative stop off the N2. The natural, hot brown water that flows through the spa offers a wonderfully relaxing and rejuvenating experience, with a number of pools to loll in, including a number of waterfall pools that offer lovely views over the surrounding farmlands. A sauna and steam room are included in the price, but you'll need to bring your own towels. It can be rather crowded over weekends, when it gets a bit grubby, but at other times you will often have the pools to yourself.

Oak and Vigne Café DS Botha St ☎ 028 254 9037. An extremely popular restaurant situated in an old cottage with an oak-shaded terrace. Fresh bread and croissants are baked daily, plus cooked breakfasts (R50) and good cocktails, such as the Greyton Mule (vodka, ginger beer and lime; R35), though service can be slow. Mon–Sun 8am–5pm.

★ **Peccadillo's** 23 Main Rd ☎ 028 254 9066. With the reputation for the best fine dining in town, *Peccadillo's* serves up food with a strong Mediterranean influence; try the local trout dishes, pork belly or wood-fired pizza (R82). A good place to try boutique wines. Thurs–Mon

noon–3pm & 6.30–10pm.

★ **Searle's Trading Post** 36 Main Rd ☎ 028 254 9550, ⓦ searles.co.za. This rambling establishment has the most appealing atmosphere in town, with a variety of places to sit indoors and outdoors, a pub, eclectic antiques and kitchenware for sale, plus the odd cat lounging on a sofa. Besides the warmth and visual appeal, the food is excellent and well priced, including thin-crust pizzas (R70) and country dishes like roasted pork belly with onions, green beans and sweet potato wedges (R95). Tues–Sat 8.30am–10pm, Sun 8.30am–5pm.

Genadendal

GENADENDAL, 6km from Greyton, was founded in 1737 by Moravians, and is definitely worth a wander about. The village's focus is around **Church Square**, dominated by a very Germanic church building constructed in 1891. The old bell outside dates back to the eighteenth century, when it became the centre of a flaming row between the local farmers and the mission station. The scrap broke out when missionary Georg Schmidt annoyed the local white farmers by forming a small Christian congregation with impoverished Khoi – who were on the threshold of extinction – and giving refuge to maltreated labourers from local farms. What really got the farmers' goat was the fact that while they, white Christians, were illiterate, Schmidt was teaching native people, whom they considered uncivilized, to read and write. The Dutch Reformed Church, under the control of the Dutch East India Company, waded in when Schmidt began baptizing converts, and prohibited the mission from ringing the bell, which called the faithful to prayer.

In 1838 Genadendal established the first teacher training college in the country, which the government closed in 1926, on the grounds that coloured people didn't need tertiary education and should be employed as workers on local farms – a policy that effectively ground the community into poverty. In 1995, in recognition of the mission's role in offering education, Nelson Mandela renamed his official residence in Cape Town "Genadendal".

Today, the population of this principally coloured town numbers around four thousand people, adhering to a variety of Christian sects – no longer just Moravianism. The **Mission Museum** adjacent to Church Square (Mon–Thurs 9am–1pm & 2–5pm, Fri 9am–3.30pm, Sat 9am–noon; free) is moderately interesting, as is a wander through the town, down to the rural graveyard, spiked with old tombstones.

Swellendam and around

SWELLENDAM is an attractive historic town at the foot of the Langeberg, 97km east of Caledon. With one of the best country museums in South Africa, it's a congenial stop along the N2 between Cape Town and the Garden Route. And because of its ample supply of good accommodation – poised between the coastal De Hoop Nature Reserve and the Langeberg – it's a suitable base for spending a day or two exploring this part of the Overberg, with the **Bontebok National Park**, stomping ground of an attractive type of antelope, close at hand to the south.

South Africa's third-oldest white settlement, Swellendam was established in 1745 by **Baron Gustav van Imhoff**, a visiting Dutch East India Company bigwig. He was deeply concerned about the "moral degeneration" of burghers who were trekking further and further from Cape Town and out of Company control. Of no less concern to the baron was the loss of revenue from these "vagabonds", who were neglecting to pay the company for the right to hold land and were fiddling their annual tax returns. Following a brief hiccup in 1795, when burghers declared a "free republic" (quickly extinguished when Britain occupied the Cape), the town grew into a prosperous rural centre known for its wagon-making, and for being the last "civilized" port of call for trekboers heading out into the interior. The income generated from this helped build Swellendam's gracious homes, many of which went up in smoke in the fire of 1865.

The town is built along a very long main road with no traffic lights; it's most attractive at either end, with a mundane shopping area in the middle. The eastern end is dominated by the museum complex and tourist information, and is nearest to the mountain reserve for hiking or horseriding.

Oefeningshuis

36 Voortrek St

The only building in the centre to survive the town's 1865 fire is the Cape Dutch-style **Oefeningshuis**, which now houses the tourist office. Built in 1838, it was first used as a place for religious activity, then as a school for freed slaves, and has surreal-looking clocks with frozen hands carved into either gable end.

Dutch Reformed Church

11 Voortrek St

The unmissable **Dutch Reformed Church**, dating from 1910, incorporates Gothic windows, a Baroque spire, Renaissance portico elements and Cape Dutch gables into a wedding cake of a building that agreeably holds its own, against the odds, and certainly still draws a good crowd on Sundays.

Drostdy Museum

18 Swellegrebel St • Mon–Fri 9am–4.45pm, Sat & Sun 10am–3.45pm • R25

On the east side of town, a short way from the centre, is the excellent **Drostdy Museum**. It's a collection of historic buildings arranged around large grounds, with a lovely nineteenth-century Cape garden. The centrepiece is the *drostdy* itself, built in 1747 as the seat of the *landdrost*, a magistrate-cum-commissioner sent out by the Dutch East India Company to control the outer reaches of its territory. The building conforms to the beautiful limewashed, thatched and shuttered Cape Dutch style of the eighteenth century, but the furnishings are of nineteenth-century vintage. From the rear garden of the *drostdy* you can stroll along a path and across Drostdy Street to **Mayville**, a middle-class Victorian homestead from the mid-nineteenth century with an old rose garden.

ARRIVAL AND INFORMATION   SWELLENDAM

By car Swellendam is 220km from Cape Town, on the N2, about three hours' drive, and 533km from Port Elizabeth, another seven hours' drive up the Garden Route.

By bus Coaches, including the Baz Bus, run between Cape Town and Port Elizabeth via Swellendam, dropping off at the *Swellengrebel Hotel*, in the centre of town.

Tourist office 22 Swellengrebel St, in one of the museum buildings (Mon–Fri 9am–5pm, Sat & Sun 9am–2pm; ☎ 028 514 2770, ⌨ swellendamtourism.co.za).

ACCOMMODATION

Anyone who enjoys the atmosphere of historic houses will be spoilt for choice in Swellendam, where places to stay in Cape Dutch and Georgian houses are ten a penny, and rates tend to be pretty reasonable.

★**Augusta de Mist** 3 Human St ☎ 028 514 2425, ⌨ augustademist.com. A 200-year-old homestead with three beautifully renovated cottages, two garden suites and a family unit, mostly with fireplaces and all with percale linen, and altogether luxurious and stylish. A rambling terraced garden and a pool complete the picture. There is a good restaurant on site, but you need to book meals in advance. R1200

★**Cypress Cottage** 3 Voortrek St ☎ 028 514 3296,

⌨ cypress-cottage.co.za. The seven charming rooms here are great value, decorated with antiques in the back garden of a grand house. The house is one of the oldest in town and the friendly owner is a brilliant gardener. R700

Eenuurkop Huisie 8km from town on the Ashton Rd ☎ 028 514 1447, ⌨ eenuurkop.co.za. Two self-catering cottages, one with three bedrooms, the other with one, in a stunning setting with great views and access to mountain walks. R800

HORSERIDING

Good horseriding is possible in the mountains and forests at the eastern edge of town in the Marloth Nature Reserve. **Two Feathers Horse Trails** (☎082 494 8279, ⓦswellendambackpackers .co.za) offer short trips for all levels (R350), and full days for experienced riders only (R1500).

Hermitage Huisies 3km from town on R60 to Ashton ☎028 514 2308 or ☎082 380 2080, ⓦwildebraam.co.za. Two restored labourers' self-catering cottages, sleeping four or five people, plus a flatlet for two, on a berry farm, with a duck pond and grazing sheep and horses, ideal for families. You'll find a couple more cottages on the farm next door, *Wildebraam* (same contact details), which are a little more upmarket. If you want to ride, you can arrange in advance to be taken up the mountain, plus there is berry picking in Nov & Dec, jams to taste and a liquor-tasting cellar at *Wildebraam*. R530
Lulu's B&B 10 Voortrek St ☎028 514 2202 or ☎082 343 4648. A well-run and centrally located B&B with three en-suite rooms and a self-catering loft apartment (sleeping up to eight people) above. It is the cheapest deal in town, though don't expect an elegant

guesthouse experience. R400
Swellendam Backpackers 5 Lichtenstein St ☎028 514 2648 or ☎082 494 8279, ⓦswellendamback packers.co.za. Swellendam's only hostel is a friendly place, well situated near the Marloth Nature Reserve, and close to the Drostdy Museum, with a large campsite, dorms and decent doubles. Staff can arrange activities including horseriding and hiking permits for Marloth. Children are welcome, as there's lots of space, and while this isn't a big party place, there is a convenient on-site bar. Dorm R130, double R410
Swellendam Country Lodge 237 Voortrek St ☎028 514 3629, ⓦswellendamlodge.com. Six garden rooms with separate entrances, reed ceilings and elegant, uncluttered decor in muted hues. There's a veranda for summer days, as well as a swimming pool and well-kept garden. R960

EATING

De Companjie 5 Voortrek St ☎083 399 0299, ⓦdecompanjie.co.za. Set in a most pleasing historic building that also functions as a lovely guesthouse. It offers breakfasts, salad-based lunches, good teatime eats and hearty dinners. They are best known for steaks (R130) and venison dishes. Wed–Sat 9am–9pm, Sun noon–9pm.
The Old Gaol Coffee Shop Church Square, 8A Voortrek St ☎028 514 3847. A great place where you can get milk tart in a copper pan and *roosterkoek*, traditional bread

made on an open fire, with nice fillings (R50). A great choice for kids, with an outdoor play area. Mon, Tues, Sat & Sun 8.30am–5pm, Wed–Fri 8.30am–10pm.
Woodpecker Deli 270 Voortrek St ☎028 514 2924. Casual and reasonably priced restaurant serving pizza, pasta, soups and burgers. A good choice if you are in town for one night and just want something simple. Mon–Sat 11.30am–9pm, Sun 11.30am–5pm.

16

Bontebok National Park
6km south of Swellendam • Daily: May–Sept 7am–6pm; Oct–June 7am–7pm • R80 • ☎028 514 2735

Set along the Breede River, **Bontebok National Park** is a compact, 28-square-kilometre reserve at the foot of the Langeberg range that makes a relaxing overnight stop between Cape Town and the Garden Route. The park was established in 1931 to save the Cape's dwindling population of bontebok, an attractive antelope with distinctive brown and white markings. By 1930, hunting had reduced the number of animals in the Cape to a mere thirty. Their survival has happily been secured and there are now three hundred of them in the park, as well as populations in other game and nature reserves in the province. There are no big cats in the park, but **mammals** you might encounter include rare Cape mountain zebra, red hartebeest and grey rhebok, and there are more than 120 **bird species**. It's also a rich environment for **fynbos**, with nearly five hundred species here, including erica, gladioli and proteas. Apart from game viewing, there are opportunities to swim in the Breede River, hike a couple of short nature trails and fish.

ACCOMMODATION   BONTEBOK NATIONAL PARK

★**Bontebok National Park** ☎028 514 2735, ⓦsanparks.org. Self-catering accommodation is available in ten, fully equipped chalets; the best have river views. There is also a campsite with very clean washing facilities

– the sites without their own electricity supply are cheaper. Stock up on supplies in Swellendam beforehand. Camping R220, chalet R910

PLETTENBERG BAY

The Garden Route

The Garden Route, a slender stretch of coastal plain on the N2 between Mossel Bay and Storms River Mouth, has a legendary status as South Africa's paradise – reflected in local names such as Garden of Eden and Wilderness. This soft, green, forested swath that stretches nearly 200km is cut by rivers that tumble down from the mountains to the north, to its southern rocky shores and sandy beaches. The Khoikhoi herders who lived off its natural bounty considered the area a paradise, calling it Outeniqua ("the man laden with honey"). Their Eden was quickly destroyed in the eighteenth century with the arrival of Dutch woodcutters, who had exhausted the forests around Cape Town and set about doing the same in Outeniqua, killing or dispersing the Khoikhoi and San in the process.

17

Birds and animals suffered too from the encroachment of Europeans. In the 1850s, the Swedish naturalist Johan Victorin shot and feasted on the species he had come to study, some of which, including the endangered narina trogon, he noted were both "beautiful and good to eat".

Despite the dense appearance of the area, what you see today are only the remnants of one of Africa's great **forests**; much of the indigenous hardwoods have been replaced by exotic pine plantations, and the only milk and honey you'll find now is in the many shops servicing the Garden Route coastal resorts. **Conservation** has halted the wholesale destruction of the indigenous woodlands, but a huge growth in tourism and the influx of urbanites seeking a quiet life in the relatively crime-free Garden Route towns threaten to rob the area of its remaining tranquillity.

The Garden Route coast is dominated by three inlets – Mossel Bay, the Knysna lagoon and Plettenberg Bay – each with its own town. Oldest of these and closest to Cape Town is **Mossel Bay**, an industrial centre of limited charm, which marks the official start of the Garden Route. **Knysna**, though younger, exudes a well-rooted urban character and is the nicest of the coastal towns, with one major drawback – unlike **Plettenberg Bay**, its eastern neighbour, it has no beach of its own. A major draw, though, is the **Knysna forest** covering some of the hilly country around Knysna.

Between the coastal towns are some ugly modern holiday developments, but also some wonderful empty beaches and tiny coves, such as **Victoria Bay** and **Nature's Valley**. Best of all is the **Tsitsikamma National Park**, which has it all – indigenous forest, dramatic coastline, the pumping **Storms River Mouth** and South Africa's most popular hike, the **Otter Trail**.

There are no serious Big Five game reserves in the Western Cape and certainly none that can offer anything like you'll get on a safari in the Kruger or a stay in one of the reserves near Port Elizabeth. Of the **game experiences** offered along the Garden Route, **Botlierskop**, inland from Mossel Bay and within half a day's drive from Cape Town, consistently gets rated as one of the best.

Most visitors take the Garden Route as a journey between Cape Town and **Port Elizabeth** (see p.239), dallying for little more than a day or two for shopping, sightseeing or a taste of one of the many outdoor activities on offer. The rapid passage cut by the excellent N2 makes it all too easy to have a fast scenic drive – and end up disappointed because you don't see that much from the road. To make the journey worthwhile, you'll need to slow down, take some detours off the highway and explore a little. Each town offers a plethora of adventure-based activities, including whale- and dolphin-spotting from land or boat and the more sedate pleasures of first-class restaurants, ultra-luxurious guesthouses and forest and beach walks.

GETTING AROUND   THE GARDEN ROUTE

The Garden Route is probably the best-served stretch of South Africa for **transport**. If time is tight, you may want to go by **plane** to George at the west end of the Garden Route, which is served by scheduled flights from Cape Town and Port Elizabeth (see p.239). Visiting Port Elizabeth from Cape Town, consider taking the magnificent interior **Route 62** to avoid having to drive the N2 in both directions.

By Baz Bus Most user-friendly among the public transport options is the daily Baz Bus (see p.23) service between Cape Town and Port Elizabeth (☎ 0861 229 287, Skype: Bazbus Reservations, ⍟ bazbus.co.za), which picks up passengers daily in Cape Town (7.15–8.30am) and Port Elizabeth (6.45–7.30am). It provides a door-to-door service within the central districts of all the towns along the way, and has the advantage over the large intercity lines that it will happily carry outdoor gear, such as surfboards or mountain bikes. Although the buses take standby passengers if there's space available, you should book ahead to secure a seat.

By intercity bus Intercape, Greyhound and Translux intercity buses (see p.24) from Cape Town and Port Elizabeth are better and cheaper for more direct journeys, stopping only at Mossel Bay, George, Wilderness, Sedgefield, Knysna and Storms River (the village, but not the Mouth, which is some distance away). These buses often don't go into town, letting passengers off at petrol stations on the highway instead.

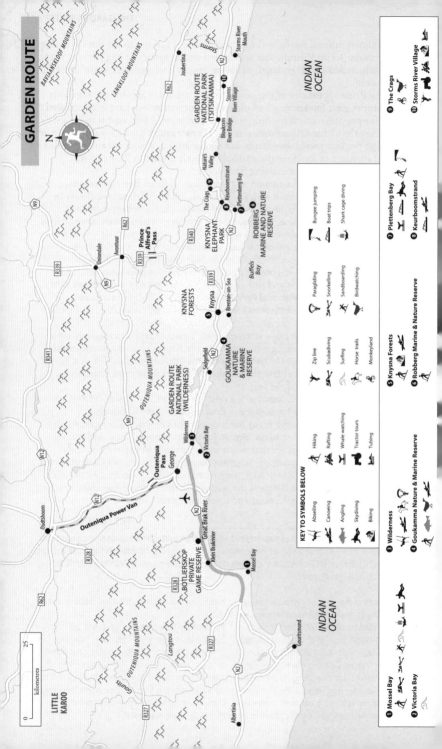

GARDEN ROUTE

N

BAVIAANSKLOOF MOUNTAINS

LANGKLOOF MOUNTAINS

OUTENIQUA MOUNTAINS

LITTLE KAROO

INDIAN OCEAN

Storms

Storms River Mouth

GARDEN ROUTE NATIONAL PARK (TSITSIKAMMA)

Joubertina

Storms River Village

Bloukrans River Bridge

Nature's Valley

The Crags

Keurboomstrand

Plettenberg Bay

KNYSNA ELEPHANT PARK

ROBBERG MARINE AND NATURE RESERVE

Buffels Bay

KNYSNA FORESTS

Knysna

Brenton-on-Sea

Prince Alfred's Pass

Avontuur

Uniondale

GOUKAMMA NATURE & MARINE RESERVE

Sedgefield

GARDEN ROUTE NATIONAL PARK (WILDERNESS)

Wilderness

Outeniqua Pass

George

Victoria Bay

Outeniqua Power Van

Oudtshoorn

Great Brak River

Klein Brakrivier

BOTLIERSKOP PRIVATE GAME RESERVE

Mossel Bay

INDIAN OCEAN

Gouritsmond

Langtou

Gouris

Albertinia

kilometres
0 — 25

KEY TO SYMBOLS BELOW

Abseiling	Hiking	Zip line	Paragliding	Bungee jumping
Canoeing	Rafting	Scubadiving	Snorkelling	Boat trips
Angling	Whale watching	Surfing	Sandboarding	Shark cage diving
Skydiving	Tractor tours	Horse trails	Birdwatching	
Biking	Tubing	Monkeyland		

1 Mossel Bay

2 Victoria Bay

3 Wilderness

4 Goukamma Nature & Marine Reserve

5 Knysna Forests

6 Robberg Marine & Nature Reserve

7 Plettenberg Bay

8 Keurboomstrand

9 The Crags

10 Storms River Village

Mossel Bay

17

MOSSEL BAY, a mid-sized town 397km east of Cape Town, gets a bad press from most South Africans, mainly because of the huge industrial facade it presents to the N2. Don't panic – the historic centre is a thoroughly pleasant contrast, set on a hill overlooking the small working harbour and bay, with one of the best **swimming** beaches along the southern Cape coast and an interesting museum. Like other Garden Route destinations it is also a springboard for numerous adventure activities. The town takes on a strong Afrikaans flavour over Christmas, when Karoo farmers and their families descend in droves to occupy its caravan parks and chalets.

If the urban nature of Mossel Bay holds no appeal, you are best heading off inland in the direction of Oudtshoorn, along the R328 Robinson Pass Road, where there are some great places to stay.

Brief history

Mossel Bay bears poignant historical significance as the place where indigenous Khoi cattle herders first encountered the Europeans in a bloody spat that symbolically set the tone for five hundred years of race relations on the subcontinent. A group of Portuguese mariners under Captain **Bartholomeu Dias** set sail from Portugal in August 1487 in search of a sea route to the riches of India, and months later rounded the Cape of Good Hope. In February 1488, they became the first Europeans to make landfall along the South African coast, when they pulled in for water to the safety of an inlet they called Aguado de So Bras ("watering place of St Blaize"), now Mossel Bay. The Khoikhoi were organized into distinct groups, each under its own chief and each with territorial rights over pastures and water sources. The Portuguese, who were flouting local customs, saw it as "bad manners" when the Khoikhoi tried to drive them off the spring. In a mutual babble of incomprehension the Khoi began stoning the Portuguese, who retaliated with crossbow fire that left one of the herders dead.

Bartholomeu Dias Museum Complex

Mon–Fri 9am–4.45pm, Sat & Sun 9am–3.45pm • R20; entry onto Dias caravel additional R20 • ⓦ diasmuseum.co.za

Mossel Bay's main urban attraction is the **Bartholomeu Dias Museum Complex**, housed in a collection of historic buildings well integrated into the small town centre, all near the tourist office and within a couple of minutes' walk of each other.

The Maritime Museum

The highlight is the **Maritime Museum**, a spiral gallery with displays on the history of European, principally Portuguese, seafaring, arranged around a full-size replica of Dias' original caravel. The ship was built in Portugal and sailed from Lisbon to Mossel Bay in 1987 to celebrate the five hundredth anniversary of Dias' historic journey. You can't fail to be awed by the idea of the original mariners setting out on the high seas into terra incognita on such a small vessel – particularly as the crew were accommodated above deck with only a sailcloth for protection against the elements.

Post Office Tree

Sixteenth-century mariners used to leave messages for passing ships in an old boot under a milkwood tree somewhere around the designated **Post Office Tree**, just outside the Maritime Museum; the plaque claims that "this may well" be the same tree. You can post mail here in a large, boot-shaped letterbox and have it stamped with a special postmark.

Shell Museum and Aquarium

Of the remaining exhibitions, the **Shell Museum and Aquarium**, next to the Post Office Tree, is the only one worth taking time to visit. This is your chance to see some of the beautiful shells found off the South African coast, as well as shells from around the

17

world. Exhibits include a history of the use of shells by humans and a fascinating display of living shellfish including cowries with their inhabitants still at home.

Santos Beach

A short walk north down the hill from the Maritime Museum gets you to **Santos Beach**, the main town strand, and purportedly the only north-facing beach in South Africa – which gives it exceptionally long sunny afternoons. Adjacent to the small town harbour, the beach provides some of the finest swimming along the Garden Route, with uncharacteristically gentle surf, small waves and a depth perfect for practising your crawl.

The Point

East of the harbour, the coast bulges south towards the **Point**, which has several places to eat and a popular restaurant bar (see p.192) with a deck at the ocean's edge, from which you may see dolphins cruising past along a surreal five-hundred-metre rocky channel known as the aquarium, which is used as a natural **tidal pool**.

St Blaize Lighthouse and Cape St Blaize Cave

A couple of hundred metres to the south of the harbour, atop some cliffs, the **St Blaize Lighthouse**, built in 1864, is still in use as a beacon to ships. Below it, the **Cape St Blaize Cave** is both a marvellous lookout point and a significant archeological site. A boardwalk leads through the cave past three information panels describing the history of the interpretation of the cave as well as the modern understanding of it. In 1801 Sir John Barrow insisted that **shells** found at the site had been brought by seagulls, while others argued that they were relics of human habitation. It turned out that Barrow's opponents were right, but it wasn't till 1888 that excavations uncovered **stone tools** and showed that people had been using the cave for something close on 100,000 years. The path leading up to the cave continues onto the Cape St Blaize trail (see opposite).

ARRIVAL AND DEPARTURE   MOSSEL BAY

By Baz Bus Only the daily Baz Bus comes right into town, dropping you off at *Mossel Bay Backpackers* and *Park House Lodge*.

By intercity bus Greyhound, Intercape, SA Roadlink and Translux buses stop at Shell Voorbaai Service Station on the N2, 7km from the centre, at the junction of the national highway and the road into town. (Voorbaai Truckport offers a centralized bus booking service ☎ 044 695 1172).

Destinations Cape Town (3 daily; 6hr); George (1–2 daily; 45min); Knysna (1–2 daily; 2hr); Oudtshoorn (1–2 daily; 1hr 15min); Plettenberg Bay (1–2 daily; 2hr 30min); Port Elizabeth (1–2 daily; 6hr 30min).

By taxi The town itself is small enough to negotiate on foot, but should you need transport, call 24/7 Taxi on ☎ 082 932 5809.

INFORMATION

Tourist information Bang in the centre, the tourist information office on the corner of Church and Market sts (Mon–Fri 8am–6pm, Sat & Sun 9am–4pm; ☎ 044 691 2202, ⓦ visitmosselbay.co.za) has shelves of brochures

about Mossel Bay and the rest of the Garden Route, and a map of the town. Their website has comprehensive listings of Mossel Bay's main attractions, businesses, accommodation and restaurants.

ACTIVITIES

Mossel Bay is a springboard for popular **activities**, including skydiving, surfing instruction, sandboarding and deep-sea fishing, all of which can be booked through the Garden Route Adventure Centre at *Mossel Bay Backpackers* (☎ 044 691 3182, ⓦ gardenrouteadventures.com). It is worth noting that although fishing is available at Mossel Bay, you should question operators about what catch they target. Some operators are known to recreationally catch threatened or endangered species that are on the Red or Orange list of WWF SASSI (World Wildlife Fund, Sustainable Seafood Initiative; ⓦ wwfsassi.co.za).

DIVING AND SNORKELLING

There are several rewarding diving and snorkeling spots

around Mossel Bay, and full facilities, including Open Water certification courses (around R3800) and one-off dives

(R400). If you haven't the time or inclination to go the whole hog, you can take a scuba crash course (R800) that allows you to go out on a dive with an instructor. These aren't tropical seas, so don't expect clear warm waters, but with visibility usually between 4m and 10m you stand a good chance of seeing octopus, squid, sea stars, soft corals, pyjama sharks and butterfly fish.

Electro Dive ⊕ 082 561 1259, ⓦ electrodive.co.za. This outfit rent out gear and provide shore- and boat-based dives to local reefs and wrecks (R240/400 including kit), certification courses, underwater hockey and guided snorkelling trips (R220).

HIKING

On the mainland you can check out the coast on the St Blaize hiking trail, an easy fifteen-kilometre walk (roughly 4hr each way; a map is available from the tourist office) along the southern shore of Mossel Bay. The route starts from the Cape St Blaize Cave, just below the lighthouse at the Point, and heads west as far as Dana Bay, taking in magnificent coastal views of cliffs, rocks, bays and coves.

SANDBOARDING AND SURFING

Billeon Surf and Sandboarding Surf Factory, Fields St ⊕ 082 97 11 405, ⓦ billeon.com. Mossel Bay is one of the best places in the country for sandboarding: the dunes are big, the sand is moist and fine and you pay roughly half what you would in Cape Town. You can take trips with these guys to the so-called "Dragon Dune", which they claim, at 320m, is the longest runnable stretch of sand in the country. The activity is suitable for all levels, from beginner to extreme – the dune tends to run faster during the winter months. They also offer surfing instruction, and Mossel Bay

has a good beach break suitable for novices (R350/person for 2hr. All gear is included in the price for both activities (R380/person for 3hr; group discounts available).

SKYDIVING

Skydive Mossel Bay Mossel Bay Airfield ⊕ 044 695 1771, ⓦ skydivemosselbay.com. For the ultimate adrenaline junkies, the Garden Route has some of the country's best sky diving. Skydive Mossel Bay offer tandem sky-dives (3000m for R2000) and skydiving courses.

SHARK ENCOUNTERS

White Shark Africa Cnr Church & Market sts ⊕ 044 691 3796, ⓦ whitesharkafrica.com. One of the better shark-cage operations in the country, they'll let you watch from a boat or go underwater in a cage for R1300. The best months for sightings are March to November, but at no time are encounters guaranteed.

WHALE-WATCHING AND SEAL ISLAND CRUISES

The Romonza ⊕ 044 690 3101, ⓦ mosselbay.co.za. Cruises around Seal Island (hourly 10am–3pm, adults R145, children R70), about 10km northwest of Santos Beach, to see the African penguin and seal colonies can be taken on the *Romonza*, a medium-sized yacht that launches from the yacht marina in the harbour. The *Romonza* is also the only registered vessel allowed to run boat-based whale-watching cruises (adults R660; children R400; 2–3hr) in Mossel Bay. As elsewhere along this coast, the whale season is variable with southern rights appearing from June till late October. If you're extremely lucky, you may also see a humpback whale.

ACCOMMODATION

Edward Charles Manor Hotel 1 Sixth Ave ⊕ 044 691 2152, ⓦ edwardcharles.co.za. An upmarket two-storey guesthouse in a central location overlooking Santos Beach with a swimming pool. There are fifteen en-suite rooms and courtesy shuttle to take you to town if you don't have your own car. R1150

Mossel Bay Backpackers 1 Marsh St ⊕ 044 691 3182, ⓦ mosselbaybackpackers.co.za. Well-run lodge with squeaky clean rooms, only 300m from the sea. They also do adventure activity bookings, and there's a swimming pool, garden and football table when you're relaxing at home. Dorm R170, double 440

Park House Lodge 121 High St ⊕ 044 691 1937,

ⓦ parkhouse.co.za. Top-notch budget accommodation in twenty rooms distributed across three buildings, one of which is a beautiful nineteenth-century sandstone manor house. Some rooms have private entrances leading onto the lush garden and doubles with a shared bathroom are very affordable (R460). Dorm R170, double R780

Protea Hotel Mossel Bay Bartholomeu Dias Museum Complex, Market St ⊕ 044 691 3738, ⓦ proteahotels .com/mosselbay. Opposite the tourist office, in an old Cape Dutch manor house, this quaint place in the town centre overlooks Santos Bay and the harbour. Breakfast is served at *Café Gannet*, Mossel Bay's nicest restaurant (see p.192). R1535

EATING AND DRINKING

You don't come to Mossel Bay for the food, but there are a number of reasonable places to eat, some of them with superb sea views. The small Point Village shopping development at the north end has a couple of inexpensive to mid-priced family restaurants, opening daily from the morning until 11pm-ish.

17

Café Gannet Market St ☎ 044 691 1885, ⓦ oldposttree .co.za. Close to the Bartholomeu Dias Museum Complex, Mossel Bay's smartest restaurant serves straightforward seafood dishes, such as grilled sole (R165), at a moderate price in a stylish garden with glimpses across the harbour; it's a good spot for sundowners. Daily 7.30am–10pm.

Delfino's Espresso Bar and Pizzeria Point Village ☎ 044 690 5247. Pasta (R65), pizza and steak as well as decent coffee all at reasonable prices, with great views of the sea. Daily 7am–11pm.

★**Kai** 4 Mossel Bay Harbour ☎ 079 980 3981, ⓦ kaai4 .co.za. Relaxed, rustic, open-air beach restaurant, with

sprawling picnic tables in a stunning location right on the beach, where you can watch your seafood braai on an open fire (R85). Although the menu is small, the servings are large and good value for money. Daily 10am–10pm (closed when raining).

King Fisher Point Village ☎ 044 690 6390, ⓦ theking fisher.co.za. A relaxed joint that, as its name suggests, specializes in seafood, from humble fish and chips to lobster thermidor and everything in between (average mains R120). There's also a kids' menu. Its elevated position above *Delfino's* means it has excellent views. Daily 11am–11pm.

Mossel Bay to Oudtshoorn

Heading inland towards Oudtshoorn from Mossel Bay on the R328 takes you over the forested coastal mountains of **Robinson Pass** into the desiccated Little Karoo. The draw of this road is some great scenery and accommodation, and an alternative, prettier route to Oudtshoorn than travelling via George. Day-visitors are welcome at **Botlierskop Private Game Reserve** (see below), with activities including game drives (R420; 3hr); elephant rides (R520; 30min) and horse rides (R270; 1hr) that can be booked in advance.

ACCOMMODATION   **MOSSEL BAY TO OUDTSHOORN**

Botlierskop Private Game Reserve 22km from Mossel Bay ☎ 044 696 6055, ⓦ botlierskop.co.za. While there is nothing wild about it, the tented accommodation here works hard to provide a safari atmosphere, with decks and outdoor seating to admire the lovely views. You will usually (although not always) see lions in their huge enclosure, and there's a good chance of spotting rhinos, elephants, giraffes and antelope too. Their packages are professionally put together and include a number of activities for both day- and overnight-visitors. Half-board, including a game drive R2400/person

Eight Bells Mountain Inn 35km from Mossel Bay ☎ 044 631 0000, ⓦ eightbells.co.za. A firm favourite with well-heeled families wanting a fully catered hotel-style holiday, with all sorts of activities laid on for children, including special meal times for younger kids, horseriding, swimming, tennis and walking. The atmosphere is friendly and it's superbly run. Out of school holidays it remains a

restful stop-off with lovely gardens and extensive grounds, close to the top of the mountainous pass. R1200

★**Outeniqua Moon Percheron Stud and Guest Farm** 23km from Mossel Bay, just below the Robinson Pass ☎ 044 631 0093 or ☎ 082 564 9782, ⓦ outeniqua moon.co.za. Comfortable and classy self-catering or B&B accommodation in four, colonial farm-style units on a working farm with beautiful views of the Outeniqua mountains. The huge, serene draft horses are given a sanctuary on the farm and you can spend time with them, petting foals or taking a carriage ride (R80 per person including tea and cake, 45min). You can swim laps in the 25m ozone pool or explore the 100 hectares of forest on the farm. If you choose not to self-cater, prepare to be spoilt with home-made bread and other farm delights. Prices are reasonable, dropping down outside of school holidays. Two-bed self-catering cottage R1000, half-board R1500

George

There's little reason to visit **GEORGE**, a large inland town 66km northeast of Mossel Bay, unless you need what a big centre offers – airport, car rental, hospital and shops. Sadly, all that's left of the forests and quaint character that moved Anthony Trollope, during a visit in 1877, to describe it as the "prettiest village on the face of the earth" are some historic buildings.

If you're pushed for time, however, George is conveniently right in the middle of the Garden Route, halfway between Cape Town and Port Elizabeth, and there are regular flights here from both Cape Town and Johannesburg. By road, the town is a 5km detour northwest off the N2 and 9km from the nearest stretch of ocean at Victoria Bay.

Dutch Reformed Church

Davidson St

17

The most notable of George's historic buildings is the beautiful **Dutch Reformed Church**, at the top end of Meade Street. Completed in the early 1840s, the church is definitely worth a stop if you happen to be passing through, with its elegantly simple classical facade, Greek-cross plan with an impressive, centrally placed pulpit and wonderful domed ceiling, panelled with glowing yellowwood.

St Mark's Cathedral

Cathedral St • ⓦ stmarkscathedral.co.za

St Mark's Cathedral, consecrated in 1850, is worth seeing, but unlike the Dutch Reformed Church, which is open to the public, it can only be visited by appointment. Ask at the tourist office for bookings (see below). It also holds regular worship services.

ARRIVAL AND INFORMATION   GEORGE

By plane Kulula and SAA fly between Johannesburg and the small George airport, 10km west of town on the N2 (8 daily; 1hr 50min). SAA also flies here from Cape Town (6 daily; 50min). Most tourists flying in rent a car from one of the companies at the airport and set off down the Garden Route.
By Baz Bus Baz Bus drops off at *Outeniqua Backpackers* on Merriman St on its daily run between Cape Town and Port Elizabeth.
By intercity buses Intercape, Translux and Greyhound intercity buses pull in at George station, adjacent to the

railway museum, and at the Sasol garage station on the N2 east of town.
Destinations Cape Town (2 daily; 7hr); Jo'burg (daily; 16hr); Knysna (2 daily; 1hr 30min); Mossel Bay (6–7 daily; 45min); Oudtshoorn (daily; 1hr 10min); Plettenberg Bay (2 daily; 2hr); Port Elizabeth (2 daily; 5hr 30min).
Tourist information The George tourist office at 124 York St (Mon–Fri 7.45am–4.30pm, Sat 9am–1pm; ☎ 044 801 9295, ⓦ visitgeorge.co.za) can provide town maps and help with accommodation bookings.

PRESIDENT BOTHA AND APARTHEID'S LAST STAND

Pieter Willem Botha believed that by setting up a powerful "Imperial Presidency" in South Africa he could withstand the inevitable tide of democracy. A National Party hack from the age of 20, Botha worked his way up through the ranks, getting elected as an MP in 1948 when the first apartheid government took power. He was promoted through various cabinet posts until he became **Minister of Defence**, a position he used to launch a palace coup in 1978 against his colleague, Prime Minister John Vorster. Botha immediately set about modernizing apartheid, modifying his own role from that of a British-style prime minister, answerable to parliament, to one of an executive president taking vital decisions in the secrecy of a President's Council heavily weighted with army top brass.

Informed by the army that the battle to preserve the apartheid status quo was unwinnable purely by force, Botha embarked on his **Total Strategy**, which involved reforms to peripheral aspects of apartheid and the fostering of a black middle class as a buffer against the ANC, while pumping vast sums of money into building an enormous military machine that crossed South Africa's borders to bully or crush neighbouring countries harbouring groups opposed to apartheid. South African refugees in Botswana and Zimbabwe were bombed, Angola was invaded, and arms were run to anti-government rebels in Mozambique, reducing it to ruins – a policy that has returned to haunt South Africa with those same weapons now returning across the border and finding their way into the hands of criminals. Inside South Africa, security forces enjoyed a free hand to murder, maim and torture **opponents of apartheid**.

Botha blustered and wagged his finger at the opposition through the late 1980s, while his bloated military sucked the state coffers dry as it prosecuted its dirty wars. Even National Party stalwarts realized that his policies were leading to ruin, and in 1989, when he suffered a stroke, the party was quick to replace him with **F.W. de Klerk**, who immediately proceeded to announce reforms.

Botha lived out his unrepentant retirement near George, declining ever to apologize for any of the brutal actions taken under his presidency to bolster apartheid. Curiously, when he died in 2006, he was given an uncritical, high-profile state funeral, broadcast on national television and attended by members of the government, including then-president, Thabo Mbeki.

17

THE OUTENIQUA POWER VAN

Sadly South Africa's main-line railways are slowly dying. The Garden Route's train line penetrated some of the region's most visually stunning back country making the Cape Town-to-Port Elizabeth run one of the great railway journeys of the world. That ended when some of the tracks were washed away and never replaced. Until 2010, you could still travel on the tourist Outeniqua Choo-Tjoe steam train that chugged between George and Mossel Bay. That too has gone – wiped away by government bean counters, who regard it as financially unviable.

Fortunately you can still get a taster of the line on the **Outeniqua Power Van**, a single cab diesel-powered train that trails into the Outeniqua Mountains just outside George. The train stops at a scenic site for a picnic before returning to the town. En route you pass through forest, negotiate passes and tunnels, and will see waterfalls and *fynbos*.

BOOKING

The train departs from the Outeniqua Transport Museum, 2 Mission Rd, George (☎082 490 5627 or ☎044 801 8239, ✉opv@mweb.co.za; Mon–Sat on demand, booking essential; R100; 2.5hr). Bring your own picnic, sunglasses, a hat and a warm jacket.

ACCOMMODATION

10 Caledon Street 10 Caledon St ☎044 873 4983, ⓦ10caledon.co.za. The pick of the mid-priced B&Bs, in a spotless guesthouse on a quiet street, featuring balconies with mountain views and a garden. The owners are superb hosts and provide an excellent breakfast. The B&B is an easy walk to the city centre. R850

Die Waenhuis 11 Caledon St ☎044 874 0034, ⓦdiewaenhuis.co.za. Mid-nineteenth-century home that has retained its period character with eleven spacious en-suite rooms, a beautiful garden and gracious hosts. English breakfasts, included in the price, are served in a sunlit dining room. R850

Mount View Resort & Lifestyle Village York St ☎044 874 5205, ⓦmountviewsa.co.za. Modern complex that lacks much character, but offers great value in its one-, two- and three-bedroom en-suite chalets and rondavels. The gardens are well-kept and pleasant and the complex also houses a wellness and beauty salon, a ten-pin bowling alley and a pool hall. Rondavels R390, chalets R1180

Oakhurst Hotel Cnr Meade & Cathedral sts ☎044 874 7130, ⓦmountviewsa.co.za. Charming, centrally located manor house with a country feel, green lawns, a peaceful garden with pool, lovely dining area and views of the Outeniqua Mountains. R1000

Outeniqua Backpackers 115 Merriman St ☎082 316 7720, ⓦouteniqua-backpackers.com. Friendly hostel in a bright and airy suburban house with comfortable dorms and doubles, some with mountain views. There's a swimming pool, and they provide free airport pick-ups. The Baz Bus pulls in here. Dorm R140, double R500

EATING AND DRINKING

Kafe Serefe 60 Courtenay St ☎044 884 1012. Hugely popular venue that does South African cuisine which, like the belly dancing on Wednesday and Friday nights, comes with a Turkish twist. Meat is the speciality, whether it's sirloin steak with blue cheese sauce, walnuts and preserved figs, or pork with goat's cheese and fig sauce (R90). There's also a good choice of meze, if you're after something lighter. Mon–Fri 9am–4.30pm & 6.30–11pm, Sat 6–11pm.

La Capannina 122 York St ☎044 874 5313. Italian restaurant that in addition to excellent pizzas and pasta, has other tricks up its sleeve such as beef fillet on a bed of polenta and distinctly un-Italian fare such as ostrich jambalaya with a hint of curry (R85). Mon–Fri noon–10pm, Sat & Sun 6–10pm.

The Old Town House Cnr York and Market sts ☎044 874 3663. There's a lovely ambience in this original town house, where the food is well cooked with attention to detail in an intimate setting. Despite the place's carnivorous inclination – they specialize in venison and beef – vegetarians are catered for and their baked pasta is delicious (R65). Mon–Fri noon–3pm & 6–10pm, Sat 6–10pm.

Victoria Bay

Some 9km south of George and 3km off the N2 lies the minuscule hamlet of **VICTORIA BAY**, on the edge of a small sandy beach wedged into a cove between cliffs, with a

17

grassy sunbathing area, safe swimming and a tidal pool. During the December holidays it packs out with day-trippers, and rates as one of the top **surfing** spots along the Garden Route. Because of the cliffs, there's only a single row of buildings along the beachfront, with some of the most dreamily positioned guesthouses along the coast (and therefore some of the priciest for what you get).

ARRIVAL AND DEPARTURE   VICTORIA BAY

By car Arriving by car, you'll encounter a metal barrier as you drop down the hill to the bay, and you'll have to try and park in a car park that's frequently full (especially in summer). If you're staying at one of the B&Bs, leave your car at the barrier and collect the key from your lodgings to gain access to the private beach road.

By Baz Bus The daily Baz Bus, which provides the only transport to Victoria Bay, drops passengers at the *Vic Bay Surf Lodge*.

ACCOMMODATION

Land's End Guest House The Point, Beach Rd ☎ 044 889 0123, ⓦ vicbay.com. En-suite rooms in what claims to be "the closest B&B to the sea in Africa", as well as self-catering accommodation a few doors away at *Bay House*, which sleeps four, and *Sea Cottage*, which sleeps five. R1300

Sea Breeze Holiday Resort Along the main road into the settlement ☎ 044 889 0098, ⓦ seabreezecabanas .co.za. A variety of budget self-catering units, including modern two-storey holiday huts and wooden chalets, sleeping two, four or eight people. The huts have no sea views, but it's an easy stroll to the beach. Note that in peak season prices quadruple. R660

Vicbay Safari Backpackers Victoria Bay Rd ☎ 044 889 0113, ⓦ vicbaysurfari.co.za. Predominately a surfers' lodge with home comforts including wi-fi, DSTV, a self-catering kitchen and BBQ areas. The lodge offers surf camps and full- or half-day surf lessons for all levels at the local easy, local right-hand point break. There's also a trampoline, pool table, table tennis, volleyball and shuttles to the beach and George, if you don't have a car. Dorm R180, double R750, family room R1100

EATING

There are no food shops or restaurants at Victoria Bay, so you'll need to bring supplies. There is a marvellous service, however, offered by Mr Delivery in George (☎ 044 873 6677) which will collect pre-ordered takeaways from George, as well as groceries bought on line at Pick n Pay, and even DVDs.

Wilderness

East of Victoria Bay, across the Kaaimans River, the beach at **WILDERNESS** is so close to the N2 that you can pull over for a quick dip with barely an interruption to your journey, though African wilderness is the last thing you'll find here. Wilderness village earned its name, so the story goes, after a young man called Van den Berg bought the property in 1830 for £183 as a blind lot at a Cape Town auction. When he got engaged, his fiancée insisted that their first year of marriage should be spent out of town in the wilderness, so he romantically (or perhaps opportunistically) named his property Wilderness and built a hut on it.

If the hut still exists, you'll struggle to find it among the sprawl of retirement homes, holiday houses and thousands of beds for rent in the vicinity. The beach, which is renowned for its long stretch of sand, is backed by tall dunes, rudely blighted by holiday houses. Once in the water, stay close to the shoreline: this part of the coast is notorious for its unpredictable currents.

ARRIVAL AND INFORMATION   WILDERNESS

By Baz Bus The Baz Bus drops off at *Fairy Knowe Backpackers*, a 20min walk into Wilderness.

Tourist office The tourist office is in Milkwood Village Mall, Beacon Rd, off the N2 opposite the Caltex garage (Mon–Fri 7.45am–4.30pm, Sat 9am–1pm; ☎ 044 877 0045, ⓦ george.org.za).

Services Wilderness's tiny village centre, on the north side of the N2, has a petrol station and a few shops.

17

ACTIVITIES

OUTDOOR ACTIVITIES

Black Horse Trails 19km into the mountains, up the Hoekwil Rd ⓣ 082 494 5642, ⓦ blackhorsetrails.co.za. Mountain and forest horseriding tours using bitless bridles (R275 for 90min or R425 for 3hr).

Eden Adventures ⓣ 044 877 0179 or ⓣ 083 628 8547, ⓦ eden.co.za. Offers daily kloofing adventures (8am–1pm, R500) and abseiling (1.30–4.30pm, R500); a full day taking in both activities costs R850. Explore the river yourself by renting a two-seater canoe from them (R50/hr).

PARAGLIDING

Cloudbase Paragliding Adventures ⓣ 044 877 1414, ⓦ cloudbase-paragliding.co.za. To see it all from the air, sign up for a tandem paragliding jump that starts from R450 for a minimum of fifteen minutes. You'll only be taken up when the weather offers absolutely safe conditions. They also offer a one-day introductory course for R950.

ACCOMMODATION

Beach House Backpackers Western Rd ⓣ 044 877 0549, ⓦ wildernessbeachhouse.com. Set on the hill, with ocean views from the hammocks on the terrace and bar, *Beach House Backpackers* has very basic dorm rooms and doubles with a communal kitchen. Internet can be sketchy when it is available and costs extra, and no alcohol can be brought from outside. Cooking classes, surf lessons and board rental are available. Dorm R150, double R450

Fairy Knowe Backpackers 6km from the village, follow signs from the N2 east of Wilderness ⓣ 044 877 1285, ⓦ wildernessbackpackers.com. The oldest home (built 1897) in the area, with a wraparound balcony and set in the quiet woodlands near the Touw River, though nowhere near the sea. Beware, during peak season it gets busy and can be very noisy near the bar. The Baz Bus drops off here. Dorm R130, double R480

Island Lake Holiday Resort Lakes Rd, 2km from the Hoekwil/Island Lake turn-off on the N2 ⓣ 044 877 1194, ⓦ islandlake.co.za. Camping and self-catering rondavels that sleep four on one of the quietest and prettiest spots on the lakes. The rondavels are basic one-room affairs with kitchenettes equipped with hotplates, microwaves and utensils, but you share communal washing and toilet facilities. Camping R220, rondavel R430

Mes-Amis Homestead Buxton Close, signposted off the N2 on the coastal side of the road, directly opposite the national park turn-off ⓣ 044 877 1928, ⓦ mesamis .co.za. Nine double rooms, each of which has its own terrace, offering some of the best views in Wilderness. Rooms are elegantly furnished with crisp white bedding and curtains and there are luxurious touches such as bathrobes and espresso machines in each room. R1400

★ **Palms Wilderness Retreat** Owen Grant Rd ⓣ 044 877 1420, ⓦ palms-wilderness.com. With lush tranquil gardens, a pool, spa and lots of private outdoor seating for curling up with a book, you will find plenty here to help you relax and unwind. Rooms with thatched roofs are stylishly decorated, equipped with coffee and tea stations and there is a plush guest lounge with satellite TV and a small library. R1900

Wilderness Bush Camp Heights Rd (follow Waterside Rd west for 1600m up the hill) ⓣ 044 877 1168, ⓦ boskamp.co.za. Six self-catering timber units with loft bedrooms, thatched roofs and ocean views. The camp, set on a hillside amid *fynbos* wilderness, is part of a conservation estate that you're free to roam around. R650

EATING

The Girls George Rd ⓣ 044 877 1648, ⓦ thegirls restaurant.co.za. Deservedly one of the most popular restaurants in the village, *The Girls* fuses classic French dishes, such as steak tartare, with North African and Middle Eastern influences. The prawns are fantastic, they do a mean steak (R150) and vegetarians get a decent look in. Tues–Sun 6pm–late.

Salinas Beach Restaurant Cnr N2 and Zundorf Lane ⓣ 044 877 001. An easy stop-off on the N2 with a great view over the beach from the tables under umbrellas on the terrace. They're known for fresh fish brought in from Mossel Bay or Knysna, good cocktails (R40) and excellent cheese cake. Daily 11am–10pm.

Serendipity Freesia Ave ⓣ 044 877 0433, ⓦ serendipitywilderness.com. A fine-dining restaurant located on the banks of the Touw River Lagoon, where you can have a fabulous dinner cooked by a husband-and-wife team, with Asian, Mediterranean and strong South African influences. Vegetarians may be seriously tempted by twice-baked goat's cheese soufflé or aubergine and pumpkin roulade. A seasonal, ever-changing five-course set menu is on offer (R380) and you need to book well ahead. Mon–Sat 7pm–late.

Zucchini Timberlake Organic Village ⓣ 044 882 1240, ⓦ zucchini.co.za. This restaurant is making strides to offer more sustainable food choices, including cooking veg from their own organic gardens and sourcing meat that is either free-range or organic. Their meals are simple and tasty with large portions – dishes include gourmet burgers like the "Dronk Bok" which is topped with brandy-soaked pears (R80), créme fraîche and home-made nut-brittle. Drinks include thirteen types of locally brewed craft beer and sulphur-free wine. Phone before you go as opening times change according to seasons. Mon–Wed 9am–5pm, Thurs–Sun 9am–9pm.

Garden Route National Park: Wilderness Section

17

Reception open 7am–5.30pm • R100 • ☎ 044 877 1197

Stretching east from Wilderness village is the **Wilderness Section of the Garden Route National Park**, an inappropriate name, as it never feels very far from the N2. It's the **forests** you should come for, and the 16km of inland waterways; the variety of habitats here includes coastal and montane *fynbos* and wetlands, attracting 250 species of **bird** – as well as many holiday-makers.

ARRIVAL AND DEPARTURE

WILDERNESS SECTION

By car Driving along the N2, follow the road signs to Wilderness National Park to get to Ebb and Flow restcamps. There is also a Western access to the park, reached by passing through the town of Wilderness, across the rail road bridge and a right turn for reception.

ACTIVITIES

Canoeing You can navigate the Touw River from the restcamp down to the beach in a canoe, which can be rented from Eden Adventures (see opposite).
Hiking There are five waymarked trails in the Wilderness Section of between two and five kilometres. A map of the trails, which also shows the location of three bird hides, is available at reception or you can download it from the SANParks website (🖥 sanparks.org).

ACCOMMODATION

There are two **restcamps**, *Ebb and Flow North*, and *Ebb and Flow South*, both on the west side of the park, which can be booked through SANparks (🖥 sanparks.org/parks/garden_route/camps/wilderness).

Ebb and Flow North Right on the river, this restcamp is cheap, old-fashioned and away from the hustle. It offers camping, fully equipped two-person rondavels with their own showers and rondavels with communal washing and toilet facilities. Camping R270, rondavel R270
Ebb and Flow South This site has camping and modern accommodation in spacious log cottages on stilts and brick bungalows for up to four people (with private kitchen and bathroom). There are also en-suite two-sleeper forest huts with communal kitchens. Camping R240, huts R625, bungalow R1235

Sedgefield

The drive between Wilderness and Sedgefield gives glimpses on your left of dark-coloured lakes which eventually surge out to sea, 21km later, through a wide lagoon at **SEDGEFIELD** a pleasantly old-fashioned holiday village – one of the last of its kind along the Garden Route – a few kilometres off the road, with miles of beautiful beaches. In fact so proud is Sedgefield of its lack of pizzazz, that the village has had itself registered as a "slow town", affiliated to the Cittaslow towns of Italy with its emblem a tortoise.

The entertainment highlight of Sedgefield's week is the **Wild Oats Community Farmers' Market** (🖥 wildoatsmarket.co.za; summer Sat 7.30–11.30am, winter from 8–11.30am), along the N2 on the west side of town, just before Swartvlei Lake, where you can pick up groceries and tasty nosh, such as preserves, cheeses, pickles and cured meats as well as delectable takeaway finger foods.

Sedgefield can be used as a base from which to explore Goukamma Nature and Marine Reserve and the western extent of Groenvlei, a freshwater lake that falls within the reserve's boundaries.

ARRIVAL AND DEPARTURE

SEDGEFIELD

By intercity bus Greyhound, Intercape and Translux buses stop in the middle of the village at the Sedgefield Garage, Main Rd, a service road running parallel to the N2, which passes through the town's shopping area.
Destinations Cape Town (2 daily; 8hr); Knysna (2 daily; 35min); Mossel Bay (2 daily; 1hr 15min); Plettenberg Bay (2 daily; 1hr 10min); Port Elizabeth (2 daily; 5hr 25min).

17

ACCOMMODATION

Afrovibe Adventure Lodge and Backpackers 2 Claude Urban Drive, Myoli Beach ☎ 044 343 3217, ⓦ afrovibe.co.za. An unattractive, rectangular building, built questionably close to the beach on the ecologically sensitive fore-dunes, but offering a stunning location. Take advantage of their wide range of adventure activities. Dorm R140, double R500

★**Teniqua Treetops** 23km northeast of Sedgefield ☎ 044 356 2868, ⓦ teniquatreetops.co.za. This is a genuinely unique and romantic retreat under the boughs of virgin forest between Sedgefield and Knysna, a patch

including 4km of woodland walks and a river with pools for swimming. Luxury tents are raised on timber decks, where, if you feel so inclined, you can leave the flaps open and wake up to dappled light filtering through the leaves; one unit is wheelchair accessible. Apart from being a chilled-out hideout, this is a fascinating example of sustainable living in practice: not a single tree was felled to build *Teniqua*; recycled materials were used where possible; water is gravity fed; showers are solar-heated; and toilets use a dry composting system that preserves precious water. R1660

Goukamma Nature Reserve

Daily 7:30am–4pm • R40, free entry for overnight visitors • ☎ 044 383 0042

An unassuming sanctuary of around 220 square kilometres, **Goukamma** ranges from near Sedgefield and stretches east to Buffalo Bay (also known as Buffels Bay) to take in Groenvlei Lake and approximately 18km of beach frontage, some of the highest vegetated dunes in the country and walking country covered with coastal *fynbos* and dense thickets of milkwood, yellowwood and candlewood trees.

The area has long been popular with anglers, while away from the water, you stand a small chance of spotting one of the area's **mammals**, including bushbuck, grysbok, vervet monkeys, mongoose, caracals and otters. Because of the diversity of coastal and wetland habitats, more than 220 different kinds of **bird** have been recorded here, including fish eagles, Knysna louries, kingfishers and very rare African black oystercatchers. Offshore, southern right whales often make an appearance during their August-to-December breeding season, and bottlenose and common dolphins can show up at any time of year.

ARRIVAL AND DEPARTURE   GOUKAMMA NATURE RESERVE

By car Two roads off the N2 provide access to the reserve. The entrance and office are on the Buffalo Bay side accessed via the Buffalo Bay road, halfway along which is the reserve office. There are no public roads within the reserve. At the

westernmost side, a dirt road that runs down to Platbank Beach takes you past the tiny settlement of Lake Pleasant on the south bank of Groenvlei, which consists of little more than a hotel and holiday resort.

ACTIVITIES

Apart from angling and birdwatching, the Goukamma offers a number of **self-guided activities**, including safe swimming in Groenvlei.

Hiking There are several day-long hiking trails that enable you to explore different habitats. A beach walk, which takes around four hours one way, traverses the 14km of crumbling cliffs and sands between the Platbank car park on the western side of the reserve and the Rowwehoek one on the eastern side. Alternatively, you can go from one end of the reserve to the other via a

slightly longer inland trek across the dunes. There's also a shorter circular walk from the reserve office through a milkwood forest.

Canoeing You can canoe on the Goukamma River on the eastern side of the reserve; a limited number of canoes can be rented from the office during the week or at the gate over the weekend. Single/double canoes R60/100 a day.

ACCOMMODATION

There are two fully equipped bush camps on the Groenvlei side of the reserve and three thatched rondavels on the east side. Book through CapeNature (ⓦ capenature.co.za). Over weekends, expect to pay roughly 25 percent more than prices quoted.

17

Fish Eagle Lodge This loft, located on the top floor of *Otters Rest Lodge*, sleeps two people in single beds. There are wonderful sea and river views, an open-plan kitchen, dining room and lounge leading onto a deck with fully equipped kitchen and private braai facilities. R850

Mvubu Thatched timber and reed bush camp on stilts at the edge of Groenvlei in a stand of milkwood trees. There are two en-suite bedrooms, both of which have doors opening onto a deck that overlooks the lake. Up to four people R1570

Otters Rest Lodge Ground-floor lodge, with views of the ocean and river, sleeping four in two rooms with two single beds in each and a shared bathroom. Facilities include an open-plan kitchen, dining room and lounge with indoor fireplace, and large deck area with braai facilities. R1460

Stumpnose, Blacktail and Kabeljou Chalets Three basic double units on the Buffalo Bay side of the reserve that sleep four people. Each has two-bed rooms with single beds, one shared bathroom and overlook the river and estuary. There's a fully equipped kitchen with solar electricity and braai facilities (wood for sale at the gate). R1260

Knysna

South Africa's 1990s tourist boom rudely shook **KNYSNA** (pronounced "Nize-na") from its gentle backwoods drowse, which for decades had made it the hippie and craftwork capital of the country. The town, 491km and six hours' drive from Cape Town and 102km east of Mossel Bay, now stands at the hub of the Garden Route, its lack of ocean beaches compensated for by its hilly setting around the **Knysna lagoon**, its handsome **forests**, good opportunities for **adventure sports**, a pleasant **waterfront development** – and some hot marketing. If you want somewhere quiet or rural, Knysna is not for you: it is busy yet sophisticated with good restaurants and ever-burgeoning housing developments.

Knysna's distinctive atmosphere derives from its small historic core of Georgian and Victorian buildings, which gives it a character absent from most of the Garden Route holiday towns. Coffee shops, craft galleries, street traders and a modest nightlife add to the attractions. That the town has outgrown itself is evident from the cars and tour buses that, especially in December and January, clog Main Street, the constricted artery that merges with the N2 as it enters the town.

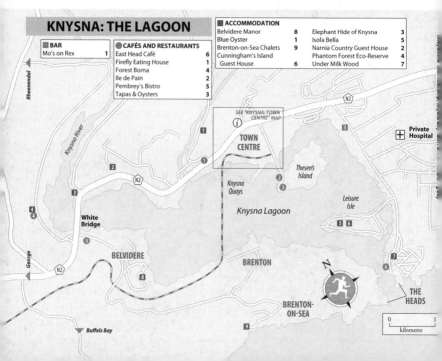

KNYSNA: THE LAGOON

■ BAR
Mo's on Rex ... 1

● CAFÉS AND RESTAURANTS
East Head Café ... 6
Firefly Eating House ... 1
Forest Boma ... 4
Ile de Pain ... 2
Pembrey's Bistro ... 5
Tapas & Oysters ... 3

■ ACCOMMODATION
Belvidere Manor ... 8
Blue Oyster ... 1
Brenton-on-Sea Chalets ... 9
Cunningham's Island Guest House ... 6
Elephant Hide of Knysna ... 3
Isola Bella ... 5
Narnia Country Guest House ... 2
Phantom Forest Eco-Reserve ... 4
Under Milk Wood ... 7

17

TOWNSHIP TOURS AND HOMESTAYS

Get a taste of Knysna's townships by joining one of the warts-and-all tours operated by **Eco Afrika** (tours daily 10am & 2pm; R400; booking essential; ☎082 558 9104, ⊕eco-afrika-tours .co.za). Tours go to five areas, where you'll be given some historical background and get a chance to walk around and chat to people. You can also include lunch with a township family as part of the package (R50).

Eco Afrika also arrange **homestays** in one of the shanty towns within the townships, where you stay with a family in a corrugated iron shack (R150). The tour operator will drop you off and pick you up the next morning.

Knysna wraps around the lagoon, with its oldest part – the town centre – on the northern side. The lagoon's narrow mouth is guarded by a pair of steep rocky promontories called **The Heads**, the western side being a private nature reserve and the eastern one an exclusive residential area (confusingly, it's also called The Heads), along dramatic cliffs above the Indian Ocean.

Main Street, which used to be the hub of Knysna, lost some of its status as the heart of the town with the development of the waterfront area. But it has begun fighting back, with extensive redevelopment that has brought with it trendy coffee bars, restaurants and shops.

Brief history

At the beginning of the nineteenth century, the only white settlements outside Cape Town were a handful of villages that would have considered themselves lucky to have even one horse. Knysna, an undeveloped backwater hidden in the forest, was no exception. The name comes from a Khoi word meaning "hard to reach", and this remained its defining character well into the twentieth century. One important figure was not deterred by the distance – **George Rex**, a colourful colonial administrator who placed himself beyond the pale of decent colonial society by taking a coloured mistress. Shunned by his peers in Britain, he headed for Knysna at the turn of the nineteenth century in the hope of making a killing shipping out hardwood from the lagoon.

By the time of Rex's death in 1839, Knysna had become a major **timber centre**, attracting white labourers who felled trees with primitive tools for miserly payments, and looked set eventually to destroy the forest. In 1872, **Prince Alfred**, on his visit to the Cape, made his small royal contribution to this destruction when he took a special detour here to hunt elephants. The forest only narrowly escaped devastation by far-sighted and effective conservation policies introduced in the 1880s.

By the turn of the twentieth century, Knysna was still remote, and its forests were inhabited by isolated and inbred communities made up of the impoverished descendants of the woodcutters. As late as 1914, if you travelled from Knysna to George you would have to open and close 58 gates along the 75-kilometre track. Fifteen years on, the passes in the region proved too much for **George Bernard Shaw**, who did some impromptu off-road driving and crashed into a bush, forcing Mrs Shaw to spend a couple of weeks in bed at Knysna's *Royal Hotel* with a broken leg.

Knysna Quays and Thesen's Island

About 500m south of Knysna Tourism, at the end of Grey St

The **Knysna Quays** are the town's waterfront complex and yacht basin. Built at the end of the 1990s, this elegant two-storey steel structure with timber boardwalks resembles a tiny version of Cape Town's V&A Waterfront. Here you'll find a mix of hotels, clothes and knick-knack shops and a couple of good eating places, some with outdoor decks, from which you can watch yachts drift past.

Riding on the success of the Quays, **Thesen's Island**, reached by a causeway at the south end of Long Street, has some stylish shops and places to eat.

17

The beaches

Don't come to Knysna for a beach holiday: the closest beach is 20km from town at **Brenton-on-Sea**. A tiny settlement on the shores of Buffels Bay, it does admittedly have a quite exceptional beach. In the opposite direction from Knysna, the closest patch of sand is at **Noetzie**, a town known more for its eccentric holiday homes built to look like castles than for its seaside.

ARRIVAL AND DEPARTURE

KNYSNA

By Baz Bus The Baz Bus drops off at *Knysna Backpackers*.
By intercity bus Knysna is connected to Cape Town, Port Elizabeth and all major towns on the Garden Route by daily services on Greyhound, Intercape and Translux buses. Intercape and Translux buses drop passengers off at the old train station in Remembrance Avenue opposite Knysna waterfront; Greyhound stops at the

Toyota garage, 9 Main Rd.
Destinations Cape Town (2 daily; 8hr); Mossel Bay (2 daily; 1hr 45min); Plettenberg Bay (2 daily; 30min); Port Elizabeth (2 daily; 4hr 30min); Sedgefield (2 daily; 30min); Storms River Bridge (2 daily; 1hr 30min); Jo'burg (daily; 17hr 30min).

GETTING AROUND

By car Renting a car is the best way to explore Knysna and the surrounding forest – there are a number of rental agencies in town including Avis (Long & Fichat sts; ☎ 044 382 2222, ⓦ avis.co.za), Europcar

(1 Waterfront Drive, Caltex Quay service station; ☎ 044 382 2733, ⓦ europcar.co.za) and Tortoise Car Hire (23 Uil St, Sedgefield; ☎ 044 343 2991, ⓦ tortoisecarhire.co.za).

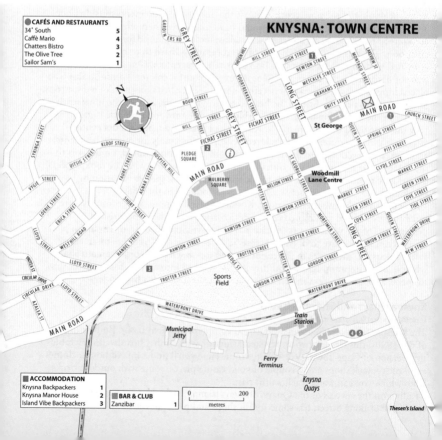

CAFÉS AND RESTAURANTS

34° South	5
Caffè Mario	4
Chatters Bistro	3
The Olive Tree	2
Sailor Sam's	1

KNYSNA: TOWN CENTRE

ACCOMMODATION

Knysna Backpackers	1
Knysna Manor House	2
Island Vibe Backpackers	3

BAR & CLUB

Zanzibar	1

0   200
metres

Thesen's Island

17

INFORMATION AND ACTIVITIES

Tourist office Knysna Tourism, 40 Main St (Mon–Fri 8am–5pm, Sat 8.30am–1pm; ☏ 044 382 5510, ☒ visitknysna.co.za), provides maps and runs a desk for booking activities around Knysna – including cruises to and abseiling down The Heads and bungee jumping from the Bloukrans River Bridge. They can also help with booking accommodation. There are a wide range of adventure activities on offer at Plett (see p.214).

Mountain biking Knysna Cycle Works, 20 Waterfront Drive (☏ 044 382 5151, ☒ knysnacycles.com), offer bikes for rent (from R170/day) and have maps and information about trails in the Harkerville Forest, which is a brilliant area to explore.

ACCOMMODATION

The best places to stay in Knysna are well away from the N2 main road, with views of the lagoon and The Heads. Out of town there are some excellent establishments as well as reasonably priced self-catering cottages right in the forest. For somewhere quieter on the lagoon, make for the western edge at Brenton-on-Sea.

TOWN CENTRE AND KNYSNA QUAYS

Island Vibe Backpackers 67 Main Rd ☏ 044 382 1728, ☒ islandvibe.co.za; map opposite. Part of the popular *Island Vibe Backpackers* group that are situated along the Garden Route, this branch has a good location, swimming pool and a deck. The facilities are not plush but it is a good cheap option and excellent place to meet buddies to join up with for adventure activities. Dorm R140, double R480

Knysna Manor House 19 Fichat St ☏ 044 382 5440, ☒ knysnamanor.co.za; map opposite. A centrally located hundred-year-old house with yellow wood floors and colonial furnishings. It is good value for money although a little dated in style. The twin, double and family rooms come with the use of a swimming pool and garden. R870

Knysna Backpackers 42 Queen St ☏ 044 382 2554, ☒ knysnabackpackers.co.za; map opposite. Spotless, well-organized hostel in a large, rambling and centrally located Victorian house that has been declared a National Monument. This tranquil establishment has five rooms rented as doubles (but able to sleep up to four people) and a dorm that sleeps eight. Dorms R140, doubles R380

LEISURE ISLE AND THE HEADS

Cunningham's Island Guest House 3 Kingsway, Leisure Isle ☏ 044 384 1319, ☒ islandhouse.co.za; map p.200. Purpose-built two-storey, timber-and-glass guesthouse with eight suites, decked out in dazzling white relieved by a touch of blue and some ethnic colour (stripy cushions and African baskets). Each room has its own entrance leading to the garden, which has a swimming pool shaded by giant strelitzias. Stylish and comfortable, its only drawback is the lack of views. R895

Under Milk Wood George Rex Drive, The Heads ☏ 044 384 0745, ☒ milkwood.co.za; map p.200. Luxury self-catering accommodation on the lagoon at the foot of The Heads with its own private beach – safe for swimming – and terrific views of the mountains and water. Three two-bedroom self-catering units, with their own sundecks, surrounded by milkwood trees; rates vary depending on position, and there are hefty off-season discounts. R1459

WEST OF TOWN

Blue Oyster Cnr Rio & Stent sts ☏ 044 382 2265, ☒ blueoyster.co.za; map p.200. Hospitable three-storey, vaguely Greek-themed B&B set high on one of the hills that rise up behind Knysna, offering fabulous panoramas across the lagoon to The Heads. The four comfortable double rooms, of which the ones on the top floor have the best views, are done out in white and blue. R1000

Elephant Hide of Knysna Cherry Lane ☏ 044 382 0426, ☒ elephanthide.co.za; map p.200. Overlooking the lagoon, 3km from the town centre, this peaceful guesthouse has seven rooms, each lavishly styled with warm and earthy textures and tones. The lagoon suites are a honeymooner's dream, each with a spa bath set with floor-to-ceiling windows overlooking the lagoon, as well as a private balcony and a king-sized bed. The guesthouse has a spacious communal lounge and a fireplace for winter; there's a dreamy swimming pool and deck area to laze on in the summer. R1960

Isola Bella 21 Hart Lane, Leisure Isle ☏ 044 384 0049, ☒ isolabella.co.za; map p.200. You can't help but gasp at the views of The Heads through the huge windows of this imposing guesthouse at the lagoon's edge. You'll either love or loathe the mildly operatic decor – repro furniture, lots of oil paintings and some floral fabrics. Either way, the rooms are undeniably luxurious. Breakfast is served on the spectacularly positioned balcony overlooking the water. Double R1850, self-catering studio R950

★Narnia Country Guest House Signed off Welbedacht Lane, 3km west of Knysna ☏ 044 382 1334, ☒ narnia.co.za; map p.200. On a hillside with far-off views of the lagoon, this is an immensely fun stone and rough-hewn timber farmhouse in a glorious garden. Decorated in a rustic-chic style, the comfortable, semi-detached two-bedroom cottage downstairs has a lounge, fireplace and kitchenette, while the Pool House sleeps three and leads out onto a large pool with a deck and lovely views. Walks on the property include one down to a small lake. R1500

Phantom Forest Eco-Reserve Phantom Pass Rd, west of town off the N2 ☏ 044 386 0046, ☒ phantomforest.com; map p.200. Breathtaking, tranquil forest lodge

17

KNYSNA CRUISES

One of the most pleasant diversions around Knysna is a **cruise** across the lagoon to The Heads. Knysna Featherbed Company (☎044 382 1693, ⦿knysnafeatherbed.com) runs a number of trips a day from Knysna Quays to The Heads, the shortest of which take 75 minutes (R110). For travel beyond The Heads, you can take a sailing trip (1hr 30min; R340) and a sunset cruise (2hr 30min; R655) with delicious food and wine. The only way to reach the private **Featherbed Nature Reserve** on the western side of the lagoon is on a four-hour Featherbed Nature Tour (R530), which includes the boat there, a 4WD shuttle to the top of the western Head and a buffet meal. There's a slightly shorter version (3hr 45min) which excludes the meal. **Bookings** are essential, and can be made at the kiosk on the north side of Knysna Quays; **departures** are from the Waterfront Jetty and municipal jetty on Remembrance Avenue, 400m west of the quays and station.

---

making extensive use of timber and glass, set on a hill in indigenous forest, with fabulous lagoon views. African fabrics and pure cotton linen reinforce the sense of unbridled luxury. Timber boardwalks wind through the forest to connect the suites to the main buildings, which feature a safari-style dining room, an open-air hot tub, a massage suite and a jacuzzi. The swimming pool teeters on the edge of the hill, cocooned by vegetation, with vervet monkeys frolicking in the forest canopy. **R4274**

THE FOREST

★**Forest Edge Cottages** Rheenendal turn-off, 16km west of Knysna on the N2 ☎082 456 1338, ⦿forestedge .co.za. Ideal if you want to be close to the forest itself, these traditional two-bedroom woodcutters' cottages have verandas built in the vernacular tin-roofed style. Self-contained, fully equipped and serviced, they sleep four, while the luxury ones, which cost an extra R300, have free wi-fi, satellite TV and a fire place. You can also sample produce from the organic veggie garden and local honey or collect fresh eggs from the chickens that are kept on the farm. Forest walks and cycling trails start from the cottages (there are several bike rental companies in the area). **R750**
Southern Comfort Western Horse Ranch 3km along the Fisanthoek Rd, 17km east of Knysna en route to Plettenberg Bay ☎044 532 7885, ⦿schranch.co.za. Affordable and suitable for large groups, accommodation here is in very basic double rooms and dorms, on a farm adjacent to the eastern section of the Knysna forest. Horseriding (8.30am and 2.30pm; one-hour ride R270, two-hour ride R370), quad-biking (4km; R270) and massages for the saddle-weary are on offer. You can self-cater or take the meals provided. Dorm **R130**, double **R300**

BELVIDERE AND BRENTON-ON-SEA

Belvidere Manor Duthie Drive, Belvidere Estate ☎044 387 1055, ⦿belvidere.co.za; map p.200. A collection of tin-roofed repro Victorian cottages, nicely positioned on the water's edge. This is the only accommodation in this exclusive leafy area, with its lush gardens and replica Norman church, built in the 1850s. **R2400**
Brenton-on-Sea Chalets C.R. Swart Drive, Brenton beachfront ☎044 381 0081, ⦿brentononsea.net; map p.200. A 15min drive from Knysna and overlooking the long curve of Brenton beach, which swings round to Buffels Bay, these three-bedroom, self-catering chalets sleep six people, and are well equipped and comfortably furnished. **R980**

EATING

As far as food goes, you'll find a lot of good restaurants catering to a wide range of palates and one or two excellent coffee shops. With so many forests, waterways and beaches, you may be tempted to have a **picnic**, and there's no shortage of tempting deli food in town. In summer and holiday periods, you'll need to make a restaurant reservation.

34˚ South Knysna Quays ☎044 382 7331, ⦿34-south .com; map p.202. An outstanding deli, café, restaurant, bar and sushi joint with imported groceries, home-made food and an extensive menu that includes seafood in all its guises – from *peri-peri* calamari heads to a red Thai curry mussel pot (R95) and tempura calamari hand rolls (R32). From here you can watch the drawbridge open to let yachts sail through. Daily 8.30am–10pm.
Caffè Mario Knysna Quays ☎044 382 7250; map p.202. An intimate Italian waterside restaurant with outdoor seating, and *paninoteca* and *tramezzini* on its snack menu as well as great pizza (R70) and pasta. The food is consistently good value. Daily 7.30am–10pm.
Chatters Bistro Cnr Gray & Gordon sts ☎044 382 0203, ⦿chattersbistro.co.za; map p.202. With an enclosed garden, a fireplace in winter and eighty wines on the drinks list, this is the place to go in Knysna for superb thin and crispy pizzas (with wheat and gluten-free bases available) and pastas (R70). Tues–Sun noon–9.30pm.
East Head Café 25 George Rex Drive ☎44 384 0933, ⦿eastheadcafe.co.za; map p.200. Very popular café

17

with an outdoor area, panoramic views of the Knysna Heads and a kids' playground. Try their simple, delicious seafood dishes (R80), classic wraps and salads or a killer mojito to boot. Note they don't take bookings and parking can be tricky. Daily 8am–3.30pm.

Firefly Eating House 152A Old Cape Rd ☎044 382 1490, ⓦfireflyeatinghouse.com; map p.200. Relaxed little bistro whose fiery-red decor and sparkling fairy lights match the mid-priced spicy menu. Delicious tapas-style dishes draw their inspiration from Malaysia, Thailand and East and South Africa (R45). Recommended if you like it hot. Tues–Sun 6–10pm.

Forest Boma Phantom Forest Eco-Reserve, Phantom Pass Rd ☎044 386 0046; map p.200. Eating is secondary to the setting here, in a forest with views of the whole estuary, which places this spot among the most beautiful in South Africa. The six-course pan-African set menu (R400) ranges from *kudu* and prune *sosatie* with herb polenta to pan-fried ostrich in black cherry sauce and tempting desserts such as brandy snap baskets. Booking essential. Daily 6.30–8.30pm.

★**Ile de Pain** Thesen Island ☎044 302 5707, ⓦiledepain.co.za; map p.200. A trendy restaurant in an artisan bakery that does salads, baguettes, oysters and pastas. Try the crusty wood-fired bread with butter and preserves for breakfast or settle for one of the delicious pastries with coffee (R60). Tues–Sat 8am–3pm, Sun 9am–1.30pm.

The Olive Tree 12 Wood Mill Lane, Main Rd; map p.202. This local favourite offers bistro dining, with fresh

ingredients and Mediterranean-influenced and beautifully plated dishes (R130 average mains). Great for vegetarians. Mon–Sat 6–10pm.

Pembrey's Bistro Brenton Rd, Belvidere ☎044 386 0005, ⓦpembreys.co.za; map p.200. Small, unpretentious and highly-rated restaurant that fuses country cooking with haute cuisine. You'll usually find ostrich, springbok and duck confit with sauces such as balsamic caramelized peaches (R160) on the daily changing menu. Their help-yourself Mediterranean-inspired salad buffet, with herbs from their garden, is a winner and appetizing starters range from fresh crab and dill ravioli (R85) to veggie-friendly options. Wed–Sun 6.30pm–late.

★**Sailor Sam's** Main Rd, opposite the post office ☎044 382 6774; map p.202. A warm-hearted, old-fashioned chippy that offers incredible value, brilliant fish and chips and the cheapest oysters in town (R10 per oyster). Don't tell a soul, but the delicious shellfish aren't local; they're shipped in from the West Coast. Mon–Sat 11am–8.30pm, Sun 11am–3pm.

Tapas & Oysters Thesen Island ☎044 382 7196, ⓦtapasknysna.co.za; map p.200. Although the branding is a bit cheesy, this is a hip local hangout with live music on Wed and Fri accompanied by half-price drinks. Inside it is open and airy with floor-to-ceiling windows showing the wraparound deck, right on the harbour. They do sushi as well as both Spanish and South African tapas, including traditional pickled fish dishes and *frikkadelletjies* (meatballs) and smoked *snoek* (R40). Daily 11am–11pm.

DRINKING AND NIGHTLIFE

Knysna has perked up over the past decade, but it still isn't somewhere you come if your main aim is to party. Having said that, there are one or two clubs in town that burn the midnight oil and where you may catch some live music or DJs.

Mo's on Rex George Rex Drive ☎044 384 0493; map p.200. A lively, local hangout with loads of atmosphere and a big outdoor beer garden. Their restaurant is also good value for money, serving up pizzas (R50) and ribs. Mon–Sat noon–late.

Zanzibar Cnr St George's & Main sts ☎044 382 0386;

map p.202. Knysna's longest-established nightclub occupies the premises of the Old Barnyard Theatre and blends everything from pop to commercial house and beyond. It continues with the Barnyard's tradition of occasional live acts that include bands, cabaret and comedy (spirit + mixer R35). Daily noon–2am.

THE FOREST ON WHEELS, WATER AND FOOT

Eleventh-hour **conservation** has ensured that some of the Knysna's hardwoods have survived to maturity in reserves of woodland that can still take your breath away. A number of walks have been laid out in several of the forests – yet the effects of the nineteenth-century timber industry means that all these reserves are some distance from Knysna itself and require transport to get to. **Knysna Forest Tours and Mountain Biking Africa** (Tony Cook; ☎082 783 8392, ⓦmountainbikingafrica.co.za and ⓦknysnaforesttours.co.za) is an adventure company offering guided forest and coastal **hikes, mountain biking and canoe trips** in the area as well as birdwatching and fly-fishing. You can also combine two activities into a full-day trip. Half-day (including refreshments) hikes start at R495 per person, biking trips at R580, kiteboarding lessons and gear rental at R1350 and a canoe trip at R595.

DIRECTORY

Emergencies General emergency number from landline ☎ 107, from mobile phone ☎ 112; Police ☎ 044 302 6600; National Sea Rescue ☎ 082 990 5956.

Hospital Life Knysna Private Hospital, Hunters Drive (☎ 044 384 1083), is well run and has a casualty department.

The Knysna forests

The best reason to come to Knysna is for its **forests**, shreds of a once magnificent woodland that was home to **Khoi** clans and harboured a thrilling variety of wildlife, including elephant herds. The forests attracted European explorers and naturalists, and in their wake woodcutters, gold-diggers and businessmen like George Rex, all bent on making their fortunes here.

The French explorer François Le Vaillant was one of the first Europeans to **shoot and kill** an elephant. The explorer found the animal's feet so "delicious" that he wagered that "never can our modern epicures have such a dainty at their tables". Two hundred years later, all that's left of the Khoi people are some names of local places. The legendary Knysna elephants have hardly fared better and are teetering on the edge of certain extinction.

Goudveld State Forest

Just over 30km northwest of Knysna • Daily sunrise–sunset • R100

The beautiful **Goudveld State Forest** is a mixture of plantation and indigenous woodland. It takes its name from the gold boom (*goudveld* is Afrikaans for goldfields) that brought hundreds of prospectors to the mining town of **Millwood** in the 1880s. The six hundred small-time diggers who were here by 1886, scouring out the hillsides and panning Jubilee Creek for alluvial gold, were rapidly followed by larger syndicates, and a flourishing little town quickly sprang up, with six hotels, three newspapers and a music hall.

However, the singing and dancing was shortlived and bust followed boom in 1890 after most of the mining companies went to the wall. The ever-hopeful diggers took off for the newly discovered Johannesburg goldfields, and Millwood was left a deserted **ghost town**. Over the years, its buildings were demolished or relocated, leaving an old store known as Materolli as the only original building standing.

Today, the old town is completely overgrown, apart from signs indicating where the old streets stood. In **Jubilee Creek**, which provides a lovely shady walk along a burbling stream, the holes scraped or blasted out of the hillside are still clearly visible. Some of the old mine works have been restored, as have the original **reduction works** around the cocopan track, used to carry the ore from the mine to the works, which is still there after a century.

The forest itself is still lovely, featuring tall, indigenous trees, a delightful valley with a stream, and plenty of swimming holes and picnic sites.

ARRIVAL AND DEPARTURE   GOUDVELD STATE FOREST

By car To get here from Knysna, follow the N2 west toward George, turning right onto the Rheenendal road just after the Knysna River, and continue for about 25km, following the Bibby's Koep signposts until the Goudveld sign.

Diepwalle Forest

Just over 20km northeast of Knysna • Daily 6am–6pm • R100 • ☎ 044 302 5606 or ☎ 044 382 9762, ⓦ sanparks.org/parks/garden _route/camps/knysna_lakes

The **Diepwalle Forest** is the last haunt of Knysna's almost extinct elephant population, although the only elephants you can expect to see here are on the painted markers indicating the three main hikes through these woodlands. However, if you're quiet and alert, you do stand a chance of seeing vervet monkeys, bushbuck and blue duiker.

Diepwalle ("deep walls") is one of the highlights of the Knysna area and is renowned for its impressive density of huge trees, especially **yellowwoods**. Once the budget timber of South Africa, yellowwood was considered an inferior local substitute in place of imported pine, and found its way into thousands of often quite modest nineteenth-century houses in the Western and Eastern Cape. Today, its deep golden grain is so sought after that it commands premium prices at the annual auctions.

The three main hiking routes cover between 7km and 9km of terrain, and pass through flat to gently undulating country covered by indigenous forest and montane *fynbos*. If you're moderately fit, the hikes should take 2hr to 2hr 30min. The nine-kilometre **Arboretum trail**, marked by black elephants, starts a short way back along the road you drove in on, and descends to a stream edged with tree ferns. Across the stream you'll come to the much-photographed **Big Tree**, a six-hundred-year-old Goliath yellowwood. The easy nine-kilometre **Ashoekheuwel trail**, marked by white

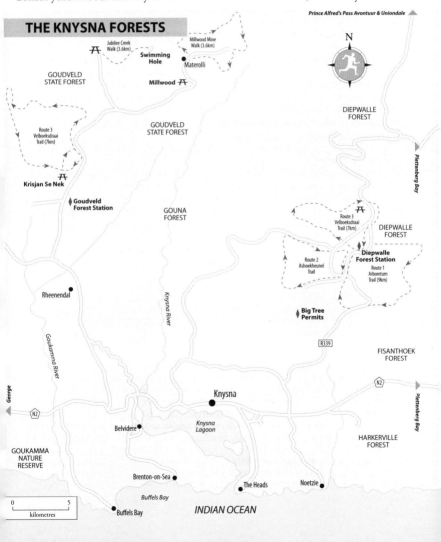

17

elephants, crosses the Gouna River, where there's a large pool allegedly used by real pachyderms. Most difficult of the three hikes is the rewarding seven-kilometre **Velboeksdraai trail**, marked by red elephants, which passes along the foothills of the Outeniquas. Take care here to stick to the elephant markers, as they overlap with a series of painted footprints marking the Outeniqua trail, for which you need to have arranged a permit (see p.214).

ARRIVAL AND INFORMATION   DIEPWALLE FOREST

By car To get there from Knysna, follow the N2 east towards Plettenberg Bay, after 7km turning left onto the R339, which you should take for about 16km in the direction of Avontuur and Uniondale.

Information The forest station is 10.5km after the tar gives way to gravel and provides a map for the park's trails, all of which begin here.

ACCOMMODATION

There are two National Parks accommodation options in the Forest, both booked through the SANparks Knysna Lakes office (Long St, Thesen Island, adjacent to Jetty; ☎ 044 302 5606). Driving directions given on booking.

★**Forest timber camping decks** Ten camp sites set within forest, each with their own deck, make this an exceptional SANParks site – you can really get in touch with nature here amid the busy Garden Route. Braai facilities, communal bathrooms and electricity available. R170
Tree Top Forest Chalet This timber chalet tucked away in forest at the head of a wide valley has luxuries including

a jacuzzi, DSTV, dishwasher and washing machine. Outdoors there's a wide viewing deck, walking trails, mountain-biking opportunities and great birdwatching. It sleeps up to four people, though the price is for two; you pay a supplement of R300 for each additional person. Book at least a month in advance. R1300

Knysna Elephant Park

Daily 8.30am–5pm • Free • Tours R250 (daily 8.30am–4.30pm; every half-hour; 1hr duration); two-hour elephant ride R885; two-hour guided nature walk with elephant R550; bookings essential • ☎ 044 532 7732, ⓦ knysnaelephantpark.co.za

Heading east from Knysna along the N2 for 20km, you come to the **Knysna Elephant Park**. The park was established in 1994 to provide a home for abandoned, orphaned and abused young elephants from all over the country, and opened to the public in 2003. The youngest of its charges are reared by park staff, who hand-feed them forty litres of baby formula a day, and sleep next to them at night. Regular tours give visitors the chance to touch and feed one of the pachyderms.

GOUDVELD HIKES

A number of clearly **waymarked hikes** traverse the Goudveld. The most rewarding (and easy going) is along **Jubilee Creek**, which traces the progress of a burbling brook for 3.5km through giant woodland to a gorgeous, deep rock pool. It's also an excellent place to encounter **Knysna turacos** (formerly known as Knysna louries); keep an eye focused on the branches above for the crimson flash of their flight feathers as they forage for berries, and listen out for their harsh call above the gentler chorus provided by the wide variety of other birdlife here. You can pick up a **map** directing you to the creek from the entrance gate to the reserve; the waymarked trail is linear, so you return via the same route. There's a pleasant **picnic site** along the banks of the stream at the start of the walk.

A more strenuous option is the circular **Woodcutter Walk**, though you can choose either the three- or the nine-kilometre version. Starting at **Krisjan se Nek**, another picnic site not far past the Goudveld entrance gate, it meanders downhill through dense forest, passing through stands of tree ferns, and returns uphill to the starting point. The picnic site is also where the nineteen-kilometre **Homtini Cycle Route** starts, taking you through forest and *fynbos* and offering wonderful mountain views. Be warned though; you really have to work hard at this, with one particular section climbing over 300m in just 3km. The tourist office in town has maps of the area.

THE KNYSNA ELEPHANTS

17

Traffic signs warning motorists about elephants along the N2 between Knysna and Plettenberg Bay are rather optimistic: there are few indigenous pachyderms left and, with such an immense forest, sightings are rare. But such is the mystique attached to the **Knysna elephants** that locals tend to be a little cagey about just how few they number. By 1860, the thousands that had formerly wandered the once vast forests were down to five hundred, and by 1920 (twelve years after they were protected by law), there were only twenty animals left; the current estimate is three. Loss of habitat and consequent malnutrition, rather than full-scale hunting, seems to have been the principal cause of their decline. The only elephants you're guaranteed to see near Knysna are at the **Knysna Elephant Park** (see opposite) or the **Elephant Sanctuary** (see p.211), both near Plettenberg Bay.

ACCOMMODATION   **ELEPHANT PARK**

Self-catering The park offers accommodation in upmarket self-catering units, which, as the management points out, are "situated on the second level of the elephant *boma* and as a result the sounds of the elephants and the cleaning of their stalls in the morning will be audible". **R1950**

Plettenberg Bay and around

Over the Christmas holidays, forty thousand residents from Johannesburg's wealthy northern suburbs decamp to **PLETTENBERG BAY** (usually called Plett), 33km east of Knysna and 520km from Cape Town, and the flashiest of the Garden Route's seaside towns. It's wise to give it a miss at this time, with prices doubling and accommodation impossible to find. Yet, during low season, sipping champagne and sucking oysters while watching the sunset from a bar can be wonderful – the banal suburban development on the surrounding hills somehow doesn't seem so bad because the bay views really are stupendous. The deep-blue **Tsitsikamma Mountains** drop sharply to the inlet and its large estuary, providing a constant vista to the town and its suburbs. The bay generously curves over several kilometres of white sands separated from the mountains by forest, which makes this a green and temperate location with rainfall throughout the year.

Nevertheless Plett remains an expensive place to stay, with no cheap chalets or camping. For these you'll have to go to nearby **Keurboomstrand**, on the east of the bay. Further east lie **The Crags** (both of them more or less suburbs of Plett) with their trio of wildlife parks: Monkeyland, Birds of Eden and the Elephant Sanctuary are all worth a visit, especially if you're travelling with kids.

Plett's town **centre**, at the top of the hill, consists of a conglomeration of supermarkets, swimwear shops, estate agents and restaurants aimed largely at the holiday trade. Visitors principally come for Plett's **beaches** – and there's a fair choice. Southern right whales appear every winter, while dolphins can be seen throughout the year, hunting or riding the surf, often in substantial numbers. Swimming is safe, and though the waters are never tropically warm they reach a comfortable temperature between November and April. River and rock fishing are rewarding all year long.

Southeast of the town centre on a rocky promontory is **Beacon Island**, dominated by a 1970s hotel, an eyesore blighting a fabulous location. Development has been halted however, on the magnificent **Robberg Peninsula**, the great tongue of headland that contains the western edge of the bay, which offers one of the Garden Route's best short **hikes**.

The beaches

Beacon Island Beach, or **Main Beach**, right at the central shore of the bay, is where the fishing boats and seacats anchor a little out to sea. The small waves here make for calm swimming, and this is an ideal family spot. To the east is **Lookout Beach** which is also one of the nicest stretches of sand for bathers, or sun lizards. Lookout Beach has the

17

added attraction of a marvellously located restaurant (see p.216), from which you can often catch sight of **dolphins** cruising into the bay. From here you can walk several kilometres down the beach towards Keurbooms and the **Keurbooms Lagoon**.

Keurboomstrand

Some 14km east of Plettenberg Bay by road, across the Keurbooms River, is the uncluttered resort of **KEURBOOMSTRAND** (Keurbooms for short), little more than a suburb of Plett, sharing the same bay and with equally good beaches, but less safe for swimming. The safest place to take the waves is at **Arch Rock**, in front of the caravan park, though **Picnic Rock Beach** is also pretty good. A calm and attractive place, Keurbooms has

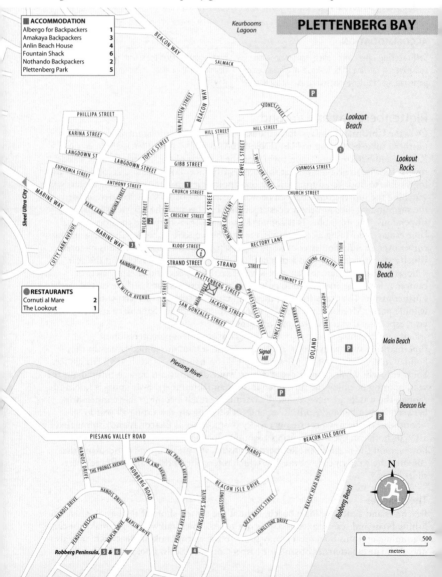

PLETTENBERG BAY

Keurbooms Lagoon

ACCOMMODATION
Albergo for Backpackers	1
Amakaya Backpackers	3
Anlin Beach House	4
Fountain Shack	6
Nothando Backpackers	2
Plettenberg Park	5

RESTAURANTS
Cornuti al Mare	2
The Lookout	1

Lookout Beach

Lookout Rocks

Hobie Beach

Main Beach

Beacon Isle

Robberg Beach

Robberg Peninsula, 5 & 6

0   500
metres

WHALING AND GNASHING OF TEETH

For conservationists, the monumental 1970s eyesore of the *Beacon Island Hotel* may not be such a bad thing, since previously the island was the site of a whale-processing factory established in 1806 – one of some half-dozen such plants erected along the Western Cape coast that year. Whaling continued at Plettenberg Bay until 1916. Southern right whales were the favoured species, yielding more oil and **whalebone** – an essential component of Victorian corsets – than any other. In the nineteenth century, a southern right would net around three times as much as a humpback caught along the Western Cape coast, leading to a rapid decline in the southern right population by the middle of the nineteenth century.

The years between the establishment and the closing of the Plettenberg Bay factory saw worldwide whaling transformed by the inventions of the Industrial Revolution. In 1852, the explosive harpoon was introduced, followed by the use of steam-powered ships five years later, making them swifter and safer for the crew. In 1863, Norwegian captain Sven Foyn built the first modern whale-catching vessel, which he followed up in 1868 with the **cannon-mounted harpoon**. In 1913 Plettenberg Bay was the site of one of seventeen shore-based and some dozen floating factories between West Africa and Mozambique, which that year between them took about ten thousand whales.

Inevitably, a rapid decline in humpback populations began; by 1918, all but four of the shore-based factories had closed due to lack of prey. The remaining whalers now turned their attention to fin and blue whales. When the South African fin whale population became depleted by the mid-1960s to twenty percent of its former size, they turned to sei and sperm whales. When these populations declined, the frustrated whalers started hunting minke whales, which at 9m in length are too small to be a viable catch. By the 1970s, the South African whaling industry was in its death throes and was finally put out of its misery in 1979, when the government banned all activity surrounding whaling.

few facilities, and if you're intending to stay here you should stock up in Plett beforehand. One of Keurbooms' highlights is **canoeing** up the river (see p.214).

Robberg Marine and Nature Reserve
Robberg Rd • Daily Feb–Nov 7am–5pm; Dec & Jan 7am–8pm; R40 • ☎ 021 483 0190, ⓦ capenature.co.za/reserves/robberg-nature-reserve

One of the Garden Route's nicest walks is the four-hour, nine-kilometre circular route around the spectacular rocky peninsula of **Robberg**, 8km southeast of Plett's town centre. Here you can completely escape Plett's development and experience the coast in its wildest state, with its enormous horizons and lovely vegetation. Much of the walk takes you along high cliffs, from where you can often look down on seals surfacing near the rocks, dolphins arching through the water and, in winter, whales further out in the bay. If you don't have time for the full circular walk, there is a shorter two-hour hike and a thirty-minute ramble; a map is provided at the entrance gate. There is one rustic hut, *Fountain Shack*, to stay overnight (see p.215).

The Crags
From Keurbooms, look out for the BP petrol station, then take the Monkeyland/Kurland turn-off and follow the Elephant Sanctuary/Monkeyland signs for 2km

The Crags, 2km east of Keurboomstrand, comprises a collection of smallholdings along the N2, a bottle store and a few other shops on the forest edge, but the reason most visitors pull in here is for the **Elephant Sanctuary**, **Monkeyland** and **Birds of Eden**.

Elephant Sanctuary
Daily 8am–5pm • Trunk-in-Hand Programme daily 7am R475; elephant ride R475; elephant brush-down experience R575 • ☎ 044 534 8145, ⓦ elephantsanctuary.co.za

The **Elephant Sanctuary** offers a chance of close encounters with its half-dozen pachyderms, all of whom were saved from culling in Botswana and Kruger National Park. On the popular one-hour Trunk-in-Hand programme you get to walk with an

17

elephant, holding the tip of its trunk in your hand and also to feed and interact with it. The programme includes an informative talk about elephant behaviour; fifteen-minute elephant-back rides and helping brush down the elephants are among the other packages on offer.

Monkeyland

Daily 8am–5pm • Free entry to viewing deck; safaris R160; combined ticket with Birds of Eden R260 • ⓦ monkeyland.co.za

Monkeyland, 400m beyond the Elephant Sanctuary, brings together primates from several continents, all of them orphaned or saved from a dismal life as pets. The place is a sanctuary, so none of the animals has been taken from the wild – and most wouldn't have the skills to survive there. Life is made as comfortable as possible for them and they are free to move around the reserve, looking for food and interacting with each other and their environment in as natural a way as possible. For your own safety and that of the monkeys, you are not allowed to wander around alone. **Guides** take visitors on walking "safaris", during which you come across water holes, experience a living indigenous forest and enjoy chance encounters with creatures such as ringtail lemurs from Madagascar and squirrel monkeys from South America.

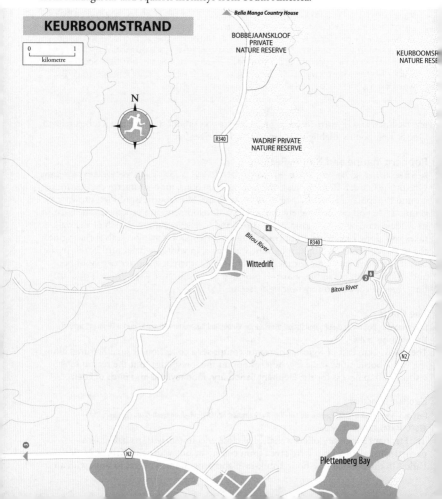

The safaris are entertaining and also feature an informed **commentary** covering issues such as the differences between monkeys and apes, primate communication and social systems. One of the sanctuary's highlights is crossing the Indiana Jones-esque **rope bridge** (at 128m, it's purportedly the longest such bridge in the southern hemisphere) spanning a canyon to pass through the upper reaches of the forest canopy, where a number of species spend their entire lives. For **refreshments** or meals, there's a restaurant with a forest deck at the day-lodge.

Birds of Eden

Daily 8am–5pm • R160; combined ticket with Monkeyland R260 • ⓦ birdsofeden.co.za

Under the same management as Monkeyland and right next door, **Birds of Eden** is a huge bird sanctuary, which took four years to create. Great effort was taken to place netting over a substantial tract of virgin forest with as little impact as possible. The result is claimed to be the largest free-flight aviary in the world. As with Monkeyland, most of Birds of Eden's charges were already living in cages and are now free to move and fly around within the confines of the large enclosure (so large in fact that you can easily spend an hour slowly meandering along its winding, wheelchair-friendly, wooden walkway).

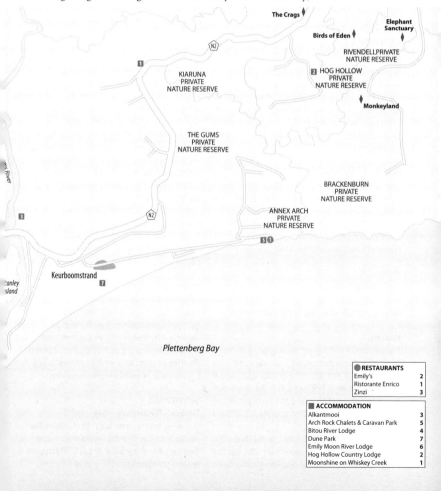

● RESTAURANTS	
Emily's	2
Ristorante Enrico	1
Zinzi	3

■ ACCOMMODATION	
Alkantmooi	3
Arch Rock Chalets & Caravan Park	5
Bitou River Lodge	4
Dune Park	7
Emily Moon River Lodge	6
Hog Hollow Country Lodge	2
Moonshine on Whiskey Creek	1

17

Although it has come in for some criticism for cutting off local birds from their traditional turf and disrupting some migration routes, the result is quite remarkable, with little lakes, waterfalls and a **suspension bridge** along the way. Most of the birds are exotics, some impossibly brightly coloured (such as the incandescent scarlet ibis from South America and golden pheasant from China), but you'll also see a number of locals, such as the Knysna lourie and South Africa's national bird, the blue crane. Watch out for the cheeky cockatoos that may alight on your shoulder and steal buttons from your shirt or beads from round your neck. A **restaurant** by one of the lakes sells light meals and liquid refreshments.

ARRIVAL AND INFORMATION

PLETTENBERG BAY

By Baz Bus The Baz Bus drops passengers off at accommodation in town.

By intercity bus Intercape, Greyhound and Translux intercity buses stop at the Shell Ultra City petrol station, just off the N2 in Marine Way, 2km from the town centre. As there's no transport around town, if you don't have your own car, you'll need to arrange for your guesthouse to collect you.

Destinations Cape Town (2 daily; 9hr); George (2 daily; 2hr); Jo'burg (2 daily; 18hr); Knysna (2 daily; 1hr 30min); Mossel Bay (2 daily; 2hr 20min); Port Elizabeth (2 daily; 3hr 30min).

Tourist information The tourist office, Shop 35, Mellville Corner, Main St (Mon–Fri 9am–5pm, Sat 9am–1pm; ☏ 044 533 4065, ⓦ plettenbergbay.co.za), has maps of the town and may be able to help with booking accommodation.

ACTIVITIES

BOAT TRIPS

Keurbooms River Ferries Signposted on the east side of the Keurbooms River Bridge ☏ 083 254 3551, ⓦ ferry.co.za. This company runs daily guided upriver boat trips (11am, 2pm, sunset; R150) with knowledgeable guides skilled at spotting rare birds – the indigenous forest comes right down to the edge. Cape Nature entrance fee is R40 per person.

BUNGEE JUMPING

Bloukrans Bungy ☏ 042 281 1458, ⓦ faceadrenalin .com. The world's highest commercial bungee jump takes place off the 216-metre Bloukrans River Bridge and costs R790 (excluding pictures or video) for the seven-second descent. For the not so brave there's a bridge walk over the jump site (R100).

CANOEING

CapeNature On the east side of the Keurbooms River Bridge along the N2 ☏ 044 533 2125. This outfit rent fairly basic craft (R120 per day for a two-person canoe).

HIKING

If you're keen on walking and the outdoors, you'll find a couple of excellent options around Plett (which tend to get less booked out than the more popular trails around Tsitsikamma National Park (see p.217). The waymarked hikes listed below are two to five days long: for permits and bookings contact ☏ 044 302 5606 or ☏ 044 302 5600 and ⓔ reservations@sanparks.org.

Harkerville Coastal Trail Closer to the roads, this circular trail doesn't feel as remote as the Otter Trail (see box, p.217) but is a good second-best, taking in magnificent rocky coastline, indigenous forest and *fynbos*. Lots of rock scrambling and some traversing of exposed, narrow ledges above the sea is required, so don't attempt this if you're unfit or scared of heights. Monkeys, baboons and fish eagles are commonly seen, and you may spot dolphins or whales. *Start and end: Harkerville Forestry Station, 12km west of Plettenberg Bay, signposted off the N2; distance: 26.5km; duration: two days; cost: R212 per person and daily conservation fee R25.*

Outeniqua Trail The main draw here is the indigenous forest, including giant yellowwood trees, pine plantations and gold-mining remains at Millwood in the Goudveld State Forest. *Start: Beervlei (the old forest station where there are eight overnight huts; directions are given when you book); end: Harkerville Forestry Station, 12km west of Plettenberg Bay; distance: 108km; duration: seven days (shorter versions possible); cost: R73 per person per day.*

ROCK CLIMBING

GoVertical Mountaineering Adventures ⓦ govertical .co.za ☏ 082 731 4696. An outfit which teaches the basics of rock climbing and takes experienced climbers out: kloofing or canyoning is the most adventurous way of exploring the deep river gorges between Knysna and Plett. Prices depend on the size of the group, and are given when you enquire. Their reach is country-wide for guided adventure expeditions.

SKYDIVING

Skydive Plettenberg Bay ☏ 082 905 7440, ⓦ skydiveplett.com. If you fancy a bit of an adrenaline rush, you can go tandem skydiving (no experience required) with these guys, who charge R1850 for a 10,000ft jump, with the option of paying extra for a DVD or video of the event.

17

TOWNSHIP TOURS

Ocean Blue Central Beach ☎044 533 5083, ⓦoceanadventures.co.za. Ocean Blue arranges relaxed tours into Plett's township with a member of the community. Outings cost R200 per person and all the takings go into a development trust, which among other things, pays teachers' salaries and funds a crèche.

WHALE- AND DOLPHIN-WATCHING

Dolphin Adventures Central Beach ☎083 590 3405, ⓦdolphinadventures.co.za. Sea kayaking is one of the best ways to watch whales, and this outfit offers unforgettable trips with experienced and knowledgeable guides in two-person kayaks (2hr–2hr 30min, R250; children R150, including all equipment) or just rentals (1hr R100; 2hr R150).

Ocean Blue Central Beach ☎044 533 4897 or ☎083 701 3583, ⓦoceanadventures.co.za. Sea-kayaking (R250) and boat-based whale-watching (R700) are among the offerings of this licensed outfit, which also runs township tours (see opposite).

Ocean Safaris Shop 3, Hopwood St ☎044 533 4963, ⓦoceansafaris.co.za. Tailor-made cruises from a licensed whale-watching company. Whale-watching by boat (R680) virtually guarantees sightings between July and September. Out of whale season it's still worth going out to see dolphins and seals (R420).

ACCOMMODATION

IN TOWN

Albergo for Backpackers 8 Church St ☎0 44 533 4434, ⓦalbergo.co.za; map p.210. Self-catering backpackers, with friendly staff and lots of little perks. There's a nice garden area, free wi-fi, a TV room and a pool table. They also book adventure activities and have free bodyboards and canoe rental. Be aware that it can get popular and noisy during high season. Camping **R100**, dorm **R175**, double **R550**

Amakaya Backpackers 15 Park Lane ☎044 533 4010, ⓦamakaya.co.za; map p.210. Located close to town and the beach, this place is well-set-up for backpackers with communal lounge areas, and outside fire pit and hammocks to while away your time. They also boast an upstairs veranda with bar and swimming pool with views of the lagoon and mountains. Note that the minimum stay over the weekend is two nights. Dorm **R175**, double **R480**

Anlin Beach House 33 Roche Bonne Ave ☎044 533 3694, ⓦanlinbeachhouse.co.za; map p.210. Stylish and comfortably kitted out garden studios, luxury suites with kitchenettes and a larger family unit with three bedrooms and a kitchen in a garden setting close to Robberg Beach. Units are serviced daily. **R1900**

Fountain Shack Robberg Nature Reserve ☎ 021 483 0190, ⓦcapenature.co.za/reserves/robberg-nature -reserve; map p.210. A renovated wooden cottage sleeping eight, magically isolated with no electricity and beautifully set above the ocean. There is no vehicle access – you need to walk two hours to reach it – though linen, cooking facilities and cutlery is provided, so you just need to bring in your food. **R1300**

Nothando Backpackers 5 Wilder St ☎044 533 0220, ⓦnothando.com; map p.210. Top-notch child-friendly hostel run by a former teacher. A 5min walk from Plett's main drag, this suburban home has seven doubles and three dorms. A jolly good breakfast is available for an extra R50. Dorm **R160**, double **R500**, family room **R820**

Plettenberg Park Near the end of Robberg Rd ☎044 533 9067, ⓦplettenbergpark.co.za; map p.210. Perched on the Robberg cliff edge, this stupendously located and very pricey boutique hotel overflows with easy luxury. Seven suites have sea views and the remaining three look onto a beautiful little lake surrounded by *fynbos*. The shower in one room is enclosed on four sides by glass, two of them exposed to the ocean. A set of meandering timber steps leads down from the pool deck to an isolated private beach far below with a lovely natural rock pool. **R7834**

KEURBOOMSTRAND AND EAST OF PLETT

Alkantmooi Keurboom Rd, Keurbooms River ☎044 535 9245, ⓦalkantmooi.co.za; map pp.212–213. Four

---

WHALE- AND DOLPHIN-WATCHING VIEWPOINTS

Elevated ocean panoramas give Plettenberg Bay outstanding vantages for watching **southern right whales** during their breeding season between June and October. An especially good vantage point is the area between the wreck of the *Athene* at the southern end of Lookout Beach and the Keurbooms River. The Robberg Peninsula is also excellent, looming protectively over this whale nursery and giving a grandstand view of the bay. Other good town viewpoints are from Beachy Head Road at Robberg Beach; Signal Hill in San Gonzales Street past the post office and police station; the *Beacon Island Hotel* on Beacon Island; and the deck of the *Lookout* restaurant on Lookout Beach. Outside Plett, the Kranshoek viewpoint and hiking trail offers wonderful whale-watching points along the route. To get there, head for Knysna, taking the Harkerville turn-off, and continue for 7km. It's also possible to view the occasional pair (mother and calf) at Nature's Valley, 29km east of Plett on the R102, and from Storms River Mouth.

17

modern one- or two-bedroom self-catering units, all varying in style, with lagoon rather than sea views, fully equipped kitchens and braai or outdoor patio facilities. Great value for money. R900

Arch Rock Chalets & Caravan Park Arch Rock ☎ 044 535 9409, ⓦ archrock.co.za; map pp.212–213. Seventeen fully-equipped chalets, some with one and the others with two bedrooms, in the best position at Keurbooms, right at the beach. Apart from the forest chalets and log cabins, which are set back among trees (R600), the rest have sea views. Camping R150, chalet R1100

Bitou River Lodge Bitou Valley Rd (the R340), about 4km from the N2 ☎ 044 535 9577, ⓦ bitou.co.za; map pp.212–213. Great value in a lovely spot on the banks of the Bitou River, this intimate establishment has five comfortable but unfussy bedrooms that overlook a pretty garden with a lily pond. Rate includes use of canoes on the river. R1450

Dune Park Keurboomstrand Rd, leading off the N2 and running along the shore to Keurbooms ☎ 044 535 9606, ⓦ dunepark.co.za; map pp.212–213. Luxury hotel whose airy bedrooms with crisp white linen are simple and stylish. Two-bedroom self-catering cottages built on top of high dunes provide great views (R1500) within spitting distance of the sea. R850

Emily Moon River Lodge Rietvlei Rd, off the N2 (turn off at Penny Pinchers) ☎ 044 533 2982, ⓦ emilymoon .co.za; map pp.212–213. That the owner of this highly imaginative and luxurious lodge, perched on a ridge looking across the Bitou Wetlands, is a dealer in ethnic art is plain to

see. The place is not only littered with Batonga sculptures and Swazi crafts, it has in places been constructed out of artworks, such as the intricate Rajasthani arched screen that is the entrance to the magnificently sited restaurant. Each of its chalets jetties out of the hillside to offer views from a private deck (and bathroom) of the oxbowing Bitou, along which small game can occasionally be seen. There is a family suite that sleeps four in which kids are accommodated at a discounted rate. R2980

★ **Hog Hollow Country Lodge** Askop Rd, 18km east of Plettenberg Bay (turn south off the N2 at the signpost) ☎ 044 534 8879, ⓦ hog-hollow.com; map pp.212–213. A touch of luxury on a private reserve where each of the chalets, done out in earthy colours and spiced up with African artefacts, has a bath or shower and its own wooden deck with vistas across the forest and Tsitsikamma Mountains; superb food is served as well. From here you could hike for a couple of hours through forest to Keurbooms beach, or drive there in 15min. R3112

Moonshine on Whiskey Creek 14km east of Plettenburg Bay along the N2, signposted north of the N2 ☎ 044 534 8515 or ☎ 072 200 6656, ⓦ whiskeycreek .co.za; map pp.212–213. Fully equipped bungalows, three wooden cabins and one creatively renovated labourer's cottage (R720), nestled in indigenous forest, with a children's play area. One of the best reasons to come here is the access to a secluded natural mountain pool and waterfall at the bottom of the nearby gorge. Note they don't have credit card facilities. R1440

EATING AND DRINKING

Restaurants come and go in Plett at a similar lick to the tides, but one or two long-standing establishments have managed to remain afloat. Locally caught fresh **fish** is the thing to look out for. And because the town is built on hills, you should generally expect **terrific views**.

Cornuti al Mare 1 Perestrella St ☎ 044 533 1277, ⓦ cornuti.co.za; map p.210. Though the quality is inconsistent, and it's not cheap, you can still get good pizzas and pasta dishes (R90) topped off with endless views of sea and sky. Daily noon–10pm.

Emily's Rietvlei Rd, off the N2 (turn off at Penny Pinchers) ☎ 044 533 2982; map pp.212–213. Boutique restaurant attached to *Emily Moon's Lodge* that many regard as the best in the area, offering stunning views of the Bitou Wetland and classical French cuisine with an edge. There's no set menu as everything is based on what seasonal ingredients are locally available on the day, but there's always a choice of five or six starters and mains with a small range of desserts. The fillet of sole is a good fish choice (R150). Booking essential, especially for a table on the deck. Mon 6.30–10pm, Tues–Sun noon–3pm & 6.30–10pm.

The Lookout Lookout Beach ☎ 044 533 1379, ⓦ lookout.co.za; map p.210. There are marvellous bay

views at this bar-restaurant, with umbrellas and outdoor tables, which focuses on seafood, including crayfish. They also do good chargrilled steaks (R130), poultry, pasta, salads and breakfasts. Daily 9am–9pm.

Ristorante Enrico Main Beach, Keurboomstrand ☎ 044 535 9818; map pp.212–213. Casual holiday-feeling restaurant right on the beach with mid-priced Italian standards – thin-based pizzas, pasta and veal (R90) where you can eat outside and enjoy the sea breeze. Summer daily noon–10pm, winter Tues–Sun noon–10pm.

Zinzi Hunter's Country House, off the N2, 10km west of Plett ☎ 044 501 1111, ⓦ zinzi.hunterhotels.com. Located at the lavish *Hunter's Country House*, *Zinzi* is happily not stuffy, with fair prices and a welcoming attitude to children. The food has distinctly international flavours with an African influence: you will find such delights as Asian pork belly, wild mushroom risotto with truffle oil (R90) and for rooibos pannacotta with Cape gooseberry compote for dessert. Daily noon–2.30pm & 6–9.30pm.

Tsitsikamma

17

The **Tsitsikamma section** of the Garden Route National Park, roughly midway between Plettenberg Bay and Port Elizabeth, is the highlight of any Garden Route trip. Starting from just beyond Keurboomstrand in the west, the section extends for 68km into the Eastern Cape along a narrow belt of coast, with dramatic foamy surges of rocky coast, deep river gorges and ancient hardwood forests clinging to the edge of tangled, green cliffs. Don't pass up its main attraction, the **Storms River Mouth**, the most dramatic estuary on this exhilarating piece of coast. Established in 1964, Tsitsikamma is also South Africa's oldest marine reserve, stretching 5.5km out to sea, with an **underwater trail** open to snorkellers and licensed scuba divers.

Tsitsikamma has two sections: **Nature's Valley** in the west and **Storms River Mouth** in the east. Each section can only be reached down a winding tarred road from the N2 (apart from hiking, there's no way of getting from one to the other). Nature's Valley incorporates the most low-key settlement on the Garden Route, with a fabulous sandy beach stretching for 3km. South Africa's ultimate hike, the five-day **Otter Trail** (see box below), connects the two sections of the park.

The nearest settlement to Storms River Mouth, some 14km to its north at the top of a steep winding road, is the confusingly named **Storms River Village**, which is outside the national park and some distance from any part of the river, though appealingly set in forest. While Storms River Village makes a convenient base for adventure activities in the vicinity and day-trips down to Storms River Mouth, the experience is very different from staying overnight at the coast.

Nature's Valley

Nature's Valley, at the western end of the Tsitsikamma Section of the Garden Route National Park, 29km east of Plettenberg Bay and two and a half hour's drive from Port Elizabeth (204km), extends inland into the rugged and hilly interior. It incorporates a settlement of wooden houses set on the stunningly beautiful Groot River Lagoon, with 20km of sandy beach and miles of indigenous forest to explore, which is highly sought

---

NATURE'S VALLEY AND STORM'S RIVER HIKES

Dolphin Trail This is the Garden Route's luxury, portered trail. The terrain through the Tsitsikamma National Park is breathtaking, covering the rugged coastal edge and the natural forest. The price includes a guide, a boat trip up the Storms River Gorge and a 4WD drive through the Storms River Pass. *Start: Storms River Mouth, Garden Route National Park (Tsitsikamma); end: Sandrif River Mouth; distance: 20km; duration: three and a half days; book accommodation through the Fernery (☎ 042 280 3588, ⊛ dolphintrail.co.za); cost: R4990 per person sharing, including food, accommodation and permits.*

Otter Trail The Otter Trail is South Africa's flagship hike; it is simply magnificent hiking a pristine stretch of coastline and forest where there is no habitation or vehicle access. If you're desperate to walk the Otter Trail and have been told that it is full, don't despair – keep checking the website for cancellations. You need to be fit for the steep sections, and an experienced hiker – you carry everything from hut to hut, and you need to be able to manage river crossings. *Start: Storms River Mouth; end: Nature's Valley; distance: 42km; duration: five days; booking through South African National Parks, at least twelve months in advance (☎ 012 428 911, ⊛ sanparks.org). The maximum number of people on the trail is twelve; cost: R925 plus park conservation fees R600 per person.*

Tsitsikamma Trail Not to be confused with the Otter Trail, this is an inland hike through indigenous forest, long stretches of open *fynbos* and the Tsitsikamma mountain range. Five overnight huts accommodate 24 people and it is a fairly strenuous hike, although you won't cover more than 17km or so per day. *Start: Nature's Valley; end: Storms River Bridge; distance: 60km; duration: two to six days; permit: MTO Ecotourism (☎ 042 281 1712, ⊛ mtoecotourism.co.za/tsitsikama.htm); cost: R135 per person per night (porterage available for additional R800 per day for a group of up to six).*

17

after among nature lovers. The strict legislation here (highly unusual in South Africa) means there are no crass holiday houses, housing developments, hotels or tour buses and only one small restaurant and village shop.

There are plenty of good **walks** at Nature's Valley, many starting from the national park campsite, 1km north of the village, where you can pick up maps and information about birds and trees. One of the loveliest places to head for is **Salt River Mouth**, 3km west of Nature's Valley, where you can swim and picnic – though you'll need to ford the river at low tide. This walk starts and ends at the café at Nature's Valley. Also recommended is the circular six-kilometre **Kalanderkloof trail**, which starts at the national park campsite, ascends to a lookout point, and descends via a narrow river gorge graced with a profusion of huge Outeniqua yellowwood trees and Cape wild bananas.

ARRIVAL AND INFORMATION

NATURE'S VALLEY

By car There is no public transport to Nature's Valley and the only way of getting there is by car, taking the beautiful Groot River Pass road that winds down through riverine forest from the N2, 2km east of The Crags. Nature's Valley is at the bottom of the pass, 11km after the turn-off. The road continues from Nature's Valley and rejoins the N2 after 9km, just west of the Bloukrans River Bridge. The detour is well worth taking in its own right – the last relic of the

meandering Garden Route as it was before the N2 sped through it – with a reasonable chance of encountering baboons and vervet monkeys along the way.

Tourist information The *Nature's Valley Trading Store* (see p.220) is effectively the village centre and acts as an informal but excellent, information bureau. If you're self-catering, stock up on supplies before you get to Nature's Valley, since their supplies are basic.

ACCOMMODATION

Accommodation in Nature's Valley itself is pretty limited, which contributes to its low-key charm, but you'll find some choice options on the road leading off the N2 into the village, just before the switchbacks begin. Other than the below, if you are self-catering you may wish to contact Meyer van Rooyen (☎ 082 772 2972) who handles a number of houses in and around Nature's Valley.

Four Fields Farm Nature's Valley Rd, 3km from the N2 along the R102 and 8km from Nature's Valley ☎ 044 534 8708, ⓦ fourfields.co.za. A welcoming and charmingly unpretentious former dairy farm, less than 10min drive from the sea. The self-catering farm house has four bedrooms (R1760 per room) simply furnished with beautiful old pieces and with French doors leading to their own private decks, which in turn open onto a much-loved garden surrounded by fields. An additional flat sleeps four (R1100) and another sleeps a couple (R660).

Lily Pond Lodge 102 Nature's Valley Rd, 3km from the N2 along the R102 and 6km from Nature's Valley ☎ 044 534 8767, ⓦ lilypond.co.za. Probably the most memorable accommodation in Nature's Valley, this lodge distinguishes itself through its commitment to luxury. The four en-suite rooms have patio doors opening onto private terraces, plus sound systems, TVs and wi-fi access, while the two spacious luxury suites also have their own lounge, under-floor heating and king-sized beds. There are three even more luxurious garden suites and a honeymoon suite that has its own private garden. **R1500**

★**Nature's Valley Restcamp** 1km to the north of the village. Campsites tucked into indigenous forest, and basic two-person forest huts with communal ablution facilities. Bookings through South African National Parks

(☎ 044 531 6700, ⓦ sanparks.org/parks/garden_route /camps/natures_valley) or if you're already in Nature's Valley, the camp supervisor ☎ 044 531 6700. Camping **R190**, hut **R450**

Rocky Road Backpackers 1.5km from the N2 along the R102, 12km from Nature's Valley ☎ 072 270 2114, ⓦ rockyroadbackpackers.com. A tranquil backpacker retreat set on a large forested property. While the setting and landscaped gardens are the big draw, it has all home comforts including free wi-fi, an outdoor pizza oven, forest bathroom and a highly social Friday braai night. There is a range of sleeping options, the most appealing being the luxury tents with soft bedding and electric blankets. Camping **R80**, luxury tent **R140**, dorm **R120**, double **R600**

Tranquility Lodge 130 St Michael's Ave (next to the shop) ☎ 044 531 6663, ⓦ tranquilitylodge.co.za. If Nature's Valley has a centre, then this comfortable lodge, next to the village's only shop, is bang in the middle of it. A two-storey brick and timber building set in a garden that feels as if it's part of the encroaching forest, it is just 50m from the beach. Breakfast is served on an upstairs deck among the treetops. All rooms are en-suite and there's also a larger honeymoon suite (R2400) with a spa bath, double shower, fireplace and private deck. **R1300**

OPPOSITE TSITSIKAMMA COASTLINE >

17

Wild Spirit Lodge and Backpackers Nature's Valley Rd, 8km from Nature's Valley ☎044 534 8888, ⓦwildspiritlodge.co.za. This lodge has an alternative focus, with accommodation in bunk-free dorms in three, two-storey garden cottages. There is free wi-fi, a kitchen for self-catering, a yoga and meditation room, book exchange, live music and drumming nights and a big outdoor braai. Camping R80, dorm R120, double R400

EATING AND DRINKING

Nature's Valley Trading Store Cnr Forest & St Michael's ☎044 531 6835. The only place in the village that does food and booze is a pretty informal and convivial spot for seafood, steaks, burgers (R60) and toasted sandwiches, and provides the only nightlife – a large-screen TV – apart from gazing at the stars. Daily 9.30am–8pm.

Storms River Mouth

55km east of Plettenberg Bay • Daily 7am–7pm • Day-visitor R80; overnight R150 • ☎042 281 1607

In contrast to the languid lagoon and long soft sands of Nature's Valley, **Storms River Mouth**, 55km from Plettenberg Bay, presents the elemental face of the Garden Route, with the dark Storms River surging through a gorge to battle with the surf. Don't confuse this with **Storms River Village** just off the N2, which is nowhere near the sea, but right in the forest.

Walking is the main activity at the Mouth, and at the visitors' office at the restcamp you can get **maps** of short, waymarked coastal trails that leave from here. These include steep walks up the forested cliffs, where you can see 800-year-old yellowwood trees with views onto a wide stretch of ocean. Most rewarding is the **three-kilometre hike** west from the restcamp along the start of the Otter Trail to a fantastic **waterfall** pool at the base of fifty-metre-high falls. Less demanding is the kilometre-long **boardwalk stroll** from the restaurant to the suspension bridge to see the river mouth. On your way to the bridge, don't miss the dank *strandloper* (beachcomber) **cave**. Hunter-gatherers frequented this area between five thousand and two thousand years ago, living off seafood in wave-cut caves near the river mouth. A modest display shows an excavated midden, with clear layers of little bones and shells. The area's most famous and popular walks, however, are the Dolphin and Otter trails (see box, p.217). **Swimming** at the Mouth is restricted to a safe and pristine little sandy bay below the restaurant, with a changing hut, though conditions can be cold in summer if there are easterly winds and cold upwellings of deep water from the continental shelf.

ARRIVAL AND DEPARTURE   STORMS RIVER MOUTH

By car Storms River Mouth is 18km south of Storms River Bridge: you'll need your own wheels to get around here as there's no public transport to the Mouth. Most people stop at the bridge, on the N2, to gaze into the deep river gorge and fill up at the most beautifully located petrol and service station in the country.

By shuttle *Tsitsikamma Backpackers* (see opposite) can arrange a shuttle service for their guests from Storms River Village to the Mouth (R100/person; minimum three passengers).

ACCOMMODATION

Storms River Mouth Restcamp ☎042 281 1607, ⓦsanparks.org/parks/garden_route/camps/storms_river. Sited on tended lawns, *Storms River Mouth Restcamp* is poised between a craggy shoreline of black rocks pounded by foamy white surf and steeply raking forested cliffs, and is the ultimate location along the southern Cape coast. It has a variety of accommodation options, not especially nice and rather modest and worn, but all with sea views and the ever-present sound of the surging surf. Advance booking through South African National Parks is essential (see p.31) and you may have to take whatever is available, as its location makes it understandably popular. Two units have disabled access. Camping R345, forest hut R565, chalet or oceanette R1100–1760

EATING

Tsitsikamma Restaurant The only place to eat at Storms River Mouth has such startling views that it can be forgiven its dreadfully mediocre fare of English breakfasts, toasted sandwiches, burgers, pastas and steak, and appallingly indifferent service. They do a reasonable range of seafood dishes (R100) and you can get a drink out on the wooden deck. Daily 8.30am–10pm.

Storms River Village

17

About a kilometre south of the national road, **STORMS RIVER VILLAGE** is a tranquil place crisscrossed by a handful of dirt roads and with a few dozen houses, enjoying mountain vistas, with easy access to stroll or hike in the state-run forest which is literally on the doorstep. The main attraction of the village is as a centre for adventure activities, of which the canopy tour zip-line is the really substantial drawing card.

ARRIVAL AND DEPARTURE
STORMS RIVER VILLAGE

By Baz Bus The only transport into Storms River Village proper is on the Baz Bus, which pulls in at the backpacker hostels daily in each direction on its way between Cape Town and Port Elizabeth.

By intercity bus Greyhound, Translux and Intercape intercity buses pull in on their daily hauls along the N2 between Cape Town and Port Elizabeth at the filling station at the Storms River Bridge, some 5km from the village.

Destinations Cape Town (2 daily; 10hr 25min); Knysna

(2 daily; 1hr 20min); Mossel Bay (2 daily; 3hr); Plettenberg Bay (2 daily; 50min); Port Elizabeth (2 daily; 2hr 30min); Sedgefield (2 daily; 1hr 40min).

By shuttle bus Some of the backpacker hostels, among them *Tsitsikamma Backpackers*, offer a free shuttle service to and from the bridge from 8am–5pm, as well as a paid shuttle to Storms River Mouth in the Garden Route National Park, the Bloukrans Bungee site, Nature's Valley and Plettenberg Bay.

ACTIVITIES

BOAT TRIPS
SANParks ☎ 042 281 1607. Runs trips for up to twelve people (R115 for 30min + conservation fee) about 1km up Storms River leaving from near the dive shop, where you book, just beneath the restaurant.

MOUNTAIN BIKING
A 22km mountain trail winds through the forest on the edge of the village and offers terrific views of the river gorge and coastline. *Tsitsikamma Backpackers* rent out mountain bikes for the day (R220).

TOURS
Woodcutters' Journey ☎ 042 281 1836, ⓦ stormsriver .com. A relaxed jaunt organized by Storms River Adventures (teatime trip R200, lunch trip R250), headquartered next to the post office. The trip takes you through the forest to the river along the old Storms River Pass in a specially designed trailer, drawn by a tractor.

TUBING
Tube 'n Axe Backpackers ☎ 042 281 1757,

ⓦ tubenaxe.co.za. *Tube 'n Axe Backpackers* operate trips down the Storms River gorge, where during the high-water season (generally winter) you ride the river and its rapids buoyed up by a small inflatable (R490 half-day, R800 full day).

ZIP LINE
Storms River Adventures ☎ 042 281 1836, ⓦ stormsriver.com. The Storms River Adventures Canopy Tour (R495) through the treetops gives a bird's-eye view of the forest as you travel 30m above ground along a series of interconnected cables attached to the tallest trees. The system has been constructed in such a way that not a single nail has been hammered into any tree.

Tsitsikamma Falls Adventures ☎ 072 030 4367, ⓦ tsitsikammaadventure.co.za. A faster, higher alternative, geared more to adrenaline junkies, is the zip-line tour across the Kruis River at Tsitsikamma Falls Adventures (R380), which at times is 50m above the ground and crisscrosses an awesome ravine, zipping over three waterfalls, with the longest slide measuring 211m.

ACCOMMODATION

The Armagh Fynbos Ave ☎ 042 281 1512, ⓦ thearmagh.com. A hospitable and very comfortable guesthouse with excellent bathrooms and bed linen, in a beautiful garden that drifts off into the *fynbos*. The rooms include two budget rooms, four standard ones, a garden cottage and an ultra luxurious and very private honeymoon room, all of which open onto the garden. There's a nice swimming pool and a decent restaurant. R1300

★**At the Woods Guest House** 49 Formosa St, along the main drag into town ☎ 042 281 1446, ⓦ atthewoods.co.za. Friendly, modern guesthouse that's

the nicest place in town, with traditional reed ceilings and large, comfortable rooms with king-sized beds and French doors that open onto garden verandas, or, upstairs, onto private decks with mountain views. Three-course home-cooked dinners can be arranged, and there's a nice communal lounge with a fireplace where you can use the internet. R990

Tsitsikamma Backpackers 54 Formosa St ☎ 042 281 1868, ⓦ tsitsikammabackpackers.co.za. Well-run hostel, whose accommodation options include luxury tents set in a beautiful garden that claims environmentally

17

friendly and fair-trade credentials. You can self-cater or order a reasonably priced breakfast or dinner and there's a bar. They offer a shuttle service to local attractions and pick up guests for free from the Storms River Bridge. Tent R340, dorm R160, double R470

Tsitsikamma Village Inn Darnell St, along the road into the village and left at the T-junction ☎ 042 281 1711, ⓦ tsitsikammahotel.co.za. A charming, old-fashioned and consistently well-run hotel in the village amid the trees and with a well-tended garden. It has 49 rooms in eleven cottage units, and the advantage of a pub and restaurant on the premises. R990

Tube 'n Axe Backpackers Cnr Darnell and Saffron sts ☎ 042 281 1757, ⓦ tubeaxe.co.za. A wacky place that works hard to compete with the bright lights of Knysna and Plett by offering drumming nights, a pool table and loads of laughs. Accommodation, besides the usual dorms and doubles, includes two-person elevated tents. Camping R85, elevated tent R300, dorm R150, double R480

EATING AND DRINKING

De Oude Martha Tsitsikamma Village Inn, Darnell St. Totally acceptable, if unexceptional, hotel restaurant that serves up unpretentious breakfasts, lunches and dinners (mains average R160), but the best thing about it is the cosy pub with a welcoming fireplace on damp winter nights. Daily 7am–9pm.

Rafters The Armagh, Fynbos Ave. The dinner menu has an emphasis on the local: South African cuisine using garden greens in their salads, fish from Plettenberg Bay and meat sourced nearby. Cape Muslim sweet and mild curries feature big on the menu (R115). Daily 8am–9pm.

THE OSTRICH FARM, OUDTSHOORN

Route 62 and the Little Karoo

One of the most rewarding journeys in the Western Cape is an inland counterpart to the Garden Route (see Chapter 17) – the mountain route from Cape Town to Port Elizabeth, largely along the R62, and thus often referred to as Route 62. Nowhere near as well known as the coastal journey, this trip takes you through some of the most dramatic passes and *poorts* (valley routes) in the country and crosses a frontier of *dorps* (villages) and drylands. This "back garden" is in many respects more rewarding than the actual Garden Route, being far less developed, with spectacular landscapes, quieter roads and some great small towns to visit.

GARDEN ROUTE
NATIONAL PARK
(WILDERNESS)

N2

N9

Klaarstroom

Stompdrif

Amos

W12

De Rust

Meiringspoort Pass

Cango Caves

R407

Prince Albert

Sand

Wilderness
Victoria
Bay
George

Oudtshoorn

Outeniqua
Pass

R328

Gamkaskloof
Pass

Swartberg
Pass

Groenfontein
Valley

R62

R328

BOTLIERSKOP
PRIVATE GAME
RESERVE

Mossel Bay

Great Brak River
Klein Brakrivier

Prince Albert Road

R407

Gamka

N1

OUTENIQUA MOUNTAINS

Dwyka

Dwyka

Gamkapoort

Calitzdorp

LITTLE
KAROO

Langtou

R327

Gourits

Gourikwa

Gourikwa

Bloed

Kerks

Elandskloof

Huis

R62

Ladismith

Albertinia

Gourritsmond

INDIAN
OCEAN

Buffls

SWARTBERG MOUNTAINS

Groot

Groot

R323

Ronnie's Sex Shop

Lemoenshoek Farm
& The Labyrinth

R62

Duivenhoks

Heidelberg

Riversdale

R305

Goukou

Stilbaai

Laingsberg

Prins

Anys

Warmwaterberg Spa

LANGEBERG MOUNTAINS

Duiwenhoks

N2

R324

R322

R322

Infanta

Matjiesfontein

Bellair

SANBONA
WILDLIFE
RESERVE

Barrydale

Tradouw Pass
Suurbraak

BONTEBOK
NATIONAL
PARK

Breede

DE HOOP
NATURE
RESERVE

Groot

GREAT KAROO

N1

Touwsrivier

Koo

Cogman's Pass

Montagu

R60

Swellendam

N2

De
Hoopvlei

Arniston

Doring

R318

R318

Ashton

Robertson

R317

Bonnievale

WESTERN
CAPE

R319

R316

Bredasdorp

R319

R316

L'Agulhas

R46

Ceres

Worcester

R43

McGregor

R60

Greyton

R406

Riviersonderend

R326

Napier

R316

OVERBERG

Elim

AGULHAS
NATIONAL PARK Soetendal

Cape Agulhas

R303

HEX RIVER MOUNTAINS

R321

Kwaggaskloof

Villiersdorp

Genadendal

R406

Caledon

N2

R320

Stanford

R43

De Kelders
Gansbaai

Nuwejaars

R46

Tulbagh

Wolseley

R301

N1

R43

Franschhoek

Houwhoek

R41

Bot River

Hermanus

ATLANTIC
OCEAN

Cape Town

0   25

With no scheduled public transport, apart from intercity buses between Oudtshoorn and Cape Town, this is a journey best done by car – combis are available in some destinations but run on demand and cannot be organized in advance.

Though it's possible to drive to Oudtshoorn from Cape Town in a day, it's worth breaking your journey to explore the pretty towns of McGregor, Montagu and Barrydale. Continuing east from Barrydale, the R62 landscape becomes more spare as you get into the **Little Karoo** (or Klein Karoo), a vast, khaki-coloured hinterland (the name is a Khoi word meaning "hard and dry") with low, wiry scrub and dotted with flat-topped hills. One unsung surprise along the way is **Calitzdorp**, a rustic little *dorp*, five hours' solid driving from Cape Town, down whose backstreets a few unassuming wine farms produce some of South Africa's best port. By contrast, the well-trumpeted attractions of **Oudtshoorn**, half an hour further on, are the ostrich farms and the massive **Cango Caves**, one of the country's biggest tourist draws. Less than 70km from the coast, with good transport connections, Oudtshoorn marks the convergence of the mountain and coastal roads and is usually treated as a leisurely day-trip away from the Garden Route. From Oudtshoorn, over the most dramatic of all passes in the Cape – the unpaved **Swartberg Pass**, 27km of spectacular switchbacks and zigzags through the Swartberg Mountains – is **Prince Albert**, a favourite Karoo village whose spartan beauty and remarkable light make it popular with artists.

18

Worcester

Worcester, the large functional hub of the region, is on the N1 just 110km from Cape Town, and worth a stop if you are interested in Cape flora. Worcester is an agricultural centre at the centre of a wine-making region, consisting mostly of co-operatives producing bulk plonk, and for most travellers it marks the place to buy petrol and deviate from the N1 onto the scenic R62. However, it's worth considering stopping for a break and a cup of tea at the peaceful botanic gardens. An interesting nugget is that J.M. Coetzee, South Africa's most acclaimed writer internationally, grew up here, though nothing yet in the town makes mention of its famous son.

Karoo Desert Botanic Gardens

Daily 7am–7pm · R20 · Restaurant daily 9am–5pm · ☎ 023 347 0785, ⓦ sanbi.org

As you enter Worcester from Cape Town, signs point to the **Karoo Botanic Gardens**, a sister reserve to Kirstenbosch in Cape Town, known for its show of indigenous spring flowers and succulents. The pleasant **restaurant** here serves light meals looking out over the gardens onto an attractive mountain backdrop. The best time to visit the gardens is from late July to early September when all the flowers people travel to see in Namaqualand bloom here in a profusion of purples, oranges and yellows. Three hiking trails meander through large wild areas, full of desert plants and prickly blooms, and in the winter, snow caps the dramatic backdrop of the Hex River mountain range.

McGregor

McGREGOR is an attractive small village, with whitewashed cottages that sparkle in the summer daylight amid the low scrub, vines and olive trees. Its quiet, relaxed atmosphere has attracted a small population of spiritual seekers and artists, and residents are urged to build in harmony with existing style and thus maintain the town's character. It makes a great weekend break from Cape Town, with a couple of decent restaurants, plenty of well-priced accommodation and a beautiful retreat centre with reasonably priced massage and other body-work. Spending a day wine tasting around McGregor and its environs is another drawing card, as long as it's not a Sunday when almost everything is closed.

McGregor gained modest prosperity in the nineteenth century by becoming a centre of the whipstock industry, supplying wagoners and transport riders with long bamboo sticks for goading oxen. There aren't too many ox-drawn wagons today, and tourism,

18

though developing, is still quite limited. One reason people come here is to walk the **Boesmanskloof Traverse** (see below), which starts 14km from McGregor and crosses to Greyton on the other side of the mountain. From McGregor you can walk a section of the trail, hiking to the main waterfall and back to the trailhead, which is a three- to four-hour round hike of exceeding beauty through the river gorge, or *kloof* in Afrikaans.

ARRIVAL AND INFORMATION   MCGREGOR

By car McGregor, 180km from Cape Town and fifteen minutes to the south of Robertson, is at the end of a minor road signposted off the R60. Don't be tempted by an approach from the south which may look like a handy back route – you'd need a 4WD for this. Allow two and a half hours for the drive from Cape Town along the N1, turning onto the R62 at Worcester for Robertson.

Tourist office Voortrekker St (Mon–Sat 9am–1pm &

2–4.30pm, Sun 9am–1pm; ☎023 625 1954, ⓦtourismmcgregor.co.za). The office can book accommodation and issue permits for walking the whole Boesmanskloof Traverse or simply for the waterfall section (R30). They will also direct you to artists' studios in town, and to complementary health practitioners offering massage and yoga, and give you times of the daily meditation sessions at Temenos Country Retreat.

ACCOMMODATION

The Barn Grewe St ☎076 411 9477, ⓦthebarn mcgregor.co.za. Beautifully restored self-catering barn sleeping six in three rooms, with a Victorian bath, antique Cape furniture, fireplace and wood-burning stove. Rates drop to R950 for two people. R1350

Green Gables Country Inn 7 Smith St ☎023 625 1626, ⓦgreengablescountryinn.co.za. Country accommodation at the edge of the village, with a swimming pool, an English-style pub and a restaurant open three nights a week. The decor is cosy if slightly cluttered, and service is warm and personal; rates are very reasonable for what you get. R700

The Old Village Lodge Voortrekker St ☎023 625 1692, ⓦoldvillagelodge.co.za. Upmarket B&B in a Victorian cottage on the main road, with a pretty garden, swimming pool and rooms furnished in an elegant and comfortable country style. R900

Rhebokskraal Farm Cottages 2km south of town ☎082 896 0429, ⓦrhebokskraalolives.co.za. Secluded cottages, each on a different part of this beautiful fruit, olive and grape farm, which is within easy reach of the restaurants in town. R500

★**Tanagra Guest Wine Farm** 4.5km northeast of

McGregor, towards Robertson ☎023 625 1780, ⓦtanagra-wines.co.za. Idyllic wine farm with stylish, light and airy cottages, all with private verandas and mountain views. One cottage is totally off the grid, with a private plunge pool, hammocks and a fireplace. There are walking trails on the farm itself or on the adjoining Vrolijkheid Nature Reserve. Bed and breakfast rates are available for an additional R250. R700

★**Temenos Country Retreat** On the corner of Bree and Voortrekker sts ☎023 625 1871, ⓦtemenos.org .za. Retreat centre with cottages dotted about beautiful gardens and walkways, a lap-length swimming pool, library and meditation spaces. Breakfast is included and it's safe and peaceful – an ideal place for solo women. R700

Whipstock Farm 7km southwest of McGregor, towards Boesmanskloof ☎073 042 3919, ⓦwhipstock.co.za. Farm accommodation in a Victorian house with five cottages, each with white-washed walls, wooden beams, fridges and tea-making facilities. Meals are served communally in a large dining room with a fireplace. It's ideal for families wanting a nature-based holiday; self-catering rates are also available. R440

EATING AND DRINKING

Deli Girls Voortrekker St. Great for picnic supplies, with smoked fish, cheese, chocolate and other tempting goodies on offer. You can sit on the back porch to savour home-made dishes, such as cottage pie and salad , tandoori pork chop or a rich cheesy pasta and veg bake with salad (R50). Daily 9am–4.30pm.

Green Gables Country Inn, 7 Smith St ☎023 625 1626, ⓦgreengablescountryinn.co.za. Alfresco dinners on the terrace overlooking vineyards and the village, with a cosy dining room and a fireplace for winter nights, plus a "village pub". There are generally three well-cooked dishes on offer, such as chicken curry, fish and chips, and lamb shank (R90). The simplicity of the dishes belies their

quality. Booking essential. Wed, Fri & Sat 6–10pm.

Karoux Restaurant Voortrekker St ☎023 625 1421. Intimate restaurant with gourmet food you wouldn't expect to find in a sleepy village, such as crispy duck with exotic mushroom wontons, and free-range chicken liver parfait with truffled blueberry vinaigrette (R60). Booking essential. Mon & Fri–Sun 7–10pm.

★**Tebaldi's at Temenos** On the corner of Bree and Voortrekker sts ☎023 625 1871, ⓦtemenos.org.za. Breakfasts and salad lunches served in a tranquil garden setting, or on the street-facing *stoep*. The *coq au vin*, served on a bed of creamy mash, is recommended (R90). Tues & Sun 9.30am–3.30pm, Wed–Sat 9.30am–3.30pm & 7–9.30pm.

Montagu

Some 190km from Cape Town, and 47km from McGregor, is **MONTAGU**, the centre of a major peach- and apricot-growing region whose soaring mountains with twisted red and ochre strata dominate the town with its pleasing Victorian architecture.

The town was named in 1851 after **John Montagu**, the visionary British Secretary of the Cape, who realized that the colony would never develop without decent communications and was responsible for commissioning the first mountain passes connecting remote areas to Cape Town. Montagu is best known for its **hot springs**, but serious **rock climbers** come for its cliff faces, which are regarded as among the country's most challenging. You can also explore the mountains on a couple of trails or, easiest of all, on a tractor ride onto one of the peaks. Montagu is also conveniently positioned for excursions along both the Robertson and Little Karoo **wine routes**.

Highly photogenic, Montagu is ideal for exploring on foot, taking in the interesting buildings or simply enjoying the setting, with the Langeberg Mountains, valleys and farms.

Montagu Museum

41 Long St • Mon–Fri 9am–5pm, Sat & Sun 10.30am–12.30pm • R10

The best thing about the **Montagu Museum**, housed in a pleasant old church, is its herbal project, which traces traditional Khoisan knowledge about the medicinal properties of local plants. Note the peach pips embedded in the floor, to give texture, and the peach kernels used to create the driveway, both of which are typical in these fruit-growing parts.

Montagu Springs Resort

3km northwest of Montagu on the R318 • Daily 8am–11pm • R100 • ⓦ montagusprings.co.za

Montagu's best known attraction, the **Montagu Springs Resort** is home to several chlorinated open-air pools of different temperatures and a couple of jacuzzis, spectacularly situated at the foot of the cliffs – an effect slightly spoilt by the neon lights of a hotel complex and fast-food restaurant. It's a nice place to take kids, but the weekends become a mass of splashing bodies: if you want a quiet time, go first thing in the morning or last thing at night. The temperatures in winter are not hot enough to be entirely comfortable, when you're better off heading to the springs at **Caledon** (p.182) or **Warmwaterberg** (p.230), which are much hotter, and in many respects preferable.

ARRIVAL AND INFORMATION   MONTAGU

By car Montagu is 190km from Cape Town; take the N1 as far as Worcester and then head southeast on the R60. The journey from Worcester (roughly 60km) takes you through Robertson and Ashton. Danie (☎ 072 750 3125) runs a very reasonably priced on-demand shuttle service (R160)

between Montagu and Cape Town.

Tourist office 24 Bath St (Mon–Fri 8am–6pm, Sat 9am–5pm, Sun 9.30am–5pm; ☎ 023 614 2471, ⓦ montagu-ashton.info).

ACCOMMODATION

★ **Aasvoelkrans** 1 Van Riebeeck St ☎ 023 614 1228, ⓦ aasvoelkrans.co.za. Four exceptionally imaginative garden rooms at a guesthouse situated on a farm with competition Arab horses grazing in the fields, in a pretty part of town. There is also a two-bedroomed self-catering cottage suitable for a family or larger group. Cottage R600, double R900

De Bos Guest Farm 8 Brown St ☎ 023 614 2532, ⓦ debos.co.za. Camping (lovely shady sites), dorms and basic doubles on a farm at the western edge of town, close to the spectacular, twisted mountain slopes, and often accommodating rock climbers who bring their own kit to tackle climbs in the area. There are also hikes on the

doorstep, but you don't have to be a climber to enjoy staying here. Camping R60, dorm R90, double R360

Montagu Rose Guest House 19 Kohler St ☎ 023 614 2681, ⓦ montagurose.co.za. All of the rooms in this well run, modern guesthouse, decorated with plenty of paintings and knicknacks, have baths and mountain views; one is wheelchair friendly, and there is a family room for four. R700

Montagu Springs Signposted off the R62, west of town ☎ 023 614 1050, ⓦ montagusprings.co.za. Large resort with fully equipped self-catering chalets, some more luxurious than others, sleeping four. The only reason to stay here is if you are travelling with children who want access to the pools and playing areas. Prices go down by roughly a

18

18

third during the week. **R940**

Mystic Tin 38 Bath St ☏ 082 572 0738, ⊛ themystictin .co.za. Two reasonably-priced upstairs family rooms and two garden rooms, simply but stylishly furnished in a rustic/ethnic manner, each with their own entrances and bathrooms. **R520**

★ **Squirrel's Corner** Cnr Bloem and Jouberts sts

☏ 023 614 1081, ⊛ squirrelscorner.co.za. A reasonably priced B&B situated two blocks from the main road, with four comfortable, spotless en-suite rooms in a friendly family house, as well as an African-themed garden suite. They do a delicious speciality omelette for breakfast, and you will be greeted with a glass of Montagu muscadel on arrival. **R600**

EATING AND DRINKING

The farm stalls as you drive through Montagu on the R62 are worth stopping at for nibbles and local produce, and there are several appealing cafés to choose from on Long Street. On Saturday mornings, don't miss the local farmers' market at the church, where you can get olives and olive oil, bread, cheese, almonds and dried fruit from the surrounding farms – all exceptionally well priced. In summer, bags of peaches and apricots are often sold from back yards or along the roadside, for next to nothing. All restaurants need to be booked ahead for dinner.

Die Stal 8km out of town on the R318 ☏ 082 324 4318. A thoroughly pleasant venue on a farm, serving breakfast, lunches and tea. A good destination if you want to see something of the surrounding orchards and farmlands. A hearty favourite is lamb rump (R105), while vegetarians can opt for the ploughman's platter (R85). Tues–Sun 9am–5pm.

★ **Mystic Tin** 38 Bath St ☏ 082 572 0738, ⊛ themystictin.co.za. Tablecloths, candlelight and a winter fireplace create a cosy atmosphere to enjoy South African specialities done with flair. The ostrich herb meat balls with roasted almonds and potato bread are worth a

try (R92) and there are a couple of appealing vegetarian options, all accompanied by hand-crafted beers brewed in their Karoo microbrewery. Mon, Wed–Sun 5–9.30pm.

Simply Delicious Restaurant Four Oaks, 46 Long St ☏ 023 614 3483, ⊛ four-oaks.co.za. A good choice for a light lunch or dinner, set in a handsome 1860 thatched house with a shady courtyard. Lunch options include a veg wrap (R55), while more substantial offerings include steak with seasonal vegetables (R100). Summer daily 12.30–2.30pm & 7–9pm; winter Mon–Sat 12.30–2.30pm & 6.30–9pm.

Barrydale

BARRYDALE, 240km from Cape Town, is perfect for a couple of days of doing very little other than experiencing small-town life in the Little Karoo, with good, reasonably priced accommodation, hot springs at **Warmwaterberg** or picnics along the Tradouw Pass. West of town you'll find big game – and correspondingly high rates – at the magnificent **Sanbona Wildlife Reserve**, though day-visitors are not accepted.

Not yet on the tourist route, Barrydale nonetheless has a number of restaurants and decent places to stay, and the sixty-kilometre drive from Montagu offers spectacular mountain scenery. There's a distinct rural feel about Barrydale: vineyards line the main road, farm animals are kept on large plots of land behind dry-stone walling, and you'll find fig, peach and quince trees thriving in the dryness.

ARRIVAL AND INFORMATION

BARRYDALE

By car Allow three to three and a half hours for the journey from Cape Town, either taking the N1 and R62, via Montagu, or the N2, and cutting inland on the R324 just east of Swellendam for the lovely drive through Suurbraak and the Tradouw Pass. Both routes are equally recommended for the scenery and ease of travel.

Tourist office The tiny visitor information centre (Mon–Fri 9am–5pm, Sat & Sun 9am–2pm; ☏ 028 572 1572, ⊛ barrydale.co.za) sits at the entrance to the village, on the R62.

Services There's a supermarket on the main drag, van Riebeeck Street, which houses an ATM and post office.

ACCOMMODATION

Inkaroo Cottage 2 Bain St, close to the Mud Gallery ☏ 028 572 1344. Beautifully restored and furnished in a contemporary style, this typical Karoo farmhouse cottage sleeps up to six people on a self-catering basis. It has dry stone-walling and seating at the back of the house under

vines, and a full kitchen and living room, with sunset views onto the mountains. **R600**

★ **Tradouw Guest House** 46 van Riebeeck St ☏ 028 572 1434, ⊛ tradouwguesthouse.co.za. One of the best accommodation places along the R62 is Leon and

18

THE LABYRINTH

The Labyrinth (daily 9am–5pm; ☎028 572 1643, ⓦmagicmountainsretreat.com),15km east of Barrydale on a small farm at Lemoenshoek, is a beautiful outdoor maze based on one at Chartres Cathedral in France . The circuit is demarcated by rose quartz stones and allows you to gaze at the mountains as you move through. On the same property is a Buddhist Peace Pagoda, a rather wonderful curiosity in this out-of-the-way place.

Denis' friendly *Tradouw Guest House*, with four simple, homely rooms with nostalgic, thick white cotton sheets and blankets in rooms with sash windows opening onto a courtyard shaded by vines where you can breakfast, while two open onto the appealing large garden. There's a roaring fire in winter in the lounge. Rates are reasonable. **R700**

EATING

Most places are only open during the day, but you will always find at least one restaurant open in the evening.

Blue Cow Signposted off the eastern side of the R62 ☎082 579 1253, ⓦfacebook.com/bluecowbarrydale. The setting, overlooking fields and a dam, is restful, and they serve pleasant cakes, milkshakes and light meals (R60). This is the best place if you are travelling with children and they need to run around. Mon–Sat 8am–5pm.

Clarke of the Karoo Mud Gallery, on R62 ☎028 572 1017, ⓦclarkeofthekaroo.co.za. A great option for tasty steaks, *bobotie* and other hearty country fare, with a starter provided on the house. Their Karoo lamb curry or venison burger on ciabatta are recommended (R90). Mon & Tues 8am–4pm, Wed–Sun 8am–8pm.

Jam Tarts On R62 ☎028 572 1017. Of the several places strung along the R62, this is the best spot for coffee and light meals; dishes include delicious soups (R50) and pizza. You can also pick up local olives and tasty jams. Mon 8am–4.30pm & 6–9pm, Tues–Sun 8am–4.30pm.

★**Mez Karoo Kitchen** van Riebeeck St ☎082 077 5980. Excellent and reasonably-priced Mediterranean food, including light tapas meals and their Greek lamb speciality (R110). Their bright pink rose-water ice cream served with pistachios and fresh mint is always delightful. You sit in Michelle's cosy kitchen in her home, though there are some outside seats too. Book ahead. Thurs–Sat 6–10pm, Sun 1–3pm.

SHOPPING

Wine A couple of wine outlets are worth a visit for tasting and buying, particularly the Southern Cape Winery in van Riebeeck Street (Mon–Fri 9am–5pm, Sat 9am–1pm; ☎028 572 1012). There are a number of interesting craft shops along the R62, including the Mud Gallery (Mon–Fri 9am–5pm, Sat & Sun 9am–1pm; ☎028 572 1950, ⓦmud .co.za), built with earth and dry stone walling, worth looking at just for the architecture, where you can find silver jewellery, paintings and metal work. In town, Magpie Studio at 27 van Riebeeck Street (Tues–Fri 10am–5pm, Sun 9am–1pm; ☎028 572 1997, ⓦmagpieartcollective .com) makes colourful light fittings and chandeliers from recycled materials; their most famous customer is Michelle Obama.

WARMWATERBERG SPA

Thirty kilometres east of Barrydale (just beyond *Ronnie's Sex Shop*, a pub and well-known landmark in the middle of nowhere), is **Warmwaterberg Spa** (☎028 572 1609, ⓦwarmwater bergspa.co.za), a Karoo farm blessed with natural hot water siphoned into two outdoor, unchlorinated hot pools and surrounded by lush green lawns and lofty palms. Primarily aimed at South Africans, it gets rather crowded and noisy during school holidays and over weekends. Indeed, the best time of day to enjoy the baths is after dark, when the steam rises into the cold, starry Karoo sky. The farm is attractively set, with mountain vistas to gaze at from the baths and fantastic bird life drawn by this oasis in the deserty landscape.

Accommodation is basic, reasonably priced and all self-catering – in wooden cabins or rooms in the main farmhouse, each of which has an indoor spa bath (R640). There are also some campsites (R325), a bar, and a restaurant serving dinners and breakfasts. Rates are lowered on weekdays and during the school term (R410). If you are driving past, and want to have a swim, day-visitors pay R40.

Sanbona Wildlife Reserve

20km west of Barrydale • R7800 • ☎ 028 572 1365, ⓦ sanbona.com

The striking semi-desert landscape of the massive Sanbona Wildlife Reserve is the backdrop for some luxurious all-inclusive lodges, *Dwyka Tented Lodge* and *Gondwana Family Lodge*. *Dwyka* is closer to where most of the game is to be found and has the more spectacular setting, while *Gondwana* is great if you are travelling with kids. The price includes all your meals and accommodation, plus two game drives a day, but, owing to the vegetation, the game is far sparser here than in the major game-viewing areas such as the Kruger National Park. Having said that, it is the only place in the Western Cape with free-roaming lions and cheetahs and there's a herd of elephants. Sanbona is worth considering only if you are set on seeing some big game and don't have time for Kruger. A two-night stay is recommended and day-visitors are not allowed – check for specials and cheaper winter rates.

18

Oudtshoorn

From Barrydale, vineyards and orchards give way to arid mountains and rocky, treeless plains vegetated with low, wiry scrub, making for a dramatic journey onwards, and another spectacular, twisting pass. **OUDTSHOORN**, 420km from Cape Town and 180km from Barrydale, has been called the "ostrich capital of the world"; the town's surrounds are indeed crammed with ostrich farms, several of which you can visit, and the local souvenir shops keep busy dreaming up 1001 tacky ways to recycle ostrich parts as comestibles and souvenirs. But Oudtshoorn has two other big draws: it's the best base for visiting the nearby **Cango Caves** (see p.234), and the town is known for its winter sunshine, when it can be raining on the Garden Route. It's boiling hot in summer, though, so make sure you have access to a pool, and nights in winter can freeze.

Oudtshoorn's town centre has little more than a couple of museums worth visiting; the town's main interest lies in its Victorian and Edwardian sandstone buildings, some of which are unusually grand and elegant for a Karoo *dorp*.

Brief history

Oudtshoorn started out as a small village named in honour of Geesje Ernestina Johanna van Oudtshoorn, wife of the first civil commissioner for George. By the 1860s, **ostriches**, which live in the wild in Africa, were being raised under the ideal conditions of the Oudtshoorn Valley, where the warm climate and loamy soils enabled lucerne, the favourite diet of the flightless birds, to be grown. The quirky Victorian fashion for large feathers had turned the ostriches into a source of serious wealth, and by the 1880s hundreds of thousands of kilogrammes of feathers were being exported, and birds were changing hands for up to £1000 a pair – an unimaginable sum in those days. On the back of this boom, sharp businessmen made their fortunes, ignorant farmers were ripped off, and labourers drew the shortest straw of all. The latter were mostly coloured descendants of the Outeniqua and Attaqua Khoikhoi and trekboers, who received derisory wages supplemented by rations of food, wine, spirits and tobacco – a practice that still

Cango Ostrich Farm, Cango Wildlife Ranch, Cango Caves, ▲ **1**, **0**, **2** & **3**

■ **ACCOMMODATION**
Backpacker's Paradise	5
Berluda	3
Buffelsdrift Game Lodge	1
De Oue Werf	2
Gum Tree Lodge	6
Kleinplaas Holiday Resort	4

● **RESTAURANTS & CAFÉS**
Bello Cibo	2
Buffelsdrift Game Lodge	1
Café Brule	3

OUDTSHOORN

continues on some farms. In the early twentieth century, the most successful farmers and traders built themselves "feather palaces", ostentatious sandstone Edwardian buildings that have become the defining feature of Oudtshoorn.

C.P. Nel Museum

Cnr Baron van Reede and Voortrekker sts • Mon–Sat 8am–5pm, Sat 9am–1pm • R15

The **C.P. Nel Museum** is a good place to start your explorations. A handsome sandstone building, it was built in 1906 as a boys' school, but now houses an eccentric collection of items relating to ostriches. It's worth a visit mainly for the story it tells of the town's feather boom and decline, and the contrast between ostrich design items of the past – including gorgeous feather trimmings – compared to what you'll see in the tacky ostrich shops today.

Le Roux Town House

Cnr Loop and High sts • Mon–Fri 9am–5pm • R15

Le Roux Town House is a perfectly preserved family townhouse, and the only way to get a glimpse inside one of the much-vaunted "feather palaces". The family's gracious, opulent style was enjoyed and appreciated by royalty and politicians alike during their visits here. The beautifully preserved furnishings were all imported from Europe between 1900 and 1920, and there is plenty to stroll around and admire, from the art nouveau glass panels inside to the corrugated iron verandas encircling the house.

Buffelsdrift Game Lodge

7km from Oudtshoorn • Free • **Elephant interactions** 10am, 11am, 1pm & 2pm • R210 • ☎ 044 272 0106, ⓦ buffelsdrift.com

The **Buffelsdrift Game Lodge**, just out of town on the Cango Caves road, offers an exciting opportunity to get close to **elephants**. Book ahead for a really worthwhile experience where you get to stroke elephants under the guidance of their handlers, and watch them at training and play. From the lodge's **restaurant** (see opposite) on the large dam, you are likely to see hippos, and may be lucky enough to see other animals coming to drink. There is safari-style accommodation too (see opposite).

Cango Wildlife Ranch

Just outside town on the Cango Rd • Daily 8.30am–4.30pm • R145 • ☎ 044 272 5593, ⓦ cango.co.za

The other wildlife activity around Oudtshoorn is **Cango Wildlife Ranch**. Guided tours lead you past white tigers and cheetahs, crocodiles and other amazing creatures from other parts of Africa, and you can pay extra to be photographed touching the animals and reptiles, and even get into the pool with the crocodiles. Don't expect it to be thrilling, though; you'll be lucky if a crocodile so much as flicks its eyes while you're in there. The ranch offers a spectacle rather than authentic wildness, but it caters well for children who can frolic in water fountains or on climbing frames while you eat lunch.

OSTRICH TOURS

Many people come to Oudtshoorn to see, or even ride, **ostriches**. You don't actually have to visit one of the ostrich farms to view Africa's biggest bird, as you're bound to see flocks of them as you drive past farms in the vicinity or past truckloads of them on their way to the slaughterhouse (feathers being no longer fashionable, these days ostriches are raised for their low-cholesterol flesh). A number of show farms offer **tours**, which include the chance to sit on an ostrich (if you are under 70kg). Best of the bunch is **Cango Ostrich Farm** on the main road between Oudtshoorn and the Cango Caves, in the Schoemanshoek Valley, which runs tours every twenty minutes, where you can sit on a bird, stand on their unbreakable eggs and look at ostrich chicks (45min; R80; ☎ 044 272 4623, ⓦ cangoostrich.co.za).

ARRIVAL AND DEPARTURE

By car Allow six hours from Cape Town for the 420km journey along the R62. Alternatively, take the N2 to George along the Garden Route and cut inland to Oudtshoorn on the N12.

By bus Intercity buses pull in at Que Voortrekker Street, across the river from the Baron van Reede Street.

INFORMATION AND ACTIVITIES

Tourist office 80 Voortrekker Rd, in front of the library (Mon–Fri 8.30am–5pm, Sat 9.30am–12.30pm; ☎ 044 279 2532, ⓦ oudtshoorn.com). Good for information about the caves, ostrich farms, and they can find you local accommodation.

Activities Backpacker's Paradise (see below) rents out bikes and arranges spectacular adventurous cycling trips down the Swartberg Pass, with motor vehicle back-up.

18

ACCOMMODATION

Oudtshoorn has a number of large hotels catering mainly to tour buses, plus plenty of good-quality B&Bs and guesthouses, a centrally located campsite with chalets, and one of the country's best-run backpacker lodges. Some of the nicest places to stay are in the attractive countryside en route to Cango Caves. Rates fall dramatically during the winter months following the week-long **Klein Karoo Nasionale Kunstefees** (KKNK; ⓦ absakknk.co.za), a major arts festival, mostly in Afrikaans, and street party in the April Easter holidays when people from all over the country take every bed in town.

Backpacker's Paradise 148 Baron van Reede St ☎ 044 272 3436, ⓦ backpackersparadise.net. A well-run two-storey hostel along the main drag, which makes an effort to go the extra few centimetres with three-quarter beds, en-suite doubles and family rooms as well as dorms. There are nightly ostrich, and veg-friendly, braais, too, and a daily shuttle from the Baz Bus drop-off in George to the hostel. The on-site adventure centre organizes cycle trips in the Swartberg Pass and there's a daily shuttle to the caves, ostrich farm and wildlife ranch, as well as horseriding. Camping R̲7̲0̲, dorm R̲1̲3̲0̲, double R̲4̲0̲0̲

Berluda On the R328, 15km from Oudtshoorn, en route to Cango Caves ☎ 044 272 8518, ⓦ berluda.co.za. An avenue of trees leads up to a fairly modern-looking farmhouse with five bedrooms and two self-catering cottages in a well-established garden. The friendly owners can organize ostrich-farm tours on their property 8km away, and there is a pool to cool off in. R̲1̲2̲6̲0̲

Buffelsdrift Game Lodge 7km from town on the road to the caves ☎ 044 272 0106, ⓦ buffelsdrift.com. The town's top stay, in luxurious en-suite safari tents overlooking a large dam with hippo in it. Breakfast, served in the grand thatched dining area, is included, and game drives or horseback rides to view rhino, buffalo, elephant,

giraffe and various antelope can be included in a package, or paid for separately. R̲2̲5̲0̲0̲

★**De Oue Werf** Signposted off the R328 to Cango Caves, 12km north of Oudtshoorn ☎ 044 272 8712, ⓦ ouewerf.co.za. Luxurious and well-priced garden rooms on a working farm, run by the very welcoming sixth generation of the family. Green lawns run down to a dam, which has a swinging slide and raft to play on, and lots of birdlife. A great option if you're visiting the caves and want to stay in the country. R̲1̲1̲2̲0̲

Gum Tree Lodge 139 Church St ☎ 044 279 2528, ⓦ gumtreelodge.co.za. Five rooms in a peaceful B&B, as well as a two-roomed self-catering cottage sleeping four, conveniently located a few minutes' walk from the centre, fronting onto a river with good birdlife. There's a pool and deck, a well-stocked pub, and rooms have modern bathrooms, a/c and TV. Double R̲8̲3̲0̲, cottage R̲1̲2̲5̲0̲

Kleinplaas Holiday Resort 171 Baron van Reede St ☎ 044 272 5811, ⓦ kleinplaas.co.za. Well-run, shady sites for camping and fully equipped self-catering brick chalets, conveniently close to town, with a swimming pool and launderette. The owners know the town well and will show you the ropes, and can provide breakfast for a little extra. Camping R̲2̲7̲5̲, chalet R̲7̲8̲5̲

EATING AND DRINKING

Oudtshoorn has a choice of several places to eat, mostly strung out along Baron van Reede Street and catering to the tourist trade, with the obligatory ostrich on the menu.

Bello Cibo 145 Baron van Reede St ☎ 044 272 3245. Relaxed and reasonably-priced Italian place with indoor and outdoor seating, making it a good choice for children. Besides pizza and pasta, there are some creative ostrich (R65) offerings. Booking advisable. Mon–Sat 5–11pm.

Buffelsdrift Game Lodge 7km out of town towards Cango Caves ☎ 044 272 0106. Have a great breakfast or

lunch on a wooden deck overlooking the waterhole, and do a spot of game viewing at the same time. The lodge is open to non-guests for meals, and you could combine it with an elephant encounter or other game activity. Breakfast buffets with some local specialities such as roesterkoek – delicious sandwiches roasted on the coals (R90). Daily 7am–3pm.

⌐e Brule Queens Hotel, 5 Baron van Reede St ☎ 044 279 2414, ⓦ queenshotel.co.za. The nicest café in town, set in the restored *Queen Hotel* which has a rather grand, colonial ambience. The menu includes generous cooked breakfasts and ostrich burgers (R60) for lunch; it's also a great spot to sip a cappuccino overlooking the main street. They make their own pastries and breads too, and their deli counter is good for picnic supplies. Mon–Fri 7am–5pm, Sat & Sun 7am–4pm.

Cango Caves

29km from Oudtshoorn • Daily 9am–4pm • R80 • ☎ 044 272 7410, ⓦ cangocaves.co.za

The **Cango Caves** number among South Africa's ten most popular attractions, drawing a quarter of a million visitors each year to gasp at their fantastic cavernous spaces, dripping rocks and rising columns of calcite. In the two centuries since they became known to the public, the caves have been seriously battered by human intervention, but they still represent a stunning landscape growing inside the Swartberg foothills. Don't go expecting a serene and contemplative experience, though: the only way of getting inside the caves is on a **guided tour** accompanied by a commentary.

San hunter-gatherers sheltered in the entrance caves for millennia before white settlers arrived, but it's unlikely that they ever made it to the lightless underground chambers. **Jacobus van Zyl**, a Karoo farmer, was probably the first person to penetrate beneath the surface, when he slid down on a rope into the darkness in July 1780, armed with a lamp. Over the next couple of centuries the caves were visited and pillaged by growing numbers of callers, some of whom were photographed cheerfully carting off wagonloads of limestone columns.

In the 1960s and 1970s the caves were made accessible to mass consumption when a tourist complex was built, the rock-strewn floor was evened out with concrete, ladders and walkways were installed, and the caverns were subsequently turned into a kitsch extravaganza with coloured lights, piped music and an indecipherable commentary. Even **apartheid** put its hefty boot in: under the premiership of Dr Hendrik Verwoerd, the arch-ideologue of racial segregation, a separate "non-whites" entrance was hacked through one wall, resulting in a disastrous through-draft that began dehydrating the caves. Fortunately, the worst excesses have now ended; concerts are no longer allowed inside the chambers, and the coloured lights have been removed.

ARRIVAL AND INFORMATION

By car The drive here from Oudtshoorn involves heading north along Baron van Reede Street, and continuing 32km along a signposted scenic, quiet road (R328) to the caves. From the caves you can continue by car on the R328 to Prince Albert via the majestic Swartberg Pass.

Information The visitors' complex includes an interpretive centre with quite interesting displays about the geology, people and wildlife connected with the caves, the decent *Caves* restaurant, and a souvenir shop. Below the complex you'll find shady picnic sites at the edge of a river that cuts its way into the mountains and along which there are hiking trails.

CAVE TOURS

Two **tours** leave every hour, and you may only enter the caves on a tour. The one-hour Standard Tour (on the hour; R80) gets you through the first six chambers, but far more interesting is the ninety-minute Adventure Tour (on the half-hour; R100) which takes you into the deepest sections open to the public, where the openings become smaller and smaller. Squeezing through tight openings with names like **Lumbago Walk, Devil's Chimney and The Letterbox** is not recommended for the overweight or claustrophobic, and you should wear oldish clothes and shoes with a grip to negotiate the slippery floors.

Calitzdorp

The small Karoo village of **CALITZDORP** hangs in a torpor of midday stillness, with its attractive, unpretentious Victorian streets and handful of wineries. There's nothing much to do here, apart from have coffee, taste some port, buy some olives and wander through the streets. Some of South Africa's best ports are produced at the three modest **wineries** signposted down side roads, a few hundred metres from the centre. Calitzdorp is at the turn-off to the beautiful Groenfontein (green fountain) Valley (see below).

ARRIVAL AND INFORMATION | CALITZDORP | 18

By car Calitzdorp is 370km from Cape Town, 50km east of Oudtshoorn on the R62. If you're driving from the capital, allow for a five-hour drive with a lunch stop; this would be a good halfway, overnight stop along the R62 if you are

travelling between Cape Town and Port Elizabeth.
Tourist office At the Shell garage on Voortrekker Street (Mon–Fri 9am–5pm, Sat 8am–1pm; ☎ 044 213 3775, ✇ calitzdorp.org.za).

ACCOMMODATION

Die Dorpshuis Opposite the church ☎ 044 213 3453, ✇ diedorpshuis.co.za. Airy, no-frills rooms in a nineteenth-century house that offer exceptional value. There is a convenient restaurant on-site that serves up reasonably priced sandwiches, teas and light meals as well as heavier traditional Karoo food, such as stews and lamb. Set across the road from the church, you can be treated to bells ringing and organ recitals. R600
Port-Wine Guest House On the corner of Queen and Station streets ☎ 044 213 3131, ✇ portwine.net. The smartest and most comfortable guesthouse in town, in a

renovated early nineteenth-century homestead with local paintings on the walls, and a veranda overlooking the Boplaas wine estate. There is a pool and rose garden at the back too. R850
Welgevonden Guesthouse St Helena Rd ☎ 044 213 3642, ✇ welgevondenguesthouse.co.za. A comfortable country-style guesthouse, on a smallholding adjacent to Boplaas wine estate, 300m from the main road. The four en-suite bedrooms, set in an 1880 outbuilding, are furnished with brass or wooden bedsteads, patchwork quilts and wooden family heirloom furniture. R640

The Groenfontein Valley

The narrow dirt road through the highly scenic **Groenfontein Valley** twists through the Swartberg foothills, past whitewashed Karoo cottages and farms and across brooks, eventually joining the R328 to Oudtshoorn. Winding through these backroads is also an option to reach the Cango Caves (see opposite) and Prince Albert (see p.236), one of the best drives you'll ever do in South Africa. Many of the roads are unsealed but are perfectly navigable in an ordinary car if taken slowly.

ARRIVAL AND DEPARTURE | GROENFONTEIN VALLEY

By car A circuitous minor route to the valley diverts just east of Calitzdorp from the R62, signposted *Groenfontein Retreat*.

ACCOMMODATION

Kruis Rivier Guest Farm 17km off the R62 (signposted turn-off 14km east of Calitzdorp) ☎ 044 213 3788, ✇ kruisrivier.co.za. Homely, simply furnished cottages right underneath the mountains, with lovely streams and waterfalls, which make an excellent base for hiking. The owners, who have a policy of keeping prices absolutely affordable, will also do breakfast on request and provide braai packs, home-made bread and wood. R400
Red Stone Hills 6km off the R62 (signposted turn-off 14km east of Calitzdorp) ☎ 044 213 3783, ✇ redstone .co.za. Four lovely period-furnished Victorian cottages on a working farm in a landscape full of red rock formations. The owners can provide dinner on request as well as breakfast.

Besides walking and cycling trails, there is birdwatching and the four horses on the farm can be ridden. R580
★ The Retreat at Groenfontein 20km northeast of Calitzdorp and 59km northwest of Oudtshoorn ☎ 044 213 3880, ✇ groenfontein.com. This isolated Victorian colonial farmstead borders the 2300-square-kilometre Swartberg Nature Reserve, an outstandingly beautiful area of gorges, rivers and dirt tracks. Accommodation is in deliciously comfortable en-suite rooms, each with its own fireplace, and rates include full board with vegetarians well catered for, and hospitable and helpful owners who turn every evening into a fine dinner party. R1420

18

Prince Albert

Isolation has left intact the traditional rural architecture of **PRINCE ALBERT**, an attractive little town 70km north of Oudtshoorn, across the loops and razorbacks of the Swartberg Pass – one of the most dramatic drives and entries to a town imaginable. Although firmly in the thirstlands of the South African interior, on the cusp between the Little and Great Karoo, Prince Albert is all the more striking for its perennial spring, whose water trickles down furrows along its streets – a gift that propagates fruit trees and gardens. Visitors mostly come to Prince Albert for the drive through its two southerly gateways – the aforementioned **Swartberg Pass** on the R328 and **Meiringspoort** on the N12, and to experience some Karoo life with the bonus of friendly locals and good arts, crafts and food.

Prince Albert is small enough to explore on foot and you'll find everything you want on the main road. The essence of the town is in the fleeting impressions that give the flavour of a Karoo *dorp* like nowhere else: the silver steeple of the Dutch Reformed church puncturing a deep-blue sky and residents sauntering along or progressing slowly down the main street on squeaky bikes.

Prince Albert Gallery

57 Church St • Mon–Fri 9am–4pm, Sat 9am–2pm, Sun 10am–1pm • Free

The town's beauty has attracted a number of artists to live here and the excellent **Prince Albert Gallery**, set in an airy Victorian building, sells paintings, sculpture, beadwork, jewellery, ceramics and etchings by local artists.

ARRIVAL AND DEPARTURE
PRINCE ALBERT

By car From Cape Town allow 5–6 hours for the 420km trip. The fastest and least scenic route is along the N1, past Laingsburg, and involves no mountain passes; turn off onto the Prince Albert Road. The most scenic route is along the R62 to Calitzdorp or Oudtshoorn, and along the R328 over Swartberg.

By train Trains between Cape Town and Johannesburg (Wed, Fri & Sun; Shosholoza Meyl; ☎ 086 000 8888) stop at Prince Albert Road station, 45km from the hamlet. Be warned that the trains are often late, and Prince Albert Road station has absolutely no facilities. Arrange to be collected by your guesthouse, or book a taxi in advance through Billy van Rooyen (☎ 072 337 3149).

By bus Greyhound (☎ 083 915 9000, ⓦ greyhound.co.za) stops daily at the *North and South Hotel* in Prince Albert Road station, on the N1, on its Cape Town-to-Johannesburg run, but you will need to arrange to be picked up (see "By train", above) for the 45km journey to Prince Albert.

INFORMATION

Tourist office Church Street (Mon–Fri 9am–5pm, Sat 9am–noon; ☎ 023 541 1366, ⓦ princealbert.org.za). Has maps with accommodation, restaurants and craft shops, and can point you to other activities in the area, such as olive oil tasting or visiting the largest fig farm in South Africa. **Internet access** You'll find wi-fi at the *Lazy Lizard* (daily 7am–5pm; ☎ 023 541 1379) in Church Street which also sells Cape Nature hiking permits for exploring the Swartberg.

ACCOMMODATION

★ **Dennehof Guest House** Off Christina de Wit St, on the outskirts of town ☎ 023 541 1227, ⓦ dennehof .co.za. Five rooms – the best two with spa baths – in a homestead that is a National Monument and one of the town's top stays. Mountain-biking and hiking trips are offered by the guesthouse; you're driven up the Swartberg, and descend the terrifying 18km on your own two wheels (R250). Renting a bike for a day around town is another, more sedate option (R100). **R1060**

Karoo Lodge 66 Church St ☎ 023 541 1467 or ☎ 082 692 7736, ⓦ karoolodge.com. You'll find reasonably priced, spacious accommodation at this B&B, run by a

---

STARGAZING

The Karoo sky is heaven for astronomers due to the lack of pollution and few lights, and you get some of the southern hemisphere's sharpest views of the firmament from here. One of the most exciting things you can do in Prince Albert, if not in South Africa, is to watch the **night skies** with resident astronomer Hans Daehne (new moon only; R300 for a lecture and viewing; ☎ 072 732 2950, ⓦ astrotours.co.za). Be sure to book far in advance.

GO TO HELL

Prince Albert is one of the best places to begin a trip into **Die Hel** (also known as Hell, The Hell or Gamkaskloof), a valley that's part of the Swartberg Nature Reserve, and not on the way to anywhere. Although it doesn't look far on the map, you'll need to allow two-and-a-half hours in either direction to make the spectacular but tortuous drive into it along a dirt road. A 4WD isn't needed, but you should definitely not attempt the drive in the killing heat of December or January without air conditioning. The valley itself is 20km long and fertile, a deep cleft between the towering Swartberg Mountains, with the Gamka River running through it.

The attraction of the place is the silence, isolation and birdlife. If you don't want to go it alone, contact Lisa from *Onse Rus* B&B (see below), who organizes tours, for a minimum of two people. You can get picked up if you want to hike a section of the road (4–12km), instead of driving it.

There's **accommodation** here in the form of spick-and-span Nature Conservation camping and cottages (camping R220; cottage R520; ☎021 483 0190, ⓦcapenature.co.za/reserves /swartberg-nature-reserve), and a restaurant (daily 7am–8pm), which serves good home-cooking and will make up picnic baskets. The restaurant owner, Annetje Joubert, also offers self-catering and camping accommodation and runs informal historical tours (camping R200, cottage R250/person; tours R50; ☎023 541 1107, ⓦgamkaskloof.co.za) about the area, which was only opened up to road transport in 1962; the valley still has no electricity supply, petrol, ATMs, cell phone reception or shops.

18

hospitable couple. Each of the suites, complete with pure cotton sheets and goose down duvets, leads onto the pool and garden filled with crimson bougainvillea. **R980**
Karoo Views Margrieta Prinsloo Rd ☎023 541 1929, ⓦkarooview.co.za. Upmarket, comfortable self-catering in four modern Karoo-style cottages on the edge of town with views of the Swartberg and surrounding countryside, but close enough to walk into town. **R850**
Mai's Guest House 81 Church St ☎023 541 1188, ⓦmaisbandb.co.za. A comfortable stay is offered in this

restored nineteenth-century house with great linen, a/c, a pool and lots of cats. A fabulous breakfast is served under the vines, dished up by the full-of-beans Irish owner. **R900**
★**Onse Rus** 47 Church St ☎023 541 1380, ⓦonserus .co.za. Cool, thatched B&B rooms attached to a restored Cape Dutch house, with welcoming and informed owners who serve you tea and cake on arrival, and do delicious home-made muesli and local yoghurt breakfasts, as well as the usual eggs. You can also arrange to visit their nearby farm and labyrinth during the day, for a picnic. **R950**

EATING

Café Photo Albert 44 Church St ☎023 541 1030. You can tuck into local dishes with a Swiss twist on the veranda of this café, such as Swiss pie with biltong (R70). It's also a good spot for a cup of Italian coffee with a freshly made waffle. You'll need to bring your own wine for dinner. Tues–Sun 9am–10pm.
★**Gallery Café** Church St ☎023 541 1197. Imaginative dishes by passionate chef Brent, who creates a relaxed ambience above Prince Albert Gallery, with balcony seating – the first choice for an evening in Prince Albert, and best

booked beforehand. Vegetarians and vegans are catered for, there are delightful starters, meat dishes including kudu (R110), springbok and chicken and home-made ice creams. Daily 6pm–10pm.
Ladida Coffee Shop and Farmstall At the southern end of the main road. You can sit on the veranda here and enjoy a coffee, or try the home-made ginger beer and the fig and blue cheese burger (R70). Their local olives are among the best in South Africa. Free wi-fi. Mon, Wed–Fri 8am–4pm, Sat & Sun 8am–3pm.

SHOPPING

Prince Albert is known for its **mohair products**: rugs, socks, scarves and other garments. Prince Albert Gallery (see opposite) is the best place to start looking for artworks and crafts, though there are a number of smaller shops on Church Street.

Gay's Guernsey Dairy Christina de Wit St ☎023 541 1274, ⓦgaysguernseydairy.yolasite.com. Award-winning home-made cheeses which you can taste before buying, as well as yoghurts and cream. If you're travelling with children, take them to watch the milking at sunrise, and walk around the farm. Mon–Fri 7–9am, 10am–noon

& 4–6pm, Sat & Sun 7–10am & 4.30–6pm.
Karoo Looms 55 Church St ☎023 541 1363, ⓦkarooweavery.co.za. The best place for mohair carpets and rugs with bright, funky designs. Also look out for cotton bath-mats off the looms. Mon–Fri 9am–5pm, Sat 9am–1pm.

CITY HALL, PORT ELIZABETH

Port Elizabeth, Addo and the private reserves

Port Elizabeth, the Eastern Cape's commercial and industrial centre, is for many visitors a place to start or end a trip along the Garden Route. On the western end of Nelson Mandela Bay (formerly Algoa Bay), the city is the transport hub of the Eastern Cape, well served by flights, trains, buses and car rental companies. Around an hour's drive inland is Port Elizabeth's biggest draw, Addo Elephant Park, the closest Big Five reserve to Cape Town, with virtually guaranteed sightings of elephants, and a good prospect of seeing other big game.

Port Elizabeth

As a city, **PORT ELIZABETH** (always referred to as **PE**) is pretty functional and easy enough to navigate. The industrial feel is mitigated by excellent and safe beaches, and beautiful **coastal walks** a few kilometres from town and in the small **historical centre**. A couple of classically pretty rows of Victorian terraces still remain in the **Central** suburb on the hill above the bay, but most of the decent accommodation and eating options are in the beachfront suburbs of **Humewood** and **Summerstrand**.

Port Elizabeth's **city centre** is marred by a network of freeways that cuts a swath across the south of town, blocking off the city from the harbour. The city's white population retreated to the suburbs some time ago, leaving the centre to African traders and township shoppers. The **suburbs** offer little to draw you away from the beachfront, unless you're a shopaholic, in which case you should make a beeline for **Newton Park**, 5km west of the centre and home to the shopping malls of **Greenacres** and **The Bridge**.

Central suburb

The city's main street, which runs parallel to the freeway as it sweeps into town, has been renamed **Govan Mbeki Avenue** in honour of the veteran activist (father of Thabo Mbeki, South Africa's former president), who died in 2001. African traders dealing a pretty standard selection of crochet and leather goods line up along the pavements giving the precinct a lively feel, but it's not safe after dark. The symbolic heart of town is the **City Hall**, standing in **Market Square**, a large empty space surrounded by some striking mid-Victorian buildings. But the dejection of the quarter, under the grimy shadow of a flyover, conspires against it ever pumping any real life into the district.

19

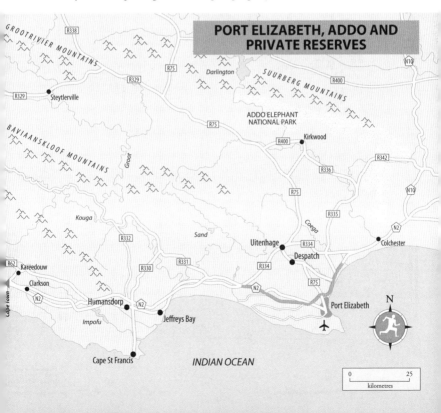

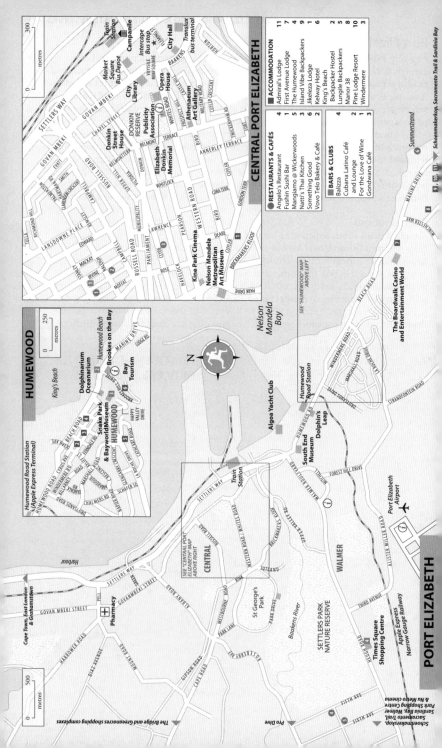

CENTRAL PORT ELIZABETH

ACCOMMODATION
Admiral's Lodge	11
First Avenue Lodge	7
The Humewood	4
Island Vibe Backpackers	9
Jikeleza Lodge	6
Kelway Hotel	1
King's Beach	6
Backpacker Hostel	2
Lungile Backpackers	5
Manor 38	8
Pine Lodge Resort	10
Windermere	3

RESTAURANTS & CAFÉS
Angelo's Restaurant	4
Fushin Sushi Bar	1
Mangiamo @ Wickerwoods	4
Natti's Thai Kitchen	3
Something Good	6
Vovo Telo Bakery & Café	2

BARS & CLUBS
Balizza	4
Cubana Latino Café and Lounge	5
For the Love of Wine	1
Gondwana Café	3

HUMEWOOD

PORT ELIZABETH

Donkin Street

Heading west up hilly **Donkin Street**, you'll come upon a curious stone pyramid commemorating **Elizabeth Donkin**, after whom PE was named. Elizabeth was the young wife of the Cape's acting governor in 1820, Sir Rufane Donkin; she died of fever in India in 1818. As you stroll up Donkin Street, you could be forgiven for thinking you were in the wrong country, the wrong continent – the raked terrace of Victorian double-storey houses would look completely at home in any town on England's south coast. The nineteen **Donkin Houses**, built in the mid-nineteenth century and declared National Monuments in 1967, reflect the desire of the English settlers to create a home from home in this strange, desiccated land.

Nelson Mandela Metropolitan Art Museum

1 Park Drive • Mon–Fri 8.30am–5pm, Sat & Sun 1–5pm • Free

The **Nelson Mandela Metropolitan Art Museum**, situated in two buildings framing the entrance to St George's Park, has a collection of contemporary local work, visiting exhibitions and a small shop selling postcards and local arts and crafts. Their Eastern Cape art section is the thing to aim for, though they do have some minor European and oriental artworks.

South End Museum

Cnr Humewood Rd and Walmer Boulevard • Mon–Fri 9am–4pm, Sat & Sun 1–3pm • Free

Based in the old Seamen's Institute, the **South End Museum** is worth a visit, recalling the bygone days of the South End, a vibrant multicultural neighbourhood whose growth had much to do with PE's then booming harbour. As a result of the Group Areas Act it was razed street by street in the 1960s, save for a handful of churches and mosques. Today, the area is full of pricey townhouses.

The beachfront and around

PE's **beaches** are its main attraction. The beachfront strip, divided from the harbour by a large wall, starts at wide **King's Beach**, somewhat marred by a jumble of coal heaps and oil tanks behind it. To the southeast lies **Humewood Beach**, across the road from which is a complex housing the **Bayworld Museum and Snake Park** (daily 9am–4.30pm; R35; snake interaction daily noon; seal and penguin talks 11am & 3pm; Ⓦ bayworld .co.za), a research and education centre where you can visit the snake park, and see seals and penguins in the Oceanarium. Brookes on the Bay and **Dolphin's Leap** nearby are complexes of restaurants, pubs and clubs with great views.

Beyond, to the south, **Hobie Beach** and **Summerstrand** are great for walking and sunbathing. Summerstrand's mammoth **Boardwalk Casino Complex** (Ⓦ suninternational .com/boardwalk) houses a casino, places to eat and shop, and a cinema, plus adventure golf and ten-pin bowling, among other things.

Marine Drive continues 15km down the coast from here to the village of **Schoenmakerskop** ("Schoenies" to the locals), along an impressive coastline that alternates between rocky shores and sandy beaches. From here you can walk the

19

THE ART IN MADIBA'S STEPS

Art Route 67 (Ⓦ mbda.co.za/route67.html) is a walk that incorporates 67 works of art by artists from the Eastern Cape, which commemorate Madiba's 67 years of fighting for democracy. The art ranges from small tile mosaics and vinyl street stickers to metal installations and towering sculptures. The route starts at the 52m-high Campanile Bell Tower (Strand St, Central; Tues–Sun 9am–12:30pm & 1–2pm), which offers views of the harbour and surrounds from the top; from here, the route continues to Vuyisile Mini Square and up the staircase at St Mary's Terrace, to meander through the Donkin Reserve, before reaching a triumphal end at the gigantic flag on top of Donkin Hill.

eight-kilometre **Sacramento Trail**, a shoreline path that leads to the huge-duned **Sardinia Bay**, the wildest and most dramatic stretch of coast in the area. To get to Sardinia Bay by road, turn right at the Schoenmakerskop intersection and follow the road until Sardinia Bay is signposted on the left.

ARRIVAL AND DEPARTURE   PORT ELIZABETH

BY PLANE
Port Elizabeth's airport is conveniently situated on the edge of Walmer suburb, 4km south of the city centre, and served by kulula (☎0861 585 852, ⓦkulula.com), SAA (☎041 507 1111, ⓦflyssaa.com) and Mango (☎086 100 1234, ⓦflymango.com). Taxis rank outside the airport and the major car rental companies are here too. Destinations: Cape Town (daily; 1hr 15min); Durban (3 daily; 1hr 15min); Johannesburg (6–7 daily; 1hr 35min).

BY TRAIN
The train station (☎041 507 2662) is centrally located on the Strand. The Shosholoza Meyl (ⓦshosholozameyl.co.za) connects Johannesburg to PE (Mon, Wed & Sun; 20hr 35min). You will need to arrange to be met by your hotel or a taxi (see below) beforehand, as this downtown area is prone to crime.

BY BUS
Intercity buses Greyhound, Intercape and Translux buses stop at Greenacres shopping mall in Newton Park suburb, 3km from the centre; it's best to arrange to be met here by your accommodation, though there are waiting taxis during business hours (see below). Leaving PE, buses stop at every major town along the Garden Route to Cape Town, and also head east to Mthatha and Durban.
Destinations: Cape Town (6–7 daily; 12hr); Durban (daily; 12hr 30min); Johannesburg (daily; 14hr 30min); Knysna (daily; 5hr), Mthatha (daily; 8hr 50min).
Baz Bus The Baz Bus will drop you off at any central location or accommodation.

INFORMATION

Tourist offices The Nelson Mandela Bay Tourism head office (Mon–Fri 8am–4.30pm; ☎041 582 2575, ⓦnmbt.co.za) is on the corner of Mitchell Street and Walmer Boulevard, South End. There are also offices at the airport (daily 7am–7pm; ☎041 581 0456); Shop 48 at the Boardwalk, Marine Drive, Summerstrand (daily 8am–7pm; ☎041 583 2030); and Donkin Reserve Lighthouse Building, Belmont Terrace, Central (Mon–Fri 8am–4.30pm, Sat 8am–3pm; ☎041 585 8884).

ACTIVITIES

Horseriding Heavenly Stables (431 Sardinia Bay Rd; ☎082 420 8855; R250/hr) offers riding on the huge beach for both beginners and experienced riders.
Sea cruises Raggy Charters (☎073 152 2277, ⓦraggycharters.co.za; R900) run cruises from PE Harbour at the Algoa Yacht Club, with opportunities to see the massive penguin colony at St Croix Island, dolphins and humpback and southern right whales (July–Nov).
Watersports Although the ocean around PE is not tropically clear and warm, the diving is good, especially for soft corals, and there is the chance of diving with Ragged Tooth Sharks. Pro Dive, 189 Main Rd, Walmer (☎041 581 1144, ⓦprodive.co.za), offer diving, snorkelling, kiteboarding, stand-up paddling, kayaking and dive courses.

GETTING AROUND

Taxis PE's minibus taxis run regularly from town to the beachfront, but are the least recommended way to travel. There are some metered taxis about, but it's better to arrange transport beforehand; try Hurter Cabs (☎041 585 5500) or King Cab (☎041 368 5559).
Tours It's possible to explore Central on foot – the tourist office (see above) can provide a map for the self-guided Heritage Walk. The best way to see the city, however, is on one of the excellent bus tours, which shed light on the culture and history of a city shaped by layers of political history. Calabash Tours (☎041 585 6162, ⓦcalabashtours .co.za) is one of the best and operates "Real City Tours" by day (R550) and *shebeen* tours by night, as well as trips to Addo.

ACCOMMODATION

The obvious place to stay is the **beachfront**, with a wide choice of hotels, self-catering suites and B&Bs. During the December and January peak holiday period the beachfront becomes the focus for most of the city's action, while February, March and April are much quieter yet offer perfect beach weather.

Admiral's Lodge 47 Admiralty Way, Summerstrand ☎041 583 1894 or ☎083 455 2072, ⓦadmiralslodge .co.za. Spacious and stylish rooms at a good B&B situated at the far end of Summerstrand, roughly 7km from the centre; airport transfers are available. There's a braai area, communal lounge, pool and a trampoline for the kids. R880

First Avenue Lodge 3 First Ave, Summerstrand ☎ 041 583 5173, ⓦ firstavenuelodge.co.za. Sixteen en-suite rooms close to the beach with their own entrances, offered on a B&B or self-catering basis, in a popular and pleasant establishment with a lawn pool and chilling-out area. R900

The Humewood 33 Beach Rd, Humewood ☎ 041 585 8961, ⓦ humewoodhotel.co.za. A large, old-fashioned hotel with more than a nostalgic hint of 1950s family seaside holidays. The rooms are large and feature wicker furniture and older-style floral prints. Service is excellent and includes laundry facilities and babysitting. There's a good bar and sun deck. Airport transfers available. R980

★**Island Vibe Backpackers** 4 Jenvey Rd, Summerstrand ☎ 041 583 1256, ⓦ islandvibe.co.za. Ideal for backpackers wanting more creature comforts without sacrificing the social atmosphere. An appealing location near the beach and nightlife spots, offering four-bed dorms with wooden bunks, as well as doubles, plus a swimming pool, jacuzzi, free wi-fi, pool table and ping pong table. Dorm R160, double R550

Jikeleza Lodge 44 Cuyler St, Central ☎ 041 586 3721, ⓦ highwinds.co.za. Friendly backpacker place, recently renovated with dorms, doubles and a family room. Its adventure centre, High Winds, can help you sort out tour and travel bookings; they do tours around Addo, as well as recommended combo tours to Addo and *Schotia* for the evening or overnight. Dorm R120, double R300

Kelway Hotel Brookes Hill Drive, Humewood ☎ 041 584 0638, ⓦ thekelway.co.za. Stylish hotel kitted out with timber panelling, seagrass chairs and handcrafted wooden tables. The pool area, swathed in green and with a natural rock wall, wooden decking and sun beds overlooking the sea, is lovely. Standard, luxury and family rooms are available, and breakfast is included. R1380

King's Beach Backpacker Hostel 41 Windermere Rd, Humewood ☎ 041 585 8113, ⓦ kingsbeachbackpackers .wozaonline.co.za. Spotless, slightly out-dated, well-established hostel, a block away from the beach, with camping facilities, dorms and double rooms, plus an outside bar and braai area. Although principally for self-catering, it lays on tea, coffee, bread and jams in the morning. The travel desk can book township and game park tours among others. Camping R70, dorm R130, double R380

Lungile Backpackers 12 La Roche Drive, Summerstrand ☎ 041 582 2042, ⓦ lungilebackpackers .co.za. Large and popular beachfront hostel with a sociable party vibe, situated in the heart of PE's nightlife strip. Perched on a hill, it has facilities for camping and a large lawn to relax on, twin rooms by the swimming pool and dorms inside the main house. Camping R90, dorm R130, double R480

Manor 38 38 Brighton Drive, Summerstrand ☎ 083 270 7771, ⓦ manorcollection.co.za. New, modern, sparklingly clean boutique hotel in an excellent location close to Summerstrand and the Boardwalk. There's a lovely pool area with sun beds, and two communal lounge areas. R1320

Pine Lodge Resort Off Marine Drive, Humewood ☎ 041 583 4004, ⓦ pinelodge.co.za. Right on the beach near the wonderful historic lighthouse and next to the Cape Recife Nature Reserve, where owls, mongooses and antelope make appearances. Accommodation is in excellent-value self-catering log cabins, some of which sleep up to eight. There's a popular bar and restaurant, and the lodge also boasts a swimming pool, gym and a games room. R875

Windermere 35 Humewood Rd, Humewood ☎ 041 582 2245, ⓦ thewindermere.co.za. Stylish hotel with just nine suites, given an almost Zen-like feel through the subtle use of off-white to oatmeal tones contrasted with dark, chocolatey hues and timber and granite surfaces. Full hotel facilities are available including a plunge pool, bar, laundry and secure parking. It's worth noting that the rooms with sea views don't have a higher price tag, so ask for one of those. R1900

19

EATING

The best area to trawl, both during the day and night, for an alfresco meal, rejuvenating coffee or tasty sandwich is **Richmond Hill**, close to Central, where the Art Deco and Victorian buildings give a historical feel, offsetting the overall industrial and bland, functional quality of PE. Another obvious choice in a seaside town for having a meal or drink is along the **beachfront**.

Angelo's Restaurant 45 Sixth Avenue, Walmer ☎ 041 501 2899; Marine Drive, Summerstrand ☎ 041 583 5862. An institution in PE, these two local Italian restaurants have different decor but come under the same name. Lunch meals including large pastas are excellent value for money (R50), although be prepared to wait, as *Angelo's* is popular and known for its slow service. Daily 8am–10pm.

Fushin Sushi Bar Stanley on Bain, Richmond Hill ☎ 082 865 2707. Sit at the long counter for the most delicious sushi in town, as well as salads (R70) and Eastern-influenced tapas-style small dishes. The next-door *Soho Fushin Lounge* stays open till midnight. Daily noon–10pm.

Mangiamo @ Wickerwoods 50 Sixth Avenue, Walmer ☎ 041 581 1107 or ☎ 082 900 0777. You can't go wrong with dinner at this welcoming, shabby, Italian pizzeria, which many locals consider to be the best restaurant in PE; as well as excellent pasta (R70), they also offer pizzas and antipasti. Tues–Sat 6–11pm.

Natti's Thai Kitchen 5 Park Lane, Central ☎ 041 373 2763. Unfailingly great restaurant, which has been going for years, serving reasonably priced, authentic Thai cuisine (average mains R75) in a relaxed atmosphere, with a BYO alcohol policy. Mon–Sat 6.30pm till late.

★**Something Good** Marine Drive ☎ 041 583 6986. Stripped-down surfer bar on the beachfront, where you can get pizzas, burgers, gourmet foot-long sandwiches (R60) and other classic roadhouse meals, served on a deck

humming with people and with a beautiful view of the sea. Mon–Sun 7am–11pm.

Vovo Telo Bakery and Café 16 Raleigh St, Richmond Hill ☎ 041 585 5606. This is a great place for breakfast and lunch, with Italian and French breads and pastries (R35), real coffee and veranda seating. Mon–Sat 7.30am–3pm.

DRINKING AND NIGHTLIFE

Balizza Times Square Shopping Centre, cnr Heugh Rd & 5th Ave, Walmer. This sprawling nightclub complex houses two bars, three lounges, two dancefloors, and serves up a range of cocktails and shooters. The DJs mix recent house anthems and oldies, and you're likely to have a good night out here (beer R18). Mon–Sun 11am–2am.

Cubaña Latino Caffè and Lounge 49 Beach Rd, Humewood ☎ 041 582 5282. A café during the day, and a lounge at night, offering a large cocktail menu (R50), Cuban music and DJ on the weekends, and an outside deck from which to watch the sea. Smart-casual dress code in the evenings (no trainers or shorts). Mon–Wed & Sun

8am–midnight, Thurs 8am–2am, Fri & Sat 8am–4am.
For the Love Of Wine 1st Floor, 20 Stanley St, Richmond Hill ☎ 072 566 2692. This smart, compact bar is situated on the first floor with a wraparound balcony that overlooks Stanley St. Despite being PE's only wine bar for the discerning, it is not overpriced and the selection is broad (from R35). Tues–Sat 1–10pm.

Gondwana Café 2 Dolphin's Leap, Main Rd, Humewood. This place is great fun; a relaxed, racially mixed restaurant by day that doubles up as a club by night, plus there's jazz on Sunday afternoons (spirits from R38). Tues–Sun 9am till late.

DIRECTORY

Cinema Kine Park Cinema, 3 Rink St; Nu Metro, Walmer Park Shopping Centre, Main Rd between 14th and 16th Sts, Walmer.

Foreign exchange American Express Foreign Exchange, Boardwalk Casino Complex (☎ 041 583 2025), Mon–Fri 8am–10pm, Sat & Sun 10am–2pm.

Hospitals St George's (private), 40 Park Drive, Settlers Park (☎ 041 392 6111).

Pharmacy Mount Road Pharmacy, 559 Govan Mbeki Ave (daily 8.15am–11pm; ☎ 041 484 3838).

Post office 259 Govan Mbeki Avenue (Mon–Fri 8am–5pm & Sat 8.30–1am; ☎ 041 508 4039).

Addo Elephant National Park

73km northeast of Port Elizabeth • Daily 7am–7pm • R216 • ⓦ addoelephantpark.com

Home to the Big Five, but best known for its hundreds of pachyderms, **Addo Elephant National Park** is close enough to Port Elizabeth to be visited on a day-trip, though a couple of nights spent here are undoubtedly more rewarding.

You can drive around Addo yourself, but if you want to be taken around in open-topped Land Rovers and given a luxury safari experience, stay in one of the nearby **private reserves** (see p.248). Another highly enjoyable way to roam the park is from atop a horse or elephant (see box, p.247).

CALL OF THE WILD

With an expansion programme under way that will see it become one of South Africa's three largest game reserves, and the only one to include coastline, Addo's PR people are now talking in terms of a "Big Seven" reserve, as the denizens of the future coastal section (adjoining the Alexandra State Forest/Woody Cape section of the park) include **whales** and **great white sharks**. **Elephants** remain Addo's most obvious drawing card, but with the reintroduction in 2003 of a small number of **lions**, in two prides (big cats last roamed here over a century ago), as well as the presence of the rest of the Big Five – **buffalo**, **hippos** and **leopards** – it has become a game reserve to be reckoned with. **Spotted hyenas** were also introduced in 2003 as part of a programme to re-establish predators in the local ecosystem. Other species to look out for include **cheetah**, **black rhino**, **eland**, **kudu**, **warthog**, **ostrich** and **red hartebeest**.

One big attraction of Addo and these private reserves is that, unlike the country's other major game parks, they benefit from the fact that the Eastern Cape is **malaria-free**. And if you've driven out this way along the Garden Route and don't fancy heading back exactly the way you came, you've the option of returning to Cape Town via the inland **Route 62** (covered in Chapter 18), branching off the N2 not far west of Port Elizabeth.

Wildlife-watching

The Addo bush is thick, dry and prickly, making it difficult sometimes to spot any of the 450 or so elephants and other game; when you do, though, it's often thrillingly close up. The best strategy is to ask where the pachyderms and the other four of the Big Five have last been seen (enquire with staff at the park reception), and also to head for the waterhole in front of the restaurant to scan the bush for large grey backs quietly moving about. The best way, though, is to go on a **guided game drive** in an open vehicle with a knowledgeable national parks driver.

19

ARRIVAL AND DEPARTURE   ADDO ELEPHANT NATIONAL PARK

By car Addo's southern gate is accessed off the N2 at the village of Colchester, 43km northeast of Port Elizabeth; the gate is about 5km from *Mathyolweni Camp*. To get to *Main Camp*, north of *Mathyolweni*, take a slow, scenic drive through the park from the southern gate, which will take at least an hour, or use the R335 that runs outside the western flank – take the N2 from Port Elizabeth east towards Grahamstown for 5km, branching off at the Addo/Motherwell/Markman signpost onto the R335 through

Addo village. The R335 is also the way to reach the majority of accommodation outside the park. The Zuurberg section is reached by taking a turn-off marked "Zuurberg" 1km before you reach *Main Camp*, and travelling for 21km along a good gravel road; this is the way to *Narina Bush Camp* and the Zuurberg horse trails. The network of roads within the section of the park between *Main Camp* and *Mathyolweni* is untarred, but in good condition.

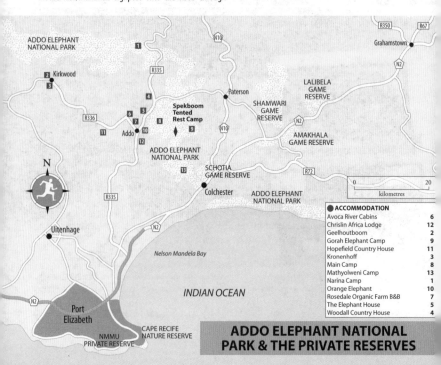

ACCOMMODATION

Avoca River Cabins	6
Chrislin Africa Lodge	12
Geelhoutboom	2
Gorah Elephant Camp	9
Hopefield Country House	11
Kronenhoff	3
Main Camp	8
Mathyolweni Camp	13
Narina Camp	1
Orange Elephant	10
Rosedale Organic Farm B&B	7
The Elephant House	5
Woodall Country House	4

ADDO ELEPHANT NATIONAL PARK & THE PRIVATE RESERVES

HORSE AND ELEPHANT RIDES

A number of interesting escorted **horse rides** are on offer in Addo. Experienced riders can head into the Nyathi area, home to the Big Five, on two-hour tours (8.30am & 2pm; R265) – though note that trails are liable to change depending on animal behaviour. Both novices and more experienced riders can explore the beautiful Zuurberg section, 21km beyond *Main Camp* (2–3 daily; beginners R180, experienced riders R255) – don't expect to see much game here, though the mountain and steep river valley scenery is beautiful (you'll need a head for heights on the longer trails). The full-day ride (9am; R275) is particularly worthwhile, and a two-day ride that overnights at *Narina Bush Camp* (R450) is also available. Advance booking for all horse rides is required (☎042 233 8657).

Elephant-back safaris are operated from a farm abutting the northern boundary of Addo (3 daily; ☎041 585 1150, ✺addoelephantbacksafaris.co.za), off the R335, and cost R975 per person.

INFORMATION AND TOURS

Maps of the park are available at reception and indicate the location of picnic and braai sites.

Eating The restaurant at *Main Camp* is open for three meals a day (daily 7:30am–10pm), while the shop is well stocked with food and drink.

Guided tours can be booked in advance at *Main Camp* or on the park's website. Two-hour guided game drives leave throughout the day and cost R280/person for day-drives,

R330/person for sunset trips (including snacks and drinks), and R310/person for night drives. The vehicles used are higher off the ground than a normal sedan to improve viewing opportunities. In PE, Calabash Tours (see p.242) run day-trips here, as do most of the backpacker hostels.

Hop-on guide You can hire the exclusive services of a hop-on guide (R180) who joins you in your own car for two hours and will direct you to where you will find game.

ACCOMMODATION INSIDE THE PARK

Bear in mind that **reservations** are essential in high season, through SANParks (☎012 428 9111, ✺addoelephantpark .com), or can be made directly with Addo if it's less than 72 hours in advance (☎042 233 8600). There are few villages in the area, so stock up on self-catering supplies in PE or Colchester.

Main Camp ☎012 428 9111, ✺addoelephantpark .com. The oldest and largest of the National Parks camps. In addition to camping facilities, there are forest cabins that sleep two people and share cooking facilities in communal kitchens, and more luxurious two-person chalets (R925) with their own kitchenettes. Some units sleep up to four people (minimum charge is for two occupants). The cheapest accommodation available is in well-designed, spacious safari tents, perfect during the summer months, with decks right next to the perimeter fence. Camping R260, safari tent R700, forest cabin R800, chalet R925

Mathyolweni Camp ☎012 428 9111, ✺addoelephant park.com. National Parks accommodation in a dozen fully equipped self-catering chalets with showers, each sleeping two. The chalets are set in a secluded valley surrounded by thicket that supports a wealth of birdlife and have nice

viewing decks. There is no restaurant, so bring food from PE or Colchester. R1300

Narina Camp ☎012 428 9111, ✺addoelephantpark .com. A small, very attractive National Parks bush camp in the mountainous Zuurberg section, comprising four safari tents that sleep four people and share ablution and cooking facilities; there is no restaurant here, so bring your own provisions. R1150

★**Spekboom Tented Rest Camp** ☎012 428 9111, ✺addoelephantpark.com. The newest and most rustic of the National Parks accommodation, consisting of five fixed tents on decks with twin beds. Each tent is equipped with camp chairs, a table and solar light, with communal showers and toilet within short walking distance. There is no electricity, so you'll need to bring torches; barbecue facilities and a communal gas fridge and stove plates are available. R670

ACCOMMODATION JUST OUTSIDE THE PARK

Outside the park, but within easy striking distance, you'll find an abundance of private B&Bs and guesthouses, especially among the citrus groves of the Sundays River Valley. Many offer day and night drives in the game reserve.

Avoca River Cabins 13km northwest of Addo village on the R336 ☎082 677 9920, ✺avocarivercabins.co.za. Reasonably priced B&B and self-catering accommodation on a farm in the Sundays River Valley. The range of

self-catering spans from budget cabins (four- and five-sleeper) to more comfortable thatched huts (some on the banks of the river); there is a swimming pool, some pleasant walks to be had on the farm, plus a zip line and treetop course for kids, and canoes are available to rent. Five-sleeper cabin R600

Chrislin Africa Lodge 12km south of Addo main gate, off the R336 ☎042 233 0022 or ☎082 783 3553, ⓦchrislin.co.za. Quirky B&B with thatched huts built using traditional Xhosa construction techniques, a lovely *lapa* (courtyard) and pool, and hearty country breakfasts, as well as dinners on request. R1100

★ **The Elephant House** 5km north of Addo village on the R335 ☎042 233 2462 or ☎083 799 5671, ⓦelephanthouse.co.za. Just minutes from Addo is one of the Eastern Cape's top places to stay, a stunning thatch-roofed lodge filled with Persian rugs and antique furniture that perfectly balances luxury with a supremely relaxed atmosphere. The eight bedrooms and six garden cottages open onto a lawned courtyard. Candlelit dinners are available, as are game drives (R800/person) into Addo and the surrounding reserves. R2800

Geelhoutboom 26 Market St, Kirkwood ☎042 230 1191, ⓦgeelhoutboom.co.za. A great value and homely B&B in the shade of a large yellowwood tree, with a/c rooms, just a 20min drive from Addo main gate. R800

Gorah Elephant Camp 9km west along the Addo Heights Rd leading from the N10 to Addo village ☎044 501 1111, ⓦgorah.hunterhotels.com. Ultra-luxurious outfit based around a Victorian homestead decked out with the appropriate paraphernalia including mounted antelope skulls above the fireplace and evocative African landscapes, and accompanied by a beautifully landscaped swimming pool. The suites are plush and there are opportunities to dine under the stars; meals are included in the price, as are game drives. Hefty low-season discounts are available. R13430

Hopefield Country House 20km southwest of Addo main gate ☎042 234 0333, ⓦhopefield.co.za. An atmospheric 1930s farmhouse set in beautiful English-style gardens on a citrus farm. The five bedrooms are imaginatively furnished with period pieces in a style the owners (a pair of classical musicians who occasionally give impromptu concerts for guests) describe as "farmhouse eclectic". R1200

Kronenhoff On the R336 as you enter Kirkwood ☎042 230 1448, ⓦkronenhoff.co.za. Situated in a small farming town, this is a hospitable, high-ceilinged Cape Dutch-style home, with spacious suites, polished wooden floors, large leather sofas and a sociable pub. In summer the sweet scent of orange blossom carries from the surrounding citrus groves. R1140

Orange Elephant On the R335, 8km from the National Park gate ☎042 233 0023, ⓦaddobackpackers.com. Budget accommodation at a comfortable hostel, whose management will help you organize outings into the surrounding game reserves – an Addo half-day tour starts from R650, and a full-day, including a braai in the park, costs R1000. The lively bar is well known for its large portions of pub grub. Dorm R120, double R300

★ **Rosedale Organic Farm B&B** On the R335, 1km north of Addo village ☎083 329 8775, ⓦrosedalebnb .co.za. Very reasonably priced accommodation in eight cottages on a certified organic farm that exports citrus fruits to the EU. Hosts Keith and Nondumiso Finnemore are seriously committed to sustainable farming and tourism – water for the cottages is solar-heated, and you'll get organic oranges and juice for breakfast. Keith offers a free one-hour walking tour of the farm to guests, on which you can get all those nagging questions about the state of the world's food industry answered. There is also a kitchen available for guests to self-cater. R800

Woodall Country House About 1km west of Addo main gate ☎042 233 0128, ⓦwoodall-addo.co.za. Excellent luxury guesthouse on a working citrus farm with eleven self-contained suites and rooms. There's a swimming pool, gymnasium and spa and sauna (massages are available, and there's a resident beautician). A lovely sundowner deck overlooks a small lake full of swans and other waterfowl. Renowned for its outstanding country cuisine, its restaurant offers three- to six-course dinners. R2750

The Eastern Cape's private game reserves

Although driving through Addo can be extremely rewarding, nothing beats getting into the wild in an open vehicle with a trained guide – something the private reserves excel at. If you want the works – game drives, outstanding food, uncompromising luxury and excellent accommodation, you'll find it at top-ranking **Shamwari**, with prices rising over R5000 per person a day. If you're in this league it's also worth considering **Kwandwe Game Reserve**, another outstanding safari destination in the Eastern Cape, near Grahamstown.

If you're on a tighter budget or pushed for time, a good option is one of the full-day safaris offered by **Amakhala** (R980/person; see opposite). Accommodation rates are listed as the cheapest for two people in high season, although specials and season variations may be available.

THE PRIVATE RESERVES

Amakhala Game Reserve 67km north of Port Elizabeth on the N2 ☎041 581 0993, ⓦamakhala .co.za. A fantastic, family-friendly reserve stocked with the Big Five as well as cheetah, giraffe, zebra, wildebeest and antelope. The Bushman's River meanders through the reserve allowing for canoe safaris and riverboat sundowner cruises. Safaris for day-visitors must be booked in advance and include two game drives, a river cruise and lunch (R980). All accommodation comprises fabulous views, whether the farmhouse lodges or the camp with beds fashioned from restored ox wagons. R5000

★**Kwandwe Private Game Reserve** On the R67, 34km north of Grahamstown and 160km from Port Elizabeth ☎046 603 3400, ⓦkwandwereserve.com. This is the Eastern Cape's top wildlife destination, with 30km of Fish River frontage and the Big Five in attendance. Apart from twice-a-day game drives, *Kwandwe's* safari activities include guided river walks, canoeing on the Great Fish, rhino tracking and fascinating cultural tours with a resident historian. Children are well catered for with family game drives, bush walks, fishing and frog safaris. There are four lodges, ranging from a quintessential luxury thatched lodge to a stunning boutique-hotel-in-the-bush ingeniously designed with glass walls for panoramic views of the terrain. R11000

Lalibela Game Reserve 90km northeast of Port Elizabeth on the N2 to Grahamstown ☎041 581 8170, ⓦlalibela.co.za. An excellent luxury choice, *Lalibela Game Reserve* is home to the Big Five and diverse flora and fauna. Safaris are included in the accommodation rate, along with all meals and drinks – you can dine on terrific Eastern Cape food and contemporary cuisine. There are three fabulous lodges with private viewing decks, swimming pools and

bomas to choose from, and they also offer an African drumming and dancing session. R9000

Schotia Game Reserve On the eastern flank of Addo ☎042 235 1436, ⓦschotiasafaris.co.za. *Schotia* is the smallest and the busiest of the private reserves, on account of the excellent value it offers. Although not (quite) a Big Five reserve, it's really only missing elephants. Day-visitors can arrange to be collected from Port Elizabeth or anywhere in the Addo vicinity; full-day safaris (R2000/person) involve a game drive through Addo and an evening game drive with lunch and dinner thrown in. If you're pushed for time or money you can opt for the afternoon game drive (R1000/person). An overnight stay here is the cheapest among the private reserves; rates include a room in one of three bush lodges or eight double rooms plus game drives into Addo and there are big low-season discounts. You pay even less if you don't go into Addo, but it would be a travesty to miss the elephants. R4000

Shamwari Game Reserve 65km north of Port Elizabeth on the N2 ☎041 509 3000, ⓦshamwari.com. The largest and best known of the private reserves, *Shamwari* has cultivated a jetsetter fan base, hosting such celebrities as Tiger Woods and John Travolta. In 2011 it won the World's Leading Safari and Game Reserve Award at the World Travel Awards (tourism's Oscars) for the fourteenth year running and in 2013, won the award for the World's Leading Eco-Lodge. The accolades are justified in the reserve's diverse landscapes, requisite animals and high standards of game-viewing. Accommodation is in colonial-style, family-friendly *Long Lee Manor* or attractive (child-unfriendly) lodges and tented camps, furnished with every conceivable comfort. R9720

19

Contexts

History

Cape Town's history is complex and what follows is only a brief account of major events in the city's past. For more detailed coverage on both Cape Town's and South Africa's history in general, see the list in "Books".

Hunters and herders

Rock art provides evidence of human culture in the Western Cape dating back nearly 30,000 years. The artists were **nomadic** hunter-gatherers, known most commonly as **San**, a relatively modern term from the Nama language with roots in the concept of "inhabiting or dwelling", to reflect the fact that these were South Africa's aboriginals. At one time, they probably spread throughout sub-Saharan Africa, after pretty well perfecting their hunting and gathering, leaving them considerable time for artistic and religious pursuits. People lived in small, loosely connected bands comprising family units and were free to leave and join up with other groups.

About two thousand years ago, this changed when some groups in territory north of modern South Africa laid their hands on fat-tailed sheep and cattle from northern Africa, thus transforming themselves into **herding communities**, known as **Khoikhoi** or simply Khoi. The introduction of livestock had a revolutionary effect on social organization and introduced the idea of ownership and accumulation. Social divisions developed, and political units, which centred around a chief, became larger.

The Cape goes Dutch

Portuguese mariners, under the command of **Bartolomeu Dias**, first rounded the Cape in the 1480s, and named it Cabo de Boa Esperanza, the **Cape of Good Hope**. Marking their progress, they left an unpleasant set of calling cards all along the coast – slaves they had captured in West Africa and had cast ashore to trumpet the power and glory of Portugal with the aim of intimidating the locals. Little wonder then, that the first encounter of the Portuguese with the indigenous Khoikhoi along the Garden Route coast was not a happy one. It began with a group of Khoikhoi stoning the Portuguese for taking water from a spring without asking permission, and ended with a Khoikhoi man lying dead with a crossbow bolt through his chest.

It was another 170 years before any European settlement was established in South Africa. In 1652, a group of white employees of the **Dutch East India Company** (Verenigde Oostindische Compagnie or **VOC**), which was engaged in trade between the Netherlands and the East Indies, pulled into Table Bay to set up a refreshment station to feed sailors on Company ships trading between Europe and the East. There were no plans at this time to set up a colony; in fact, the Cape post was given to the station commander **Jan van Riebeeck** because he had been caught with his hand in the till. Van Riebeeck dreamed up a number of schemes to keep "darkest Africa" at bay, including the very Dutch solution of building a canal that would cut the Cape Peninsula adrift. In the end he had to satisfy himself with planting a **bitter almond**

30,000 years ago	2000 years ago	1652 AD
Hunter-gatherers occupy Cape Peninsula	Khoikhoi herders with fat-tailed sheep migrate from the north	Dutch East India Company establishes supply station for trade ships sailing to Indies

hedge (still growing in Cape Town's Kirstenbosch Gardens) to keep the natives at arm's length.

Despite Van Riebeeck's view that the indigenous Khoikhoi were "a savage set, living without conscience", the Dutch were dependent on them to provide livestock, which were traded for trinkets. As the settlement developed, Van Riebeeck needed more **labour** to keep it going, and bemoaned the fact that he was unsuccessful in persuading the Khoikhoi to discard the freedom of their herding life to work for him. Much to his annoyance, the bosses in Holland had forbidden Van Riebeeck from enslaving the locals, and refused his request for slaves from elsewhere in the Company's empire.

Creeping colonization

Everyone at the Cape at this time was under stringent contract to the VOC, which effectively had total control over all persons' activities and movements – a form of indentureship. But a number of Dutch men were released from their contracts in 1657 to farm as **free burghers** on land granted by the Company; they were now at liberty to pursue their own economic activities, although the VOC still controlled the market and set prices for produce. This annexation of the lands around the mud fort, which preceded the construction of the more solid Castle of Good Hope, ultimately led to the inexorable process of **colonization**.

The only snag was that the land granted didn't belong to the Company in the first place, and the move sparked the first of a series of **Khoikhoi–Dutch wars**. Although the first campaign ended in stalemate, the Khoikhoi were ultimately no match for the Dutch, who had the tactical mobility of horses and the superior killing power of firearms. Campaigns continued through the 1660s and 1670s and proved profitable for Dutch raiders, who on one outing in 1674 rounded up eight hundred Khoikhoi cattle and four thousand sheep.

Meanwhile, in 1658, Van Riebeeck had managed successfully to steal a shipload of **slaves** from West Africa, which whet his insatiable appetite for this form of labour. The VOC itself became the biggest slaveholders at the Cape and continued importing slaves, mostly from the East Indies, at such a pace that, by 1710, there were more slaves than burghers in the colony. With the help of this ready workforce, the embryonic Cape colony expanded outwards and trampled the peninsula's Khoikhoi, who by 1713 had lost everything. Most of their livestock (nearly fifty thousand animals) and the majority of their land west of the Hottentots Holland Mountains had been gobbled up by the VOC. Dispossession, and diseases like smallpox, previously unknown in South Africa, decimated their numbers and shattered their social system. By the middle of the eighteenth century, those who remained had been reduced to a condition of miserable servitude to the colonists.

Kaapstad

During the early eighteenth century, **slavery** became the economic backbone of the colony, which was now a rude colonial village of low, whitewashed, flat-roofed houses. Passing through in 1710, Jan van Riebeeck's granddaughter, Johanna, commented contemptuously that the settlement was "a miserable place. There is nothing pretty along the shoreline, the Castle is peculiar, the houses resemble prisons", and "one sees here peculiar people who live in strange ways".

1657	1658	1713	1795
Company releases indentured labourers to farm as free burghers	First slaves brought to settlement	Khoikhoi dispossessed of all livestock by Company and free burghers are reduced to servitude	Company goes bust and English becomes official language when British take Cape

Dutch global influence began to wane in the early 1700s, but at the same time the Cape settlement began to develop an independent identity and a little prosperity, based on its pivotal position on the European–Far East trade route. People now began referring to it as "**Kaapstad**" (Cape Town) rather than "the Cape settlement", and by 1750 it had a thousand buildings, with over three thousand diverse inhabitants. Some of these were indigenous Khoikhoi people, but the largest number were VOC employees, dominated by an elite of high-ranking Dutch-born officials. The lower rungs were filled by the poor from all over Europe, including Scandinavia, Germany, France, England, Scotland and Russia, while slaves came from East Africa, Madagascar, India and Indonesia. There was also a transient population from passing ships, which by the second half of the century were largely manned by Indian, Javanese and Chinese crews. If nothing else, the constant **maritime traffic** injected some life into this intellectual desert, which couldn't boast a single printing press, let alone a newspaper. Entertainment consisted mainly of carousing, whoring and gambling.

Britain takes the Cape

By the 1790s, the VOC was more or less bankrupt, and its control over the restive Cape burghers had become tenuous. As Dutch maritime influence declined, Britain and France were tussling for domination of the Indian Ocean. The outbreak of the French Revolution in 1789 and the establishment of a Francophile republic in the Netherlands a few years later made the **British** distinctly jittery about their strategic access to Cape Town. In August 1795, Rear Admiral George Keith Elphinstone was sent in haste with four British sloops of war to secure Cape Town; by mid-September the ragtag Dutch garrison had capitulated.

The British occupation heralded a period of **free trade** in which exports from the Cape multiplied, as tariffs were slashed, with the result that Cape wines, the largest Cape export, were meeting ten percent of British wine consumption by 1822. The tightly controlled and highly restrictive Dutch regime was replaced with a more tolerant government, which brought immediate **freedom of religion**, the abolition of the slave trade in 1808, and the **emancipation** of slaves in 1834.

Although British-born residents were a minority during the first half of the nineteenth century, their influence was huge, and Cape Town began to take on a British character through a process of cultural, economic and political dominance. **English** became the language of status and officialdom, and by 1860 there were eight newspapers, six of them in English. A vibrant press fed a culture of **liberalism** which led Capetonians to thwart British attempts to transport convicts to the Cape (see box, p.44) – the first time since the American Revolution that an outpost of empire had successfully defied Whitehall. This gave the colonists the confidence to demand **self-government** and, in 1854, males, regardless of race, who owned property worth £25 or more won the right to vote for a lower house of parliament, which was based in Cape Town. A significant development of the second half of the nineteenth century was the rapid growth of **communications**, both within Cape Town and into the interior, which reinforced the city's status as the principal centre of a Cape Colony that by now extended 1000km to the east. The road from Cape Town to Camps Bay across Kloof Nek was started in 1848 and a telegraph line between Cape Town and

1834	1864	1901	1899–1901
Emancipation of slaves leads many Dutch to leave Cape and establish two Boer republics	Completion of Cape Town–Wynberg rail line facilitates development of outlying suburbs	First segregated black location, Ndabeni, established after bubonic plague outbreak	Britain defeats Afrikaner republics in Anglo-Boer War

Simon's Town was laid in 1860, but most significant of all was the introduction of steam. The first **rail line** from central Cape Town to Wynberg was completed in 1864, which opened up the southern peninsula to the growth of **middle-class suburbia**.

From backwater to breakwater

The development of an urban infrastructure wasn't enough to lift Cape Town from its backwater provinciality. That required the discovery, in 1867, of the world's largest deposit of **diamonds** around modern-day Kimberley. Coinciding with this, the city's breakwater was started, and the **harbour** was completed just in time to accommodate the massive influx of fortune-hunters and immigrants who flooded into Cape Town en route to the diggings. More significant still was the **discovery of gold** around Johannesburg in the Boer-controlled South African Republic in the 1880s, which gave Cape Town a new significance as the gateway to the world's richest mineral deposits.

From the 1870s, growing middle-class self-confidence was reflected in the erection of grand **Victorian frontages** on the city centre's shops, banks and offices. Echoing Victorian London, this prosperous public facade hid a growing world of poverty, inhabited by immigrants, Africans and people of mixed race (see box, p.42) who made up a cheap labour force. The degradation and vice that thrived in Cape Town's growing slums were disquieting to the Anglocentric middle class, which would have preferred Cape Town to be like a respectably homogenous Home Counties town, rather than a cultural melting pot.

As the twentieth century dawned, the authorities attempted to achieve a closer approximation to the white middle-class ideal by introducing laws to stem **immigration**, other than from Western Europe, while other statutes sought to protect "European traders" against competition from other ethnic groups. Racial segregation wasn't far behind, and an outbreak of bubonic plague in 1901 gave the town council an excuse to establish **Ndabeni**, Cape Town's first black ghetto, near present-day Pinelands.

Industrialization and segregation

Apart from contributing to Cape Town's development as a trading port, the discovery of gold had more significant consequences for the city. By the end of the nineteenth century, a number of influential capitalists, among them **Cecil John Rhodes** (prime minister of the Cape from 1890 to 1897), were convinced that it would be a good idea to annex the two Boer republics to the north to create a unified South Africa under British influence. In 1899, Britain marched on the Boer republics, in what was rashly described by Lord Kitchener as a "teatime war", but became known internationally as the **Anglo-Boer War**, Britain's most expensive campaign since the Napoleonic Wars. Eventually, three years later, the war ended with the Boers' surrender. What followed was nearly a decade of discussions, at the end of which the two Boer republics (the South African Republic and the Orange Free State) and two British colonies (the Cape and Natal) were federated in 1910 to become the **Union of South Africa**, in which Cape Town gained a pivotal position as the **legislative capital** of the country.

Africans and coloureds, excluded from the cosy deal between Boers and Brits, had to find expression in the workplace. They flexed their collective muscle on the docks in

1910	1920s	1948
Parliament comes to Cape Town when Afrikaner republics and British colonies (Cape and Natal) federate	Influx of Africans leads to building of segregated township Langa, surrounded by barbed-wire fence	National Party, with its former-Nazi members, wins election and goes full throttle on segregation

1919, where they formed the mighty **Industrial and Commercial Union**, which boasted 200,000 members in its heyday. Cape Town began the process of becoming a modern industrial city and, with the building of the South African National Gallery, promoted itself as the urbane cultural capital of the country. Accelerated **industrialization** brought an influx of Africans from the rural areas, and soon Ndabeni was overflowing. Alarmed that Africans were living close to the city centre in District Six and were also spilling out into the Cape Flats, the authorities passed the **Urban Areas Act**, which compelled Africans to live in what were named "locations" and empowered the city council to expel jobless Africans – measures that preceded apartheid by 25 years. In 1927, the new location of **Langa** (which ironically means "sun") was opened next to the sewage works. Laid out along military lines, with barrack-style dormitories for the residents, it was surrounded by a security fence.

World War II

During the 1930s, Cape Town saw the growth of several fascist movements, the largest of which was the **Greyshirts**, whose favourite meeting place was the Koffiehuis (coffee house) next to the Groote Kerk in Adderley Street. Its members included Hendrik Verwoerd, a Dutch-born intellectual who became a fanatical Afrikaner Nationalist and South African prime minister from 1958 to 1966. When **World War II** broke out, there was a heated debate in parliament, which narrowly voted for South Africa to side with Britain against Germany. Members of all South African communities volunteered for service, and the **ANC** (**African National Congress**, founded in 1912) argued that their support should be linked to full citizenship for blacks. Afrikaners were deeply divided, and **Nazi sympathizers**, among them John Vorster (Verwoerd's successor as prime minister), were jailed for actively attempting to sabotage the war effort. *Die Burger*, Cape Town's Afrikaans-language newspaper, backed Germany throughout the war.

The war brought hardship, particularly to those at the bottom of the heap, leading to an increased influx of Africans and poor white Afrikaners from the countryside to the cities. This changed the demographics of the city of Cape Town, which lost its British colonial flavour and, for the first time in 150 years, had more black (mostly coloured) than white residents. New townships were built to accommodate the burgeoning African population.

Cape Town became a mixed bag of ad hoc official **segregation** in some areas of life, while in others, such as on buses and trains, there was none.

Apartheid and defiance

In postwar South Africa, ideological tensions grew between those pushing for universal civil rights and those whites who feared black advancement. In 1948, the **National Party** came to power, promising its fearful white supporters that it would reverse the flow of Africans to the cities. In Cape Town, the government introduced a policy that favoured coloureds for certain unskilled and semi-skilled jobs, admitting only African men who were already employed and forbidding the construction of family accommodation for Africans – hence the townships turned into predominantly male preserves.

During the 1950s, the National Party began putting in place a barrage of laws that would eventually constitute the structure of apartheid. Early **onslaughts on civil rights**

1952	1960	1962	1966
Nelson Mandela leads defiance campaign against apartheid legislation	Robert Sobukwe heads march from Langa against enforced carrying of passes by Africans	Mandela, Sobukwe and ANC leadership imprisoned on Robben Island	Coloureds and Africans evicted from "white areas" and relocated to Cape Flats townships

included the Coloured Voters Act, which stripped coloureds of the right to vote; the Bantu Authorities Act, which set up puppet authorities to govern Africans in rural reserves; the Population Registration Act, which classified every South African at birth as "white, Bantu or coloured"; the Group Areas Act, which divided South Africa into ethnically distinct areas; and the Suppression of Communism Act, which made anti-apartheid opposition (communist or not) a criminal offence. Africans, now regarded as foreigners in their own country, had at all times to carry **passes** – one of the most reviled symbols of apartheid.

The ANC responded in 1952 with the **Defiance Campaign**, whose aim was to grant full civil rights to blacks. A radical young firebrand called **Nelson Mandela** was appointed "volunteer-in-chief" of the campaign, which had a crucial influence on his politics. Up to that point, he had rejected political association with non-Africans, but the campaign's interracial solidarity brought him round to the conciliatory inclusive approach for which he became famous. The government swooped on the homes of the ANC leadership, which resulted in the detention and then banning of over a hundred ANC organizers. Unbowed, the ANC pressed ahead with the **Congress of the People**, held near Johannesburg in 1955. At a mass meeting of nearly three thousand delegates, four organizations – representing Africans, coloureds, whites and Indians – formed a strategic partnership.

From within the organization, a group of Africanists criticized cooperation with white activists, leading to the formation in 1958 of the breakaway **Pan Africanist Congress** (**PAC**), under the leadership of the charismatic **Robert Mangaliso Sobukwe**. Langa township became a stronghold of the PAC, which organized peaceful **anti-pass demonstrations** in Johannesburg and Cape Town on March 21, 1960. Over a period of days, work strikes spread to all Cape Town's locations, and a temporary nationwide suspension of the pass laws was achieved – the calm before the storm. As the protests gathered strength, the government declared a **State of Emergency**. They sent the army in to crush the strike, restored the pass laws and banned the ANC and PAC. Nelson Mandela continued to operate in secret for a year until he was finally captured in 1962, tried and imprisoned – together with most of the ANC leadership – on **Robben Island**.

Soweto and the Total Strategy

With resistance stifled, the state grew more powerful, and for the majority of white South Africans, business people and foreign investors, life seemed perfect. The panic caused by the 1960 uprising soon became a dim memory, and confidence returned. For black South Africans, poverty deepened – a state of affairs enforced by apartheid legislation.

In 1966, the notorious **Group Areas Act** was used to uproot whole coloured communities from many areas, including District Six, and to move them to the s oulless **Cape Flats**, where, in the wake of social disintegration, gangsterism took root (see box, p.83). It remains one of Cape Town's most pressing problems. Compounding the injury, the National Party stripped away coloured representation on the Cape Town city council in 1972.

The **Soweto Revolt** of June 16, 1976, signalled the start of a new wave of anti-apartheid protest, when black youths took to the streets against the imposition of Afrikaans as a medium of instruction in their schools. The protests spread to Cape

1976	1978	1981
Police open fire on black school pupils opposing government; 128 Capetonians are killed	Hawkish P.W. Botha becomes president in palace coup	Botha moves Mandela to mainland prison, but also sends massed troops into townships to suppress rolling protest

Town where, as in Jo'burg, the government responded ruthlessly by sending in armed police, who killed 128 and injured 400 Capetonians.

Despite naked violence, protest spread to all sections of the community. The government was forced to rely increasingly on armed police to impose order. Even this strategy was unable to stop the mushrooming of new liberation organizations, many of which were part of the broadly based **Black Consciousness movement**. As the unrest rumbled on into 1977, the government responded by banning all the new black organizations and detaining their leadership.

From the mid-1960s to the mid-1970s, Prime Minister **John Vorster** had relied on the police to maintain the apartheid status quo, but it became obvious that this wasn't working. In 1978, he was deposed in a palace coup by his minister of defence, **P.W. Botha**, who conceived a complex military-style approach that he called the **Total Strategy**. The strategy was a two-handed one: the reform of peripheral aspects of apartheid, alongside the deployment of the armed forces in unprecedented acts of repression. In 1981, as resistance grew, Botha began contemplating change and moved Nelson Mandela and other ANC leaders from Robben Island to Pollsmoor Prison in mainland Cape Town. This was a symbolic gesture, as Pollsmoor had lower security, less harsh conditions and it was easier to access for (potential) negotiations. At the same time, however, he poured ever-increasing numbers of troops into the townships.

In 1983, Botha concocted what he believed was a master plan for a so-called **New Constitution**, in which coloureds and Indians would be granted the vote – in racially segregated chambers with no executive power. The only constructive outcome of this project was the extension of the Houses of Parliament to their current size.

Apartheid suffers a stroke

As President Botha was punting his ramshackle scheme in 1983, fifteen thousand anti-apartheid delegates met at Mitchell's Plain, on the Cape Flats, to form the **United Democratic Front (UDF)**, the largest opposition gathering in South Africa since the Congress of the People, in 1955. The UDF became a proxy for the banned ANC, and two years of strikes, boycotts and protest followed. As the government resorted to increasingly extreme measures, internal resistance grew and the international community turned up the heat on the apartheid regime. The Commonwealth passed a resolution condemning apartheid, the US and Australia severed air links, Congress passed disinvestment legislation and finally, in 1985, the Chase Manhattan Bank called in its massive loan to South Africa.

Botha declared his umpteenth **State of Emergency** and unleashed a last-ditch storm of tyranny. There were bannings, mass arrests, detentions, treason trials and torture, as well as assassinations of UDF leaders by sinister hit squads. At the beginning of 1989, **Mandela** wrote to Botha from prison describing his fear of a polarized South Africa and calling for negotiations. An intransigent character, Botha found himself paralyzed by his inability to reconcile the need for radical change with his fear of a right-wing backlash. When he suffered a stroke later that year, his party colleagues moved swiftly to oust him and replaced him with **F.W. de Klerk**.

Faced with the worst crisis in South Africa's history, President de Klerk realized that repression had failed. Even South Africa's friends were losing patience, and, in September 1989, US President George Bush Sr told de Klerk that if Mandela wasn't released within

1983	1989	1990
15,000 delegates form ANC proxy the United Democratic Front, leading to escalation of violence	Botha has stroke and is replaced by F.W. de Klerk, who unbans ANC and releases Mandela	Mandela walks free and makes first public speech from City Hall

six months, he would extend US sanctions. Five months later, de Klerk lifted the ban on the ANC, PAC, the Communist Party and 33 other organizations, and released Mandela.

On February 11, 1990, Cape Town's history took a neat twist when, just hours after being released from prison, **Nelson Mandela** made his first public speech from the balcony of City Hall to a jubilant crowd spilling across the Grand Parade – the site of the very first Dutch fort.

A tale of two cities

Four protracted years of negotiations followed, which eventually led to South Africa's current constitution. Following the country's first-ever **democratic elections** in 1994, Mandela voted in national elections for the first time in his life – and became South Africa's president. One of the anomalies of the 1994 election was that while most of South Africa delivered an **ANC landslide**, the Western Cape, purportedly the most liberal region of the country, returned the **National Party**, who had implemented apartheid, as its provincial government. Politics in South Africa were not, it turned out, divided along a fault line that separated whites from the rest of the population, as many had assumed; the majority of coloureds had voted for the very party that had once stripped them of the vote, regarding it with less suspicion than the ANC. Apart from the period between 2002 and 2006, when Capetonians elected an ANC mayor and administration, the Western Cape and its capital have consistently bucked South Africa's national trend of overwhelming ANC dominance, by repeatedly returning administration run by the National Party and, after its dissolution, the economically liberal **Democratic Alliance** (**DA**).

During the ANC's first term in national government under Mandela (1994–1999), affirmative action policies and a racial shift in the economy led to the rise of a **black middle class**, but even so this represented a tiny fraction of the African and coloured population, and many felt that transformation hadn't gone far enough. Indeed, after two decades of non-racial democracy, Cape Town is still a very divided city.

On the one hand, the Mother City has been titivating itself for tourists and investors, helped by the establishment of the Cape Town Partnership in 1999, which has overseen the regeneration of the city centre. The post-apartheid period led to a wave of economic confidence expressed by investors in a number of monumental developments. Among these was the megalomaniacal **Century City** (1997) in the northern suburbs, a garish retail, residential and office complex that adopted faux Tuscan architecture and Venice-inspired canals. More tasteful was the expansion of the **V&A Waterfront** to include the hugely symbolic **Nelson Mandela Gateway** (2001), from where the ferry to Robben Island now embarks. In conjunction with South Africa's hosting of the 2010 FIFA World Cup, the iconic **Cape Town Stadium** (2009) went up on Green Point Common, and Cape Town International Airport got a brand-new **Central Terminal Building** (2009), which at last provided a facility that could cope with the city's expanding air traffic. To cap it all, the state-of-the-art **Cape Town Film Studio** (2010) was completed and went on to attract an increasing number of major international productions, such as the 2012 hit *Chronicle*, *Safe House* starring Denzel Washington, futuristic 3D drama *Dredd*, *The Giver* with Meryl Streep and TV pirate drama *Black Sails*.

On the other hand, as the biggest city within a thousand kilometres, Cape Town continues to attract a steady **influx** of people seeking a better life, mostly from the rural

1994	1997–2011	2006
ANC wins election and Mandela becomes president, but Western Cape returns National Party provincial government	City constructs several prestige developments and regenerates centre	Liberal Democratic Alliance takes control of Western Cape and Cape Town

Eastern Cape, but also from all over Africa, making it one of the subcontinent's fastest-growing cities, with shacks proliferating wherever there are available open spaces in the townships. The city estimates that nearly a quarter of its households live in so-called "**informal dwellings**", ie shacks. In 2005, the ANC national housing minister launched the **N2 Gateway Project** to replace some of the shacks that lined the N1 from the airport to the city with brick buildings. Whether it was a serious attempt to alleviate the housing shortage, or just grandstanding for the electorate and eye candy for tourists arriving by air in the Mother City, is a moot point. Either way, **housing** is still one of the biggest problems facing the metropolis (and the whole of South Africa), and it's a growing one: between 1998 and 2012 Cape Town's housing **backlog** grew from 150,000 to 400,000. At present rates of construction it would take 66 years to meet the existing shortfall – and that's without taking population growth into account.

With current birth rates and the influx of fifteen thousand families from the rural areas into the city each year, planners project that by 2030 the city's **population** will grow from its present 3.5 million to between five and six million inhabitants. The housing shortage means that hundreds of thousands of Capetonians have limited **access to services**, such as running water, waterborne-sewerage and electricity. It's also symptomatic of the city's slew of other problems: poverty, unemployment, rampant crime and high infection rates for HIV and TB.

In response to the tardy pace of transformation throughout the country since the end of apartheid, **street protests** became an increasingly common means for citizens to register dissatisfaction, and lack of housing provision still tops the list of complaints. While millions of South Africans were reduced to living in shacks, over R200m of taxpayers' money had been lavished on upgrading President Jacob Zuma's private residence at **Nkandla** in KwaZulu-Natal. This and the **death of Nelson Mandela** in late 2013 signalled a symbolic end to the ideals of the Freedom Charter, which had inspired the ANC for over half a century. It underlined the intractability of economic apartheid and the creeping entrenchment of corruption and political patronage.

The ANC went to the polls for the **2014 general election**, handicapped, one might have thought, by the Nkandla scandal and a record of poor delivery. However, despite losing some support, the ANC still managed to win the national election. Victory was by a smaller margin than five years previously, but by a 62 percent majority nonetheless.

In the **Western Cape**, the ANC fared less well, and the DA strengthened its dominance with 59 percent of the poll, reiterating the province's distinct demographic and political character. The DA's success may in part be due to its better-than-average record of delivery – a survey published in 2014 showed that seven of South Africa's ten best-performing municipalities were in the Western Cape. This included Cape Town, which was the only large city on the list.

However, this is by no means reason enough for this rapidly growing metropolis to rest on its laurels. Burgeoning joblessness remains a pressing problem. The expansion of industry is a common route for urbanizing societies to rapidly create **employment**; the first signs of this are noticeable in Cape Town, such as with an increase in oil refineries. And yet, industrialization comes at an ecological cost, and Cape Town's **environment** is one of its greatest assets – through tourism, it is a tangible source of income and employment. But on its own, it's not enough. The city's planners and politicians face some tough choices.

2008	**2010**	**2013**
Planners worry about growing housing backlog and that a quarter of Cape Town homes are shacks	City stages glittering FIFA World Cup extravaganza in new Cape Town Stadium	South Africa – and the world – mourns the death of Nelson Mandela

Books

For a country with a relatively small reading public, South Africa generates a huge number of books, particularly novels and politics and history titles.

FICTION

Tatamkhulu Afrika *The Innocents*. Set in the struggle years, this novel examines the moral and ethical issues of the time, from a Muslim perspective.

Mark Behr *The Smell of Apples*. Powerful first novel set in the 1970s recounts the gradual falling of the scales from the eyes of an eleven-year-old Afrikaner boy, whose father is a major-general in the apartheid army.

Andre Brink *A Chain of Voices*. Superbly evocative tale of eighteenth-century Cape life, exploring the impact of slavery on one farming family, right up to its dramatic and murderous end.

★**J.M. Coetzee** *Disgrace*. A subtle, strange novel set in a Cape Town university and on a remote Eastern Cape farm, where the lives of a literature professor and his farmer daughter are violently transformed. Bleak but totally engrossing, this novel won the Booker Prize in 1999. Coetzee is something of a national treasure (see box below).

Achmat Dangor *The Z Town Trilogy*. One of the best writers from Cape Town, Dangor sets his trilogy in a town much like it, during one of apartheid South Africa's many states of emergency, which is burrowing in intricate ways into the psyches of his characters. The book portrays a brittle family, a dysfunctional society, and how we address – or fail to address – the past's deepest wounds.

Damon Galgut *In a Strange Room*. The writer, some say, best placed to fill J.M. Coetzee's literary shoes, Damon Galgut has scooped several literary awards: *In a Strange Room* was shortlisted for the 2010 Man Booker Prize for Fiction. Unusually for Galgut, this novel is set outside South Africa and describes the global travels and relationships of a protagonist named, like the author, Damon. Quirky, beautifully written and highly readable.

Lily Herne *Deadlands*. South Africa's street-smart answer to *Twilight* follows the adventures and romance of seventeen-year-old Lele as she navigates the shattered, zombie-infested suburbs of a postapocalyptic Cape Town.

Rayda Jacobs *The Slave Book*. A carefully researched historical novel dealing with love and survival in a slave household in 1830s Cape Town, on the eve of the abolition of slavery.

J.M. COETZEE

To read a **J.M. Coetzee** novel is to walk an emotional tightrope from exhilaration to sadness, with a sense throughout of being guided by a strong creative intellect and an exceptionally shrewd observer of human experience.

Coetzee's taut, measured style strikes some readers as cold and bloodless; he is relentlessly unsentimental, and plots tend to end on an unsettling note. But despite his reputation as a "difficult" writer, Coetzee never fails to involve us absolutely in the fates of his characters; in the words of Nadine Gordimer, Coetzee "goes to the nerve-centre of being".

Born in Cape Town in 1940 and trained as a linguist and computer scientist in South Africa and the US, Coetzee began to write fiction in the early 1970s. *Dusklands* and *In the Heart of the Country*, his first two novels, were dense and often overwrought dissections of settler psychology, but his prose reached a soaring maturity with *Waiting for the Barbarians* (1980), in which an imaginary desert landscape is the setting for a chilling exploration of the dynamics of imperial power.

In 1983, *The Life and Times of Michael K*, following the wanderings of a reclusive refugee across a future South Africa ravaged by civil war, won the Booker Prize. The novel ends with a passage of extraordinary beauty and subtlety, and stands as a postmodern masterpiece that now bears ironic testimony to South Africa's actual future. After *Michael K* came the novels *Foe*, *Age of Iron* and *The Master of Petersburg* and two nonfiction books: an anthology of criticism, *White Writing*, and a moving childhood memoir, *Boyhood*.

When Coetzee won an unprecedented second Booker Prize for *Disgrace* in 1999, he became famous beyond literary circles for the first time. This has meant exasperation for soundbite-hungry media hounds, since Coetzee abhors publicity – he chose not to attend the Booker Prize award ceremony and is notoriously cagey in social interactions. In 2002, Coetzee emigrated to Australia, where he lives in Adelaide. In 2006, he became an Australian citizen.

Ashraf Jamal *Love Themes for the Wilderness*. The inhabitants of a bohemian subculture are lovingly observed in this funny and free-spirited novel set in mid-1990s Observatory.

Pamela Jooste *Dance with a Poor Man's Daughter*. The fragile world of a young coloured girl during the early apartheid years is sensitively imagined in this hugely successful first novel.

Alex La Guma *A Walk in the Night*. One of the truly proletarian writers South Africa has produced, La Guma, before his long exile in Cuba, focused on the conditions of life in Cape Town, particularly the inner-city areas like District Six. His social realism is gritty yet poignant, and it gives us many indelible portraits of Cape Town in the mid-twentieth century.

Anne Landsman *The Devil's Chimney*. A stylish and entertaining piece of magic realism about the Southern Cape town of Oudtshoorn, in the days of the ostrich-feather boom.

Sindiwe Magona *Mother to Mother*. Magona adopts the narrative voice of the mother of the killer of Amy Biehl, an American student murdered in a Cape Town township in 1993. The novel is a trenchant and lyrical meditation on the traumas of the past.

Songeziwe Mahlangu *Penumbra*. Semi-autobiographical debut novel that etches a unique vision of Cape Town through the eyes of a young man employed by a large insurance company. Torn by turns between mindless web-surfing, drug-induced mania and charismatic Christianity, Manga charts his course through the southern suburbs of the Mother City.

Deon Meyer *Thirteen Hours*. A riveting read from South Africa's hottest crime writer, which may be uncomfortably close to the bone for some – one thread follows Detective Benny Griessel's quest to find and save the life of an American backpacker on the run from Cape Town gangsters after her travelling companion's murder.

Mike Nicol *Payback*. This hard-boiled thriller, one of several by established novelist Nicol (who has been compared to Elmore Leonard and Cormac McCarthy), follows a pair of gun-runners drawn back from retirement into Cape Town's dark underworld.

Margie Orford *Water Music*. One of the Clare Hart novels by internationally acclaimed crime writer Orford, this riveting read, set in picturesque Hout Bay, delves into the dark depths of child abuse.

Patricia Schonstein Pinnock *Skyline*. Set in a crumbling apartment block in central Cape Town, Pinnock's novel examines a young girl's coming-of-age, her encounters with migrants from elsewhere in Africa, and the rising xenophobia in South Africa.

Richard Rive *Buckingham Palace, District Six*. The unique urban culture of District Six is movingly remembered in this short novel about the life of a now-desolate street and its inhabitants.

Linda Rode (ed) *Crossing Over*. Collection of 26 stories by new and emerging South African writers on the experiences of adolescence and early adulthood in a period of political transition.

Jann Turner *Heartland*. A white farmer's daughter and a black labourer's son are childhood companions on a Boland fruit farm; a betrayal occurs, and years later the boy returns from political exile, ready to stake his claim to the land. An ambitious and popular novel.

Zoe Wicombe *You Can't Get Lost in Cape Town*. The author of a book of primarily short stories, Wicombe is remarkable for her sense of realism and the subtle way in which she produces her work. Social concern is transparent, humour is demonstrable, and yet none of it consents to the heavy-handed treatment anti-apartheid protest literature usually follows.

GUIDES AND REFERENCE BOOKS

G.M. Branch *Two Oceans*. Don't be put off by the coffee-table format; this is a comprehensive guide to southern Africa's marine life.

★ **Richard Cowling and Dave Richardson** *Fynbos: South Africa's Unique Floral Kingdom*. Lavishly illustrated hardback which offers a fascinating layman's portrait of the *fynbos* ecosystem.

Mike Lundy *Best Walks in the Cape Peninsula*. An invaluable, not-too-bulky book for casual walkers, which

contains plenty of possibilities for an afternoon's stroll.

L. McMahon and M. Fraser *A Fynbos Year*. Exquisitely illustrated and well-written book about the Western Cape's unique floral kingdom.

★ **Philip van Zyl** (ed) *John Platter South African Wines*. One of the best-selling titles in South Africa – an annually updated pocket book that rates virtually every wine produced in the country. No aspiring connoisseur of Cape wines should venture forth without it.

HISTORY, POLITICS AND SOCIETY

★ **Vivian Bickford-Smith, Elizabeth van Heyningen and Nigel Worden** *Cape Town: The Making of a City* and *Cape Town in the Twentieth Century*. The first book is richly illustrated and exhaustively researched, and recounts the growth of Cape Town, from early Khoisan societies to the end of the nineteenth century. The second volume is a thorough and elegant account of modern Cape Town, which

interweaves rich local history with international events.

Andrew Brown *Street Blues*. Advocate, police-reserve sergeant and award-winning novelist, Brown paints a gritty, and sometimes witty, picture of life on the beat, tackling the mean streets of Cape Town.

Richard Calland *Anatomy of South Africa: Who Holds the Power*. An incisive dissection of politics and power in South

Africa today, from one of the country's most respected commentators.

John Carlin *Playing the Enemy: Nelson Mandela and the Game that made a Nation*. Gripping account of Nelson Mandela's use of the 1995 Rugby World Cup to unite a fractious nation, in danger of collapsing into civil war. It was also published as *Invictus*, the title of the Clint Eastwood film, which starred Matt Damon and Morgan Freeman.

Andrew Feinstein *After the Party: Corruption, the ANC and South Africa's Uncertain Future*. A personal account of where South Africa's government has lost its way, by a former ANC member of parliament. Feinstein resigned in 2001 in protest at the government's cover-up of graft and corruption in negotiating the country's cripplingly expensive arms deal.

★ **Peter Harris** *In a Different Time: The Inside Story of the Delmas Four*. This brilliantly told, true historical drama is about four young South Africans sent on a mission by the ANC-in-exile, which ultimately led to Death Row. As their defence lawyer, Harris had unique and sympathetic insight into their personalities and motivations.

Hermann Giliomee and Bernard Mbenga *A New History of South Africa*. A comprehensive, reliable and entertaining account of South Africa's history, published in 2007.

★ **Antjie Krog** *Country of My Skull*. An unflinching and harrowing account of the Truth and Reconciliation Commission's investigations. Krog, a respected radio journalist and poet, covered the entire process, and skilfully merges private identity with national catharsis.

Hein Marais *Pushed to the Limit*. An assessment of why the privileged classes remain just that – a handful of conglomerates dominate the South African economy – and how this relates to Jacob Zuma's rise to power.

Alan Mountain *An Unsung Heritage: Perspectives on Slavery*. An account of the nature of slavery in the Cape, and the contribution imported slaves made to the fabric of the

area today. Best of all is the guide to slave heritage sites in the Cape Peninsula, Winelands and West Coast and along the Garden Route, with attractive photos and illustrations.

Mike Nicol *Sea-Mountain, Fire City: Living in Cape Town*. One of the few books in that rare category: living in Cape Town at the beginning of the new millennium. Nicol hinges his documentary narrative on the apparently prosaic business of moving house from one part of the city to another, and maps many of those fissures, not to say abysses, that make Cape Town the divided city that it is.

Nigel Penn *Rogues, Rebels and Runaways*. A hugely entertaining collection of essays on deviant types in the eighteenth-century Cape. Tragi-comic and written in a wry, engaging style.

Robert C-H Shell *Children of Bondage*. Definitive social history of Cape slavery in the eighteenth century – a compelling academic text that is accessible to the lay reader.

Allister Sparks *The Mind of South Africa* and *Beyond the Miracle: Inside the New South Africa*. In the first book, Sparks, an authoritative journalist and historian traces the rise and fall of the apartheid state in a lively, economical and serious work. *Beyond the Miracle: Inside the New South Africa* examines the prospects for South Africa, looking beyond the initial buoyancy of democracy to emerging patterns in its government.

Stephen Taylor *The Caliban Shore: The Fate of the Grosvenor Castaways*. A gripping account of the wreck of the *Grosvenor* in the eighteenth century, along the Eastern Cape's aptly named Wild Coast. Meticulously researched history, it has the depth and pace of a well-crafted novel.

★ **Desmond Tutu** *No Future Without Forgiveness*. This is Tutu's gracious and honest assessment of the Truth Commission that he guided. It's an important testimony, from one of the country's most influential thinkers and leaders.

Frank Welsh *A History of South Africa*. Solid scholarship and a strong sense of overall narrative mark this publication as a much-needed addition to South African historiography.

BIOGRAPHY AND AUTOBIOGRAPHY

★ **J.M. Coetzee** *Boyhood*. A moving and courageous childhood memoir by South Africa's greatest novelist.

★ **Sindiwe Magoma** *To My Children's Children*. A fascinating autobiography – initially started so that her family would never forget their roots – which traces Magoma's life from the rural Transkei to the hard townships of Cape Town.

Nelson Mandela *Long Walk to Freedom*. Superb best-selling autobiography of the former president and national icon, which is wonderfully evocative of his early years and intensely moving about his long years in prison.

★ **Benjamin Pogrund** *How Can Man Die Better? The Life of Robert Sobukwe*. The story of one of the most important

anti-apartheid liberation heroes, the late leader of the Pan Africanist Congress and a contemporary of Nelson Mandela. Sobukwe was so feared by the white government that they passed a special law – The Sobukwe Clause – to keep him in solitary confinement on Robben Island after he'd served his sentence.

★ **Anthony Sampson** *Mandela, The Authorised Biography*. Released to coincide with Mandela's retirement from the presidency in 1999, Sampson's authoritative volume competes with *A Long Walk to Freedom* in both interest and sheer poundage. Firmly grounded in exhaustive research and interviews, it offers a broader perspective and sharper analysis than the autobiography.

THE ARTS

Marion Arnold *Women and Art in South Africa*. Comprehensive, pioneering study of women artists from the early twentieth century to the present.

Thorsten Deckler, Anne Graupner, Henning Rasmuss *Contemporary South African Architecture in a Landscape of Transition*. Lavishly illustrated coverage of fifty outstanding architectural projects that have been completed since 1994.

S. Francis and Rico *Madam and Eve*. Various annual volumes of telling and witty cartoons that convey the daily struggle between an African domestic worker and her white madam in the northern suburbs of Johannesburg. These cartoons say more about post-apartheid society than countless academic tomes.

Steve Gordon *Beyond the Blues: Township Jazz of the Sixties and Seventies*. Portraits, in words and pictures, of the country's jazz greats, such as Kippie Moeketsi, Basil Coetzee and Abdullah Ibrahim (Dollar Brand).

★**Andy Mason** *What's So Funny? Under the Skin of South African Cartooning*. Insightful, fascinating and thoroughly collectable wade through the history of South African visual satire from the colonial period to the present.

Ralf-Peter Seippel *South African Photography: 1950–2010*. South Africa's history has provided a rich vein of material for photographers, and this volume covers the work of some of the country's most celebrated lensmen.

Sue Williamson *South African Art Now*. A survey of South African art from the "Resistance Art" of the 1960s to the present, covering movements, genres and leading artists such as Marlene Dumas and William Kentridge, by one of the country's most influential commentators and an accomplished artist in her own right.

Zapiro Umpteen annual cartoon collections by South Africa's leading political cartoonist. In a country where satire is in notoriously short supply, Zapiro consistently reveals what needs to be exposed (🕸 zapiro.com).

POETRY

Ingrid de Kok *Transfer*. This technically adroit and always moving work was created by probably the most intelligent of South Africa's feminist poets.

Finuala Dowling *Notes from the Dementia Ward*. At once cynical, humorous and sad, Dowling's award-winning collection explores the death of her brother and mental decline of her mother against the clearly delineated backdrop of Cape Town.

★**Denis Hirson** (ed) *The Lava of This Land: South African Poetry 1960–1996*. Comprehensive anthology of South African poetry that includes work from the oral period, as

well as translations from Afrikaans and other languages.

Ingrid Jonker *Selected Poems*. One of the few Afrikaans-language poets whose work has been translated into a standard of English that does justice to her work. The poems display a remarkable rawness in depicting the outrage of 1960s apartheid, as well as a grief-stricken lyricism from a poet who drowned herself off Sea Point in 1965.

★**Stephen Watson** *The Other City* and *The Light Echo*. No one better evokes Cape Town's changeable beauty, though Watson (who died of cancer in 2011) also writes about matters of the heart and great universal themes.

TRAVEL WRITING

Richard Dobson *Karoo Moons: A Photographic Journey*. If you need encouragement to explore the desert interior of South Africa, these enticing images should do the trick.

★**Sihle Khumalo** *Dark Continent, My Black Arse*. Insightful and witty account by a black South African who quit his well-paid job to realize a dream of travelling from the Cape to Cairo by public transport.

★**Ben Maclennan** *The Wind Makes Dust: Four Centuries of Travel in South Africa*. A remarkable anthology of fascinating travel pieces, meticulously unearthed and researched.

Julia Martin *A Millimetre of Dust: Visiting Ancestral Sites*. Sensitively crafted narrative that begins on the Cape Peninsula and takes the author, her husband and two children on a journey to important archeological sites in the Northern Cape, raising ethical, ecological and philosophical questions along the way.

Paul Theroux *Dark Star Safari: Overland from Cairo to Cape Town*. Theroux's powerful account of his overland trip from Cairo to Cape Town, with a couple of chapters on South Africa, including an account of meeting writer Nadine Gordimer.

Music

Cape Town's most proclaimed musical treasure is Cape jazz, the greatest exponent of which is Abdullah Ibrahim, a supremely gifted pianist and composer, born in the Cape Flats, who for decades has produced a hypnotic fusion of African, American and Cape Muslim idioms. Other Cape Town jazz legends include saxophonists Winston "Ngozi" Mankunku and the late Basil Coetzee and Robbie Jansen, plus guitarist Errol Dyers, pianist Hotep Galata and bassist Spencer Mbadu. Three young stars stand out as heirs to the Cape jazz tradition: the astronomically cool guitarist Jimmy Dludlu; subtle, mellow pianist Paul Hanmer; and pianist Kyle Shepherd, who was taught by Robbie Jansen – catch them live if you can.

Among African township youth, one of the biggest sounds is **kwaito** and local **hip-hop**. In an accurate reflection of the depressed and nihilistic mood of township youth culture, *kwaito*'s vibe tends to be downbeat, and the music frequently carries a strong association with gangsterism and explicit sexuality. Although the supporters of local hip-hop eagerly proclaim that it is now replacing *kwaito*, the reality is more nuanced, and the difference between the two isn't always clear-cut.

DJ-mixed South African **house** manages to cross racial and cultural boundaries, attracting practitioners and fans from all sectors of the country, though it is dominated by black DJs such as **DJ Fresh**, **Glen Lewis**, **DJ Mbuso**, **Thibo Tazz**, **DJ Fosta** and **Oskido**. Meanwhile, South African **rap** has enjoyed sustained popularity since the early 1990s, but has remained almost completely ghettoized within the coloured community of the Western Cape. Heavily influenced by African-American rappers, performers often exude a palpable sense of being "Americans trapped in Africa". Pioneers of the style were the heavily politicized **Prophets of Da City**, several members of which made names for themselves as solo artists after the group's break-up, most notably **Rahim**, **Junior**

ENTER DIE ANTWOORD

Die Antwoord (meaning "the answer") – an unknown crew from Cape Town's northern suburbs **rapping** in Cape Flats slang – was an overnight sensation that stormed the internet in 2010. This was the true grit from the streets of the Mother City: a lowlife rap genre known as **zef** (from an Afrikaans word that denotes trashy style). That, at least, was the story.

Their **success** was real enough: in February 2010, traffic to their website (Ⓦ dieantwoord .com), which was streaming their debut album *o*, was so heavy (fifteen million hits) that it crashed, and they had to move to a US server. Their signature foul-mouthed lyrics aside, there's nothing rough and ready about their output. If you aren't convinced, look at the tight machine-gun vocal style (likened by *Rolling Stone* to "Eminem's *Lose Yourself* on mescaline"), the slick art-direction, the careful choreography and the cool Keith Haring-esque graphics on their *Enter the Ninja* video.

Far from being the band that came from nowhere, Die Antwoord, made up of frontman Ninja, helium-voiced Yo-landi Vi$$er and DJ Hi-Tek, is the latest surreal vehicle for **Watkin Tudor Jones** (**Ninja**), whose previous excursions included hip-hop outfits Max Normal and the Constructus Corporation. Jones's history of taking on personas has led detractors to express disappointment that Die Antwoord "aren't real" (whatever that means in show business), while fans declare him a creative genius. Does it matter? The fact is, Die Antwoord deliver an unmistakeably Cape Town sound that really cooks.

Solela and **Ishmael.** Other groups and performers who have since emerged include the group **Brasse vannie Kaap** (who rap in Afrikaans) and DJ **Reddy D.** Less easy to confine under the rubric of rap is **E.J. von Lyrik** (of the hip-hop crew **Godessa**), who jams rap, reggae and funk influences into her sound. By far the most successful of the lot are **Die Antwoord**, who have stormed the world with their foulmouthed style known as **zef**, which is a mixture of English, Afrikaans and Cape Flats slang (see box opposite). Back home, their one-time collaborator **Isaac Mutant**, with genuine roots in the Cape Flats, projects a menace-to-society image.

English-speaking South Africans have successfully replicated virtually every popular Western musical style going, back to the late nineteenth century. Some have found fame in the outside world, but there are still many gifted performers who remained in the Mother City, including **Goldfish**, the **Parlotones**, string-maestro **Steve Newman** and **Tananas**, a string trio Newman plays with for a couple of months each year. A new Mother City talent worth catching is folk singer **Jeremy Loops**, who hit the number-one spot on the South Africa iTunes store in 2014 with his skilful artistry on loop pedal, guitar, harmonica and beatbox.

Afrikaans music, on the other hand, is a world unto itself, but from the late 1920s until the 1960s, American country was its greatest outside influence. Following the end of apartheid, a general concern about the future of the Afrikaans language and culture spurred a revival of interest in Afrikaans music. There is undoubtedly more stylistic variety now than ever before: witness the house/disco of **Juanita**, the heavy rock of **Karen Zoid** and **Jackhammer**, the Neil Diamond-esque songs of **Steve Hofmeyer** (the bestselling Afrikaans music artist), as well as the punk-rock riffs of **Fokofpolisiekar** and the studied banality of rapper **Jack Parow**, both of whom have collaborated with Die Antwoord.

Arguably the place where many contemporary South African artists sit most comfortably is the catch-all category known as **Afropop**. Characterized by a knack for combining various local African styles with Western popular influences, and the eschewing of computer-generated backing in favour of actual instruments, Afropop has the ability to attract a multiracial audience. Cape Town's most successful proponents of the style are **Freshlyground**, who, because of their broad appeal and engaging sound, were chosen to accompany Shakira in jamming to a billion viewers at the opening and closing ceremonies of the 2010 Fifa World Cup. The group are still going strong, with plenty of live performances – their bedrock – and album *The Legend* released in 2013.

ESSENTIAL CAPE TOWN SOUNDS

Abdullah Ibrahim *African Marketplace* (Discovery/WEA). Ibrahim's best album – a wistful, nostalgic, other-worldly journey.

Basil Coetzee *Monwabisi* (Mountain). Smoky, intensely energetic jazz record from the greatest of Cape jazz saxophonists.

Brenda Fassie *African Princess of Pop* and *Memeza* (CCP). The former is a posthumous survey that covers the entire career of South Africa's very own Madonna; the latter, featuring the massive hit "Vul'Ndlela", was Brenda's most commercially successful effort.

Dantai *Operation Lahlela* (Nebula BOS). R&B-flavoured *kwaito* from one of Cape Town's up-and-coming dance acts.

Die Antwoord *O* (Rhythm Records). The signature album of the *zef* rave rap style that brought the trio to the world's attention and features their addictive and weird anthem track, *Enter the Ninja*.

Fokofpolisiekar *Swanesang* (Rhythm Records/The Orchard). One of South Africa's most successful live bands has helped redefine Afrikaner identity for the post-apartheid generation with its punk-rock-influenced sound, while repeatedly outraging the conservative establishment, starting with their name, which translates as "fuck off police car".

Freshlyground *Ma'Cheri* (Freeground Records/Sony BMG). Voted Album of the Year at the 2008 SA Music Awards, *Ma'Cheri* sees the most enduring of South Africa's Afropopsters do to a tee what they're known for: crossing national and stylistic boundaries to deliver catchy hooks and accessible melodies.

Goldfish *Perceptions of Pacha* (Pacha Recordings/Finetunes). This Cape Town-based jazz-boogie duo weave acoustic sounds into their predominantly electronica-based grooves to crank out one addictively upbeat track after the other.

Jeremy Loops *Trading Change* (Sheer Sound). Debut folk

album, which shot to number one on the South Africa iTunes store in 2014 and trounced international divas Toni Braxton and Shakira.

Jimmy Dludlu *Essence of Rhythm* (Universal). Dludlu is the essence of smooth jazz, and is arguably the single most popular representative of what is in turn the most commercially successful jazz style in South Africa.

Paul Hanmer *Trains To Taung* (Sheer Sound). This album is constructed around Hanmer's dreamy, piano-based compositions. Now considered a classic, and one of the first expositions of the new jazz of the post-apartheid era.

Prophets of Da City *Ghetto Code* (Universal). South Africa's rap supremos' finest release, full of tough but articulate rhymes and some seriously heavy samples, all in true Cape Flats style.

Ringo *Sondelani* (CCP). A superb modern reworking of traditional Xhosa sounds by this bald Capetonian heart-throb, including the hit track "Sondela", which has become one of South Africa's most well-liked love songs.

Robbie Jansen *Nomad Jez* (EMI). Great, if slightly flawed, album from veteran saxophonist Jansen, playing with other luminaries of the local jazz scene including Hilton Schilder and Errol Dyers.

Springbok Nude Girls *Afterlife Satisfaction* (Sony Music). Springbok Nude Girls, who performed as the opening act for U2 during their 2011 tour of South Africa, deliver a powerful, if not particularly original, belting rock set in this album.

Winston Mankunku *Crossroads* (Nkomo/Sheer). Sinuous, upbeat township jazz from the veteran Cape Town saxman.

ESSENTIAL SOUTH AFRICAN SOUNDS

Bayete *Umkhaya-Lo* (Polygram). A seminal fusion of South African sounds with laidback soul and funk, blended by lead singer Jabu Khanyile's unique mixing talent and spiced with his beautifully soothing vocals.

Gloria Bosman *Tranquillity* (Sheer/Limelight). A young and compelling jazz vocalist, Bosman juggles African and American styles with consummate ease. Paul Hanmer arranges and tickles the ivories.

Ladysmith Black Mambazo *Heavenly* (Gallo/Spectrum). An inspired and commercially successful foray into Afropop, featuring solo versions of various pop classics as well as vocal collaborations with Dolly Parton and Lou Rawls.

Lucky Dube *Prisoner* (Gallo). Originally a township jive singer, the late Dube made a switch to reggae that was both artistically and commercially inspired. *Prisoner* was South Africa's second-bestselling album ever, full of stirring Peter Tosh-style roots tunes.

Mfaz'Omnyama *Ngisebenzile Mama* (Gallo). The title

means "I have been working, Mum", and is amply justified by this superb set, which features some of the best *maskanda* ever recorded.

Moses Taiwa Molelekwa *Genes and Spirits* (Melt2000). Fascinating jazz/drum'n'bass fusion by a talented young pianist, who died tragically in 2001.

Pops Mohamed *How Far Have We Come?* (Melt2000). An exciting celebration of traditional African instruments: *mbiras*, *koras*, mouthbows and various percussion instruments are supplemented by bass and brass in this ethereal but funky album.

Sibongile Khumalo *Ancient Evenings* (Sony Music). Though a classically trained opera singer, Khumalo takes on both jazz and a variety of traditional melodies on this wonderful album, demonstrating why she is currently one of South Africa's best-loved singers.

Vusi Mahlasela *Silang Mabele* (BMG). Lush harmonies and lilting melodies abound in this album by South Africa's sweet-voiced township balladeer.

Language

In Cape Town and along the Garden Route, you'll rarely, if ever, need to use any other language than English. Forty percent of whites are mother-tongue English speakers, many of whom believe that they are (or at least should be) speaking standard British English. In fact, South African English has its own distinct character, and is as different from the Queen's English as Australian. Its most notable characteristic is its unique words and usages, some of which are drawn from Afrikaans and the indigenous African languages. The hefty *Oxford Dictionary of South African English* makes for an interesting browse.

Afrikaans, although a language you seldom need to speak, nevertheless remains very much in evidence in South Africa, and you will certainly encounter it on official forms and countless signs, particularly on the road (see p.270).

The other main language spoken in Cape Town is **Xhosa**, the predominant mother tongue of the city's African residents and easily distinguished by the clicks that form part of the words. It is also Nelson Mandela's mother tongue, which he shares with seven million other South Africans, predominantly in the Eastern Cape.

The glossary below is far from comprehensive, but it does include some of the more common words that are unique to South African English. Words whose spelling makes it hard to guess how to render them have their approximate pronunciation given in italics. Where **gh** occurs in the pronunciation, it denotes the **ch** sound in the Scottish word lo**ch**. Sometimes we've used the letter "r" in the pronunciation, even though the word in question doesn't contain this letter; for example, we've given the pronunciation of "Egoli" as "*air-gaw-lee*". In these instances the syllable containing the "r" is meant to represent a familiar word or sound from English; the "r" itself shouldn't be pronounced.

GLOSSARY

African In the context of South Africa, an indigenous South African

Afrikaner Literally "African": a white person who speaks Afrikaans

Aloe Family of spiky indigenous succulents, often with dramatic orange flowers

Apartheid (apart-hate) Term used from the 1940s for the National Party's official policy of "racial separation"

Arvie Afternoon

Baai Afrikaans word meaning "bay"; also a common suffix in place names, eg Stilbaai

Bakkie (bucky) Light truck or van

Bantu (bun-too) Unscientific apartheid term for indigenous black people; in linguistics, a group of indigenous southern-African languages

Bantustan Term used under apartheid for the territories such as Transkei, reserved for Africans

Bergie A vagrant living on the slopes of Table Mountain; a hobo on the streets of Cape Town

Big Five A term derived from hunting that refers to the trophy animals hunters most want to bag: lion, leopard, buffalo, elephant and rhino; often now used generically to indicate top big game country (as opposed to game reserves that only have antelope and other small mammals)

Black Imprecise term that sometimes refers collectively to Africans, Indians and coloureds, but more usually is used to mean Africans

Boer (boor) Literally "farmer", but also refers to early Dutch colonists at the Cape and Afrikaners

Boland (boor-lunt) Southern part of the Western Cape

Bottle store Off-licence or liquor store

Boy Offensive term used to refer to an adult African man who is a servant

Bundu (approximately boon-doo, but with the vowels shortened) Wilderness or backcountry

Burgher Literally a citizen, but more specifically a member of the Dutch community at the Cape in the seventeenth and eighteenth centuries; free burghers were VOC employees released from contract to farm independently on the Cape Peninsula and surrounding areas

Bush See **bundu**

Bushman South Africa's earliest, but now almost extinct, inhabitants who lived by hunting and gathering

Cape Doctor The southeaster that brings cool winds during the summer months

Cape Dutch Nineteenth-century, whitewashed, gabled style of architecture

Cape Dutch Revival Twentieth-century style based on Cape Dutch architecture

CBD The Central Business District of central Cape Town

Coloured People of mixed race

Dagga (dugh-a) Marijuana

Dagha (dah-ga) Mud used in indigenous construction

Dassie (dussy) Hyrax

Disa (die-za) One of twenty species of beautiful indigenous orchid, most famous of which is the red disa or "Pride of Table Mountain"

Dominee (dour-min-ee) Reverend (abbreviated to Ds)

Dorp Country town or village (derived from Afrikaans)

Drostdy (dross-tea) Historically, the building of the landdrost or magistrate

Fundi Expert

Fynbos (fayn-boss) Term for vast range of fine-leafed species that predominate in the southern part of the Western Cape (see box, p.104)

Girl Offensive term used to refer to an African woman who is a servant

Gogga (gho-gha) Creepy-crawly or insect

Griqua Person of mixed white, Bushman and Hottentot descent

Group Areas Act Now-defunct law passed in 1950 that provided for the establishment of separate areas for each "racial group"

Homeland See bantustan

Hottentot Now-unfashionable term for indigenous Khoisan herders encountered by the first settlers at the Cape

Indaba Zulu term meaning a group discussion and now used in South African English for any meeting or conference

Is it? Really?

Jislaaik! (yis-like) Exclamation equivalent to "Geez!" or "Crikey!"

Jol Party, celebration

Just now In a while

Kaffir Highly objectionable term of abuse for Africans

Karoo Arid plateau that occupies a large proportion of the South African interior

Khoikhoi (ghoy-ghoy) Self-styled name of South Africa's original herding inhabitants

Khoisan A conflation of the terms "Khoikhoi" and "San" used to collectively refer to South Africa's aboriginal inhabitants; the two were socially, but not ethnically, distinct, the Khoikhoi having been herders and the San hunter-gatherers

Kloof (klo-ef) Ravine or gorge

Knobkerrie Wooden club

Koppie Hillock

Kramat (crum-mutt) Shrine of a Muslim holy man

Krans (crunce) Sheer cliff face; plural kranse

Lapa Courtyard of group of Ndebele houses; also used to describe an enclosed area at safari camps, where braais are held

Lekker Nice

Lobola (la-ball-a) Bride price, paid by an African man to his wife's parents

Location Old-fashioned term for segregated African area on the outskirts of a town or farm

Madiba Mandela's clan name, used affectionately

Malay Misnomer for Cape Muslims of Asian descent

Mbira (m-beer-a) African thumb piano, often made with a gourd

MK Umkhonto we Sizwe (Spear of the Nation), the armed wing of the ANC, now incorporated into the national army

Mlungu (m-loon-goo) African term for a white person, equivalent to honkie

Moffie (mawf-ee) Gay person

Mother City Nickname for Cape Town

Muti (moo-tee) See umuthi

Nkosi Sikelel' iAfrika "God Bless Africa", anthem of the ANC and now of South Africa

Pass Document that Africans used to have to carry at all times, which essentially rendered them aliens in their own country

Pastorie (puss-tour-ee) Parsonage

Platteland (plutta-lunt) Country districts

Poort Narrow pass through mountains along river course

Protea National flower of South Africa

Raadsaal (the "d" is pronounced "t") Council or parliament building

Robot Traffic light

Rondavel (ron-daa-vil, with the stress on the middle syllable) Circular building based on traditional African huts

San A more common term for Bushmen (see above)

Sangoma (sun-gom-a) Traditional spirit medium and healer

Shebeen (sha-bean) Unlicensed township tavern

Southeaster Prevailing wind in the Western Cape

Spaza shops Small stall or kiosk

Stoep Veranda

Strandloper Literally "beach walkers"; Bushman or San social group who lived along the shores of the Western Cape and whose hunting and gathering consisted largely of shellfish and other seafood

Tackies Sneakers or plimsolls

Township Area set aside under apartheid for Africans

Transkei (trans-kye) Now-defunct homeland for Xhosa speakers

Trekboer (trek-boor) Nomadic Afrikaner farmers, usually in the eighteenth and nineteenth century

Umuthi (oo-moo-tee) Traditional herbal medicine

Vlei (flay) Swamp

VOC Verenigde Oostindische Compagnie, the Dutch East India Company

Voortrekkers (the first syllable rhymes with "boor") Dutch burghers who migrated inland in their ox wagons in the nineteenth century to escape British colonialism

FOOD AND DRINK

Amarula Liqueur made from the berries of the marula tree

Begrafnisrys (ba-ghruff-niss-race) Literally "funeral rice"; traditional Cape Muslim dish of yellow rice cooked with raisins

Biltong Sun-dried salted strip of meat, chewed as a snack

Blatjang (blutt-young) Cape Muslim chutney that has become a standard condiment on South African dinner tables

Bobotie (ba-boor-tea) Traditional Cape curried mince topped with a savoury custard and often cooked with apricots and almonds

Boerekos (boor-a-coss) Farm food, usually consisting of loads of meat and vegetables cooked using butter and sugar

Boerewors (boor-a-vorce) Spicy lengths of sausage that are de rigueur at braais

Bokkoms Dried fish, much like salt fish

Braai or **braaivleis** (bry-flace) Barbecue

Bredie Cape vegetable and meat stew

Cane or **cane spirit** A potent vodka-like spirit distilled from sugar cane and generally mixed with a soft drink such as Coke

Cap Classique Sparkling wine fermented in the bottle in exactly the same way as Champagne; also called Méthode Cap Classic

Cape gooseberry Fruit of the physalis; a sweet yellow berry

Cape salmon or **geelbek** (ghear-l-beck) Delicious firm-fleshed sea fish (unrelated to northern-hemisphere salmon)

Cape Velvet A sweet liqueur-and-cream dessert beverage that resembles Irish Cream liqueur

Denningvleis (den-ning-flace) Spicy traditional Cape lamb stew

Frikkadel Fried onion and meatballs

Geelbek See **Cape salmon**

Hanepoort (harner-poort) Delicious sweet dessert grape

Kabeljou (cobble-yo) Common South African marine fish, also called kob

Kerrievis (kerry-fiss) See **pickled fish**

Kingklip Highly prized deepwater fish caught along the Atlantic and Indian ocean coasts

Kob See **kabeljou**

Koeksister (cook-sister) Deep-fried plaited doughnut, dripping with syrup

Maas or **amasi** or **amaas** Traditional African beverage consisting of naturally soured milk, available as a packaged dairy product in supermarkets

Maaskaas Cottage cheese made from **maas**

Mageu or **mahewu** or **maheu** (ma-gh-weh) Traditional African beer made from maize meal and water, now packaged and commercially available

Malva Very rich and very sweet traditional baked Cape dessert

Mampoer (mum-poor) Moonshine; home-distilled spirit made from soft fruit, commonly peaches

Mealie See **mielie**

Melktert (melk-tairt) Traditional Cape custard pie

Mielie Maize

Mielie pap (mealy pup) Maize porridge, varying from a thin mixture to a stiff one that can resemble polenta

Mqomboti (m-qom-booty) Traditional African beer made from fermented sorghum

Musselcracker Large-headed fish with powerful jaws and firm, white flesh

Naartjie (nar-chee) Tangerine or mandarin

Pap (pup) Porridge

Peri-peri Delicious hottish spice of Portuguese origin commonly used with grilled chicken

Perlemoen (pear-la-moon) Abalone

Pickled fish Traditional Cape dish of fish preserved with onions, vinegar and curry; available tinned in supermarkets

Pinotage A uniquely South African cultivar hybridized from Pinot Noir and Hermitage grapes and from which a wine of the same name is made

Potjiekos or **potjie** (poy-key-kos) Food cooked slowly over embers in a three-legged cast-iron pot

Putu (poo-too) Traditional African **mielie pap** (see above) prepared until it forms dry crumbs

Rooibos (roy-boss) tea Indigenous herbal tea, made from the leaves of a particular *fynbos* plant

Rooti Chapati

Salmon trout Freshwater fish that is often smoked to create a cheaper and pretty good imitation of smoked salmon

Salomie Roti

Sambals (sam-bills) Accompaniments, such as chopped bananas, green peppers, desiccated coconut and chutney, served with Cape curries

Samp Traditional African dish of broken maize kernels, frequently cooked with beans

Skokiaan (skok-ee-yan) Potent home-brew

Smoorsnoek (smore-snook) Smoked **snoek**

Snoek (snook) Large fish that features in many traditional Cape recipes

Sosatie (so-sah-ti) Spicy skewered mince

Spanspek (spon-speck) A sweet melon

Steenbras (ste-en-bruss) A delicious white-fleshed fish

Van der Hum South African **naartjie**-flavoured liqueur

Vetkoek (fet-cook) Deep-fried doughnut-like cake

Waterblommetjiebredie (vata-blom-a-key-bree-dee) Cape meat stew made with waterlily rhizomes

Witblits (vit-blitz) Moonshine

Yellowtail Delicious darkish-fleshed marine fish

AFRIKAANS STREET SIGNS

Derde	Third	**Perron**	Station platform
Doeane	Customs	**Polisie**	Police
Drankwinkel	Liquor shop	**Poskantoor**	Post office
Eerste	First	**Regs**	Right
Geen ingang	No entry	**Ry**	Go
Gevaar	Danger	**Sentrum**	Centre
Goof	Main	**Singel**	Crescent
Hoog	High	**Stad**	City
Ingang	Entrance	**Stad sentrum**	City centre
Inligting	Information	**Stadig**	Slow
Kantoor	Office	**Stasie**	Station
Kerk	Church	**Strand**	Beach
Kort	Short	**Swembad**	Swimming pool
Links	Left	**Verbode**	Prohibited
Lughawe	Airport	**Verkeer**	Traffic
Mans	Men	**Versigtig**	Carefully
Mark	Market	**Vierde**	Fourth
Ompad	Detour	**Vrouens**	Women
Pad	Road	**Vyfde**	Fifth
Padwerke voor	Roadworks ahead		

Small print and index

A ROUGH GUIDE TO ROUGH GUIDES

Published in 1982, the first Rough Guide – to Greece – was a student scheme that became a publishing phenomenon. Mark Ellingham, a recent graduate in English from Bristol University, had been travelling in Greece the previous summer and couldn't find the right guidebook. With a small group of friends he wrote his own guide, combining a highly contemporary, journalistic style with a thoroughly practical approach to travellers' needs.

The immediate success of the book spawned a series that rapidly covered dozens of destinations. And, in addition to impecunious backpackers, Rough Guides soon acquired a much broader readership that relished the guides' wit and inquisitiveness as much as their enthusiastic, critical approach and value-for-money ethos.

These days, Rough Guides include recommendations from budget to luxury and cover more than 120 destinations around the globe, as well as producing an ever-growing range of ebooks.

Visit **roughguides.com** to find all our latest books, read articles, get inspired and share travel tips with the Rough Guides community.

Rough Guide credits

Editors: Helen Abramson, Eleanor Aldridge, Emma Gibbs
Layout: Jessica Subramanian
Cartography: Rajesh Chhibber
Picture editor: Lisa Jacobs
Proofreader: Diane Margolis
Managing editor: Keith Drew
Assistant editor: Sharon Sonam

Production: Charlotte Cade
Cover design: Nicole Newman, Dan May, Sarah Steward Richardson, Jessica Subramanian
Editorial assistant: Rebecca Hallett
Senior pre-press designer: Dan May
Programme manager: Helen Blount
Publisher: Joanna Kirby

Publishing information

This fifth edition published February 2015 by
Rough Guides Ltd,
80 Strand, London WC2R 0RL
11, Community Centre, Panchsheel Park,
New Delhi 110017, India
Distributed by Penguin Random House
Penguin Books Ltd,
80 Strand, London WC2R 0RL
Penguin Group (USA)
345 Hudson Street, NY 10014, USA
Penguin Group (Australia)
250 Camberwell Road, Camberwell,
Victoria 3124, Australia
Penguin Group (NZ)
67 Apollo Drive, Mairangi Bay, Auckland 1310,
New Zealand
Penguin Group (South Africa)
Block D, Rosebank Office Park, 181 Jan Smuts Avenue,
Parktown North, Gauteng, South Africa 2193
Rough Guides is represented in Canada by Tourmaline
Editions Inc. 662 King Street West, Suite 304, Toronto,
Ontario M5V 1M7
Printed in Singapore by Toppan Security Printing Pte. Ltd.

Help us update

We've gone to a lot of effort to ensure that the fifth edition of **The Rough Guide to Cape Town** is accurate and up-to-date. However, things change – places get "discovered", opening hours are notoriously fickle, restaurants and rooms raise prices or lower standards. If you feel we've got it wrong or left something out, we'd like to know, and if you can remember the address, the price, the hours, the phone number, so much the better.

Please send your comments with the subject line "**Rough Guide Cape Town Update**" to ⊕ mail @uk.roughguides.com. We'll credit all contributions and send a copy of the next edition (or any other Rough Guide if you prefer) for the very best emails.

Find more travel information, connect with fellow travellers and plan your trip on ⓦ roughguides.com

ABOUT THE AUTHORS

Barbara McCrea was born in Zimbabwe and taught African literature at the University of Natal. She lived in London for fifteen years, working on Rough Guides to Zimbabwe, South Africa and Cape Town, before returning to Southern Africa. She lives close to the beach in Cape Town, where she swims, rides horses and climbs mountains to keep sane.

Tony Pinchuck lives in Cape Town, where he works as a graphic designer and writer.

Acknowledgements

Barbara McCrea: Barbara McCrea would like to gratefully thank Rosie Downey for her hard work and upbeat contributions to nightlife and other essential aspects of life in the urban hub; thanks to the editors Helen, Emma and Ellie for holding it all together, to Tony for steering and maps, to Gabriel for being a good teenage critic, to the people who gave us accommodation and information in the Winelands, Whale Coast and Garden Route, and thanks to everyone else in the network of help and support whom I haven't mentioned by name.

Tony Pinchuck: Thanks to our editor Ellie Aldridge for keeping the show on the road, to my co-author Barbara McCrea for doing much of the heavy lifting on this edition, and to all the unmentioned people who contributed to this book.

Readers' updates

Thanks to all the readers who have taken the time to write in with comments and suggestions (and apologies if we've inadvertently omitted or misspelt anyone's name):

Stewart and Catherine Ashurst, Elizabeth Bains, Ingrid Brough, Michael Brierley, John Dale, Terry Foley, Mary Gallagher, Stephan Huber, Josefin, John and Rosemary Reeves, Niall Saynor, Meryl Spencer, Wendy Stiff, Wendy Taylor, Jonathan Virden, Roger Whetton, Susan Wishart and Ron Zuiderwijk

Photo credits

All photos © Rough Guides except the following:
(Key: a-above; b-below/bottom; c-centre; f-far; l-left; r-right; t-top)

Index

Maps are marked in **grey**

Map index

Listings key

- ■ Accommodation
- ● Restaurant/café
- ■ Bar/club
- ● Shop

City plan

The **city plan** on the pages that follow is divided as shown:

N

0	300

metres

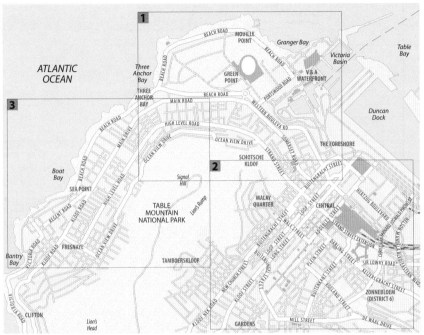

Map symbols

International boundary	✈	Airport	♦	Place of interest	禾	Picnic site
Province boundary	★	Bus/taxi	⊺	Garden	⚓	Swimming area
Chapter division boundary	P	Parking	🍇	Vineyard	▦	Building
Major road	⊠	Post office	🏌	Golf course	□	Market
Minor road	ⓘ	Information office	🏛	Monument	⇄	Church
Motorway road	⊞	Hospital	⚓	Ship wreck	◯	Stadium
Path	🕌	Mosque	🗼	Lighthouse	□	Park
Railway	✡	Synagogue	🌀	Windmill	●‒●	Cable car
Ferry route	⊠	Entrance gate	▲	Mountain peak	⊢⊢⊢	Funicular
River	〰	Mountain range	◠	Cave		

BEACH ROAD

Green Point

Green Point Lighthouse

SUBREY PLACE

FRITZ SONNENBERG ROAD

ROTHESAY PL.

BAY ROAD

KIEWIET STREET

STEPHAN WAY

KIEWIET STREET

PARK ROAD

BEACH ROAD

Green Point Park

VLEI ROAD

GREEN POINT

Three Anchor Bay

BAY ROAD

STANLEY PLACE

BILL PETERS DRIVE

Urban Park

THREE ANCHOR BAY

HELEN SUZMAN BOULEVARD

BEACH ROAD

THREE ANCHOR BAY ROAD

BOWLERS WAY

MAIN ROAD

FORT ROAD

ST BREDE'S ROAD

RICHMOND ROAD

CLYDE ROAD

PINE ROAD

VARNEY'S ROAD

SYDNEY STREET

AVONDALE ROAD

GLENGARIFF ROAD

CAMBERWELL ROAD

GRIMSBY ROAD

ANTRIM ROAD

ANTRIM ROAD

ST GEORGES ROAD

CROXTETH STREET

DYSART ROAD

YORK

HOFMEYR ROAD

GRIMSBY ROAD

MUTLEY ROAD

HATFIELD ROAD

SCHOLTZ ROAD

HILL ROAD

RAVENCRAIG ROAD

CLYDEBANK ROAD

CLYDE ROAD

BRAESIDE ROAD

TORBAY ROAD

PINE ROAD

WIGTOWN ROAD

HAYTOR ROAD

CANVALCADE ROAD

THORNHILL

FRERE ROAD

BLACK HEATH ROAD

CHEVIOT PLACE

MODENA RD

MUTLEY ROAD

HIGH LEVEL ROAD

KEVIN ROAD

JOUBERT ROAD

HIGH LEVEL RO

BLACK HEATH ROAD

GLENGARIFF ROAD

BEN NEVIS ST

DUDLEY RD

OCEAN VIEW DRIVE

ROOS ROAD

RHINE ROAD

MAIN DRIVE

BATTERY CRESCENT

SPRINGBOK ROAD

OCEAN VIEW DR

HIGH LEVEL ROAD

CALAIS ROAD

ANTWERP ROAD

ILKLEY CRES

OCEAN VIEW DRIVE

MERRIMA

Table Mountain National Park

▲
Signal Hill (350m)

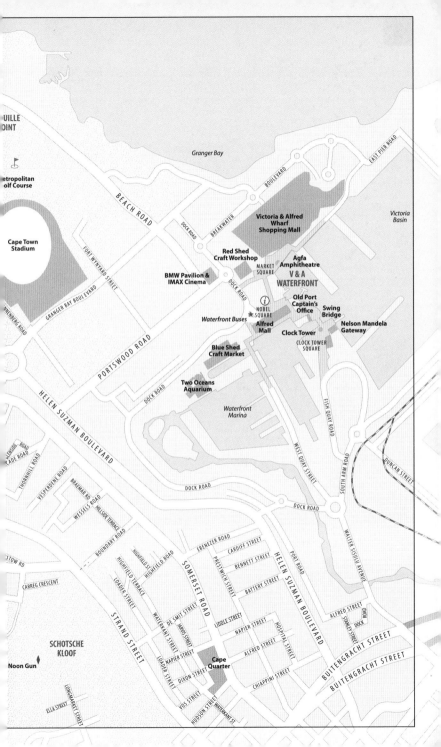

Granger Bay

Victoria Basin

EAST PIER ROAD

BOULEVARD

BEACH ROAD

DOCK ROAD

BREAKWATER

Victoria & Alfred Wharf Shopping Mall

Red Shed Craft Workshop

MARKET SQUARE

Agfa Amphitheatre

V & A WATERFRONT

BMW Pavilion & IMAX Cinema

DOCK ROAD

i NOBEL SQUARE

Old Port Captain's Office

Swing Bridge

Waterfront Buses

Alfred Mall

Clock Tower

Nelson Mandela Gateway

CLOCK TOWER SQUARE

Blue Shed Craft Market

Two Oceans Aquarium

Waterfront Marina

FISH QUAY ROAD

DOCK ROAD

WEST QUAY STREET

SOUTH ARM ROAD

DUNCAN STREET

PORTSWOOD ROAD

DOCK ROAD

DOCK ROAD

HELEN SUZMAN BOULEVARD

FORT WYNYARD STREET

GRANGER BAY BOULEVARD

WHENBERG ROAD

Cape Town Stadium

etropolitan olf Course

UILLE OINT

WALTER SISULU AVENUE

PORT ROAD

HELEN SUZMAN BOULEVARD

THORNHILL ROAD

VESPERDENE ROAD

BRAEMAR RD

WESSELS ROAD

HILLSIDE TERRACE

BOUNDARY ROAD

CADE ROAD

NSIDE ROAD

STOW RD

CARREG CRESCENT

HIGHFIELD ST

HIGHFIELD ROAD

HIGHFIELD TERRACE

LOADER STREET

SOMERSET ROAD

DE SMIT STREET

JARVIS STREET

WATERKANT STREET

LOADER STREET

NAPIER STREET

DIXON STREET

EBENEZER ROAD

CARDIFF STREET

PRESTWICH STREET

BENNETT STREET

BATTERY STREET

LIDDLE STREET

NAPIER STREET

ALFRED STREET

CHIAPPINI STREET

HOSPITAL STREET

ALFRED STREET

STANLEY STREET

DOCK ROAD

BUITENGRACHT STREET

BUITENGRACHT STREET

SCHOTSCHE KLOOF

◆ Noon Gun

STRAND STREET

ELLA STREET

LONGMARKET STREET

VOS STREET

HUDSON STREET

WATERKANT ST

Cape Quarter

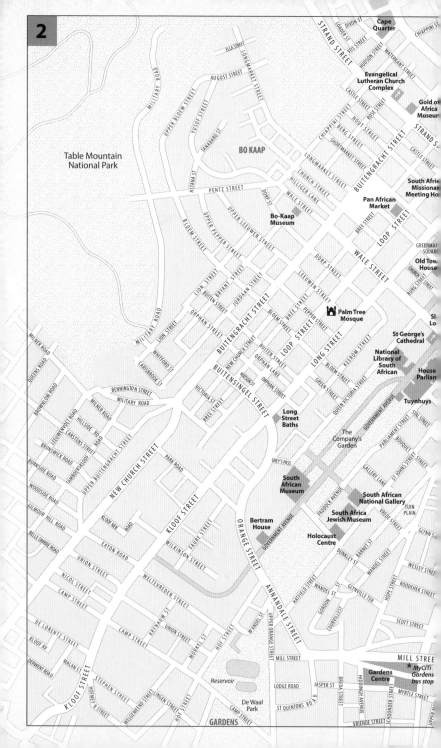

2

STRAND STREET

Cape Quarter

CHIAPPINI ST

DIXON ST

LOADER ST

JOS ST

HUDSON ST

WATERKANT STREET

Evangelical Lutheran Church Complex

Gold of Africa Museum

ELLA STREET

LONGMARKET STREET

AUGUST STREET

CASTLE STREET

ROSE STREET

HOUT STREET

STRAND STREET

MILITARY ROAD

UPPER BLOEM STREET

YUSUF STREET

CHIAPPINI STREET

BERG STREET

SHORTMARKET STREET

BO KAAP

LONGMARKET STREET

CHURCH STREET

BUITENGRACHT STREET

CASTLE STREET

South African Missionary Meeting House

Table Mountain National Park

TANBARU ST

ASTANA ST

PENTZ STREET

HILLIGER LANE

WALE STREET

DORP ST

Pan African Market

BREE STREET

LOOP STREET

BLOEM STREET

UPPER PEPPER STREET

UPPER LEEUWEN STREET

Bo-Kaap Museum

WALE STREET

GREENMARKET SQUARE

Old Town House

DORP STREET

LION STREET

BRYANT STREET

JORDAAN STREET

LEEUWEN STREET

BREE STREET

PEPPER STREET

CHURCH STREET

BURG STREET

BUITEN STREET

BLOEM STREET

Palm Tree Mosque

St George's Cathedral

MILITARY ROAD

LION STREET

ORPHAN STREET

BUITENGRACHT STREET

NEW CHURCH STREET

BUITEN STREET

LOOP STREET

LONG STREET

KEEROM STREET

St Lo

WHITFORD ST

CARISBROOK ST

ORPHAN LANE

WATSON ST

BLOEM STREET

National Library of South African

MILNER ROAD

QUEENS ROAD

BENNINGTON STREET

MILITARY ROAD

BUITENSINGEL STREET

VICTORIA ST

ORPHAN STREET

GREEN STREET

QUEEN VICTORIA STREET

House of Parlian

BROWNLOW ROAD

MILNER ROAD

HILLSIDE ROAD

LEEUWENVOET ROAD

CARSTENS STREET

BREE STREET

Long Street Baths

Tuynhuys

GOVERNMENT AVENUE

PARLIAMENT STREET

STAL STREET

BRUNSWICK ROAD

TAMBOERSKLOOF ROAD

UPPER BUITENGRACHT STREET

GREY'S PASS

The Company's Garden

GALLERY LANE

ST JOHNS STREET

BOUQUET ST

BURNSIDE ROAD

WOODSIDE ROAD

PARK ROAD

NEW CHURCH STREET

GILMOUR HILL ROAD

KLOOF STREET

KLOOF NEK ROAD

South African Museum

PADDOCK AVENUE

GOVERNMENT AVENUE

South African National Gallery

TUIN PLAIN

BELLE OMBRE ROAD

FAURE STREET

WILKINSON STREET

ORANGE STREET

Bertram House

South Africa Jewish Museum

VREDE STREET

GLYNN ST

UNION STREET

EATON ROAD

WELTEVREDEN STREET

Holocaust Centre

DUNKLEY ST

BARNET ST

WANDEL STREET

WESLEY STREET

NICOL STREET

CAMP STREET

KRYNAUW ST

UNION STREET

MORKEL ST

HATFIELD STREET

WANDEL ST

GORDON

GLYNVILLE TER

COURVILLE ST

NOPE STREET

ROODEHEK STREET

DE LORENTZ STREET

CAMP STREET

STEPHEN STREET

WANDEL ST

UPPER ORANGE STREET

ANNANDALE STREET

SCOTT STREET

KLOOF AV

MALAN ST

MILL STREET

MILL STREE

★ MyCiTi Gardens bus stop

DERWENT ROAD

KLOOF STREET

HOFMEYR STREET

WELGEMEEND STREET

LINGEN STREET

HOF STREET

CAMP STREET

Reservoir

LODGE ROAD

ST QUINTONS RD

De Waal Park

JASPER ST

Gardens Centre

BREDA STREET

HIDDINGH AVENUE

SCHOONDER STREET

MYRTLE STREET

GARDENS

VRIENDE STREET

ATLANTIC
OCEAN

Boat
Bay

**Sea Point Pavillion
Swimming Pool**

SEA POINT

Queen's
Beach

Sea Point

Saunders
Rocks

Bantry
Bay

FRESNAYE

LONDON RO

MARAIS ROAD

OLIVER ROAD

GRAHAM ROAD

ELLIS ROAD

MILTON ROAD

WORCESTER ROAD

GRAHAM ROAD

ARTHUR'S ROAD

MAIN DRIVE

ST JOHNS ROAD

ARTHUR'S R

INEZ ROAD

DUNCAN RO

CHURCH ROAD

IRWINTON ROAD

GORLESTON ROAD

ALGARKIRK ROAD

CLARENS ROAD

FRANCAIS AVENUE

CLARENS ROAD

HANOVER ROAD

AVENUE NORMANDIE

CHATEAU DE L'

AVENUE DE L'E

BEACH ROAD

SEA POINT PROMENADE

BEACH ROAD

ST ANDREWS RD

CASSELL STREET

CASSELL ST

KEI APPLE ROAD

KLOOF ROAD

REGENT ROAD

SOLOMONS ROAD

QUANTOCK ROAD

TRAMWAY ROAD

QUENDON ROAD

AVENUE DISANDT

AVENUE DE LONGUEVILLE

AVENUE LE SUEUR

HIGH LEVEL ROAD

AVENUE NORMAN

ALEXANDER STREET

QUEENS ROAD

KINGS ROAD

ILLFORD STREET

AVENUE DES HUGUENOTS

AVENUE FRESNAYE

AVENUE PROTEA

BRANSOME

BEACH ROAD

CRAIGROWNIE ROAD

SAUNDERS ROAD

SEACLIFFE RD

BANTRY ROAD

EDGEWATER ROAD

FIR ROAD

PORTMAN ROAD

AVENUE ALEXANDRA

ST PATRICK'S RD

PRINCESS RD

AVENUE LE SUEUR

AVENUE FRESNAYE

OCEAN VIEW DRIVE

AVENUE SAINT CHARLES

VICTORIA ROAD

KLOOF ROAD

ROCHESTER

BROMPTON AVENUE

QUEENS ROAD

BELLWOOD ROAD

AVENUE BRITTANY

AVENUE SAINT LOUIS

CŒUR DE LION

AVENUE LA CROIX

AVENUE SAINT BARTH

AVENUE SAINT BARTH

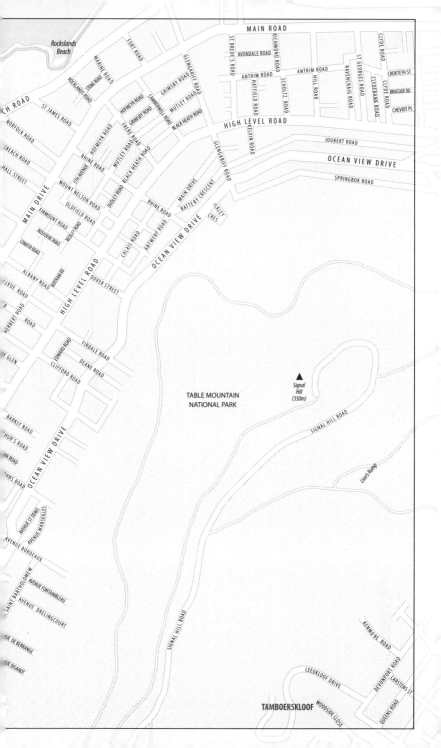

MYCITI ROUTE MAP

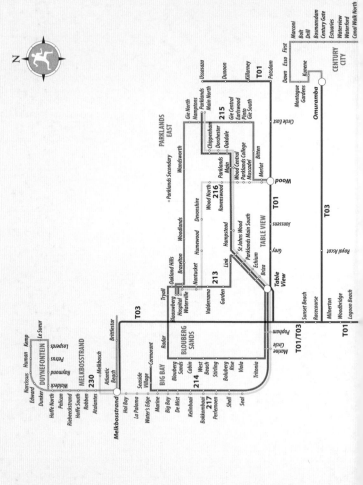

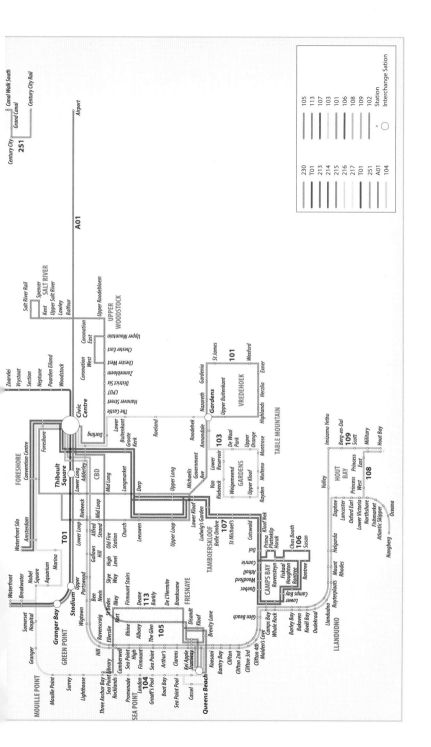

A ROUGH GUIDE TO
ROUGH GUIDES

Published in 1982, the first Rough Guide – to Greece – was a student scheme that became a publishing phenomenon. Mark Ellingham, a recent graduate in English from Bristol University, had been travelling in Greece the previous summer and couldn't find the right guidebook. With a small group of friends he wrote his own guide, combining a highly contemporary, journalistic style with a thoroughly practical approach to travellers' needs.

The immediate success of the book spawned a series that rapidly covered dozens of destinations. And, in addition to impecunious backpackers, Rough Guides soon acquired a much broader and older readership that relished the guides' wit and inquisitiveness as much as their enthusiastic, critical approach and value-for-money ethos.

These days, Rough Guides feature recommendations from shoestring to luxury and cover more than 200 destinations around the globe. Our ever-growing team of authors and photographers is spread all over the world, particularly in Europe, the US and Australia.

Rough Guides now number around 200 titles, including Pocket city guides, inspirational coffee-table books and comprehensive country and regional titles, plus technology guides from iPods to Android. As well as print books, we publish groundbreaking apps and eBooks for every major digital device.

Visit ⓦ roughguides.com to see our latest publications.

Rough Guide travel images are available for commercial licensing at ⓦ roughguidespictures.com.